World Economic and Financial Surveys

Global Financial Stability Report

Market Developments and Issues

April 2005

International Monetary Fund
Washington DC

Production: IMF Multimedia Services Division
Cover: Phil Torsani
Photo: Padraic Hughes
Figures: Theodore F. Peters, Jr.
Typesetting: Choon Lee

ISBN 1-58906-418-6
ISSN 0258-7440

Price: US$49.00
(US$46.00 to full-time faculty members and
students at universities and colleges)

Please send orders to:
International Monetary Fund, Publication Services
700 19th Street, N.W., Washington, D.C. 20431, U.S.A.
Tel.: (202) 623-7430   Telefax: (202) 623-7201
E-mail: publications@imf.org
Internet:http://www.imf.org

recycled paper

CONTENTS

Tables

Figures

The following symbols have been used throughout this volume:

. . . to indicate that data are not available;

— to indicate that the figure is zero or less than half the final digit shown, or that the item does not exist;

– between years or months (for example, 1997–99 or January–June) to indicate the years or months covered, including the beginning and ending years or months;

/ between years (for example, 1998/99) to indicate a fiscal or financial year.

"Billion" means a thousand million; "trillion" means a thousand billion.

"Basis points" refer to hundredths of 1 percentage point (for example, 25 basis points are equivalent to ¼ of 1 percentage point).

"n.a." means not applicable.

Minor discrepancies between constituent figures and totals are due to rounding.

As used in this volume the term "country" does not in all cases refer to a territorial entity that is a state as understood by international law and practice. As used here, the term also covers some territorial entities that are not states but for which statistical data are maintained on a separate and independent basis.

PREFACE

The *Global Financial Stability Report* (GFSR) assesses global financial market developments with the view to identifying potential systemic weaknesses. By calling attention to potential fault lines in the global financial system, the report seeks to play a role in preventing crises, thereby contributing to global financial stability and to sustained economic growth of the IMF's member countries.

The report was prepared by the International Capital Markets Department (ICM), under the direction of the Counsellor and Director, Gerd Häusler. It is managed by an Editorial Committee comprising Hung Q. Tran (Chairman), W. Todd Groome, Jorge Roldos, and David J. Ordoobadi, and benefits from comments and suggestions from Axel Bertuch-Samuels. Other ICM staff contributing to this issue include Renzo Avesani, Geoffrey Bannister, Nicolas Blancher, Elie Canetti, Jorge Chan-Lau, Peter Dattels, Michael Gapen, Toni Gravelle, François Haas, Anna Ilyina, William Lee, Pipat Luengnaruemitchai, Chris Morris, Shinobu Nakagawa, Li Lian Ong, Hiroko Oura, Lars Pedersen, Rupert Thorne, Laura Valderrama, Christopher Walker, Mark Walsh, and Luisa Zanforlin. Other contributors included a staff team of the Monetary and Financial Systems Department (MFD) that included Robert Corker, S. Kal Wajid, Daniel Hardy, Alexander Tieman, Kalin Tintchev, and a number of other contributors on individual countries. Martin Edmonds, Ivan Guerra, Silvia Iorgova, Herman Kamil, Oksana Khadarina, Yoon Sook Kim, Ned Rumpeltin, and Peter Tran provided analytical support. Caroline Bagworth, Norma Cayo, Rosemarie Edwards, Vera Jasenovec, Elsa Portaro, and Ramanjeet Singh provided expert word processing assistance. Archana Kumar of the External Relations Department edited the manuscript and coordinated production of the publication.

This particular issue draws, in part, on a series of informal discussions with commercial and investment banks, securities firms, asset management companies, hedge funds, insurance companies, pension funds, stock and futures exchanges, and credit rating agencies, as well as regulatory authorities and academic researchers in many major financial centers and countries. The report reflects information available up to February 16, 2005.

The report has benefited from comments and suggestions from staff in other IMF departments, as well as from Executive Directors following their discussions of the *Global Financial Stability Report* on March 18, 2005. However, the analysis and policy considerations are those of the contributing staff and should not be attributed to the Executive Directors, their national authorities, or the IMF.

CHAPTER I

OVERVIEW

Assessment of Global Financial Stability

The resilience of the global financial system has further improved in the past six months, largely because of solid global economic growth, buoyant financial markets, and continued improvement in the balance sheets of the corporate, financial, and household sectors in many countries. The ongoing improvement in the economic fundamentals of many emerging market countries—including efforts to enhance the credibility of their policy framework and the quality of their debt structure—has led to a string of upgrades of sovereign credit ratings, contributing to the benign financial market conditions. (See Chapter II for a detailed analysis of these and other market developments.)

In particular, the overall excellent profitability of the corporate and financial sectors over the past few years has been an important factor in strengthening their balance sheets. The ratio of liquid assets to debt in their balance sheets has risen and stayed at a relatively high level for some time now. So far, the preference for liquidity reflects the caution exercised by corporate executives in making investments—also mergers and acquisitions have picked up only quite recently. This cautious approach has contributed to the slow growth in employment in many countries. By the same token, it has helped to contain the risk of creating investment excesses that in the past have helped trigger sharp market corrections.

At the same time, financial institutions have improved their profitability and strengthened their capital base as well as their risk management systems. In particular, the insurance sector in many countries has improved its solvency ratio. These developments have made financial institutions better prepared to cope with potential future shocks, and have significantly improved the health of the financial system up to the early part of 2005.

Our positive assessment of financial stability is underpinned by the favorable prospect for the world economy. The April 2005 issue of the IMF's *World Economic Outlook* forecasts that the global economy is likely to enjoy solid growth in the foreseeable future, with inflation under control. Such an environment will allow financial institutions, and other market participants, to further improve their financial conditions. This assessment obviously refers to the financial system as a whole and does not exclude the possibility that individual financial intermediaries or sovereign borrowers may encounter serious difficulties.

Looking ahead, while there is no particular reason to believe that this benign scenario might come to an end any time soon, we see a number of risks that could test the resiliency of the financial system. At a time when the financial sector is in solid shape, the risks are—by definition—more on the downside.

Risks in the Period Ahead

If history is any guide, the single most important risk factor for financial markets in good times is complacency. As discussed below and more extensively in Chapter II, current risk premiums for inflation and credit risks leave little or no margin for error in terms of financial asset valuations. The combination of low risk premiums, complacency, and untested elements of risk management systems dealing with complex financial instruments could ultimately become hazardous to financial markets.

At present, it is not easy to see which single event, short of a "major devastating geopolitical incident or a terrorist attack" as highlighted in the September 2004 issue of the

Global Financial Stability Report (GFSR), could possibly trigger a sharp and abrupt reversal of this positive assessment. However, because we are more advanced in the economic, profit, and credit cycles, disappointments or negative surprises are more likely to occur. Possibly, a combination or correlation of several less spectacular events might cause markets to reverse their course, and create a less hospitable environment for investors and borrowers who have become accustomed to low rates. Such risks include disappointing developments as to the narrowing of the U.S. current account deficit, continuing rises in commodity and oil prices feeding through to inflation, larger-than-expected rises in interest rates, as well as negative surprises for corporate earnings and credit quality.

Currency adjustments to address the growing global imbalances have taken place in an orderly fashion in the past two years. So far, there is no visible sign of a sustained decline in capital flows into the United States. There is an emerging view among market participants that currency adjustments on their own are insufficient to reduce the global imbalances and that some reduction in growth differentials between the United States and several of its major trading partners is needed. However, market participants are also acutely aware that the financing of the U.S. current account deficit—at least for the time being— hinges, to a certain degree, on the willingness of central banks, especially in Asia, to accumulate further dollar assets. Undue delays in addressing the global imbalances through adjustments in domestic policies or any serious doubts about the willingness of central banks to accumulate dollars could spark strong incentives for investors, private and possibly even public, to reduce future dollar purchases or even reduce their existing dollar holdings. This could trigger a further significant decline of the dollar and an increase in U.S. interest rates that might reduce U.S. domestic demand. The sharp dollar depreciation could also have a negative effect on

European and Japanese growth. These developments could lead to weaker economic growth worldwide.

While financial markets have largely priced in a moderate and gradual monetary tightening, they might be less prepared if market interest rates—especially long-term rates— were to go up more abruptly, either because of a sharp decline of the dollar or worse-than-expected inflation data. This would lead to the unwinding of many investment positions predicated on low or gently rising rates, leading to corrections in many asset markets.

After growing strongly in the past two years, corporate earnings growth is likely to decelerate in the future. In a similar vein, banks may not be able to count on a reduction in credit provisions to increase their reported profit. Earnings disappointments relative to market expectations are likely to occur and may cause equity markets to decline, perhaps together with rising volatility. Such corrections in major equity markets could weaken a stabilizing factor that has helped improve the solvency of many financial institutions, such as insurance companies in several countries.

Another possible source of concern could be a confluence of credit events, such as a downgrading of a major global company to subinvestment grade for reasons that may not be linked to negative events in the global economy. Such a credit event could burden the high-yield market investor base, leading to a widening of high-yield credit spreads.

The growing sophistication of financial market participants over the past years has largely reduced the risk of "knee-jerk contagion" that characterized previous crises. Despite low credit spreads, markets have demonstrated their ability to restrict their pricing reactions to several specific credit events of last year, without spillover effects on the credit markets at large. However, it is also clear that a general reassessment of risk appetite of large investors and intermediaries, due to a worsening of the general economic and financial situation, could have knock-on effects for related asset classes due to relative value considerations.

Developments such as those described above would not be entirely unexpected: similar scenarios have been used in stress tests conducted by many financial institutions and their supervisors. However, the resulting market corrections could be amplified by interactions between these risks in unanticipated ways that could change the general perception of risk.

Moreover, otherwise normal market fluctuations could be amplified through liquidity problems. An increasingly relevant contributor to this liquidity risk is the recent proliferation of complex and leveraged financial instruments, including credit derivatives and structured products such as collateralized debt obligations (CDOs). While secondary trading for these products exists, these instruments still rely on quantitative models for relative value assessment, investment decisions, and pricing. Therefore, there is a risk that models that are overly similar in their construction could cause investors to rush to exit at the same time, leading to market liquidity shortages.

While risk management at many financial institutions has been strengthened and become more sophisticated in recent years, the risk management process still hinges, to a crucial extent, on the ability of market participants, in times of market stresses, to execute trades quickly without having prices move too much against them. However, most recent risk management models dealing with the new and complex credit instruments have not yet been put to a live test, that is, whether in time of need, the anticipated counterparties will stand ready to absorb the additional market and credit risks from those who would like to shed it. This issue is becoming more relevant given the recent trend of concentration in the financial sector that reduces the number of large intermediaries in various markets.

The question of a liquidity shortage as a potential amplifier for market price shocks is still one of the major "blind spots" in our financial market landscape. The interactions of liquidity risk and other potential amplifiers of market shocks with changes in global capital flows will have to be at the forefront of all future effort to further improve the global financial architecture.

Policy Measures to Mitigate Risks

The financial strength of major private international financial institutions is the first line of defense against financial risks. As mentioned earlier, strong capital positions and balance sheets of key financial institutions put them in a good position to deal with and absorb the risks described above. Nevertheless, senior management of these institutions and their supervisors should ensure that risk management practices are robustly implemented and that prudential counterparty standards are not being relaxed due to competitive pressure. In particular, liquidity risks and precautionary measures that need to be put in place to address potential liquidity shortages should receive heightened attention from market participants and supervisors alike.

Authorities can contribute to mitigate the above-mentioned risks in several ways. On a macroeconomic level, the authorities need to minimize risks by maintaining market confidence through taking credible policy measures to facilitate an orderly adjustment of global imbalances. According to recent issues of the IMF's *World Economic Outlook*, such measures include increasing national savings in the United States, implementing structural reforms and fostering stronger growth in the euro area and Japan, and allowing more currency flexibility in many Asian countries.

By the same token, central banks should continue to gradually raise policy rates to a neutral level. This will make it less compelling for financial intermediaries and investors to engage in carry trades and various aspects of leveraging. Although the prime responsibility for risk management lies with individual firms and investors, it is apparent that they perceive the generous supply of liquidity as a "collective action problem": cheap liquidity is too tempting not to exploit, especially if everyone else engages in doing so. It should be in the public interest to help avoid sudden reversals of risk appetite among financial intermediaries and investors, which have at times proven to be destabilizing. The policies of gradually raising policy rates in a way that is well anticipated by markets could buy some insurance against potentially volatile and destabilizing developments.

On a microeconomic level, supervisors and regulators must be particularly vigilant about the risk profile of financial intermediaries—particularly concentration risk—and their vulnerability to abrupt market price shocks.

All in all, there is merit in reminding investors publicly about the risks they are engaging in and the consequences they face without the expectations of being bailed out.

Risk Transfer to the Household Sector

The importance of risk management has motivated us to analyze the flow of risk through various sectors of the financial system, their changing risk profiles, and their ability to manage risk. The April and September 2004 issues of the GFSR examined the reallocation of risk from the banking sector to the insurance and pension sectors. Chapter III of this GFSR concludes the series with a study of the allocation of risk to the household sector, by examining the changes in the balance sheets and risk profiles of households, and their ability to manage risk. This chapter examines the transfer of market risk to the household sector arising from changes in the behavior of financial institutions and from pension reform. It does not evaluate either existing pension systems or ongoing pension reforms in different countries.

Households, as stakeholders in the financial system, have always been exposed to financial risks, but usually indirectly. In the past, the household sector held financial assets with intermediaries such as banks that absorbed investment risks and provided households with fixed nominal returns through simple products such as bank deposits and savings accounts. Households were exposed to the credit risk of the banks, but this risk was mitigated by deposit insurance programs and sometimes eventual government support. Households held life insurance contracts, mainly of the guaranteed return variety where the insurance companies bore the investment risk. Pension provisions were mainly through defined benefit plans, where the investment and longevity risks stayed with the pension plan sponsors. In other words, the household sector was largely insulated from financial market and investment risk as well as longevity risk. Households may have eventually paid a price for this protection as taxpayers, when public resources were used to support failed financial institutions or to provide pension benefits; however, taxes were broadly diffused throughout the population—present and/or future generations—and not directly targeted to those exposed to financial risks.

As the populations of major industrialized countries age and their life expectancy rises, the cost of providing defined pension benefits has become more difficult to sustain. This has led both corporate and government pension plan sponsors to switch—at a different pace in different countries—from defined benefit to defined contribution plans, and from pay-as-you-go to funded plans. Such changes have brought benefits and reduced some risks, including the credit risk of plan sponsors. At the same time, the household sector has taken on more responsibility for ensuring sufficient contributions to their defined contribution plans, for generating adequate investment return from those plans, and for coping with the longevity risk as well as the risk of rising costs of health care and long-term care.

At the same time, the emphasis on risk management has led banks to shed many market and credit risks to other market participants. Life insurance companies and pension funds have also begun to de-risk their portfolios by offering products that share or return market risk to their retail customers. Finally, growing use of mutual funds and direct holdings of stocks and bonds by retail investors have exposed the household sector to marked-to-market fluctuations, made transparent in their monthly account statements. This transparency will sensitize households to the investment risks to which they are exposed and eventually will influence household behavior. In short, the household sector has increasingly and more directly become the "shock absorber of last resort" in the financial system.

Given the growing relevance of the household sector in assessing financial stability and the incomplete and fragmented data on household balance sheets that is currently available, national authorities and the financial services industry should try to improve the collection and dissemination of such data. International organizations, such as the IMF or the OECD, can also play a role in supporting these efforts.

Overall, the transfer of risk from the banking sector to nonbanking sectors, including the household sector, appears to have enhanced the resiliency and stability of the financial system—mainly by widely dispersing financial risks, including throughout the household sector. Policymakers may now need to take the next logical step by helping households to improve on their financial education and to obtain quality advice and products necessary to manage their financial affairs. In fact, there is a growing consensus, in both the public sector and the financial services industry, on the importance of promoting the financial education of households. Clearly, households will remain responsible for their investment decisions.

Specifically, households need to understand the financial responsibility they have to shoulder and have ready access to information—including unbiased and quality financial advice—about investment and saving options, as well as available products to manage their risks. As the improvement of the financial sophistication of households is likely to require a long-term effort, encouraging and coordinating activities in this field are likely to become public policy issues.

In case of widespread failure of the household sector to manage complex investment risks, or if households suffer severe losses across the board on their retirement investments due to sustained market downturns, there could be a political backlash demanding government support as an "insurer of last resort." There could also be a demand for the re-regulation of the financial industry or, at the very least, more litigation would ensue. Thus, the legal and reputation risks facing the financial services industry would increase.

In addition to promoting financial education of households, governments can consider the use of tax and other regulatory incentives (such as IRA and 401(k) plans in the United States) to encourage saving for retirement and stable, long-term investment behavior by households. They can also play a role in facilitating the development of appropriate financial products, designed to fulfill the need of households to manage their risks, including longevity risk. For example, some governments are studying the possibility of issuing long-term or inflation-indexed bonds and longevity bonds to help the financial sector better manage the risks involved in supplying some of the retail products, such as annuities.

The series of GFSR chapters on the flow of risk through different sectors of the financial system has highlighted the importance of gaining a more thorough and complete understanding of all the factors that drive the global asset allocation process. Important factors include changes in regulatory and accounting standards, as well as efforts by institutions, such as pension funds and insurance companies, to better match their assets with their liabilities. Consequently, the global asset allocation process will continue to shift risk between different actors in the financial system, not only between various sectors of the economy but also across borders, and trigger global capital flows that ultimately will have important implications for financial stability. These issues will be further explored in forthcoming issues of the GFSR.

Financing Prospects and Risks Facing Emerging Market Countries

Emerging market sovereign borrowers have enjoyed much-improved financing conditions in the past two years. The favorable environment can be attributed to improvements in economic fundamentals in emerging markets, a reduction in external borrowing requirements, the abundant global liquidity that has allowed many sovereigns to prefinance their 2005 external financing needs, and more reliance on domestic capital markets. International investors' acceptance of local currency bonds, either issued internationally (Colombia) or domestically,[1] is an important and positive development in helping emerging market countries better manage their debt. Sovereign borrowers, except for some countries still burdened by a large debt overhang, are thus in a better position than in the past to cope with the potential market corrections discussed above. Nevertheless, they should not be complacent and should use the currently favorable financial conditions to implement strong economic policies and deepen reforms, so as to enhance their resiliency to future shocks.

Despite an overall improvement in their credit quality since 2000, corporate sectors in many emerging markets continue to face considerable maturity and currency mismatches on their balance sheets. Chapter IV documents this trend, using a new comprehensive

database, which combines balance sheet data for emerging market companies and financing flow data. Emerging market corporates, therefore, remain vulnerable to interest rate and foreign exchange risks, which so far have tended to materialize together: when the exchange rate is under pressure, local interest rates also rise sharply.

Another salient fact is that corporate borrowers in 2004 accounted for 60 percent of international bond issuance by emerging market borrowers—the third year in a row that corporate issuance exceeded sovereign issuance. This phenomenon has reflected a strengthening of the balance sheets of emerging market corporates, and their desire to borrow at lower rates (compared with domestic rates), as well as international investors' search for yield.

Taken together, these developments suggest that there is a need to closely monitor emerging market corporate sector vulnerabilities in order to achieve a more fully informed assessment of overall financial stability. To be effective, such monitoring should follow an integrated approach, which takes into account the interaction between interest rate, foreign exchange, and credit risks. Even though international bond investors may have held more credit risk recently, emerging market corporate insolvencies that could be triggered by a major devaluation of the local currency still present significant credit risks and costs to the domestic banking sector. The fact that some international investors may be new to the emerging market corporate sector could also amplify the volatility of such a potential sell-off.

The authorities in emerging market countries can address the potential vulnerabilities of the corporate sector, as well as help to develop more balanced and efficient financing of their corporates, in several ways:

---

[1]Local currency bonds of selected investment-grade emerging market countries (Chile, the Czech Republic, Hungary, Mexico, Poland, Slovenia, and South Africa) were recently included in the Lehman Global Aggregate Index.

- They should continue to reform and improve their legal and regulatory framework, emphasizing corporate governance and risk management. In particular, disclosure requirements should be upgraded and more vigorously enforced. This will enable the supervisors to better monitor risks and vulnerabilities in the corporate sector. Equally important, more transparency through better disclosure would allow market participants—mainly institutional investors, both domestic and international—to exercise market discipline via the appropriate pricing of corporate credit risks. While this seems to have happened to some extent in some countries, there is still room for improvement.
- They should also continue efforts to develop domestic capital markets, including markets for interest rate and exchange rate hedging instruments. This will allow emerging market companies to have access to more balanced sources of financing and to be able to hedge their balance sheet mismatches. In recent years, a few countries have made good progress in this direction, mainly by further developing local institutional investors such as pension funds, insurance companies, and mutual funds. These countries have also adopted and implemented international best practices in many institutional underpinnings, which are needed to improve the functioning of capital markets. These steps include adopting international accounting standards and implementing modern market infrastructures such as clearing and settlement platforms. These recent experiences offer rich lessons to many emerging market countries and will be analyzed in more detail in forthcoming issues of the GFSR.

CHAPTER II

GLOBAL FINANCIAL MARKET DEVELOPMENTS

This chapter assesses current financial market conditions and risks, in particular the effects of continued abundant global liquidity and improving credit quality on mature and emerging financial markets, and highlights the compression of inflation and credit risk premiums, and low volatility, that have been the key features across major markets. The external economic and financial environment for emerging markets has been exceptionally favorable. The domestic banking and financial systems of emerging market countries are showing signs of increased resilience as well. Many emerging market countries have appropriately used this environment to address vulnerabilities stemming from the level and structure of their liabilities. While financial markets and institutions remain resilient, risks could arise from growing global macroeconomic imbalances and the strong incentive for continued leveraged risk taking.

This chapter also analyzes key structural financial market developments and issues. Given the importance and relatively high volatility of energy markets, it updates earlier work on energy trading, which gained prominence following the sharp run-up in oil prices in 2004, by looking at the broadening of the investor base for energy-related commodities. It assesses developments in the rapidly growing hedge fund industry and uses market-based indicators to appraise the market and credit risks for banks and life insurance companies in the mature markets. It concludes with a report on the trend toward convergent accounting standards.

Market Developments

Financial market conditions remain benign. Favorable fundamentals, including expecta-

tions for solid, if slowing, global economic and earnings growth, limited inflationary pressure, sustained corporate balance sheet strength in the mature markets, and continued improvements in the credit quality of emerging market borrowers, are supporting financial market stability. Against this backdrop, market volatility, mature government bond yields, and global credit spreads have remained low—perhaps even too low.

Low short-term interest rates and low volatility are encouraging investors to move out along the risk spectrum in their search for relative value. The incentive to use leverage to boost returns is still strong. The premiums for inflation and credit risk appear compressed. There is little cushion for bad news regarding asset valuations if expectations for continued favorable fundamentals change.

Risks include a spike in U.S. interest rates, resulting from unanticipated inflationary pressure or a reduction in the exceptionally large foreign portfolio inflows into U.S. fixed income markets. So far, the expectation that U.S. monetary policy will be tightened gradually has provided a firm anchor to financial markets. A continued measured withdrawal of stimulus remains appropriate, and it will likely contribute to continued stability. But it remains important to be vigilant about concentrated exposures or leveraged positions that have been encouraged by low rates and low volatility. The unwinding of these conditions represents a potential source of turbulence.

Persistent global imbalances reflect underlying vulnerabilities that could increase the risk of sharp currency movements and spillovers into other asset markets if not addressed. Portfolio inflows, originating increasingly from the official sector and destined largely for U.S. bond markets, have so far facilitated an orderly, if unbalanced, decline of the dollar. Such flows cannot be counted on indefinitely. Nor should dollar depreciation be the sole means of adjustment. Policy action—including measures to raise U.S. domestic savings, structural reforms to boost domestic demand growth in Europe, and increased exchange rate flexibility in Asia—is needed to reduce the risk of global imbalances triggering market turbulence or impairing global growth.[1]

Financial risk taking encouraged by a prolonged period of abundant liquidity may have created unsustainable valuations and pushed volatility across a wide range of markets to artificially low levels. Past tightening cycles have revealed hidden vulnerabilities as the incentive to reach for yield was withdrawn. The locus of such vulnerabilities has typically become fully apparent only after the fact. In some past cycles, emerging markets have experienced turbulence in the wake of tightening monetary conditions. In this cycle, the search for yield has contributed to the compression of inflation and credit risk premiums and encouraged the rapid growth of structured products, including credit derivatives. The combination of compressed risk premiums and the rapid growth of instruments that lack transparency and afford the potential for taking leveraged positions in the credit markets is a potential source of vulnerability that merits attention.

Emerging market economies have enjoyed an exceptionally favorable economic and financing environment throughout 2004 and in early 2005. Solid global growth has boosted export demand and commodity prices. Interest rates and credit spreads have remained low. With liquidity abundant, investor appetite for new issues from emerging market borrowers has been quite healthy, permitting a high level of issuance at low cost. However, as in the credit markets of mature economies, the factors contributing to low interest rates and low spreads may have peaked, and less easy financing conditions are to be expected. Underlying interest rates are set to rise, and credit spreads are more likely to widen than narrow.

It therefore remains essential for emerging market borrowers to continue to use the favorable external environment to improve their resilience. To ensure continued investor confidence, these borrowers must persevere with measures designed to remove structural impediments to noninflationary growth and strengthen public finances. From the point of view of financial markets, a fundamental source of vulnerability would be eased by reducing the level, and improving the structure, of public debt. In this regard, actions to lengthen the average maturity of debt and reduce the share of public debt linked to short-term interest rates or foreign currencies are particularly important. Fortunately, a number of countries have taken steps to improve their debt structures and to deepen local capital markets to facilitate the issuance of fixed-coupon, long-term bonds. In the case of external financial markets, some countries have appropriately used the favorable environment to improve the maturity profile of their debt through liability management. Moreover, there has been further, though still modest, progress in issuing bonds denominated in local currencies in international capital markets.

Developments and Risks in Mature Financial Markets

Impact of Monetary Tightening Offset by Market Movements

Abundant global liquidity has been a key influence on financial market developments (Figure 2.1 and Box 2.1). Low short-term

---

[1]The cooperative international effort needed to achieve an orderly reduction of global imbalances is considered in the April 2005 issue of the IMF's *World Economic Outlook*.

Figure 2.1. Global Real Interest Rates and Excess Liquidity

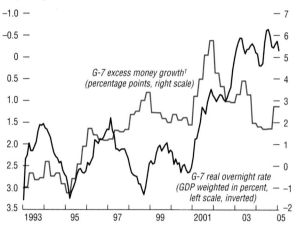

Sources: Organization for Economic Cooperation and Development; and IMF staff estimates.
[1]Excess G-7 money growth is defined as the difference between broad money growth and estimates of money demand in each of the countries of the G-7, weighted by their respective GDPs.

Figure 2.2. Policy Rates
(In percent)

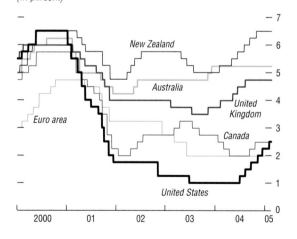

Source: Bloomberg L.P.

interest rates, especially in the United States, have contributed to a quest for yield that has kept longer-term yields and credit spreads low.

Starting from the exceptionally low level of 1 percent, which was adopted to forestall the threat of deflation, the U.S. monetary authorities have increased the federal funds rate on six occasions from mid-June 2004 through February 2005 (Figure 2.2). Over the same period, policy rates have remained constant in Australia (where a tightening cycle was initiated earlier), and the euro area and Japan (which have yet to raise rates), but have risen in Canada, New Zealand, and the United Kingdom.[2] The process of returning the federal funds rate to more normal levels is expected to continue through this year. Consensus expectations for the federal funds rate now center on 3–4 percent by end-2005.

In an unusual development, longer-term U.S. government bond yields have fallen as short-term interest rates were raised, resulting in a marked flattening of the U.S. yield curve. Market developments since the first U.S. rate increase in June—the decline of longer-term U.S. treasury yields, corporate credit spreads, mortgage rates, and the dollar—have mitigated the impact of rate increases (Figure 2.3). Consequently, financial conditions have remained accommodative (see Box 2.1).

In early 2005, the federal funds rate remained below headline consumer price inflation and was roughly in line with core consumer price inflation. Interest rates in the United States have remained below consumer price inflation for longer than might have been expected based on experience with past

[2]After this publication's data cut-off date of February 16, 2005, the Reserve Bank of Australia raised its benchmark overnight cash rate by 25 basis points to 5.5 percent on March 2. In addition, the Reserve Bank of New Zealand raised its benchmark official cash rate another 25 basis points to 6.75 percent on March 10, and the U.S. Federal Reserve raised the fed funds rate an additional 25 basis points on March 22 to 2.75 percent.

tightening cycles. Real interest rates are stimulative in the United States, and only slightly less so in the euro zone.

With key short-term interest rates near or below the rate of inflation, the real yield on inflation-indexed bonds in the United States and other mature markets has remained low, notwithstanding the rebound in global economic activity and strong U.S. productivity growth (Figure 2.4). Japan is a special case where the authorities have driven nominal interest rates to zero and have stressed that they intend to maintain that rate until core price inflation and inflation expectations become positive again. For now, given the persistence of deflation, Japanese short-term interest rates are slightly positive in real terms.

Longer-term U.S. treasury yields appear low given the pace of nominal economic growth (Figure 2.5). Several factors are contributing to the low level of yields in the United States and elsewhere.[3] A sudden shift in one or more of these factors could result in higher government bond yields and a reassessment of valuations in other markets.

First, the credibility and transparency of the U.S. Federal Reserve are key anchors to longer-term yields. In the view of the market, the greater the credibility of monetary policy, the less responsive bond markets need to be. The inflation risk premium has thus fallen to low levels. As a result, longer-term interest rates did not follow policy rates higher, but actually fell as the tightening cycle started.

Second, macroeconomic developments—chiefly limited inflationary pressure and moderating but still solid global economic growth—have reinforced the market view that inflation poses little threat. Inflation expectations based on survey data and on the spread between conventional government bonds and

[3]The April 2005 issue of the IMF's *World Economic Outlook* provides further perspective on this issue. See, in particular, Box 1.2: "Why Are U.S. Long-Term Interest Rates So Low?"

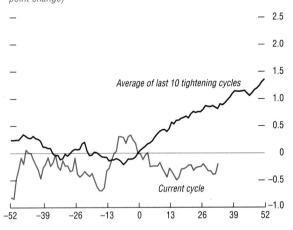

Figure 2.3. U.S. Tightening Cycles: Movement in 10-Year Treasury Yields
(In weeks before and after first Fed rate increase, percentage point change)

Average of last 10 tightening cycles

Current cycle

Sources: J.P. Morgan Chase & Co.; and IMF staff estimates.

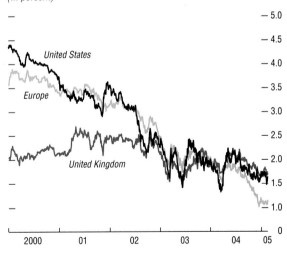

Figure 2.4. Real Yields on Inflation-Indexed Bonds
(In percent)

United States

Europe

United Kingdom

Source: Bloomberg L.P.

Figure 2.5. U.S. Economic Growth and Treasury Yields
(In percent)

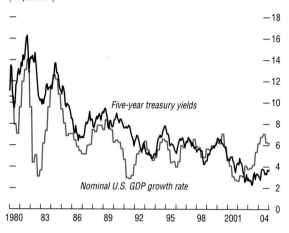

Source: Bloomberg L.P.

Figure 2.6. Foreign Ownership of U.S. Securities
(In percent of total outstanding)

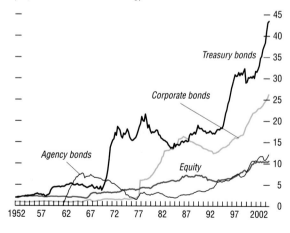

Sources: U.S. Board of Governors of the Federal Reserve System, *Flow of Funds Accounts of the United States*; and IMF staff estimates.

their inflation-indexed counterparts have remained subdued. The persistent though declining output gap, continued strong productivity growth, and competitive pressure have helped dampen inflation expectations.

Third, there remains some market uncertainty about the prospects for growth. Financial markets interpreted last year's surge in energy and commodity prices as a tax on growth rather than an inflationary impulse. In addition, some market analysts consider that there may be structural issues—the low rate of domestic savings and high external current account deficit—that may pose a future drag on growth.

Fourth, foreign flows—including, in particular, flows from Asian central banks—into U.S. government and other bonds have been substantial. These flows have contributed to keeping yields and credit spreads low. Foreign purchases of U.S. government bonds in 2004 were roughly equivalent to total net new issuance of U.S. treasury securities. Foreign holdings of the outstanding stock of U.S. fixed income assets have risen substantially (Figure 2.6).

Fifth, substantial foreign demand for U.S. fixed-income assets has coincided with limited supply from the corporate sector, because high-grade issuance has remained relatively low. As earnings recovered in the United States and elsewhere, corporations remained cautious (see below) and continued to contain costs and limit capital expenditure. As a result, the U.S. corporate sector has been a net supplier of funds to the economy, helping to keep interest rates and credit spreads low, despite the large U.S. fiscal deficit and low household savings rate.

Finally, as has been explained in previous issues of the *Global Financial Stability Report*, pension fund sponsors in Europe and the United States are adjusting their asset allocation policies to reduce a perceived mismatch between their assets and liabilities (Box 2.2, see p. 38). These institutional investors are generally seeking longer-term fixed-income

Box 2.1. Gauging Global Liquidity Conditions

Various measures of liquidity suggest that despite the tightening of policy rates in the United States and other major countries, overall liquidity conditions—based on both quantity and price measures—remain highly accommodative, though differences arise across regions.

Cost of Central Bank Liquidity: Policy Rates

The central banks of most industrialized countries directly set the cost of borrowing and lending of central bank funds traded in the interbank market—known as the policy rate—and thereby indirectly influence other financial rates in the economy. This cost of central bank liquidity is usually looked at relative to inflation to give an indication of whether liquidity conditions are accommodative or restrictive. Weighting the real policy rates of G-7 countries by their respective GDPs (see first figure) shows that despite increases in nominal policy rates, central bank liquidity (with the exception of the United Kingdom) has remained highly accommodative with a cost below zero.

Supply of Central Bank Liquidity: Base Money

Base money—currency and deposits held at the central bank by financial institutions forming the payments system—is the most liquid form of

Global Central Bank Liquidity Index
(1993 = 100)

Sources: IMF, *International Financial Statistics*; EconData Pty. Ltd.; Bloomberg L.P.; and IMF staff estimates.

purchasing power and means of settlement of economic transactions. The supply of the base money in relation to economic activity is therefore another measure of monetary accommodation. In the major economic areas, annual growth in base money has exceeded nominal GDP, sometimes substantially since 2001, highlighted by an index of cumulative central bank liquidity, suggesting accommodative liquidity conditions.[1] Japan's figures reflect quantities of central bank money aimed at breaking entrenched deflation (see second figure). In Europe, growth in base money has exceeded the pace of nominal economic activity during the past two years. Broadly, rising central bank liquidity is also consistent with low real policy rates.

Household and Corporate Liquidity: Broader Monetary Aggregates

Banks provide liquidity to the economy as their liabilities—held by the corporate and household sector in the form of deposits—are money-like. Monetary aggregates—deposit liabilities of banks plus currency liabilities of the

[1]Index of central bank liquidity is the cumulative sum of the annual percent growth of base money less the annual percent growth in nominal GDP.

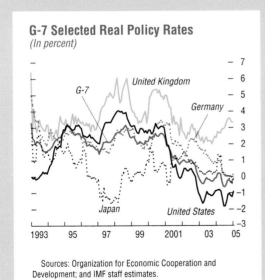

G-7 Selected Real Policy Rates
(In percent)

Sources: Organization for Economic Cooperation and Development; and IMF staff estimates.

Box 2.1 *(concluded)*

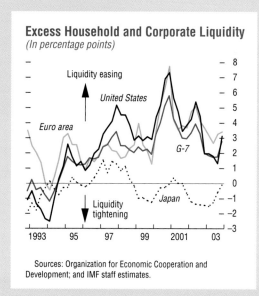

Excess Household and Corporate Liquidity
(In percentage points)

Sources: Organization for Economic Cooperation and Development; and IMF staff estimates.

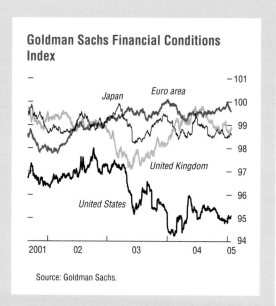

Goldman Sachs Financial Conditions Index

Source: Goldman Sachs.

central bank—are therefore a measure of an economy's liquidity. One approach to gauging household and corporate liquidity measures money demand in relation to economic activity. This measure suggests that household and corporate liquidity in the G-7, while declining from its peak at the end of 2001, remains high and has shown signs of rising in the latter half of 2004.[2] In Japan, household and corporate liquidity has not expanded along with the increase in central bank liquidity (see third figure).

Composite Measures of Liquidity: Financial Conditions Index

The channels through which the setting of monetary policy is transmitted to financial markets and to the real economy are complex and no single monetary or interest rate measure has shown a reliable link. For this reason, some central banks have sought to combine the

[2]Excess liquidity is defined by the difference between broad money growth and estimates for money demand. Estimates for money demand are derived from trend velocity growth using average velocity growth during 1980–2002 in the respective economies, except for the euro area, where it is based on the mid-value of the range for velocity growth as derived by the European Central Bank.

estimated influences of exchange rates and interest rates on the economy into a single measure to provide a gauge of monetary conditions. Some researchers have found that including capital market variables—such as stock market valuations—more fully captures the effect of financial wealth and liquidity on the economy. One such indicator is the Goldman Sachs Financial Conditions Index, which is a weighted combination of the real three-month interbank lending rate, the interest rate on corporate bonds, the market capitalization of equities in relation to GDP, and the real effective exchange rate. Indicators of financial conditions suggest that despite the increase in the fed funds rate, overall financial conditions in the United States have loosened as equity markets have risen, the exchange rate has depreciated, and credit spreads have narrowed (see fourth figure). In Europe, by contrast, financial conditions have actually tightened, reflecting in part the appreciation of the euro.

Global Liquidity: International Reserves

Globalization of finance and trade has brought with it a rise in cross-border ownership of real and financial assets. Cross-border claims of tradable financial assets might therefore serve

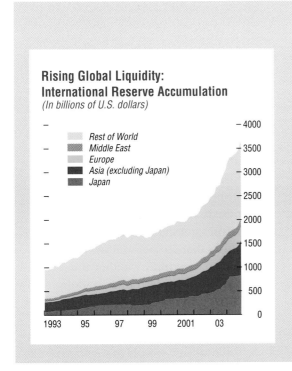

**Rising Global Liquidity:
International Reserve Accumulation**
(In billions of U.S. dollars)

Rest of World
Middle East
Europe
Asia (excluding Japan)
Japan

as a very broad measure of global liquidity. Such holdings of global liquidity—a financial asset that represents a claim on a foreigner that could be turned readily into foreign exchange—can be held by the private or the public sector. Increases in public holdings in the form of foreign exchange reserves held by the central bank create central bank liquidity in the domestic currency. To the extent that such creation of domestic liquidity is not sterilized by the central bank, excess liquidity in one country can spill over to another country. The sharp rise in international liquidity—measured by reserve accumulation—especially in Asia is a result of strong trade performance and sizable intervention (see fifth figure). The investment of the bulk of these reserves into U.S. treasuries and agencies has contributed to the low yields in global fixed income markets.

investments that better match their liabilities. In some cases, especially in Europe, regulatory changes have encouraged these investors to adjust their asset allocation targets, by increasing their holdings of longer duration bonds. As a consequence, institutional investors have been eager to seek assets at the longer end of the maturity spectrum, notwithstanding the low yields they offer in many cases.

Solid Corporate Earnings and Balance Sheets Support Corporate Bond Markets

Corporations in the United States, the euro area, and Japan have enjoyed an increase in earnings and cash balances. These factors have supported the compression of credit spreads in corporate bond markets (Figures 2.7 and 2.8). Low interest rates on less risky assets and the low level of market volatility have encouraged investors to increase their exposure to credit risk, contributing to falling spreads. In addition, life insurance companies have continued to invest in corporate bonds

as a means of better aligning their assets and liabilities (Box 2.3, see p. 40). With the exception of U.S. automobile manufacturers, which face potential further credit rating downgrades, the dispersion of spreads in credit markets has been compressed, raising the possibility of reduced investor discrimination.

The narrowing of spreads has been helped by the improvement in the creditworthiness of borrowers and the shortage of high-grade corporate paper supply. With cash flows strong, debt-service ratios low, and companies paying down short-term debt, default rates have fallen to low levels (Figure 2.9). However, rating agencies have noted that default rates are low given the stage in the economic cycle and in absolute terms. Rating agencies have warned that easy money has allowed weaker, higher-yielding credits to obtain financing, and that this may contribute to a higher incidence of default and restructurings in the future.

The rapid growth of structured products, including credit derivatives, has been a cen-

Figure 2.7. High-Grade Corporate Bond Spreads
(In basis points)

Source: Merrill Lynch.

Figure 2.8. High-Yield Corporate Bond Spreads
(In basis points)

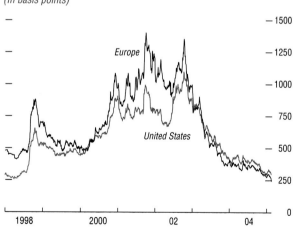

Source: Merrill Lynch.

tral element in the quest for yield (Figure 2.10).[4] The growth of credit derivatives has many positive elements (Box 2.4, see p. 42). These instruments provide a liquid and convenient vehicle for trading and hedging credit risk and provide information on market views of creditworthiness. Such instruments, however, also provide a means of taking leveraged credit exposure. Moreover, their off-balance-sheet nature and complexity reduce transparency, and potentially mask the risks to which investors and counterparties are exposed. Thus, the rapid growth of the market raises questions as to whether there may be risks that are not well understood. It is difficult to determine whether the recent expansion of credit derivatives is motivated by the liquidity or leverage that they offer. But it is likely that the rapid expansion of credit derivative instruments has increased the possibility of leveraged losses for some investors, should the current benign credit environment deteriorate.

The near-term outlook for the U.S. corporate bond market remains favorable. The risk of a credit event in the U.S. corporate bond market spreading into other mature and emerging credit markets appears low. However, the factors that have underpinned a fundamental improvement in credit quality have likely peaked. Corporate earnings growth is expected to slow, and default rates are expected to rise modestly from current low levels, in part because of the recent spate of high-yield issuance. The recent pickup in mergers and acquisitions activity could put ratings under greater pressure, possibly leading to a rise in default rates as companies increase borrowing to make acquisitions. Moreover, the gradual withdrawal of monetary stimulus is expected to contribute to more difficult financing conditions for firms.

---

[4]At end-June 2004, the total notional principal outstanding of over-the-counter derivatives contracts totaled US$220 trillion, of which credit derivatives represented US$4.5 trillion.

Solid Earnings and Balance Sheets Support Major Equity Market Valuations

Corporate earnings in major markets are beginning to slow, following recent strong gains. Fundamental reasons for slower earnings growth include a maturing cycle and the difficulty of obtaining additional cost reductions after years of aggressive cuts. For S&P reporting companies, analysts forecast earnings gains to slow to 10 percent in 2005, compared with 25 percent gains in 2004. For members of the FT Europe index, gains are expected to slow to a 12 percent rate for the year overall, and for the Japanese Topix index, earnings gains are expected to slow as well, but to a still-high 22 percent rate. Although prospective earnings gains are less buoyant than earlier, the valuation of current earnings in the major markets remains broadly conservative (Figure 2.11).

Slower earnings growth prospects may encourage managers and owners to increase company leverage. After several years of efforts to reduce gearing, managers may use solid company balance sheets and easy financial market conditions to borrow for capital expenditure or acquisitions in a bid to boost earnings. Alternatively, high cash holdings could be used for equity buybacks or increased dividend payments.

Both the opportunities for corporate releveraging and current stock market valuations depend on continued low real rates of interest. At current low risk-free rates of interest in the key mature markets, earnings appear fairly valued to slightly undervalued (Figures 2.12 and 2.13). A normalization of interest rates would make valuations appear less attractive.

Financial Market Volatility Remains Subdued

Financial market volatility has fallen to low levels (Figure 2.14). As in the case of low yields, prolonged periods of low market volatility can encourage investors to seek higher returns through leverage or by taking

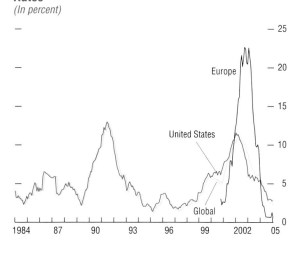

Figure 2.9. Speculative Grade Corporate Default Rates
(In percent)

Source: Moody's.

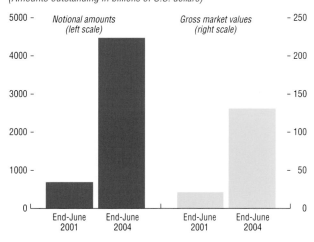

Figure 2.10. Credit Derivatives Market
(Amounts outstanding in billions of U.S. dollars)

Source: Bank for International Settlements.

Figure 2.11. Price-Earnings Ratios

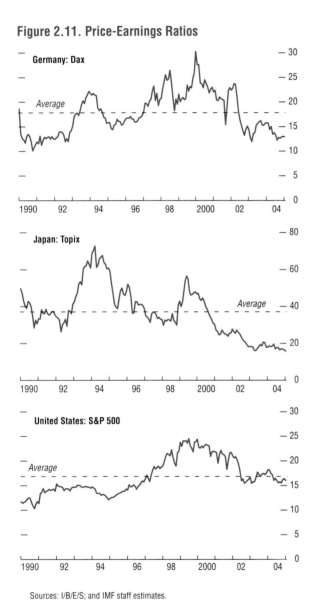

Sources: I/B/E/S; and IMF staff estimates.

positions in riskier assets. Both structural and cyclical factors explain some of this trend.

The growth of the credit derivatives market has made it much easier for banks to shed the credit risks they no longer want, and for risks to be subdivided and allocated to those willing to bear them. With many assets traded electronically, and other markets becoming more liquid, mispricings, at least as revealed by the standard pricing models, are swiftly arbitraged away. In addition, the low interest rate environment may have encouraged the sale of options as a means of boosting income. Hedge funds and others providing yield-enhanced instruments to individual and institutional investors appear to have used embedded options to help increase yields, at least initially. The increased use of these instruments, which in effect increase the supply of options, could also be contributing to reduced option premiums and implied volatility.

Cyclical factors may also have temporarily suppressed volatility to low levels. The current pace of near-trend global growth and firmly entrenched expectations for continued solid noninflationary growth could be contributing to low financial market volatility. In the mid-1990s, for example, implied volatilities, especially for equities, were low and global growth was near trend.

In addition, stronger corporate balance sheets and more robust earnings have contributed to declining volatility (Figures 2.15 and 2.16). Bond and equity volatility were elevated before the turn of the century by the precarious state of corporate balance sheets. Many companies have since repaired those balance sheets and are, therefore, less likely to slip toward bankruptcy. Lower equity and bond volatilities probably reflect these improvements.

However, even as implied volatility has fallen to historically very low levels, it has lagged the even steeper decline in actual volatilities (Figure 2.17). The gap between implied and actual volatilities increased during 2004. This suggests that many market participants do not fully accept that the factors driving down volatility are permanent. They are therefore tending to price options with some degree of risk margin in case actual volatility were to spike back up to less unusually low levels. The low level of implied volatility across a range of assets is not necessarily a cause for comfort: actual and implied volatilities have in the past increased unexpectedly from low levels, and at least part of the decline in implied volatilities appears to be linked to the quest for yield.

Markets Adjust to Persistent Global Imbalances

Despite the broadening of the global economic recovery, global imbalances among major economies have continued to increase (Figure 2.18). Broadly speaking, exchange rates and financial asset markets have, so far, smoothly intermediated cross-border flows and the divergent growth of net external assets and liabilities, while contributing to the process of shifting relative prices toward promoting a rebalancing of external conditions. One form of partial adjustment has been the depreciation of the U.S. dollar against its trading partners. Over time, this should support external adjustment through changes in relative prices of tradable and nontradable goods, thereby creating incentives for a rebalancing of global demand, leading to a narrowing of the U.S. trade deficit.[5]

Since its peak in early 2002, the dollar has depreciated substantially against the euro, the sterling, and yen. However, in real effective terms, dollar depreciation has been more modest as the extent of depreciation has been limited by the relative stability of the U.S. currency vis-à-vis the currencies of its main emerging market trading partners.

In the last quarter of 2004, emerging Asian economies experienced strong inflows of capi-

[5]See the IMF's *World Economic Outlook*, 2005.

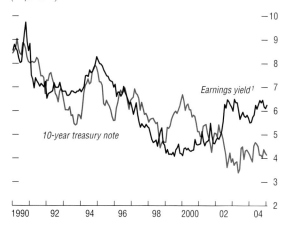

Figure 2.12. U.S. Equity and Benchmark Government Yields
(In percent)

Source: Bloomberg L.P.
[1]Earnings yield is the inverse of the price-earnings ratio.

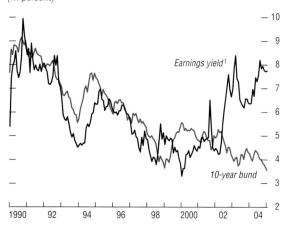

Figure 2.13. German Equity and Benchmark Government Yields
(In percent)

Source: Bloomberg L.P.
[1]Earnings yield is the inverse of the price-earnings ratio.

Figure 2.14. Implied Volatilities
(In percent)

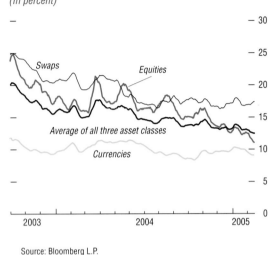

Source: Bloomberg L.P.

Figure 2.15. Equity Volatility

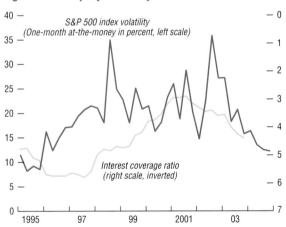

Sources: Bloomberg L.P.; and Credit Suisse First Boston.

tal and pressure for their currencies to appreciate. Reserve accumulation in Asia has soared (Figure 2.19). Currencies in Asia appreciated modestly in those countries with a degree of currency flexibility and markets expect a further appreciation during 2005 (Figure 2.20).

In this connection, a revaluation of the Chinese renminbi is seen as the key to a broadening of the adjustment process. A revaluation of the renminbi would probably create headroom for other Asian currencies to strengthen, and pressures on them to do so would intensify. As yet, however, there are no indications that a removal of the peg is imminent. At the end of February 2005, the (fairly illiquid) nondeliverable forwards market signaled expectations of appreciation over the next 12 months of only about 5 percent, and this varied considerably over 2004 (Figure 2.21).

Interest rate differentials are moving in the direction of supporting inflows of capital to the United States. Longer-term U.S. treasury yields have risen relative to yields on comparable bonds in the euro area and Japan (Figure 2.22). This move in relative interest rates should encourage continued foreign flows into U.S. fixed-income markets, while at the same time inducing U.S. investors to curb purchases of foreign government bonds.

Currency market volatility has remained relatively modest, suggesting that markets expect further currency adjustments to remain moderate (Figure 2.23). The pricing of options implied that markets believe the most likely outcome, by far, is a gradual continuation of the current trends. Disorderly moves are given a very low probability (i.e., the probability distributions are not as "fat-tailed" as they have been at times in the past).

The financial system and global financial flows are functioning in a manner that gives policymakers time to implement credibly the policies that will be necessary to correct macroeconomic imbalances. Despite the current market calm, the relatively low probability of a sharp dollar decline, and the continued apparent attraction of U.S. capital markets to foreigners, the size, source, and destination of the flows financing the U.S. current account deficit are areas of market concern. At some point, markets may become impatient with the pace of change, and asset prices will start to play a more forceful role in bringing about the needed adjustments. In that event, U.S. government bond yields and credit spreads on corporate bonds would likely increase sharply. Equity valuations that appear reasonable in the current low interest rate environment will appear less attractive as the cost of capital to corporations rises. Higher yields and spreads in the U.S. fixed-income markets would also likely spill over to emerging market bonds, contributing to a deterioration of the external financing environment for emerging markets.

It is difficult to forecast when markets might grow restive. However, the persistence of large U.S. external current account deficits, financed in part by official flows from Asia, may eventually reach a limit. One possible indication that such a limit is approaching would be if countries with rapid increases in external reserves began to experience excessive money growth and inflation. In that case, markets would begin to anticipate reduced intervention. In addition to complicating the implementation of monetary policy, reserve levels can also grow to a point at which they impose disproportionately high fiscal costs. In this case, the benefits of accumulating reserves for prudential (or other) purposes may be offset by the costs to the budget of financing a high level of reserves.[6] Moreover, as reserve levels rise, questions about whether their accumulation represents an optimal allocation of resources are likely to increase. Markets are sensitive to these potential constraints on reserve accumulation and are likely

[6]Reserves are typically held in instruments that yield less than the cost of government borrowing.

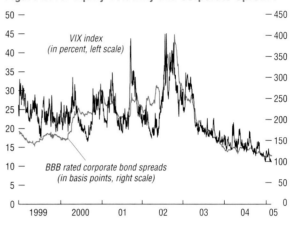

Figure 2.16. Equity Volatility and Corporate Spreads

VIX index
(in percent, left scale)

BBB rated corporate bond spreads
(in basis points, right scale)

Sources: Bloomberg L.P.; and Merrill Lynch.

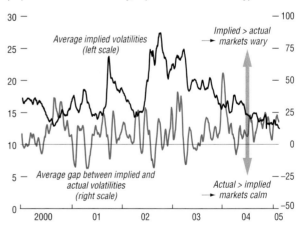

Figure 2.17. Implied Versus Actual Volatility
(Implied minus actual volatility, in percent of actual volatility)

Average implied volatilities
(left scale)

Implied > actual
→ markets wary

Average gap between implied and
actual volatilities
(right scale)

Actual > implied
→ markets calm

Sources: Bloomberg L.P.; and IMF staff estimates.

to react in anticipation of a change in the pace or composition of reserve accumulation. At the moment, however, these limits are not seen to be binding.

Developments and Vulnerabilities in Emerging Markets

Spreads on emerging market bonds have continued to narrow and remain near eight-year lows in early 2005. Improvements in domestic fundamentals, accommodative monetary policy and low returns in mature markets, and an appetite for risk reinforced by low financial market volatility have contributed to the compression of spreads (Figure 2.24).

The investor base for emerging markets has also expanded. Low interest rates in mature markets and the attractive risk-adjusted returns of emerging markets in recent years have attracted new investment flows. Since 2000, emerging market bonds have been one of the best performing assets, and emerging market equities have generated higher risk-adjusted returns than mature equity markets (Figure 2.25). In addition, credit rating upgrades, particularly for those countries that have garnered investment grade ratings, have widened the universe of potential investors in emerging market bonds.

Emerging Market Valuations Near Record Levels

Emerging market bond spreads have narrowed across the board, leading to reduced differentiation among riskier credits. In particular, the spread between B and double-B rated credits has narrowed considerably (Figure 2.26). The same phenomenon can be seen in the high returns for the riskiest credits and in the fact that the ongoing search for yield has attracted new and possibly riskier borrowers into the asset class, notably on the corporate side (Figure 2.27).

Emerging market debt valuations now appear stretched relative to their historical

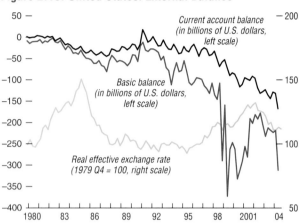

Figure 2.18. United States: External Balance

Sources: Bloomberg L.P.; and IMF staff estimates.

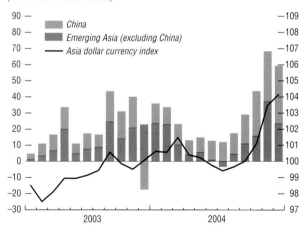

Figure 2.19. Emerging Asia Reserve Accumulation[1]
(In billions of U.S. dollars)

Sources: Bloomberg L.P.; J.P. Morgan Chase & Co.; and IMF staff estimates.
[1]Includes China, Hong Kong SAR, India, Indonesia, Korea, Malaysia, Philippines, Singapore, Taiwan Province of China, and Thailand.

relationship with fundamentals and liquidity. Spreads are more than 100 basis points narrower than forecast on the basis of a staff model that incorporates ratings and a measure of liquidity as determinants of spreads (Figure 2.28).[7] Nonetheless, these valuations reflect common trends across all credit markets. As a result, spreads against comparably rated U.S. corporate bonds remain attractive (Figure 2.29).

Improved Credit Quality Supports Valuations and Helps Broaden Investor Base

The average credit quality of J.P. Morgan Chase's EMBI Global (EMBIG) has reached a new high, more than recouping the decline in average quality after Korea graduated from the index at end-April 2004. Upgrades have outnumbered downgrades by an increasing margin since 2003. As a result, an estimated 49 percent of the combined dollar- and euro-denominated EMBIG indices (by market capitalization) are now investment grade. Moreover, a well-known private sector model suggests several sovereigns are candidates for upgrades for 2005, while none is a strong candidate for a downgrade (Credit Suisse First Boston, 2005).

A broadening investor base has also been a critical element of the emerging market rally, and it has helped buoy demand for new issues in the primary market.

• Pension funds and insurance companies have allocated an increasing proportion of their assets to emerging markets. The inclusion of some emerging market borrowers in major global bond indices has contributed to this trend, as have credit rating upgrades to investment grade for a number of countries. Strategic allocations from these investors reportedly remained strong throughout 2004, reaching an estimated $12 billion,

[7]See the *Global Financial Stability Report*, April 2004, Appendix I.

Figure 2.20. Asia (Excluding Japan) Currency Index

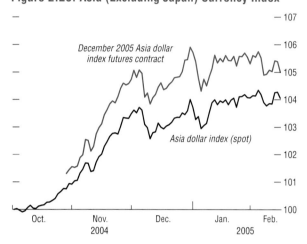

Sources: Bloomberg L.P.; and J.P. Morgan Chase & Co.

Figure 2.21. Chinese Yuan 12-Month Forward Rates
(In yuan per U.S. dollar)

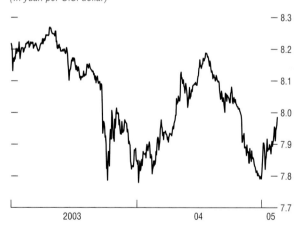

Source: Bloomberg L.P.

Figure 2.22. United States: 10-Year Rate Spread and Current Account Balance

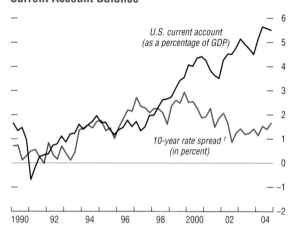

Source: Bloomberg L.P.
[1]U.S. treasury yields minus average of bund and JGB yields.

Figure 2.23. Currency Volatilities
(Three-month forwards, in percent)

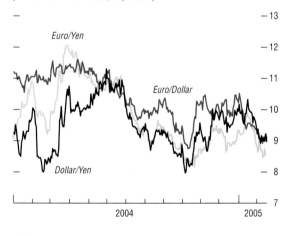

Source: Bloomberg L.P.

about one-quarter of sovereign emerging bond issuance that year. Anecdotal evidence suggests that the pipeline for new strategic investments planned for 2005 is equally substantial. Decisions to make allocations to emerging markets appear to be predicated on an understanding that such markets have performed well over the long run in spite of periodic crises. This suggests that, barring a very sharp market deterioration, these investors are likely to stay invested in emerging markets through a downturn.

- Evidence concerning investors following more short-term trading strategies remains difficult to come by.[8] Nonetheless, it is clear that the number of such investors has increased considerably in the last two years. Many investment banks have reopened or enlarged proprietary emerging market trading desks. Also, the number of hedge funds has proliferated, and many are reported to be on the forefront of the drive to invest in local markets.

- Dedicated emerging market mutual funds continue to receive steady, if modest, net inflows, though these funds (at least in the United States) have not yet recouped all of the heavy net outflows experienced in the spring of 2004.

Search for Yield Extends to Local Emerging Markets

Over the past year, foreign investment flows into local currency instruments have increased substantially. Flows have been concentrated in the most liquid local currency markets,

---

[8]Such investors, including hedge funds and investment banks' proprietary desks, are generally characterized by a total return objective (i.e., as opposed to returns relative to a benchmark) and the use of significant leverage. They are also frequently able to take advantage of a wide array of investment strategies, including the ability to short markets, and employ leverage, and can thus take on greater risk. Their use of leverage suggests that they are more vulnerable to forced closures of underperforming positions.

including government bonds in Brazil, Hungary, Mexico, Poland, and Turkey. The proportion of government bonds held by foreign investors in these markets doubled in aggregate over the past year, and ranges from a still-small 4 percent in Brazil to 20 percent of the market in Poland, and 30 percent in Hungary (Figure 2.30).

The demand for local currency government bonds has been whetted by the decline of yields on hard-currency-denominated credit instruments, including emerging market external bonds. As valuations on other assets become increasingly stretched, investors have ventured further out on the risk spectrum in a search for relative value. In addition, some investors have been attracted by the possibility of currency gains. Reflecting these factors, recent data suggest that trading of local emerging market bonds has increased significantly (Figure 2.31).

Local currency investment has been facilitated by the development and deepening of local markets.[9] Part of this process has involved the introduction of derivatives instruments to hedge foreign exchange risk. More recently, countries have also taken advantage of growing liquidity to extend the local yield curve, addressing the need of local and foreign investors for higher duration instruments, and the need of local corporate issuers for longer maturity benchmark bonds. Brazil and Turkey have issued fixed-rate local currency bonds at longer maturities, of up to five years, with strong interest from foreign investors. In the case of Brazil, this complements the extension of the inflation-indexed bond curve out to 40 years. Mexico also extended its yield curve significantly in 2004 by issuing a 20-year peso-denominated bond, which is estimated to be about 70 percent owned by foreign investors.

[9]See the March 2003 *Global Financial Stability Report,* Chapter IV, for a discussion of the policies needed to deepen local securities markets.

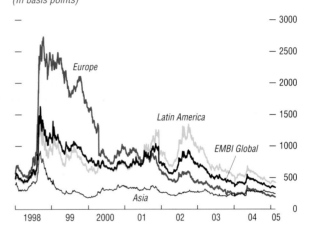

Figure 2.24. EMBIG Sovereign Spreads
(In basis points)

Source: J.P. Morgan Chase & Co.

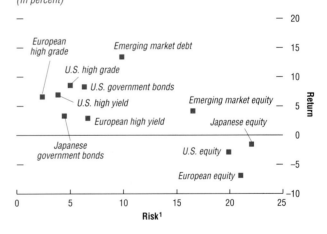

Figure 2.25. Risk-Return Trade-off
(In percent)

Sources: Bloomberg L.P.; Merrill Lynch; and IMF staff estimates.
[1]Five-year average of annualized standard deviations of total returns.

Figure 2.26. Emerging Market Credit Bucket Spread Difference
(In basis points)

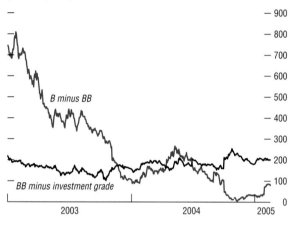

Source: J.P. Morgan & Chase Co.

Figure 2.27. EMBI Global Performance, 2004
(In percent)

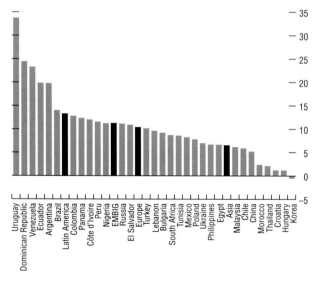

Source: J.P. Morgan Chase & Co.

Due to the high correlation between external and domestic debt, moving into some local currency markets offers little additional diversification benefit. The exceptions to this are the markets of low-yielding investment grade countries such as Mexico and Poland, where the correlation between external and domestic debt is low (Figure 2.32). For higher-yielding credits such as Brazil and Turkey, the credit risk premium is high and changes in country risk affect yields on external debt, the exchange rate, and yields on domestic debt at the same time, resulting in high correlations among these assets, particularly in times of stress.[10]

For borrowers, attracting foreign investors into local currency markets provides an opportunity to reduce exposure to currency risk and diversify the investor base, potentially lowering interest costs and resulting in more stable access to financing. The development of local market instruments has facilitated their inclusion in global bond indices that are used by a broad range of investors as benchmarks. For example, the local currency bonds of selected investment-grade emerging market countries (Chile, the Czech Republic, Hungary, Mexico, Poland, Slovenia, and South Africa) were recently included in the Lehman Global Aggregate Index. This has made it easier for longer-term investors to hold emerging market local currency bonds.

Despite increased investor interest in local currency instruments, access to some local markets remains limited by registration requirements, taxes, and regulations that require a minimum length of time before investments can be unwound. In some cases, investors have circumvented these obstacles through the use of structured notes and credit derivatives to gain access to local currency exposure without having to hold the underly-

---

[10]For example, see the discussion on shifting interest rate expectations and their effect on emerging market local currency bond yields in the September 2004 *Global Financial Stability Report,* Chapter II.

ing securities. Although difficult to quantify, anecdotal evidence suggests that the use of such instruments for local currency exposure increased rapidly last year.

Spike in U.S. Interest Rates Could Roil Emerging Markets

Expectations of a gradual reduction of global liquidity are helping to keep global credit spreads low. However, a spike in interest rates, which could lead to a rapid decompression of credit spreads and a less hospitable external financing environment, remains the key risk for emerging markets. The possible catalysts for a decompression of spreads include the following:

• Higher-than-anticipated inflation would cause markets to raise interest rates across the maturity spectrum and could lead to an increase in the inflation risk premium from current low levels. An increase in underlying interest rates would also cause a decompression of credit spreads. However, it is unlikely that the change in inflationary expectations would be so large as to cause a major dislocation in markets.

• There is also a low probability that heightened risk aversion arising from uncertainty over the financing of global imbalances could create turbulence in the currency markets that could spill over to the U.S. bond markets, leading to higher underlying interest rates and a decompression of spreads.

• It is also possible that the global compression of credit spreads could be reversed by adverse developments in the U.S. corporate bond market. In that event, investors could seek to reduce their exposure to credit risk more broadly.

Emerging Market Financing

Gross issuance by emerging market countries hit a record high in 2004 (Table 2.1 and Figure 2.33). Bond issuance rose in response

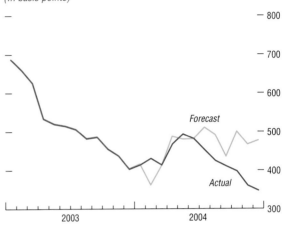

Figure 2.28. Forecast and Actual EMBIG Spread
(In basis points)

Sources: J.P. Morgan Chase & Co.; and IMF staff estimates.

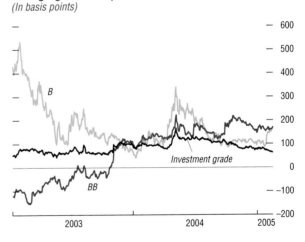

Figure 2.29. Differentials Between Corporate and Emerging Market Spreads
(In basis points)

Sources: J.P. Morgan Chase & Co.; and Merrill Lynch.

Figure 2.30. Foreign Participation Rates in Local Markets
(In percent)

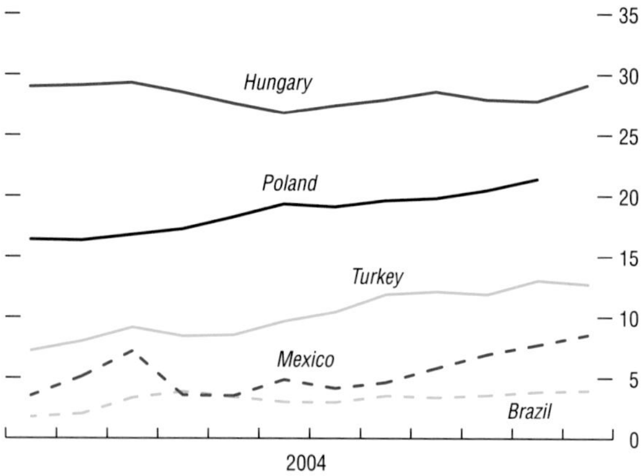

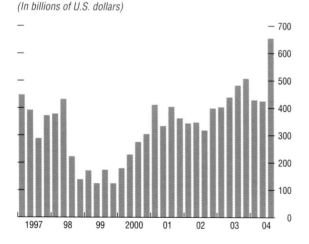

Sources: National central banks; and IMF staff estimates.

Figure 2.31. Trading Volumes in Local Emerging Market Instruments
(In billions of U.S. dollars)

Sources: EMTA; and IMF staff estimates.

to strong demand for emerging market assets, low global bond yields, and the tightening of spreads during 2004. Issuers brought forward issues planned for 2005 and 2006. By early February 2005, emerging market sovereigns had already completed about half of their planned external issuance for 2005. Equity issuance exceeded the previous highs recorded in 2000, especially in Asia and the EMEA region (Europe, Middle East, and Africa). The higher growth in emerging market economies, particularly in Asia, relative to mature markets and an increasing interest by investors in local currency exposure facilitated increased equity issuance. Syndicated lending remained below previous highs, but was still well above recent years.

Net issuance also rose, notwithstanding high bond amortizations, but it did not exceed the previous high of 1997 (Figure 2.34). Net issuance continued to be low in Latin America, as it has been since the withdrawal of Argentina from the market in 2001.

Bond Issuance

Bond issuance remained strong for the second half of 2004, though not as high as in the first half (Figure 2.35). The increase in issuance was dominated by Asia and EMEA credits, with Latin America remaining close to the historical trend. In the EMEA region, sovereign issuance reached record highs, while in Asia there was increased access by corporates to the market. Collective action clauses were typically included in new issues (Box 2.5, see p. 43).

The increase in private corporate issuance was notable. In the last half of 2004, the proportion of such issuance in the total reached about 50 percent, above the quarterly average in previous years (Figure 2.36). The increased demand for emerging market corporate bonds represents a move out along the risk spectrum in the search for yield. This could represent an additional risk to the market to the extent that investors are less familiar with, and less able to evaluate, emerging market corporates' risk.

The changing currency composition of bond issuance was also a significant development. In 2004, emerging market issuance in euros reached about 25 percent of total issuance, almost double the level of euro issuance in 2003 (Figure 2.37). Sovereigns issued over two-thirds of the total, with many from Latin America and Asia that would not normally seek to issue in euros. Funding in euros was facilitated by significant demand from European mutual funds, pension funds, insurance companies, and banks. For emerging market countries, euro issuance serves to diversify the currency composition of their debt, reducing the risk of saturating the dollar-denominated market. Such issuance may also open the possibility of tapping new investors.

The issuance of global notes in local currency was a recent innovation in the market (Box 2.6, see p. 44). The extent to which local-currency-denominated global bonds represent a new channel for overcoming the "original sin" of being unable to issue long-term, fixed-coupon debt in domestic currency remains an open question. The number and size of such issues remains limited. Moreover, recent successful issues have been made in a particularly hospitable external financing environment. The successful issue of local currency notes is linked to the increased demand for higher-yielding local market assets as well as expectations of currency gains related to the weakening U.S. dollar.

Equity Issuance

Equity issues in the second half of 2004 continued to be dominated by Asia, as in the first part of the year, but significant issuance was also seen from the EMEA region in the fourth quarter. In contrast, Latin American equity issuance remained at historically low levels, only about 4.7 percent of the total, in keeping with the tradition of financing from retained earnings or borrowing (Figure 2.38).

Figure 2.32. Correlations Between Local and External Debt

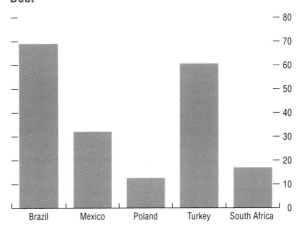

Source: Citibank.

Figure 2.33. Emerging Market Financing
(In billions of U.S. dollars)

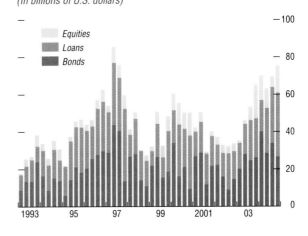

Source: Capital Data.

Table 2.1. Emerging Market Financing

	2001	2002	2003	2004	2003 Q1	Q2	Q3	Q4	2004 Q1	Q2	Q3	Q4	Nov.	Dec.	2005[1] Jan.
								(In billions of U.S. dollars)							
Gross issuance by asset	**162.1**	**135.6**	**199.3**	**280.3**	**35.0**	**46.0**	**53.2**	**65.1**	**69.9**	**63.0**	**69.3**	**78.1**	**24.9**	**25.4**	**22.2**
Bonds	89.0	61.6	98.8	131.5	20.1	27.9	24.6	26.1	40.0	28.6	33.9	29.0	9.8	5.7	18.8
Equities	11.2	16.4	28.3	43.4	1.2	2.0	7.1	18.0	13.1	10.4	5.6	14.4	5.1	4.5	1.5
Loans	61.9	57.6	72.2	105.3	13.7	16.1	21.5	20.9	16.8	24.0	29.9	34.7	10.0	15.1	1.8
Gross issuance by region	**162.1**	**135.6**	**199.3**	**280.3**	**35.0**	**46.0**	**53.2**	**65.1**	**69.9**	**63.0**	**69.3**	**78.1**	**24.9**	**25.4**	**22.2**
Asia	67.5	53.9	88.0	121.3	12.9	15.7	25.1	34.3	33.1	29.7	25.5	33.0	12.6	8.0	6.4
Latin America	53.9	33.4	42.8	53.0	7.8	12.1	9.1	13.8	14.4	9.6	15.9	13.1	3.8	4.3	5.3
Europe, Middle East, Africa	40.8	48.3	68.5	106.0	14.3	18.2	19.1	17.0	22.4	23.7	27.9	32.0	8.5	13.2	10.5
Amortization by asset	**148.0**	**129.3**	**124.2**	**135.5**	**22.1**	**34.3**	**29.6**	**38.2**	**38.4**	**33.2**	**31.9**	**31.0**	**8.5**	**12.7**	**4.3**
Bonds	60.0	59.8	61.8	76.0	10.5	17.5	15.6	18.2	25.0	17.9	17.1	16.0	4.4	5.8	2.5
Equities	0.0	0.0	0.0	1.0	0.0	0.0	0.0	0.0	0.0	0.0	0.0	0.0	0.0	0.0	0.0
Loans	88.0	69.5	62.4	58.5	11.6	16.8	14.0	20.0	13.5	15.3	14.7	15.0	4.1	6.9	1.8
Amortization by region	**148.0**	**129.3**	**124.2**	**134.5**	**22.1**	**34.3**	**29.6**	**38.2**	**38.4**	**33.2**	**31.9**	**31.0**	**8.5**	**12.7**	**4.3**
Asia	66.5	56.2	49.4	53.2	8.3	12.0	14.5	14.7	16.1	13.2	11.9	11.9	4.1	4.2	2.4
Latin America	45.9	41.2	40.8	47.7	7.6	10.1	8.0	15.1	12.7	13.4	10.6	11.0	2.0	5.4	1.4
Europe, Middle East, Africa	35.5	31.9	33.9	33.6	6.2	12.2	7.1	8.4	9.6	6.6	9.4	8.0	2.3	3.0	0.4
Net issuance by asset	**14.2**	**6.4**	**75.1**	**144.8**	**12.9**	**11.7**	**23.6**	**26.8**	**31.4**	**29.8**	**37.5**	**47.1**	**16.4**	**12.7**	**17.9**
Bonds	29.1	1.8	37.0	55.5	9.6	10.4	9.0	8.0	15.1	10.7	16.8	13.0	5.4	−0.1	16.4
Equities	11.2	16.4	28.3	42.4	1.2	2.0	7.1	18.0	13.1	10.4	5.6	14.4	5.1	4.5	1.5
Loans	−26.1	−11.8	9.8	46.9	2.1	−0.7	7.5	0.9	3.3	8.8	15.1	19.7	5.8	8.3	0.0
Net issuance by region	**14.2**	**6.4**	**75.1**	**145.8**	**12.9**	**11.7**	**23.6**	**26.8**	**31.4**	**29.8**	**37.5**	**47.1**	**16.4**	**12.7**	**17.9**
Asia	0.9	−2.3	38.5	68.2	4.7	3.7	10.6	19.6	17.0	16.5	13.6	21.0	8.4	3.7	4.0
Latin America	7.9	−7.8	1.9	5.3	0.2	2.0	1.0	−1.3	1.7	−3.8	5.3	2.1	1.8	−1.1	3.9
Europe, Middle East, Africa	5.3	16.4	34.6	72.3	8.1	6.0	12.0	8.5	12.7	17.1	18.5	24.0	6.2	10.1	10.0
Secondary markets															
Bonds															
EMBI Global (spread in basis points)	728	725	403	347	626	515	486	403	414	482	409	347	363	347	356
Merrill Lynch High-Yield (spread in basis points)	795	871	418	310	757	606	543	418	438	404	384	310	403	310	329
Merrill Lynch High-Grade (spread in basis points)	162	184	93	83	156	120	110	93	94	97	91	83	93	83	85
U.S. 10-yr. treasury yield (yield in %)	5.05	3.82	4.25	4.22	3.80	3.52	3.94	4.25	3.84	4.58	4.12	4.22	4.12	4.22	4.13
								(In percent)							
Equity															
DOW	−7.1	−16.8	25.3	3.1	−4.2	12.4	3.2	12.7	−0.9	0.8	−3.4	−1.9	0.3	−0.9	−2.7
NASDAQ	−21.1	−31.5	50.0	8.6	0.4	21.0	10.1	12.1	−0.5	2.7	−7.4	1.9	−2.6	3.2	−5.2
MSCI Emerging Market Free	−4.9	−8.0	51.6	22.4	−6.8	22.2	13.5	17.3	8.9	−10.3	7.4	−0.2	3.9	5.5	0.0
Asia	4.2	−6.2	47.1	12.2	−9.3	21.4	14.9	16.3	7.6	−12.2	4.2	−0.5	4.3	4.0	1.4
Latin America	−4.3	−24.8	67.1	34.8	−0.9	22.6	12.4	22.4	6.2	−9.2	16.6	−1.1	4.3	7.9	−1.9
Europe, Middle East, Africa	−20.9	4.7	51.2	35.8	−5.3	23.7	9.3	11.7	13.2	−7.4	7.8	1.0	3.0	6.9	−1.4

Sources: Bloomberg L.P.; Capital Data; J.P. Morgan Chase & Co.; Morgan Stanley Capital International; and IMF staff estimates.
[1]Issuance data (net of U.S. trust facility issuance) are as of January 31, 2005, close-of-business London. Secondary markets data are as of January 31, 2005, close-of-business New York.

Syndicated Lending

Syndicated lending, both on a net and on a gross basis, remained well above average in the second half of 2004, led by EMEA and Asia. Lending to Latin America increased but remained well below the flow to other regions (Figure 2.39). Lending to European corporates made up the biggest increase in flows in the second and third quarters of 2004, with flows concentrated in Russia and Turkey. In Asia, flows continued to be dominated by Hong Kong SAR and China.

Foreign Direct Investment

There was a modest recovery in foreign direct investment (FDI) in emerging markets in 2004 (Figure 2.40).[11] As in previous years, Asia continued to receive the largest share, driven by flows into China, supported by strong economic growth and world demand for its exports. Latin America also had a significant increase, led by Mexico and Brazil. In these countries, FDI flows were boosted by increased cross-border merger and acquisition activity in the banking and manufacturing sectors, respectively. Flows into Eastern and Central Europe were led by increased flows into Russia.

Banking Sector Developments in Emerging Markets

Banking systems in emerging markets generally show improving capital positions, asset quality, and earnings (Table 2.2, see p. 35).[12] Most market-based measures, including market valuations of bank stocks relative to the broader market indices and computations of distance to default derived from a standard valuation model (Box 2.7, see p. 46), also reveal a generally positive picture. In Asia, banks further improved their financial positions with the ongoing economic expansion, and banks in Latin America are showing stronger results, especially in countries that were not recently afflicted by crises. The expansion by foreign banks in a number of countries in emerging Europe is driving strong results. Performance has been more mixed in banking systems in the Middle East, Central Asia, and Africa.

Regulatory attention in many emerging markets is focused on improving institutions and risk management capacity. Immediate concerns are the risks posed by rapid credit

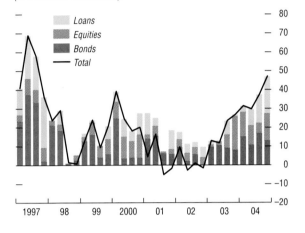

Figure 2.34. Quarterly Emerging Market Net Issuance
(In billions of U.S. dollars)

Sources: Capital Data; and IMF staff estimates.

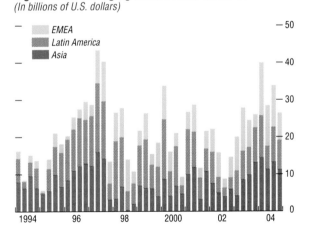

Figure 2.35. Emerging Market Bond Issuance
(In billions of U.S. dollars)

Source: Capital Data.

---

[11]Based on World Bank estimates.

[12]Classifications and definitions of various financial soundness indicators are not uniform across countries. Thus, any cross-country comparisons should be considered only indicative.

Figure 2.36. Share of Emerging Market Bond Issuance
(In percent)

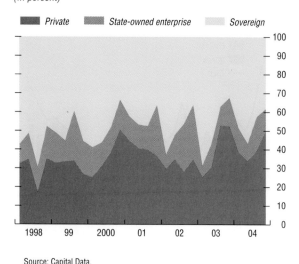

Source: Capital Data.

Figure 2.37. Emerging Market Bond Issuance by Currency
(In percent)

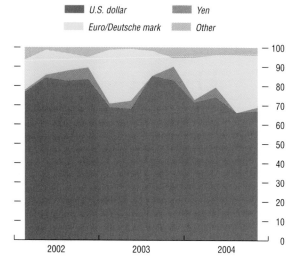

Source: Capital Data.

growth and the potential effects of higher interest rates. Longer-term reforms are progressing slowly.

Asia

In the Asian emerging markets, banks' earnings, asset quality, and capital adequacy have generally improved over the last two years under favorable macroeconomic conditions. Performance has also been bolstered by greater operational efficiency and government-supported dispositions of impaired assets in key countries. The generally positive developments are reflected in higher ratings of banks by private sector rating agencies, considerable improvement in distance-to-default measures, and a modest improvement in relative market valuations of bank stocks (Figure 2.41).[13]

Authorities in a number of countries in the region are moving to address structural issues in their banking systems. Efforts are being made to tighten regulation and supervision and recapitalize and restructure financial institutions. However, there remains considerable scope for further strengthening balance sheets and risk management of domestic financial institutions. In particular, nonperforming loan (NPL) ratios in the region, while declining, remain high despite restructuring and takeover of loans by government-sponsored asset management companies. Problem loans are especially pronounced at state-owned banks in some cases, where lending activities tend to be prone to outside pressures. Corporate restructuring is also lagging behind other regulatory reforms in some of the countries in the region.

In some cases, balance sheets of financial institutions are exposed to interest rate risk.

[13]As explained in Box 2.7, the distance-to-default measure is computed as the sum of the ratio of the estimated current value of assets to debt and the return on the market value of assets divided by the volatility of assets.

Having benefited from a benign interest rate environment, a number of institutions continue to carry substantial government securities in their portfolios, which may be affected by a reversal of the low interest rate environment. While in some countries the authorities have moved to require additional buffers to absorb the effects of increases in interest rates, in others the capacity to cushion the effects remains limited.

Generally, there is a need for faster convergence to international best practices in supervision and regulation. Issues warranting attention to varying degrees in some countries include proper enforcement of prudential regulations, alignment of capital adequacy requirements with the international standard, consolidated supervision, supervisory independence, prompt corrective action provisions, effective bankruptcy arrangements, and transparency.

Europe

Market-based indicators for the banking sector show a faster improvement in the European emerging markets than elsewhere in the region, with a declining likelihood of default, higher profitability, and prospects for long-term growth (Figure 2.42).[14] The strong earnings performance was sustained in 2004, and asset quality and capital adequacy strengthened. The favorable prospects are reflected in continued strong bank ratings. While banking systems in the region generally seem poised for continued strong performance, rapid credit growth, especially in the retail sector, poses a risk in some countries. In addition, credit expansion in some cases is denominated in foreign exchange and to sectors with no foreign exchange earnings, thereby increasing the risks.

[14]The rise in the distance-to-default measure in Figure 2.42 indicates a decline in the prospects for banking system insolvency.

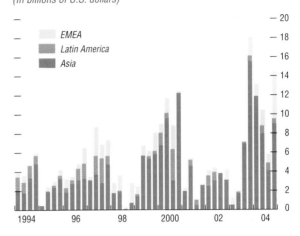

Figure 2.38. Emerging Market Equity Issuance
(In billions of U.S. dollars)

Source: Capital Data.

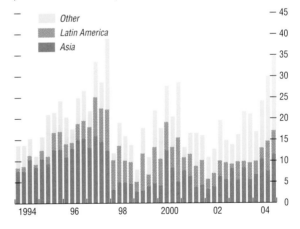

Figure 2.39. Emerging Market Syndicated Loan Commitments
(In billions of U.S. dollars)

Source: Capital Data.

Figure 2.40. Foreign Direct Investment
(In billions of U.S. dollars)

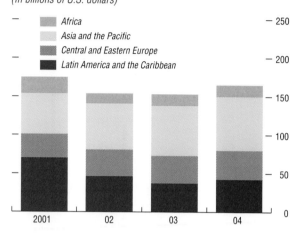

Source: World Bank.

**Figure 2.41. Asian Emerging Markets:
Market Indicators**
(January 3, 2000 = 100)

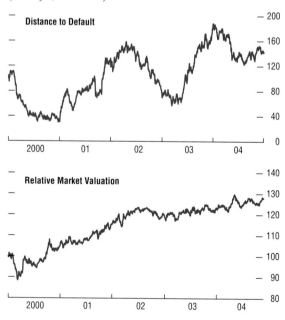

Sources: Datastream; and IMF staff estimates.

In many emerging European countries, the level of financial intermediation is lower than in developed economies, so that rapid credit growth, to an extent, may be structural. However, growth rates of well over 40 percent experienced in some countries have the potential to create problems in credit screening and pricing. The substantial growth of foreign currency credits increases the exchange-rate-induced credit risk in the banking system. Also, since mortgage credit has been a major component, banks have become more exposed to the real estate market.

Most emerging European countries have improved their supervisory structures. A number of EU accession countries have implemented legislative reforms aimed at harmonizing their laws with those in the EU. Effective implementation of legislative changes concerning the operational independence of supervisory authorities, strengthening supervisory oversight, and tightening the bankruptcy process is part of the unfinished agenda of financial sector reforms in some countries.

Western Hemisphere

The financial systems in much of the region appear healthy with the exception of those emerging from financial crises. Stock indicators, such as capitalization and NPL ratios, and flow indicators, such as profitability, are stable or improving. Market-based measures suggest that the financial position of banking institutions has been strengthening, as has investor confidence in them (Figure 2.43). These trends are evident in most of the larger economies of Latin America. The improvement is somewhat tentative in countries emerging from banking crises, where fundamental reforms still need to be fully implemented.

Three of the main factors contributing to the positive outlook are
• A benign macroeconomic environment, characterized by rising growth rates, moder-

Table 2.2. Emerging Market Countries: Selected Bank Financial Soundness Indicators
(In percent)

	Return on Assets			Nonperforming Loans to Total Loans			Regulatory Capital to Risk-Weighted Assets		
	2002	2003	2004[1]	2002	2003	2004[1]	2002	2003	2004[1]
Emerging Asia									
Mean	0.8	1.0	1.5	12.7	11.2	10.1	14.5	15.2	14.8
Median	0.8	1.0	1.4	13.1	10.9	9.5	13.2	13.8	13.7
Standard deviation	0.4	0.5	0.6	8.9	8.2	8.2	3.3	3.9	3.8
Emerging Europe									
Mean	1.5	1.6	1.7	9.3	8.0	7.8	17.5	17.1	16.0
Median	1.4	1.4	1.6	7.7	5.1	5.4	16.2	14.9	15.2
Standard deviation	0.5	0.7	0.6	7.0	8.2	7.9	4.4	5.6	4.2
Latin America									
Mean	−2.6	1.0	1.4	12.5	10.1	8.6	13.2	14.3	16.2
Median	1.0	1.2	1.2	8.7	7.7	5.3	14.2	14.1	14.8
Standard deviation	10.9	2.2	1.8	10.3	8.4	8.1	6.1	2.7	5.6
Middle East[2]									
Mean	1.1	1.3	. . .	15.4	15.2	. . .	15.6	15.0	. . .
Median	0.8	1.2	. . .	16.1	14.0	. . .	16.7	15.9	. . .
Standard deviation	0.7	0.7	. . .	4.6	5.9	. . .	4.5	4.9	. . .
Sub-Saharan Africa									
Mean	2.7	3.0	. . .	19.9	17.3	. . .	17.7	15.7	. . .
Median	2.4	2.3	. . .	22.1	19.1	. . .	17.6	17.0	. . .
Standard deviation	2.4	2.1	. . .	9.4	9.7	. . .	4.4	4.1	. . .

Source: National authorities; and IMF staff estimates.
[1]Refers to gross nonperforming loans (NPLs). For 2004, the latest available figures.
[2]Including Azerbaijan and the Kyrgyz Republic.

ate or low inflation, and low real interest rates. Global interest rates have begun to increase, but from levels that were seen to be exceptionally low, and the pace of increase has been moderate. For many countries in the region, higher U.S. rates were offset by lower country risk premiums. The depreciation of the U.S. dollar may have contributed to financial strengthening, for example, in the export sector in countries with currencies tied to the dollar.

- Improved loan quality, as indicated by lower NPL ratios and lower provisioning, has translated into higher profitability. While in some cases an overhang of NPLs has been carried forward from past economic downturns, the flow of new impaired credits has been moderate.

- Fast growth in consumer and mortgage lending. Lending to the household sector has been vigorous, and relatively profitable. In much of Latin America, this line of busi-

ness has been developing from a very low base, and lenders can enjoy high demand once institutional hindrances are overcome.

Available indicators suggest that banking systems are well placed to handle a rebound in interest rates and direct credit risk, for example, from consumer and mortgage lending.

Financial system performance in many of the larger Latin American countries has been satisfactory. In particular, the financial system in countries not affected by crises is benefiting from and contributing more to an overall economic upswing. A number of measures have been taken to strengthen the prudential regulatory framework, in some cases following recommendations made in the context of the joint IMF–World Bank Financial Sector Assessment Program. The countries most affected by major financial crises have seen a rebound in financial intermediation and bank soundness.

Figure 2.42. Emerging Europe: Market Indicators
(January 3, 2000 = 100)

Sources: Datastream; and IMF staff estimates.

Figure 2.43. Latin America: Market Indicators
(January 3, 2000 = 100)

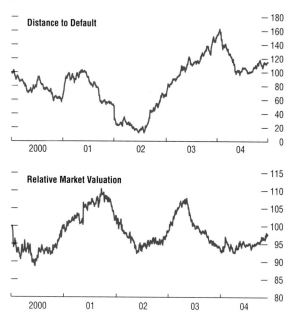

Sources: Datastream; and IMF staff estimates.

Middle East and Africa

Data limitations suggest greater caution in interpreting regional aggregate financial soundness indicators in the Middle East, Central Asia, and Africa. These indicators point to a marginal weakening in banks' performance in the Middle East, although individual country experiences vary. Favorable economic developments augur well for banking reforms in some countries in the region. There are indications that in some countries the authorities are moving to address structural weaknesses, including in the legal and regulatory areas, asset quality, and capital adequacy at state-owned banks. Large exposure to the sovereign and high degree of dollarization remain the main risks in some countries. Generally, in the oil-rich countries, the banking systems remain highly liquid, profitable, and well capitalized. In a number of African countries, the banking systems continue to be burdened by serious weaknesses, and implementation of reform measures remains slow.

Structural Issues in Mature Markets

Recent Developments in Energy Markets

The run-up in crude oil and other energy prices during 2004 has increased investor interest in the energy sector. The following will update our previous analysis of the energy markets, published in the September 2004 *Global Financial Stability Report.*

Investor Perceptions of Structural Shifts in Energy Markets

Perceived structural shifts in energy markets have increased interest and participation in energy-related commodities. Industry analysts have noted that the rise in absolute and relative crude oil prices during 2004 reflected investor perceptions of declining excess capacity among global producers, particularly in specific grades of crude oil and downstream products, in light of upward revisions to current and prospective global demand from non-OECD countries, such as China. Investor flows have been spread along the entire energy supply chain, with signs of tight capacity and bottlenecks in production, refining, and distribution. Indeed, the reason most frequently cited by market participants for the rise in oil prices is the lack of spare capacity, particularly for light sweet crude oil and related refining capabilities, following 20–25 years of underinvestment.[15]

Investors do not perceive a general or global shortage of crude oil, but over the medium term, they appear increasingly concerned about potential bottlenecks. For example, investors believe that existing production and refining capacity places a premium on light sweet grades, whose available supplies are being questioned.[16] Recent changes in market prices appear to confirm investor perceptions: as crude oil prices in general rose during 2004, prices for various grades of light sweet crude oil rose relatively more than heavier grades. Moreover, when the absolute price of crude oil retreated from recent highs in October 2004, the spread between light and heavy grades continued to rise and/or

(continued on p. 41)

[15]During the 1970s, sustained high oil prices, and various tax and other incentives, encouraged capital expenditure on exploration and infrastructure development. Indeed, overinvestment in these facilities contributed to a decline in oil prices during the 1980s and discouraged, to some extent, infrastructure development. More recently, as exploration and production (E&P) companies adjust oil price expectations upward, there has been growing interest in expanding oil reserves through either exploration or acquisition.

[16]Industry analysts have noted that much of the current global crude oil production is based on aging oil fields, and that fields abundant in light sweet crude have peaked (Texas fields peaked during the 1970s) or may be nearing their peak productive age (e.g., Brent production in the North Sea). Moreover, recent exploration has yielded smaller and more difficult-to-access replacement fields that generally produce heavier, or more sour, grades of crude oil. The April 2005 *World Economic Outlook* discusses in greater detail the general erosion of spare oil production capacity during 2004, and medium- and long-term outlooks for supply and demand factors affecting the oil market.

Figure 2.44. Arab Light/Heavy, Brent, and West Texas Intermediate Crude Oil Pricing
(In U.S. dollars a barrel)

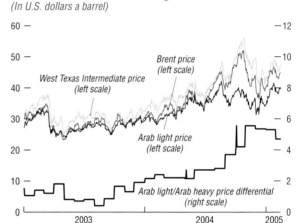

Source: Bloomberg L.P.

Box 2.2. Pension Fund Update

Pension funds have the opportunity to enhance financial stability by acting as a stable, long-term investor base. However, they face a number of challenges as populations in many industrialized countries age. The September 2004 GFSR discussed the risk management and investment strategies of pension funds, which can have significant effects on capital markets, and highlighted several ways through which policymakers can enhance such practices and their role as long-term investors.

Funding Developments

In 2004, global funding levels recovered marginally, with increased contributions primarily helping with improvements in the funding gap. Between 2000 and 2002, the equity market and interest rate declined sharply, reducing the funding ratios of many pension funds. In 2003 and 2004, the impact of relatively strong equity returns was largely offset by that of the continuing decline in corporate bond yields (increasingly used to discount liabilities), and improvements in funding positions at year-end 2004 were primarily the result of increased contribution rates. In the United States, analysts estimate that the defined benefit plans of the Fortune 100 companies were 88 percent funded on average at the end of 2004, up from 78 percent at the end of 2002. Similarly, in the Netherlands, the equity market recovery and increased contributions since 2003 have also helped with the average funding ratio, up from about 105 percent at the end of 2002 to an estimated 118 percent at the end of the third quarter of 2004. In January 2005, however, the combination of a decline in long-term bond yields and negative equity returns led to what some observers described as the most significant monthly decline in funding ratios in recent years (i.e., over 4 percent for a typical U.S. pension fund).

While no significant shift from equities to bonds has been observed in the most recent period, some pension funds have invested a growing share of their portfolio in alternative asset classes. In the United States, a recent Pensions & Investments survey indicated that the top 200 plan sponsors did not drastically change their asset mix in 2004, continuing to hold relatively large equity portfolios. Meanwhile, like other institutional investors, many pension funds have sought to benefit from risk-adjusted returns provided by markets and products that are less correlated with conventional equity or bond indices. In the United States, some market participants estimate that increasingly corporate and public pension funds are devoting 10 percent or more of their assets to alternative asset classes, such as hedge funds (including funds with an energy or commodities focus), private equity, distressed debt, and venture capital.

Policy Initiatives

Awareness of the economic, financial, and household challenges associated with the implications of aging has continued to grow. Ongoing reforms of pension and other benefit systems are increasingly being debated in the general public and in policymaking spheres. The debate has progressed most significantly in the United Kingdom in the last six months, as is evident in the release of the Interim Report of the Pensions Commission and the ongoing discussions about the creation of a pension fund guarantee scheme. The Interim Report highlights three possible ways forward in the United Kingdom: (1) a major revitalization of the voluntary system, (2) significant changes in the state system, and/or (3) an increased level of compulsory private savings. The Final Report of the Pensions Commission, to be released in the fall of 2005, will focus on analyzing these factors. (See also Chapter III for further discussion of the Interim Report.)

On the supervisory front, significant changes have been implemented in the Netherlands. The formal merger of the Nederlandsche Bank (DNB) with the Pensions and Insurance Supervisory Authority on October 30, 2004, marked the completion of a process to develop a more integrated supervisory framework. In

October 2004, the DNB issued a consultation document proposing a Financial Assessment Framework (FAF) for pensions. The FAF is expected to be submitted to the parliament during 2005, and to be implemented in the beginning of January 2006. The framework's major proposals include (1) the introduction of fair value accounting for pension fund assets and liabilities, in order to report what the authorities see as a more realistic measure of pension financial positions, and (2) new funding measures aimed at increasing the level of confidence that pension funds will remain properly funded, and facilitating corrective measures to avoid underfunding (see the September 2004 GFSR, Box 3.4, p. 104).

In the United States, the financial position of the pension guarantee fund has prompted further reform considerations. The funding situation of the Pension Benefit Guaranty Corporation (PBGC) deteriorated for the fourth consecutive year in 2004, with a deficit of about $23 billion. In early 2005, the administration outlined a pension reform proposal aiming to bring stability and flexibility to funding rules, and to encourage fully funded plans. The proposed regulatory changes focus on three aspects: (1) funding rules and incentives to encourage funding cushions (e.g., allowing plan sponsors to make additional deductible contributions); (2) disclosure to workers, investors, and regulators about pension plan status (e.g., replacing multiple measures of pension liabilities with one measure); and (3) insurance guarantee premiums to better reflect a plan's risks and to better support the PBGC's financial solvency (premiums to be determined by plan funding levels and PBGC's expected losses).

New Financial Instruments for Pension Funds

The development of markets for long-dated and index-linked bonds, which are essential to risk management in the pension fund industry, is progressing. Such instruments are an important complement to a more risk-based regulatory framework: they facilitate and encourage pension funds to better match their assets and long-term liabilities. In February 2005, the French Trésor introduced a new 50-year euro-denominated bond, in response to the positive feedback received from a survey of investors, including pension funds, regarding the demand for a long-dated bond. In Japan, the authorities issued index-linked bonds with a 10-year maturity in 2004; they intend such instruments to represent about 2 percent of their total public debt issuance in 2005. In the United Kingdom, the Debt Management Office announced in March 2005 that, from May 2005, it would issue 50-year conventional gilts, and that later in the year, it may also issue 50-year index-linked gilts. Prior to this decision, the longest dated government debt instrument was a 30-year bond. Consultations with market participants have confirmed the demand from the U.K. pension industry (and other investors) for long-dated, high-quality bonds, and that such demand is likely to increase in the future. The German authorities have also indicated their intention to issue index-linked debt securities during 2005.

A very interesting development has been the planned issuance of a "longevity bond" by the European Investment Bank, aimed at helping pension funds manage longevity risk. The instrument, which is described in Chapter III of the GFSR, is designed to help U.K. pension funds (and others) hedge longevity risk. Further developments of similar or related instruments would enhance the risk management and capital capacity of pension funds and insurance companies in this area, and potentially increase the supply of annuity products.

The above developments are in line with several of the key policy recommendations made in the September 2004 GFSR. In many countries, pension funds continue to face important challenges, including the adequacy of their funding levels, and the need to ensure that they will be in a better position to absorb market movements. In this context, we welcome the above measures aimed at further focusing the industry and its regulators on risk management and the development of prudent funding cushions, and therefore on further promoting financial stability.

Box 2.3. Insurance Industry Update

As noted in recent issues of the GFSR, insurance firms in a number of mature markets have increasingly taken on credit risks that were formerly borne by banks and other market participants. At the same time, regulatory authorities in several countries have moved to implement more market-sensitive and risk-based capital adequacy standards. In response, insurers have generally improved their own risk management systems and, in some cases, moved to de-risk their balance sheets.

On the regulatory front, the Solvency II project continues to progress, with the adoption of a discussion paper (MARKT/2515/04). It had been anticipated that the Solvency II framework would be ready for adoption in 2007, but it now appears that finalization may be delayed. Modeled on the Basel II capital adequacy standards for banks, Solvency II envisions a similar "three pillar" approach to insurance regulation. More broadly, the goal is to have solvency standards that reflect more closely the balance sheet risks of insurers.

On January 1, 2005, the United Kingdom put into effect the risk-based solvency standards for life insurance companies as set out in Consultative Paper 195 (CP195), by including the proposed requirements in its Integrated Prudential Sourcebook (PSB) for insurers. As described in the April 2004 GFSR, the new standards encompass two important developments in the regulation of life insurers. The first is a "twin peaks" solvency approach for "with-profits" products (policies that pay a bonus depending on the firm's investment results),[1] which entail applying the more stringent of a (traditional) minimum capital requirement, and an "enhanced capital requirement," which takes account of expected bonus payments and other contingent liabilities. The second development is an individual capital adequacy standard, under which each life insurer develops the appropriate capital standard for its own self-assessed risk.

In addition to imposing more risk-oriented capital standards, the new PSB regime is likely to encourage the use of more sophisticated risk management practices. In addition, a few U.K. insurers at the end of 2004 issued capital instruments that are designed to satisfy the PSB definition of Innovative Tier 1 capital for insurers. The instruments are a form of subordinated debt, with clauses permitting cumulative deferral of interest payments and, in some cases, principal repayment, in the event of certain adverse financial developments, thus allowing the securities to be counted as Tier 1 capital under the new standards.

Elsewhere, the Netherlands issued a consultation paper in December proposing a more risk-based solvency standard. The Netherlands also merged the Pensions and Insurance Supervisory Authority with the Netherlands central bank on October 30, so as to create a unified regulator for financial institutions. No major initiatives appear to be currently under way in the United States or Japan, both of which already apply risk-based capital (RBC) solvency standards. However, there has been some informal discussion of further refining the U.S. NAIC standards, including potentially applying differing risk weightings for equity holdings, similar to the system used for fixed-income investments.

As insurance firms reshape their balance sheets, there are implications for financial markets. For life insurers in particular, the evolving regulatory environment may encourage more duration matching, probably entailing greater bond holdings—especially in Europe—and more trading of derivatives to hedge the embedded options in their balance sheets. Flow of funds figures suggest that insurers in the United Kingdom and Japan have continued to shift their asset portfolios toward bonds (government and corporate), as opposed to equities, mortgages, or (in Japan's case) corporate loans. Insurers in the United States have a longer history of investment in corporate bonds, and have continued to allocate a substantial portion of their investment portfolios to credit instruments.

[1]The twin peaks calculation is compulsory for life insurers with aggregate with-profits liabilities of 500 million pounds or more.

A series of natural disasters in the latter part of 2004 affected the general insurance industry. Industry sources estimate the insurance liabilities for the hurricanes that struck Florida and the southeast United States in 2004 at $20–$28 billion. Analysts view such events as likely to prolong the existing "hard" market for catastrophic risk (i.e., relatively high premiums and pricing power for insurers), but as not likely to significantly push up rates or threaten solvency ratios for larger insurers. A series of typhoons in Japan resulted in insurance claims of about $4.9 billion and a sharp drop in earnings for non–life insurers in the first half of fiscal 2004 (April–September). Japan also suffered a major earthquake in October 2004 that resulted in about $130 million in claims, almost all of which was covered by the Japan Earthquake Reinsurance Company, a state-reinsured joint venture of the 20 leading private Japanese non–life

insurers.[2] The terrible earthquake and related tsunami disaster in South Asia at the end of 2004 may raise the political urgency of global preventive action, including support for reinsurance coverage for developing countries vulnerable to natural disaster. However, because the countries affected had very little insurance coverage, the effect on the capital adequacy or earnings of major insurers is expected to be quite small.

[2]The Japanese government bears about 83 percent of the potential insurance liability of the company, which is currently capped at 4.5 trillion yen ($43 billion). The California Earthquake Authority (CEA) is an insurance pool with a different form of state involvement. The state of California provides no funding for the CEA and bears no potential liability for CEA exposure, but it does set CEA rates and fees. The Florida Hurricane Catastrophe Fund, however, is a public sector entity, with which all insurers writing hurricane and related policies in Florida are required to reinsure.

(continued from p. 37)

remained at an elevated level (Figure 2.44).[17] Although OPEC is traditionally considered the swing producer and major source of the world's excess production capacity, investors' suspicions of potential bottlenecks for light sweet crude gained credibility during the fourth quarter of 2004 when light sweet crude prices rose sharply, and the incremental supply from OPEC was mainly composed of heavier and more sour grades of crude oil (see the April 2005 *World Economic Outlook* for further details).

Natural gas is another energy source in which investors perceive supply constraints. As a potential (environmentally preferred) substitute for oil and coal in generating electricity and in home heating, its price move-

ments are often influenced by price dynamics from other markets, particularly oil. Most simply, natural gas supply has limited distribution facilities. Although pipelines have been built to connect gas reserves (e.g., in Russia) with many of the major end markets (e.g., continental Europe), environmental concerns related to construction activity frequently limit the ability to expand existing pipelines and storage facilities. Shipping of liquified natural gas (LNG) is one way to transport the product, but environmental and local safety concerns have limited the development of LNG ports, especially along the East Coast of the United States, which is one of the largest natural gas markets. Currently, much of the observed price vola-

(continued on p. 45)

[17]Comparing the spread between Arab light and Arab heavy crude is often a preferred measure among oil analysts for comparisons of lighter benchmark grades (e.g., West Texas Intermediate (WTI) or Brent) to heavier benchmark grades (e.g., Dubai) because the Arab light/heavy spread eliminates transportation costs and other market-specific shocks (e.g., hurricanes and other local disruptions) that can distort the spread.

Box 2.4. Credit Derivatives Market Came of Age in 2004

The agreement among the leading credit derivatives market makers on standardization of credit default swap (CDS) indices (DJ iTraxx in Europe and DJ Trac-x in the United States), improved liquidity and brought about a large reduction in CDS bid/ask spreads. The number of quoted reference entities increased particularly in 2004, and was mostly concentrated in high-yield names. As a consequence bid/ask spreads on high-yield names were reduced to values comparable with those of higher-quality names. The reduction of bid/ask spreads also facilitated the development of new derivative products.

As a result of increased liquidity, CDSs started to be consistently quoted and traded for the three- and 10-year maturities (in addition to the five-year sector), providing the basis of a more complete credit spread curve. The existence of several quoted points on the curve allowed the development of the forward credit spread curve, thus supplying another powerful tool for managing credit positions. Consistent quotations for CDSs on subordinated debt are now also available.

Strong trading liquidity in standardized synthetic collateralized debt obligations (CDO) tranches, and related hedging needs, opened the way for correlation trading. Correlation became a significant operational issue for market makers only when CDO tranches began to be structured to meet specific investment and risk management needs of clients. At that point, dealer books became, from time to time, more unbalanced, and there was a need to rebalance positions. Liquidity in index tranches trading (i.e., the DJ iTraxx and DJ Trac-x) allowed dealers to derive consistent implicit correlation values from market prices, enabling them to identify the needed hedge. Correlation is also a driving factor for pricing other credit derivative's products. For example, in a first-to-default (FTD) basket, an investor can buy or sell protection against the first default of one of the credits referenced in the basket. Therefore, the cost of the FTD depends not only on the default probability and recovery rates associated with each issuer but also on the correlation of credit events affecting them.

The very low level of credit spreads encouraged the development of new financial instruments, such as credit spread options, first and Nth-to-default baskets, constant maturity CDSs (CMCDSs), and constant maturity collateralized debt obligations (CMCDOs). Credit spread options provide an effective way to buy or sell protection on credit spread movements for the reference name. The type of options currently traded (usually European-style) encompass payer and receiver swaptions and straddles on all the indices, as well as single-name CDSs of different maturities. The investor who sells protection with CMCDSs and CMCDOs is exposed to counterparty default risk, but is partially insulated from credit spread movements. The received coupon is in fact floating, and periodically readjusted to reflect current spread levels of CDSs of the same maturity.

The credit derivatives market has continued to develop in terms of participants and organizational structure. There are now at least 20 market makers with quite distinct levels of sophistication, risk appetite, and product capacity providing pricing and liquidity. Market depth and liquidity have been, so far, large enough to manage a variety of credit events (e.g., Parmalat in 2003), without serious disruptions and with continuous two-way pricing. Efforts to automate settlement procedures among market makers, who execute about half of the daily transactions in the market, has reduced the backlog in confirmation procedures.

Despite its rapid pace of development, the credit derivatives markets remain vulnerable. There are two major sources of vulnerability, according to market participants. First, it is difficult to assess whether credit derivatives markets, as well as the underlying credit market, will continue to operate smoothly in the event of a major credit event (e.g., a credit event related to a major automobile manufacturer). Second, for some reference names some market participants perceive that the amount of protection bought or sold exceeds the value of the underlying assets. Therefore, if a credit event occurs, there may not be enough deliverable assets for all the claimants.

Box 2.5. Collective Action Clauses

Since the first Mexican issue with collective action clauses (CACs) in New York in March 2003, the use of CACs in international sovereign bonds issued under New York law has generally become market practice. In 2004, sovereign bond issues that include CACs under New York law by emerging market countries represented more than 90 percent of total value of new issues, and 44 percent of the value of the outstanding stock of bonds by emerging market countries.

Market practice for CACs in bonds issued under New York law has rapidly converged toward using a voting threshold of 75 percent of outstanding principal for majority restructuring provisions.[1] This has been the case across both investment-grade and noninvestment-grade sovereign bonds. In this context, Guatemala and Venezuela, following Brazil's move in June 2004, lowered the voting threshold in their recent sovereign issues from 85 percent to 75 percent, to reflect market practice.

Since September 2004, two more emerging market countries—Hungary and El Salvador—included CACs in their international sovereign

bonds issued under New York law, while nine emerging market countries—Brazil, Colombia, Guatemala, Lebanon,[2] Mexico, Panama, Peru, Turkey, and Venezuela—continued with their established practice of including CACs in their bonds issued under New York law. China did not include CACs in its recent bonds issued under New York law.[3] There were no new issues by mature market countries in that jurisdiction. The inclusion of CACs in bonds issued under New York law continued to bear no observable impact on pricing.

There have been several issues that included CACs under English law, following market practice in that jurisdiction: Brazil, Hungary, Jordan, and Turkey among the emerging market countries, and Austria and Finland among the mature market countries. Jamaica was the only country that issued under German law. As is customary in that jurisdiction, this issue did not include CACs. There were no issues under Japanese law.

[2]The Lebanon bonds include only majority restructuring provisions.
[3]Israel did not include CACs in its October 2004 bond issued under New York law, which is fully guaranteed by the United States with respect to principal and interest.

[1]See IMF's "Guidelines for Public Debt Management, Amended 2003."

Emerging Markets Sovereign Bond Issuance by Jurisdiction[1]

	2002				2003				2004[2]			
	Q1	Q2	Q3	Q4	Q1	Q2[3]	Q3	Q4	Q1	Q2	Q3	Q4
With CACs [4]												
Number of issuance	6	5	2	4	9	31	10	5	25	19	21	14
Of which: New York law	...	...	...	...	1	22	5	4	14	12	14	12
Volume of issuance	2.6	1.9	0.9	1.4	5.6	18.0	6.4	4.3	18.5	15.9	12.2	9.1
Of which: New York law	...	...	...	...	1.0	12.8	3.6	4.0	10.6	9.5	7.7	7.7
Without CACs[5]												
Number of issuance	17	12	5	10	14	4	7	7	2	2	1	4
Volume of issuance	11.6	6.4	3.3	4.4	8.1	2.5	3.5	4.2	1.5	0.4	0.3	2.7

Source: Capital Data.
[1]Number of issuance is in number. Volume of issuance is in billions of U.S. dollars.
[2]Data as of January 3, 2005.
[3]Includes issues of restructured bonds by Uruguay.
[4]English and Japanese laws, and New York law where relevant.
[5]German and New York laws.

Box 2.6. Issuing Global Bonds in Local Currencies: Toward the Absolution of Original Sin?

Colombia took a step in 2004 toward overcoming what has been termed the "original sin" of emerging markets: the inability to issue international bonds in their own currencies.[1] Colombia was only the fourth emerging market issuer and the second sovereign to issue such a bond. In November 2002 Bancomext, a Mexican bank specializing in foreign trade finance, issued a Mexican-peso-denominated Eurobond for 1 billion pesos ($100 million). Uruguay issued the equivalent of $200 million in inflation-protected local currency bonds in October 2003. After Colombia's issue, four Brazilian banks issued real-denominated international bonds.[2]

The structure of the Colombian bond is innovative. It is denominated in local currency, with the interest and principal calculated in local currency, but payable in U.S. dollars at the spot exchange rate around the day when interest or principal falls due. The bond is thus equivalent to investing in local government debt, except investors do not have to undertake a spot currency transaction at each point when cash flow is generated to turn the local currency proceeds into dollars.

The bond offers advantages for both the investor and the issuer. For the investor:

- It provides a vehicle to take exposure in high-yielding local currency markets. The Colombian global peso-denominated bond yields 11.875 percent annually, compared with around 6.9 percent on a Colombian dollar–

bond of a similar kind. In addition, investors are also attracted by the possibility that the Colombian peso could continue to appreciate.

- It is protected against convertibility risk. Because it is a global bond payable in dollars, the investor does not have to worry about exchange controls.
- Because it is a global bond, it is governed by the legal statutes of the state of New York, which some investors might find more favorable than local Colombian law in the event of a default.
- It allows investors to take exposure in local Colombian government debt without having to fulfill local registration requirements or pay local taxes.
- The bond is cleared through Euroclear, an international clearing system that facilitates the transfer and payment of funds. A global bond issue settled through Euroclear widens the investor base to funds lacking the facilities or the mandate to invest in local emerging markets.

The size of the issue and the final price reflect these advantages. The issue was initially planned for $250 million, but generated orders for up to $1.1 billion, and was subsequently increased to $325 million. The issue was reopened in January 2005 for another $150 million equivalent. In terms of pricing, the bond was originally issued to yield almost 50 basis points less in pesos than the local Colombian TES treasury bond of equivalent duration. This discount reflects the relative benefits foreign investors receive from global bonds in terms of reduced transaction costs for local currency exposure, protection against convertibility risk, and jurisdictional benefits, compared with investing in Colombia's local market. One concern for investors, however, is the relatively small size of the issue, which may restrict its liquidity in the secondary market.

Advantages for the Colombian government include the following:

- The structure provides a way of sharing the currency risk between the investor and the government: it eliminates the convertibility

---

[1]"Original sin" is the term used by Eichengreen, Hausmann and Panizza (2003).

[2]Banco Votorantim, the financial arm of Brazil's largest industrial group, issued an 18-month $75 million equivalent external real bond in late November at a yield of 18.5 percent. Unibanco followed shortly thereafter with a similar 18-month $75 million equivalent external real bond at 17.9 percent. These were followed by two additional three-year real-linked bonds, one by ABN Amro ($75 million at 17.9 percent) and another by Banco Bradesco ($100 million equivalent at 17.5 percent). The government of Colombia issued in February 2005 another $300 million equivalent of peso-denominated global bonds maturing in 2015.

risk for the investor, but transfers the exchange rate risk from the sovereign to the creditor.

- It reduces the mismatch between assets in pesos and liabilities in dollars on the government's balance sheet, one of the main consequences of original sin, and reduces the share of dollar debt in GDP, thus reducing the sensitivity of the debt-to-GDP ratio with respect to changes in the exchange rate.
- It reduces the effect that short-term capital inflows may have on the volatility of the local government debt market.
- It allows the government to diversify the investor base for investors who are interested in Colombian local currency debt but unwilling or unable to undergo the complicated procedures for buying local paper. The 50 basis point interest rate discount on the global bonds represents the tangible benefit to the government of widening the investor base.
- The bond may provide a benchmark for corporate issuers considering similar operations.

How far does the bond go in solving the problem of original sin? An important source of original sin, according to Eichengreen, Hausmann, and Panizza (2003), is the lack of liquidity in small country currencies. Investors prefer dollars, euros, or yen because they can be used around the world as a means of exchange. Thus, a country's ability to issue bonds in its own currency may depend fundamentally on its size in the international market. While liquidity may still be a concern for some investors, the significance of Colombia's issue lies in the fact that it was able to place an international bond in local currency in spite of the fact that no previous market existed in these bonds and that their liquidity in secondary markets is low. This suggests that a lack of liquidity may not be an insur-

mountable barrier for emerging markets attempting to overcome original sin.

Another aspect of original sin is the inherently volatile nature of emerging financial markets. Even with exemplary policies, emerging market countries tend to be small, relatively open, and subject to external current or capital account shocks. These shocks tend to have large effects on the exchange rate, domestic interest rates, prices, and output, and thus on the ability of the sovereign to service its debt.

Colombia's ability to issue local currency bonds without protection for exchange rate risk reflects the country's improved macroeconomic policy environment, which augurs well for its continued stability and growth. But it is also a reflection of the current external environment for emerging markets, which is extraordinarily favorable. The widespread perception that the dollar is set to decline against major currencies over the medium term is also an important factor in the investors' decisions.

Despite Colombia's success, it is unlikely that local currency bonds for emerging market counties will become a standard part of investors' portfolios soon. They remain specialized instruments for those willing to take exposure on particular local currencies, with knowledge of the local conditions that influence those currencies. In addition, they cannot correct for the fact that emerging markets live in a volatile economic and financial environment. The fact that Colombia's bonds have met with high demand indicates that investors expect the country's policy frameworks and credit conditions to remain stable for some years to come. But it is also a reflection of the extraordinarily favorable environment for emerging market debt and the unprecedented search for yield by foreign investors in local markets that existed in 2004.

tility in natural gas is seasonal, induced by limited storage facilities and peak demand during winter heating season. However, investors in natural gas anticipate price increases, comparable to (or greater than)

those expected for crude oil in the medium term, as demand for environmentally superior energy sources, such as natural gas, continues to outpace the growth of supply and distribution capacity.

Box 2.7. Distance-to-Default Measures of Bank Soundness

Banking sector soundness can be gauged by distance-to-default (DD) measures derived from the information contained in bank equity prices. In a standard valuation model, DD measure is determined by (1) the market value of a firm's assets, V_A, a measure of the present value of the future free cash flows produced by the firm's assets; (2) the uncertainty or volatility of the asset value (risk), σ_A; and (3) the degree of leverage or the extent of the firm's contractual liabilities, measured as the book value of liabilities at time t, D_t (with maturity T), relative to the market value of assets.

Distance to default measure is computed as the sum of the ratio of the estimated current value of assets to debt and the return on the market value of assets, divided by the volatility of assets. The formula is given by

$$DD_t = \frac{\ln(V_{A,t}/D_t) + (\mu - 1/2\sigma_A^2)\,T}{\sigma_A\sqrt{T}},$$

where μ measures the mean growth of V_A.

Using market data of equity and annual accounting data, the market value V_A and the volatility of assets σ_A are typically estimated using Black and Scholes (1973) and Merton (1974) options pricing model. The DD measure therefore broadly captures the prospects for bank insolvency. A higher DD indicates reduced chances of a bank's insolvency and an improvement in financial soundness, although the measure is sensitive to underlying assumptions.

For simplicity, in this exercise, the value of assets is estimated to be equal to the sum of the market value of equity and the book value of debt. Distance-to-default measures are computed daily for the portfolio of systemically important banks in each country, making up for the majority of the country's banking system equity. The DD indicators are then indexed, with the first day of year 2000 as the base.

Investors and industry analysts have noted that, during 2004, market volatility was heightened by the frequent revisions of global demand estimates, and the paucity of data on supplies of crude oil. The lack of accurate and timely data causes financial markets to become vulnerable to information shocks. This may be particularly true when the perceived gap between global supply and demand is relatively small, as it is in the oil markets today, and geopolitical uncertainties are relatively high, especially in energy-producing countries.

Energy Investors

Recent investors in energy markets (e.g., pension and hedge funds) represent a variety of investment horizons and objectives. For example, some institutional investors, such as pension funds, have sought to diversify their portfolios into a variety of alternative investments, including commodities, seeking assets that are less correlated to their largely long-only equity and bond portfolios. Such "non-commercial" investors are generally not considered speculators (see discussion below) and indeed are usually deemed highly desirable investors. Such investors often use index-related strategies, increasing the demand for short-dated futures contracts, which may cause additional upward pressure on prices at the margin.[18]

Macro hedge funds are among those that have generated flows into commodity markets.

---

[18]Much of the new capital invested by pension and hedge funds has been through index funds, frequently associated with indices such as the Goldman Sachs Commodity Index (GSCI), which are heavily weighted in energy-related products (e.g., the GSCI is weighted 66 percent in energy, with 25 percent of the energy component represented in crude oil).

These investors typically seek to arbitrage inefficiencies in market valuations, often arising from their perception of structural shifts in underlying fundamentals not yet recognized by broader market participants. Macro funds characteristically build positions before other investors recognize such trends (for example, entering in late 2002 and early 2003) and typically close or reduce positions ahead of other investors (for example, many macro funds reduced positions as WTI spot prices approached $50 in October 2004). Many large global macro hedge funds are also registered with the Commodity Futures Trading Commission (CFTC) as commodity pools, and their investment style is typically characterized by market observers as one that contrasts with more specialized commodity trading firms (e.g., commodity pool operators (CPOs) and commodity trade advisors (CTAs)) that rely primarily on statistical and directional models. To be sure, many successful commodity investors, whether they are hedge funds or CPOs, combine elements from both of these investment styles.

In the wake of deregulation, specialized energy trading firms emerged as significant energy market participants, in addition to the more recent entry of investment firms purchasing power generation facilities (as discussed in the September 2004 GFSR). These energy traders are quite different from pure financial investors and investment banking firms who are also energy traders. Many are integrated power producers, active in arbitraging power markets throughout the supply chain, connecting inputs (e.g., oil, natural gas, and coal) with commercial and retail energy outputs (e.g., electricity). Their comparative advantage comes from the ownership of power-generating plants and distribution networks, which provide natural long positions in various products along the energy supply chain, as well as superior market information.

Integrated power producers are able to arbitrage the liquid markets for hub delivery with less-liquid off-hub and OTC markets. A typical trade may involve selling electricity to an off-hub utility for its peak demand periods at a fixed price, and hedging this commitment (to some extent) with long positions in the forward market. They can commit to forward positions that exceed their own generating capacity by hedging in the forward markets (as far as five years out), and employing supplemental supply contracts from other power generators, based on their market and industry intelligence. Industry-specific knowledge, combined with portfolio management skills, is considered crucial for managing such trades, which involve both trading and operational risks.[19] By owning power-generating facilities and other long positions in power, an integrated power company can participate in trades that are not feasible for financial firms (i.e., typical investment banks) or traders with smaller holdings of (hub-based) generating facilities (i.e., including those investment firms that have recently purchased power-generating assets). A variation on this trade is one where positions are established in the forward market for power (final outputs) that are in backwardation.[20] The forward prices appreciate as contracts mature for delivery in the

---

[19]Operational risks are amplified by the fact that electricity cannot be stored, and delivery requirements are complicated by limited transportation capabilities of regional power grids and by physically segmented markets (e.g., the West Coast U.S. electricity market is physically separated from central and eastern U.S. electricity markets by the Rocky Mountains).

[20]Some energy markets, such as crude oil, exhibit backwardation most of the time. This is where spot prices are higher than futures prices, which get lower as the date of delivery moves farther into the future. Relatively higher spot prices reflect the "convenience yield" for holding inventories of (and extracting) oil today as a hedge against supply shortages in the future. (See Litzenberger and Rabinowitz, 1995, for a recently developed analytical framework that derives the necessary and sufficient conditions for futures prices to exhibit backwardation, which highlights the central role of uncertainty. Indeed, the Hotelling rule is shown to be a special case applicable in a world without uncertainty.)

Figure 2.45. West Texas Intermediate Crude Oil Futures Price Volatility
(In percent)

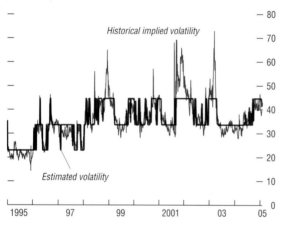

Sources: Bloomberg L.P.; and IMF staff estimates.

spot market. The most profitable part of this trade is the arbitrage between the liquid spot prices for hub delivery with prices in less-liquid off-hub locations.

Trading Activity and Price Volatility

Some observers identify "speculative" activity as contributing to market volatility and price movements. However, the only classification scheme that attempts to sort traders into speculative and nonspeculative categories, albeit imprecisely, is the CFTC report of large traders. As part of its market surveillance program, the CFTC classifies traders into two main categories, noncommercial and commercial traders. Commercial traders are the larger of the two, and consist of companies "engaged in business activities hedged by the use of the futures or options markets."[21] However, in the view of many experienced commodity investors and traders, changes in the positions of commercial and noncommercial traders do not provide an accurate picture of nonspeculative and speculative activities, respectively. This market belief has been supported by the following: (1) the CFTC data on noncommercial and commercial positions are viewed as only approximations for speculative and nonspeculative activities; (2) it is increasingly difficult to distinguish or categorize investors in the energy markets, especially when, for example, financial firms have purchased physical energy generating assets; and (3) many noncommercial players are known to be long-term investors and should not be considered speculators (e.g., pension funds generally invest

---

[21]The aggregate of all large-traders' positions reported to the CFTC usually represents 70–90 percent of the total open interest in any given market. Data for February 1, 2005 indicated that commercial traders held 67.1 percent of the open long positions, but also 69.2 percent of the short positions in crude oil futures on the NYMEX. Market participants have observed that commercial traders occasionally take speculative short-term positions, particularly during periods of larger price swings.

with long-term objectives and only change their allocations infrequently).

Notwithstanding reports that noncommercial traders contribute to price volatility, there is little evidence to support this view. In recent periods, implied volatility in crude oil futures prices has risen since mid-October 2004 to a plateau just beyond the upper end of its historic range of 35–46 percent, after having been generally range-bound since 2000 (Figure 2.45).[22] However, during this latter period, total open interest and long positions of noncommercial traders declined (Figure 2.46). Indeed, since mid-2004, when noncommercial traders were generally reducing their long positions, implied volatility in oil futures prices either remained in their estimated "middle state" or rose to a higher state. Consequently, apart from transitory jumps, there is little or no evidence of a sustained or trend increase in volatility associated with increases in long positions held by noncommercial traders.

Industry analysts have emphasized that infrastructure investment plans are highly influenced by the perceived "permanence" of oil price increases. Analysts have observed that infrastructure investments of large E&P oil companies depend primarily on whether or not they believe oil price changes will persist, since such investments may not become productive for several years. Infrastructure investment plans are generally not affected by volatility related to transitory oil price fluctuations, unless it also changes perceptions about the permanence or size of oil price changes. By contrast, financial investments may or may not be affected significantly by a rise in price volatility, which under some circumstances may be beneficial for some financial invest-

[22]A three-state statistical model was estimated to test whether volatility has recently increased. Our estimates indicate that implied volatility for WTI oil futures was generally close to the historic average during the period when noncommercial open interest rose sharply, and oil prices peaked (April 2003 through the first half of October 2004).

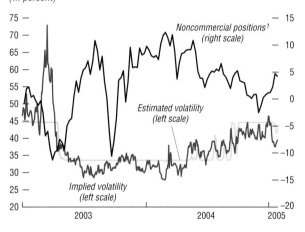

Figure 2.46. Implied Volatility of Oil Futures Prices and Crude Oil Positions of Noncommercial Traders
(In percent)

Sources: Bloomberg L.P.; and IMF staff estimates.
[1]Long positions as a percentage of total open interest.

ments.[23] In any event, market participants have noted that certain forms or sources of price volatility may curtail investment. For example, some noncommercial traders report having reduced their energy market positions during 2004 because of increased intraday volatility and price gapping (e.g., discontinuous jumps in bid and ask prices), which made it increasingly difficult to execute market orders in an efficient manner or at a desired price.[24]

Summary and Conclusions

Market participants believe structural changes have been the primary influence on oil price increases during the past year. Investor perceptions of bottlenecks and relatively tight capacity in the production, refining, and distribution of key energy products are likely to continue until new investments in infrastructure come online, or demand persists at lower levels. Investors also frequently cite the increased potential for supply disruptions, not only from geopolitical uncertainties but also from the more challenging and costly techniques to develop and deliver energy.

Investors have increasingly sought more diversified investment portfolios, including commodities. As perceptions of tight capacity persist, new investments will likely continue in the energy markets. Pension and hedge fund investors have often utilized indexed funds, whose constituents were largely represented by energy futures contracts. Nevertheless, the recent rise in implied futures market volatility has been within historical ranges, which sug-

gests there is little evidence of a sustained increase in volatility attributable to speculative behavior or the expanding energy-related financial markets.

Surveillance in these markets would be improved with more timely and reliable data on global demand and supply conditions. As spare capacity in energy markets diminishes, in reality or perception, markets may become more vulnerable to overshooting. As such, those charged with providing projections of global and local energy market conditions may consider publishing the degree of uncertainty associated with their point estimates to assist market understanding of relative supply and demand conditions.

Hedge Funds: An Update

Growth and Performance

Hedge funds have continued to receive significant investment flows, as institutional investors globally continue to search for diversification and higher returns. Assets under management by hedge funds grew by about 20 percent globally in 2004, approaching the $1 trillion level. Notably, according to research by Greenwich Associates, during 2003–2004, the percentage of institutional accounts investing in hedge funds jumped from 18 to 40 percent in Japan, with most of the increase in equity-related hedge funds. In Asia, more generally, assets under management doubled in 2004 from 2003, to an estimated $60 billion.[25] In Europe, the share of

---

[23]For example, a modest rise in implied volatility of crude oil futures prices would change the profile of prices for crude oil futures contracts in a predictable manner. Indeed, investors in shorter-dated futures contracts plan their investments knowing that volatility has the largest impact on the near-dated contracts; shorter-dated futures contracts are generally the most liquid and most volatile. This is sometimes referred to as the Samuelson effect (i.e., volatility is higher at the front end of the futures curve, and declines as the contract and time to maturity lengthens).

[24]Use of an electronic trading system rather than an open outcry exchange was suggested by several market participants and observers as a way to reduce intraday volatility and price gapping, even though local traders in an open outcry system may account for half of the intraday volume, and are acknowledged by many observers to be an important source of market liquidity.

[25]The relatively less-developed local markets in the region, and their relatively higher volatility, create opportunities for many hedge funds, but have also restricted them from offering the full range of strategies found elsewhere. As a result, smaller hedge funds (often less than $50 million in assets under management) are typical in Asia, and long/short equity and multistrategy funds tend to dominate in Asia.

Table 2.3. Recent Inflows, Performance, and Leverage of Hedge Funds

	2004			2003		
Strategy	Estimated Share of New Investments (In percent)	Range of Estimated Returns (Net of fees)	Asset-Weighted Average Leverage	Estimated Share of New Investments (In percent)	Range of Estimated Returns (Net of fees)	Asset-Weighted Average Leverage
Long/short equity (directional)	24.2	11–13	1.1	9.5	38–52	2.9
Mortgage-backed securities	14.8	7–14	4.1	4.5	6–8	4.3
Global macro	10.4	3–4	2.8	13.5	20–21	2.4
Equity hedge	7.7	7–7.5	1.4	2.1	21–23	1.4
High yield	7.4	3.5–10	3.4	3.9	9–13.5	3.3
Emerging markets	7.2	14–19	1.4	6.3	39–41	1.4
Fixed-income arbitrage	7.0	3–6	8.4	4.0	12–19	2.1
Fixed-income diversified	5.3	4.5–6	9.4	21.8	11.5–12	8.3
Distressed securities	1.6	15–19	1.2	9.5	30–34.5	1.2

Sources: Van Hedge Fund Advisors International; Hedge Fund Research; Centre for International Securities and Derivatives Markets; and IMF staff estimates.

institutional investors participating in hedge funds, usually through funds of hedge funds, has grown from 23 to 32 percent. By comparison, the growth of U.S. institutional investors was relatively slower (28 percent used hedge funds in 2004, compared with 23 percent in 2003). However, the absolute size of allocations by U.S. institutional investors was larger than those by investors in Europe and Japan.

Investor flows during 2004 were directed toward the best performing strategies of 2003, which generally failed to repeat their strong performance (Table 2.3). Directional equity and fixed-income strategies approximated the return of the major equity and fixed-income benchmark indices. The more directional equity strategies returned 11–13 percent in 2004, less than one-third of the returns they achieved in 2003. However, these funds attracted close to 25 percent of new hedge funds investments in 2004, compared with less than 10 percent in 2003. Macro funds, which received more than 10 percent of new investment in 2004, also failed to repeat their strong performance of the previous year. Among fixed-income strategies, investors moved from diversified funds to high-yield, arbitrage funds and mortgage-backed securi-

ties funds (MBS), with contrasting benefits. Emerging market funds were among the best performers in 2003 and 2004, but did not experience a significant increase in investment. Despite posting a strong performance in 2003, distressed debt strategies also failed to attract new investment in 2004, and again outperformed most other strategies.[26]

Leverage appears to have remained largely unchanged for most strategies during 2004. However, leverage appears to have increased among hedge funds pursuing fixed-income strategies, which we previously identified as typically more leveraged than other strategies. Industry observers have noted that the higher leverage employed by fixed-income funds likely represents an effort to maintain higher returns despite narrowing credit spreads (particularly for newer investment flows).

The "institutionalization" of the hedge fund industry was highlighted in the September 2004 GFSR. The growing presence of large banks and brokers in the hedge fund business has continued to develop. Some financial institutions have favored the acquisition of established hedge funds. Recently, BNP Paribas Asset Management merged its hedge fund group with Fauchier Partners, taking a

---

[26]Activity in the distressed debt market seems to have been increasingly dominated by hedge funds in recent periods; according to some market estimates, they represent up to 80 percent of trading in the secondary market.

majority stake in the new company; J.P. Morgan Chase took a majority stake in Highbridge Capital Management, and developed their hedge fund administration business, with the acquisition of Dublin-based Tranaut. Other participants, such as Citigroup, appear to favor building in-house hedge fund expertise, at least for a while.

Regulatory Developments

On October 26, 2004, the Securities and Exchange Commission (SEC) adopted Rule 203(b)(3)-2, requiring the registration of certain hedge fund advisers under the Investment Advisers Act of 1940. According to the rule, an adviser of a "private fund" managing $30 million or more, for 15 clients or more, will be required to register with the SEC by February 2006. For the purpose of the new rule, the adviser is required to "look-through" the fund in order to determine the exact number of investors.[27] A private fund is defined as a fund exempt from SEC registration as an investment company, and allows investors to redeem their interests in the fund within two years.[28] Opinions are mixed as to whether the requirements of the Advisers Act of 1940 will provide investors and the SEC with better transparency into hedge fund activities. Ultimately, the initial and ongoing legal and internal costs associated with registration and compliance with the Advisers Act may also represent a barrier to entry for new/smaller funds.

In various continental European countries, the regulatory framework has been amended to facilitate the development hedge funds, including funds of hedge funds (FOFs) for retail investors. In Germany, the Investment Modernization Act, enacted on January 1, 2004, provided the legal framework for the development of domestic (and the distribution of foreign) hedge funds and FOFs; while shares of FOFs can be distributed to individual investors without requiring a minimum investment, single hedge funds may be distributed only through private offerings or to institutional investors. However, the flow of funds into the industry has been viewed as disappointing. At the end of 2004, total assets under management with hedge funds and FOFs were estimated to be approximately €1 billion in Germany, significantly below the amount expected at the beginning of the year. In France, the regulatory framework for hedge funds was implemented in November 2004, with the adoption of rules providing for the development of new hedge fund vehicles.[29] The so-called contractual funds and ARIA/EL mutual funds (investment funds with reduced investment rules and the ability to employ more leverage) will be accessible to qualified investors and wealthier individuals.[30]

In the United Kingdom, although the Financial Services Authority (FSA) has ruled out allowing the distribution of hedge fund products to retail investors, "Qualified Investor Schemes" (QISs), set up in April 2004, are expected to give eligible investors access to hedge fund type investments. The QISs can invest in derivatives markets, short

---

[27]Since 1985, the SEC allowed an investment adviser to count an investment pool, such as a hedge fund, as a single client, irrespective of the effective number of investors in the fund. Advisers of funds of hedge funds are also required to "look-through" the funds, to the underlying clients. Similarly, offshore advisers are required to register with the SEC if they have 15 or more U.S. clients.

[28]Most hedge funds have lock-up periods of less than two years, and hence will qualify as private funds. However, we are aware of longer lock-up periods by some hedge funds, particularly the largest and most successful funds, in response to current strong investor demand. Private equity funds are largely unaffected by these changes, as they usually impose lock-up periods of more than two years (e.g., often five or more years).

[29]Rules for the development of funds of hedge funds were established in 2003.

[30]These funds are, in theory, accessible to all investors: no minimum investment thresholds are set for "qualified" and institutional investors, whereas minimum investment thresholds for retail investors are defined in relation to their financial wealth and/or expertise (the minimum required investment declines with wealth and expertise), and depend on the riskiness of the fund (thresholds for contractual funds are higher than thresholds for ARIAs).

sell securities and use leverage, and are allowed to charge performance fees. However, their development has been impaired by the absence of a clear tax regime for such investment vehicles.

Summary

Despite relatively poor return performance in 2004 compared with 2003, new investments continued to flow into hedge funds, as investors, particularly institutional investors, sought diversification and less or uncorrelated risk-adjusted returns. As the hedge fund industry continues to grow, it is likely to "institutionalize" further, with major banks and brokers increasing their presence in these businesses and investment vehicles.

Accounting

The global trend toward convergence in accounting standards for financial institutions (as well as nonfinancial corporates), as described in the September 2004 GFSR, has continued to advance on several fronts. The United States and international accounting standards have moved closer together, while a growing number of countries have taken the International Financial Reporting Standards (IFRS) as a reference point or adopted them wholesale. Areas of particular importance, where more significant progress is needed and expected, include accounting for insurance firms and pension funds, and the treatment of financial derivatives.

A significant development at the beginning of 2005 has been the implementation in the European Union of the IFRS, promulgated by the International Accounting Standards Board (IASB).[31] The adoption of the IFRS marks a significant convergence in accounting practice between the EU and the United States, as well as other countries. While generally acknowl-edged as work in progress, the IFRS represent a promising move toward more uniform disclosure.

Much attention has centered on international accounting standard (IAS) 39 regarding the treatment of derivatives and other financial instruments. The standard represents a convergence with U.S. Generally Accepted Accounting Principles (GAAP), with extensive similarities between IAS 39 and the recently revised U.S. Financial Accounting Standard (FAS) 133. While the European Union adopted IAS 39 at of the beginning of 2005, the version adopted includes two "carve outs," at least for the moment.

One of the exceptions made by the EU to IAS 39 is in hedge accounting (particularly in relation to bank deposits). The deletions with respect to hedge accounting are primarily to allow (mainly continental European) banks to use demand deposits as a portfolio hedge for interest rate risk, which is prohibited by the full IAS 39. From the banks' perspective, adoption of IAS 39 would introduce "artificial" earnings volatility.

Even critics of the carve out acknowledge the difficulty. Some observers note that banks and other financial institutions in the United States have addressed FASB rules (similar to the IAS 39 standard) on this issue by structuring derivatives on their balance sheets to neutralize the accounting impact of showing deposits at near-zero duration. In any case, such an adjustment may not be ideal, as it represents a financial position to accommodate an accounting-induced mismatch, raising again the question of accounting relative to economic reality, and the role of risk management.

The other EU exception is the application of fair value accounting to liabilities—the "full fair value option." Concerns within the EU include prudential and regulatory worries by

---

[31]The adoption covered 32 International Accounting Standards and 5 new International Financial Reporting Standards. As of January 2005, 92 countries had either adopted IFRS or decided to allow the use of IFRS as an accounting framework.

various national authorities, concerns about financial stability, and some uncertainty as to whether financial institutions currently have the resources and data to assign fair values to many liabilities. EU authorities also note that the use of full fair value accounting for liabilities may conflict with current regulations in some member countries.

The absence of the option to measure financial liabilities at fair value affects some banks, insurers, and other companies that have economically matching portfolios of financial assets, liabilities, and derivatives. Some institutions had been hoping to use the fair value option to get a degree of natural offset, rather than having to work through the onerous requirements to qualify for hedge accounting. This is no longer possible. The effect of this carve out may be to increase reported earnings volatility.

Authorities in Japan, which has implemented some accounting reforms in recent years, have indicated that, while there is some resistance to the idea of full convergence toward the IFRS, there may already have been benefits to the reforms that have been put in place. Market practitioners believe these accounting reforms have contributed to bank efforts to address balance sheet issues, including nonperforming loans. In January 2005, the IASB and the Japanese accounting standards board announced a joint project aimed at reducing differences between the Japanese and IASB standards.

Although IAS 39 is generally regarded as comprehensive, the current version excludes "insurance contracts," acknowledging that insurance firms face special difficulties in applying fair value accounting to their policy liabilities. In recognition of this difficulty, the IASB has adopted a two-step approach to setting insurance standards, with Phase I going into effect at the beginning of 2005, and Phase II expected to be implemented by the end of 2007. As such, until 2008, insurers will report assets but not liabilities at market value.

In addition to IAS 39, a revised version of IAS 19, which covers employee benefits, went into effect in the EU on January 1, 2005. As discussed in the September 2004 GFSR, the new version of IAS 19 requires employee pension funds to mark assets to market, but it permits the use of some smoothing mechanisms to limit fluctuations in liabilities. Due to the long duration of pension liabilities, moderate shifts in interest rates can have large effects on the present value of expected liabilities and therefore on solvency (to the extent that liability and asset durations are not matched). Smoothing mechanisms, such as those provided by IAS 19 and U.S. FAS 87, can reduce the impact of such market changes. IAS 19 has also provided for the use of high-grade corporate bond rates for discounting pension liabilities, as currently utilized by FASB regulations.

As it has with financial instruments and derivatives accounting under IAS 39, the United Kingdom has opted for more mark-to-market accounting on pension funds than most other countries. The United Kingdom's revised FRS 17, which implements IAS 19, goes further in its reporting requirements, mandating fair value accounting for pension fund liabilities as well as assets, generally without smoothing. Similar to IAS 19, companies applying FRS 17 have the option of amortizing unexpected gains and losses over several years, rather than reporting them in their earnings statements. However, FRS 17 requires the full amount of shortfalls (or gains) from expected earnings to be reported in a separate Statement of Total Recognized Gains and Losses (STRGL). This option has now been included in the revised IAS 19. As the pro forma effects of FRS 17 have been disclosed in reports for several years, U.K. markets and investors have been prepared for the possible impact of FRS 17 on earnings, and many companies appear sanguine about the transition.

Proponents of the international accounting standards cite several potential benefits from harmonization and convergence to "best practice." It is maintained that international convergence will lead to sounder risk disclosure and better comparability of accounts. That, in turn, will increase the ability to raise capital globally, especially in major financial centers (particularly in the United States). It is also sometimes argued that convergence would lower the cost of capital for most firms. This last claim may be more debatable. On balance, the clearest benefits, as suggested above, may arise from comparable disclosure.

Market and Credit Risk Indicators for the Mature Market Financial System

This issue of the GFSR expands on our review of mature market financial systems with Market Risk Indicators (MRI) and Credit Risk Indicators (CRI). First, the MRI Index now attempts to capture institution-specific risks, measured as a share of market capitalization. Second, the credit risk analysis includes default probabilities associated with first-to-default baskets of CDSs on financial institutions. The set of financial institutions used in this analysis is the same as defined in the September 2004 GFSR, with the exception of Bank One, now part of the J.P. Morgan Chase Group.[32] Finally, risk indices for the life insurance sector are introduced.

Banking Groups

Consolidation in the banking sector has produced several large and complex financial institutions (LCFIs). Among the large global banks, some are engaged in investment banking, while others focus more on commercial and retail banking activities.

Some observers argue that the diversified set of activities in which LCFIs are involved represents a natural hedge against possible shocks, and allows them to act as a dependable and efficient intermediator of savings and investment, a key activity for a healthy financial system (see Corrigan, 2004; and Kwan and Laderman, 1999). Many LCFIs have a substantial retail component in their business mix, which may act to offset the volatility of earnings from other lines of business, such as corporate lending or capital markets activities (Azarchs, 2004).

In any case, the operational complexity of these institutions may make them more difficult to manage and monitor than smaller deposit-taking units, given the various sources of business and market risk the management team must address (De Ferrari and Palmer, 2001). In addition, because of their large size and often their global reach, they may more significantly affect financial stability in the case of an adverse market shock. The following analysis will try to highlight the distinct behavior of LCFIs and commercial banks according to different risk measures under various market conditions.

Market Indicators

The following MRI attempt to highlight the specific risks related to a particular institution, since we factor out the effects of world and domestic market volatility from the original equity data (Hawkesby, Marsh, and Stevens, forthcoming). A comparison between the current (VaR-beta) and the September 2004 MRI (VaR) for the complete portfolio of banks as defined above may explain the impact of gen-

---

[32]The definition of LCFIs is the same as applied by the Bank of England in the *Financial Stability Review*, December 2003, and comprises ABN Amro, Bank of America, Barclays, BNP Paribas, Citigroup, Credit Suisse Group, Deutsche Bank, Goldman Sachs, HSBC Holdings, J.P. Morgan Chase, Lehman Brothers, Merrill Lynch, Morgan Stanley, Société Générale, and UBS. The commercial banks selected for our portfolio are Australia and New Zealand Banking Group, Banca Intesa, Banco Bilbao Vizcaya Argentaria, Bank of East Asia, Bank of Nova Scotia, CIBC, Commerzbank, Crédit Agricole, Development Bank of Singapore, HBOS, HVB Group, Mitsubishi Tokyo Financial, Mizuho Financial, National Australia Bank, Nordea, Royal Bank of Canada, Royal Bank of Scotland, SanPaolo IMI, Santander Hispano Group, Skandinaviska Enskilda Banken, Sumitomo Mitsui Financial, Svenska Handelsbanken, Toronto Dominion, UFJ Holdings, UniCredito, Wachovia, and Westpac Banking Corp.

Figure 2.47. Value at Risk (VaR) for Complete Portfolio of Banks: Total VaR and VaR Without World Market and Local Market Effects (VaR-Beta)
(In percent)

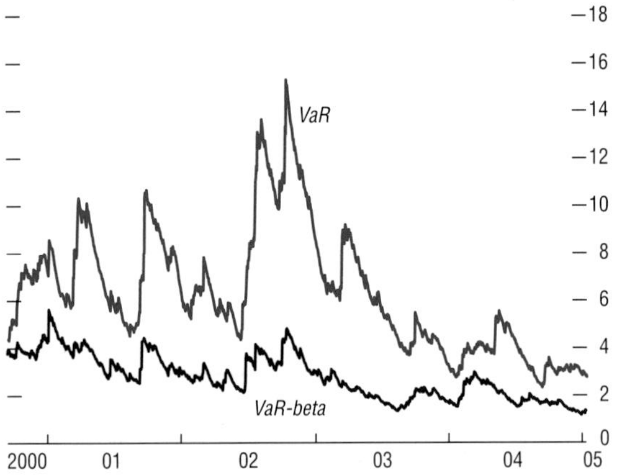

Sources: Bloomberg L.P.; and IMF staff estimates.

Figure 2.48. Bank and LCFI Portfolios: Value at Risk Without World Market and Local Market Effects (VaR-Beta)[1]
(In percent)

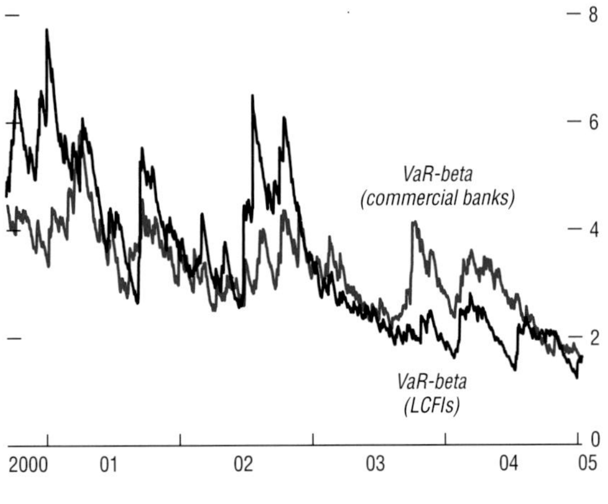

Sources: Bloomberg L.P.; and IMF staff estimates.
[1]LCFIs are large complex financial institutions.

eral market dynamics on MRI, and highlight firm-specific risk factors (Figure 2.47).

Clearly, world and local market conditions have a significant influence on the institutions in our portfolio, often contributing as much as, and sometimes more than, the institution's individual risk to total value at risk (VaR). Once the broad market effects are removed, the major events represented in the data, and discussed in the September 2004 GFSR, still stand out, but with a different ranking in terms of their relative impact or importance.

For example, the equity market decline in early 2001 had the greatest influence on the risk profile of the full portfolio of institutions, especially on LCFIs (Figure 2.48). The surge in volatility related to September 11 and the credit events of 2002 were almost entirely because of overall market movements, while financial sector/bank-specific factors played a more minor role. Uncertainty regarding the evolution of U.S. monetary policy, which surfaced in late 2003, had a much greater influence on commercial banks, possibly because of their perceived higher sensitivity to interest rate risk.

Focusing on bank-specific factors, the VaR profile of Japanese banks shows two significant events when market perceptions of bank creditworthiness became more pessimistic. The two peaks in bank value at risk were observed in October 2002 and the last quarter of 2003 (Figure 2.49). The former is associated with heightened concerns about bank creditworthiness due to the announcement of a far-reaching bank reform plan by the FSA aimed at reducing by half major banks' non-performing loan ratio to approximately 4 percent by March 2005. The second is associated with the market's reaction to the failure of a large regional bank.

Increased diversification, as measured by the ratio between diversified and undiversified VaR, reduces the potential impact of external shocks on the financial sector. After eliminating the broad market effects, our diversification measure becomes higher and more stable

(Figure 2.50). In fact, wide equity market movements, such as the ones experienced from 2000 to 2002, tend to dominate bank-specific dynamics, simultaneously driving all equity prices in one direction and reducing the degree of diversification.

In our portfolio, the diversification measure does not differ much between commercial banks and LCFIs. In May 2004, in relation to the FOMC meeting that signaled the intention to increase short-term official rates, the overall diversification index shows a sudden drop. Even though such a move by the U.S. Federal Reserve had been anticipated, the elimination of the residual uncertainty prompted a discrete unidirectional adjustment of positions. As highlighted in the September 2004 GFSR, the current relatively low level of the overall diversification index indicates a certain vulnerability of the financial sector to a market shock.

Credit Risk Indicators

The large reduction in credit spreads and low volatility levels observed over the last two years has led market participants to question whether risks from increasingly leveraged positions are building or are possibly understated. Therefore, more attention has been paid to different measures of credit risk.

One widely used measure is "distance to default," which indicates the number of standard deviations the asset value of a certain institution is away from default.[33] However, a major shortcoming of this measure is that it does not account for changes in default correlations among different institutions, as may likely be the case from a general market shock. Also, especially in a low credit spread environment, policymakers may wish to stress test risk indices or indicators, an exercise that is not easy to implement using distance to default.

[33]See Duffie and Singleton (2003); Bank of England (2004); and European Central Bank (2004).

Figure 2.49. Japanese Banks: Value at Risk (VaR) Without World Market and Local Market Effects (VaR-Beta)
(In percent)

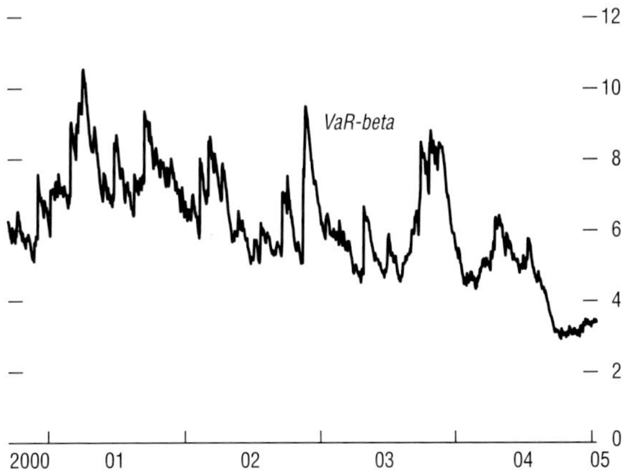

VaR-beta

Sources: Bloomberg L.P.; and IMF staff estimates.

Figure 2.50. Total Diversification Effect and Diversification Without Market Effects (Diversification-Beta) for LCFIs and Commercial Banks[1]
(In percent)

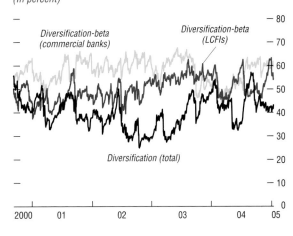

Diversification-beta (commercial banks)

Diversification-beta (LCFIs)

Diversification (total)

Sources: Bloomberg L.P.; and IMF staff estimates.
[1]LCFIs are large complex financial institutions.

One way to account for the correlation of defaults is by estimating the first-to-default (FTD) probability from a basket of CDSs on LCFIs and large commercial banks.[34] In particular, we monitor the evolution of the FTD probability up to a two-year horizon (see Box 2.4). This approach may be useful for bank supervisors who oversee large and complex institutions in order to identify common or emerging weaknesses among a group of (similar) institutions (DeFerrari and Palmer, 2001).

In our data set, which starts in July 2002, the credit outlook has improved steadily from October 2002, as the probability of observing a single default has greatly diminished (Figure 2.51). During this period, the term structure of default probabilities from the three-month to the five-year maturities has flattened, indicating that the market perceives the recent favorable credit environment as rather stable. However, expectations of possibly aggressive interest rate policy actions from the U.S. Federal Reserve (November 2003–June 2004) had some influence on default probabilities. Throughout this period, LCFIs demonstrated a higher sensitivity than the subset of commercial banks we are using in this analysis.

We also conducted a stress test to evaluate the response of default probabilities to a substantial and sudden worsening of the credit environment. To do so, we chose the worst 10 percent cases from the distribution of all possible scenarios (Gibson, 2004). In this case, the probability of observing a default in the group of all financial institutions (i.e., the portfolio of commercial banks and LCFIs) over a one-year period, in fact, rises from 7 to 22 percent, and on a two-year horizon, from 11 to 33 percent. For LCFIs, the probability of

Figure 2.51. Probability of Observing a Default Over a Two-Year Period

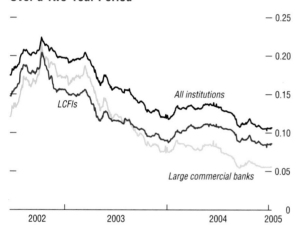

Sources: Bloomberg L.P.; and IMF staff estimates.

---

[34]The institutions analyzed include the LCFIs and nine other large banks within our portfolio for which CDSs quotations were available: Commerzbank, Crédit Agricole, HVB Group, Royal Bank of Scotland, Sanpaolo IMI, Santander Hispano Group, UFJ Holdings, UniCredito, and Wachovia.

observing a default increases from 6 to 16 percent over a one-year horizon, while for commercial banks the probability rises from 3 to 9 percent. Based on this analysis, as well as other studies, it would be difficult to draw significant conclusions on the relative stability or resiliency of LCFIs and large commercial banks. We intend to continue developing the analysis and monitoring activity in upcoming issues of the GFSR.

Insurance Sector

Market Risk Indicators

Insurance companies' relevance to financial stability considerations has often been debated, but it may have increased in recent years because of the expanding volume of complex financial transactions in which they participate (CDSs, CDOs, long-dated swaps, longevity risk, reinsurance, etc.). Insurers can be distinguished according to the line of business in which they are active: life insurance, property and casualty insurance, and reinsurance. Each of these different subgroups, because of the specific asset and liability structure of their businesses, require a somewhat different and specific analysis. For the time being, we have concentrated on life insurance companies, because of the extent of their investment activities, relative balance sheet size, and thus their relevance to the broader financial system, as highlighted in the April 2004 GFSR.[35] As also discussed in Chapter III of the GFSR, the structure of solvency regimes, together with the risk management practices of different institutions, result in different responsiveness to market events. In particular, the relatively larger equity holdings by European insurance companies appear to have translated into a higher sensitivity to

[35]The firms included in the sample are Aegon, Aviva, AXA, Friends Provident, Hartford, Irish Life, Legal & General, Metlife, Prudential Financial, Prudential PLC, and Swiss Life.

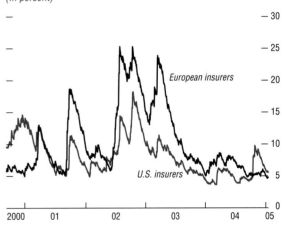

Figure 2.52. Insurance Portfolio Value at Risk (VaR)
(In percent)

Sources: Bloomberg L.P.; and IMF staff estimates.

broad market events than their U.S. peer group has.

Our market risk indicator shows that the risk profile of U.S. life insurers is markedly different from European life insurers, especially before mid-year 2002 (Figure 2.52). The credit events of 2001 and 2002 (i.e., the September 11 incident and several large corporate bankruptcies related to fraud, respectively) were broadly manifest in the equity markets. However, the impact of these events on the U.S. life insurers was short lived, in part because of the insurers' relatively larger holdings of credit rather than equity. By contrast, European insurers have a much larger share of their assets concentrated in equities. Our indicators provide supporting evidence about the market participants' greater concerns about the creditworthiness of the European companies compared with their U.S. counterparts following these events.

Finally, the October 2004 announcement by New York Attorney General Eliot Spitzer regarding his investigation of the relationship between insurance companies and brokers had a very strong influence on U.S. insurers' equity volatilities, which has by now almost completely dissipated.

Credit Risk Indicators

The amount of information available in the credit derivative markets for individual insurance companies is still very limited, as market quotes for many of the companies in our portfolio started only in mid-2003. Nonetheless, even in this relatively short period, it is possible to detect a spread reduction, indicating that the insurance sector is also benefiting from an improvement in the general credit outlook. As the credit derivative market provides greater opportunities for analysis, we will expand our review of the insurance sector.

Conclusions

Since the publication of the September 2004 GFSR, the financial market indicators

reflect a continued decline in market volatility and the market's perception of risk, albeit only slightly. Nonetheless, both VaR analysis and evidence from stress testing on the probability of a first-to-default basket of banks and LCFIs indicate that severe market-wide credit events could have a very significant impact on financial institutions. This suggests that while the soundness of an individual financial institution is of course important to supervisors, increasing attention should also be paid to monitor and detect stress situations developing in the wider financial system.

References

Azarchs, Tanya, 2004, *Retail Sector Anchors Large Complex Banks in U.S.*, Standard & Poors Ratingsdirect (October 4).

Black, Fisher, and Myron Scholes, 1973, "The Pricing of Options and Corporate Liabilities," *Journal of Political Economy*, Vol. 81, No. 3, pp. 637–59.

Bank of England, 2004, *Financial Stability Review* (London, December).

Corrigan, E. Gerald, 2004, *Large Integrated Financial Intermediaries and the Public Interest* (New York: Goldman Sachs & Co., April).

Credit Suisse First Boston, 2005, "CSFB's EM Ratings Model," January 24.

DeFerrari, L.M., and D.E. Palmer, 2001, "Supervision of Large Complex Banking Organizations," *Federal Reserve Bulletin* (February).

Duffie, Darrell, and Kenneth J. Singleton, 2003, *Credit Risk: Pricing Measurement and Management* (Princeton, NJ: Princeton University Press).

Eichengreen, Barry, Ricardo Haussman, and Ugo Panizza, 2003, "The Mystery of Original Sin," revised paper presented at the IDB Conference, "Currency and Maturity Matchmaking: Redeeming Debt from Original Sin" (Washington, November).

European Central Bank, 2004, *Financial Stability Review* (December).

Gibson, Michael S., 2004, "Understanding the Risk of Synthetic CDOs," Finance and Economics Discussion Paper No. 36 (Washington: Federal Reserve Board, May).

Hawkesby, Christian, Ian Marsh, and Ibrahim Stevens, 2005, "Comovements in the Prices of

Securities Issued by Large Complex Financial Institutions," Bank of England Working Paper (London, forthcoming)

Kwan, Simon H., and Elizabeth S. Laderman, 1999, "On the Portfolio Effects of Financial Convergence—A Review of the Literature," Federal Reserve Bank of San Francisco, *Economic Review*, No. 2, pp. 18–31.

IMF, 2003, *Global Financial Stability Report,* World Economic and Financial Surveys (Washington, March).

———, 2004a, *Global Financial Stability Report,* World Economic and Financial Surveys (Washington, April).

———, 2004b, *Global Financial Stability Report,* World Economic and Financial Surveys (Washington, September).

———, 2005, *World Economic Outlook,* World Economic and Financial Surveys (Washington, April).

Litzenberger, Robert H., and Nir Rabinowitz, 1995, "Backwardation in Oil Futures Markets: Theory and Empirical Evidence," *The Journal of Finance*, Vol. 50 (December), pp. 1517–45.

Merton, Robert C., 1974, "On The Pricing of Corporate Debt: The Risk Structure of Interest Rates," *The Journal of Finance*, Vol. 29, No. 2, pp. 449–70.

United Kingdom, Debt Management Office, 2004, "Issuance of Ultra-Long Gilt Instruments," Consultation Document (London). Available via the Internet: *http://www.dmo.gov.uk/gilts/public/consdoc/cons021204.pdf.*

———, Her Majesty's Stationery Office, 2004, "Pensions: Challenges and Choices," The First Report of the Pensions Commission. Available via the Internet: *http://www.pensionscommission.org.uk/publications/2004/annrep/appendices-all.pdf.*

Vassalou, Maria, and Yuhang Xing, 2004, "Default Risk in Equity Returns," *The Journal of Finance*, Vol. 59, No. 2 pp. 831–68.

CHAPTER III

HOUSEHOLD BALANCE SHEETS

This is the third and final installment of a series of chapters in the *Global Financial Stability Report* (GFSR) discussing the transfer, reallocation, and management of financial risk. Throughout this series we have highlighted the flow and reallocation of risks throughout the financial system, and the ability of certain market participants to manage new types of risks. Traditional assessments of financial stability tend to concentrate on the condition or resiliency of systemically important institutions, most often banks. In this series, we have expanded the analysis and highlighted the changing flow of risks among market participants, often as a result of policies or standards intended to improve the ability to manage, monitor, or measure risks in a particular sector. However, such policies and standards frequently redirect the flow of risk to less-monitored or less-measured sectors, such as the household sector. As such, the question arises whether, as a result of these policies, the financial system as a whole has become or is becoming more stable, or whether new risks and sources of instability may be emerging.

In the previous two chapters in the series, we analyzed the flow and management of financial risks in the life insurance sector and in private sector occupational pension funds.

- In the *life insurance industry*, we examined the transfer of risk from banks to insurers (largely as a result of risk-based banking regulation), highlighting the need for improved risk management skills. Our focus was on the structural influences on insurers' behavior, such as market structure (e.g., variety of financial instruments available), regulation, accounting, and the role of rating agencies. In part, we recommended that the introduction of risk-based capital or similar regulatory standards would contribute

significantly to improving the risk management practices of insurers. Indeed, as such standards are increasingly being proposed or implemented, we observe that many life insurers are seeking to de-risk their balance sheets (e.g., more fixed-income investments, and fewer sales of guaranteed or with-profits policies).

- With regard to *pension funds*, we observed risk management practices often inconsistent with the goal of meeting long-term liabilities. We found few regulatory or tax incentives that encouraged modern risk management practices or the building of even modest overfunding cushions. At the same time, proposed fair value accounting principles have been cited by market participants as a primary factor contributing to the de-risking of balance sheets by employers through the closure of defined benefit plans and the transfer of various long-term saving, investment, and other risks (e.g., longevity and inflation) to the household sector.

As banks, insurers, and pension funds seek to reduce the volatility of their balance sheets and its impact on earnings, a variety of risks traditionally managed within these institutions are flowing more directly to the household sector. The channels for these risk flows are multiple, including mortgage loans, unit-linked insurance products, and defined contribution and other self-directed pension plans. The types of financial risks increasingly being borne more directly by the household sector vary somewhat by country, but include (1) market risks (i.e., interest rate, equity, and credit, as well as derivatives embedded in structured products); (2) inflation risk (as governments and corporates adjust or eliminate benefit indexation); (3) investment planning and reinvestment risk (i.e., operational risk); and (4) longevity risk (as public and private annuity income streams are reduced or eliminated). At the same time, the transfer of risks has to be considered together with potential benefits to households from these changes, including greater choice, portability of certain benefits, and access to a broad range of financial products. Furthermore, there are also risks to *not* investing, including the erosion of asset values through inflation.

This chapter deliberately focuses on an assessment of the shift in market risks to the household sector, which results from changes in the behavior of financial institutions and from pension reform. In particular, this chapter evaluates neither existing pension systems nor ongoing pension reforms in various countries. Such reforms have changed the positions and risk profiles of the household sector. They have brought benefits and reduced some risks, but at the same time increased other risks. In particular, the move from defined benefit to defined contribution pension plans has led households to take on more market and longevity risks, while shedding other risks, such as the credit risk of the corporate plan sponsor. In addition, the portability of defined contribution and hybrid plans is widely considered an attractive feature of these pension schemes—as it could contribute to labor market mobility. More generally, demographic and/or fiscal pressures will always weigh on pension systems, regardless of their nature. Maintaining a given level of benefits will require more resources to be put into any pension plan. This means either higher contribution rates under defined benefit schemes, or higher saving rates under defined contributions schemes. Therefore, the move from defined benefit to defined contribution schemes does not in itself cause a rise in contribution or saving rates. More broadly, the move from defined benefit to defined contribution plans may contribute to the consolidation of public and corporate finances, thus helping to sustain economic growth that benefits households. In several emerging market countries, such as Chile and Mexico, pension reforms, including the establishment of corporate defined contribution plans, have helped to develop an important local institutional investor class, which in turn has fostered the development of local capital markets.

Households, as the "shareholders" of the public and private financial systems, have always been the ultimate bearers of financial risks. However, traditionally these various risks and exposures have been intermediated to differing degrees by governments and private financial and nonfinancial institutions, and households have borne these risks in different capacities, including as taxpayers, depositors, employers or business owners, pension or insurance beneficiaries, or increasingly as holders of equity or debt securities. The goal of this chapter is to increase the awareness among policymakers of how the risk profile of households (more than the aggregate risk level) has possibly changed or may change going forward. It can be argued that policymakers have improved, and are continuing to improve, financial stability by improving the resiliency of banks, insurers, and pensions; however, this chapter examines whether such policies have sufficiently considered how risks flow through the system, particularly to the household sector.

The household sector is often excluded from traditional analysis and considerations related to the stability of the financial system. However, we believe issues related to the household sector should be an important aspect of financial stability considerations. This is not to say that we anticipate widespread instability in the household sector, as in many jurisdictions households currently seem to enjoy relatively high net worth. However, the financial landscape is changing, and in certain respects households may not appreciate or be adequately prepared for such changes. Policies designed to improve the financial stability of systemically or otherwise important institutions need to also consider the consequent flow of risks to households and their ability to absorb or manage such risks.

Households are relevant to the financial stability debate in numerous ways, including the following considerations: (1) potential public sector costs related to household shortfalls in long-term saving and investment; (2) the broader role of government as "insurer of last resort"; (3) the need to facilitate or more actively develop markets and market solutions, or alternatively, to re-regulate institutional behavior to achieve the desired risk sharing; (4) moral hazards, for example, from excessive risk taking by institutions based on the belief that governments will support market values in an effort to protect household balance sheets (i.e., markets are seen as "too important to fall"); and (5) the impact of more direct risk exposures on household behavior, including consumption and saving patterns. This chapter will not discuss each of these issues in detail, but we will attempt to highlight the changing flow of risk and risk profile of households, and how this may impact some of these considerations.

In this study, we continue our comparative analysis and approach, looking at these trends and influences on household behavior in selected industrialized countries, notably France, Germany, Japan, the Netherlands, the United Kingdom, and the United States. We will also discuss Denmark and Sweden, where many of these issues have received significant consideration.

We recognized from the outset that this study should highlight current and potential trends in household net worth, risk profiles, and investment behavior, and, where possible, present such trends using timely data. However, aggregate household data are frequently one or more years out of date, or do not exist in sufficient detail, and often are not comparable across jurisdictions. The timeliness of disaggregated household data

(i.e., income groups and age cohorts) has been a particular concern, since numerous market practitioners and analysts note that a variety of changes in the risk profile and financial behavior of different household groups or cohorts may be occurring, particularly in recent periods. Therefore, such behavior may not yet be fully reflected in government data or academic studies. Indeed, there appears to be tremendous scope for international organizations such as the IMF or the OECD and others to promote efforts to improve the timely gathering and comparability of household data.[1]

The following section will discuss comparative and national trends in household net worth, financial holdings, and financial behavior, including, where available, such trends for different income groups and age cohorts. We will also discuss certain future or potential obligations that are rarely, if ever, included in official data or considered in academic studies (e.g., prospective changes to pension provisions, and health care and education costs), which households in many countries increasingly may be expected to assume as governments and employers reduce benefits. This may be an important consideration for policymakers and an area for further study, as many outstanding studies have assumed little or no change in existing institutional structures and programs when evaluating the current financial position of households.

The next section will focus on household saving and asset allocation behavior. It will analyze how such behavior may be affected by changes to household risk profiles, and examine the products and services that the financial industry has developed, or may need to develop, to help households meet these new challenges. It will also discuss possible public policy initiatives on the promotion of a broader range of payout instruments and structures.

---

[1]An OECD working group is currently considering ways to improve the coverage of household financial data in national accounts.

The following section focuses on communication and education, which has been broadly recognized as an area needing significant attention, and one in which there seems to be a vital role for governments. The public sector may be best positioned to ensure that households are made aware of the increasing demands on their savings, and to coordinate public and private sector actions to provide the basic understanding and financial skills needed to address these new demands. Such considerations, and steps to address these needs, are occurring to some degree, albeit at varying levels of detail, in most industrialized countries.

Throughout this series of chapters, including this one, we have sought to provide a comparative analysis of the major issues, and as such we do not seek to propose a single "best way forward." Possibly, more than with any other sector, policy considerations regarding the appropriate risk sharing and risk profile of the household sector reflect the different cultural, social, and political choices of individual countries or regions. While recognizing this diversity of national approaches, we intend to highlight below how households may cope with this changing flow of risks, and its policy implications.

Household Balance Sheets

This section discusses the principal influences on the household sector's risk profile, and assesses national and global trends for selected industrialized countries. The discussion also illustrates the need for more up-to-date and detailed data at the household level, and how the lack of data may limit our ability to monitor the impact of policy changes on the household sector. Partly because of data limitations, we have restricted the discussion

of household balance sheet developments to a select group of countries: France, Germany, Japan, the Netherlands, the United Kingdom, and the United States. Even among this group of countries, there are large differences in coverage at the aggregate and individual household level.[2]

Components and Evolution of Household Balance Sheets

Assessing household risk profiles entails examining how well they have managed their balance sheets, along with the associated returns and risks (e.g., credit, market, liquidity, and longevity risks). It involves assessing not only the magnitude of various portfolio items but also their risk profiles, as illustrated by their volatility and diversification benefits. Government statistics and survey data only take account of explicit financial assets (e.g., bank deposits and savings accounts, market securities, and private pension and insurance reserves) and liabilities (e.g., mortgage and consumer debt), and nonfinancial assets (e.g., housing) when computing household net worth. However, these data do not include all current or likely future household assets and obligations.

It is important to consider a wider range of future assets and obligations in order to fully capture the scope of household risk management challenges. This section focuses in particular on a number of additional costs and obligations that may significantly increase households' savings needs, as well as change their risk profiles and investment behavior. The potential costs and obligations include those arising from changes (or likely changes) in state and private pension arrangements, or subsidies for medical and long-term health care or education. At the same time, to deal

---

[2]Japan and the United States have the most complete coverage, including relatively long time series of aggregate flow-of-funds data and microsurvey data (e.g., income and age cohorts) of household finances. By comparison, many of the continental European countries do not have data that are as timely or complete (in particular for nonfinancial assets), and have little comparable subgroup data.

Figure 3.1. Household Sector: Net Worth and Net Financial Assets in Domestic Currencies[1]

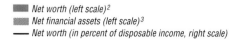

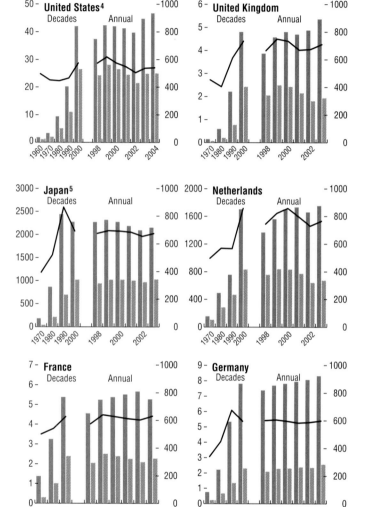

Sources: U.S. Board of Governors of the Federal Reserve System; Bank of England, U.K. Office of National Statistics, National Institute of Economic and Social Research; Bank of Japan, Economic and Social Research Institute; De Nederlandsche Bank; Banque de France, INSEE; Bundesbank; OECD; and IMF staff estimates.

[1]Net worth is calculated as sum of nonfinancial assets and financial assets minus financial liabilities. Net financial assets are financial assets minus financial liabilities.

[2]Net worth for United States, in trillions of U.S. dollars; for United Kingdom, in trillions of pounds sterling; for Japan, in trillions of yen; for Netherlands, in billions of euros; and for France and Germany, in trillions of euros.

[3]Net financial assets for United States, in trillions of U.S. dollars; for United Kingdom, in trillions of pounds sterling; for Japan, in trillions of yen; for Netherlands, in billions of euros; and for France and Germany, in trillions of euros.

[4]Data for 2004 are only available through the third quarter.

[5]Figures for financial assets and liabilities are for the fiscal year beginning April 1.

with such costs and obligations, households will also rely on future incomes and assets that would also need to be taken into account in a systematic assessment of the challenges ahead. However, this chapter does not attempt to provide such a comprehensive approach; it focuses primarily on the transfer of risks to the household sector.

Household Risk Profiles: Comparative Developments

Comparisons across countries reveal a variety of themes and trends in the composition of household balance sheets, reflecting different influences (market structure, regulation, cultural preferences, etc.) on household behavior.

Net Worth

Average household net worth grew faster than disposable income in most industrialized countries throughout the 1980s and 1990s, and has largely recovered from the bursting of the equity market bubble. In most countries, net worth to disposable income levels are close to historical highs, with growth since 1990 spurred by strong increases in the value of real estate and equity holdings (Figure 3.1). Housing wealth has grown strongly in the Netherlands and the United Kingdom, with net worth rising to 765 percent and 710 percent of disposable income in 2003, respectively.

In both France and Germany, the ratio of net worth to disposable income has stayed near historic highs, at about 600 percent, and has not changed materially in recent years. In contrast with others, Germany has experienced slower growth in house prices, and has not experienced a notable increase in the share of housing assets in household portfolios. In addition, households in France and Germany have noticeably lower levels of debt. Meanwhile, market-sensitive assets have formed a relatively small share of household portfolios.

Japan's net worth has shown a distinctly different trend. In the period from 1970 to 2003, the growth of household net worth outpaced that of disposable income by a modest amount. Of course, this 30-year period is composed of two distinct periods, with rapid net worth growth in the 1980s, and a steady decline in net worth during much of the 1990s, largely because of a continuing decline in house prices throughout the later period.

In the United States, steady gains in household net worth have stemmed more from increases in the market value of assets than from increased savings. Despite a relatively higher exposure to asset market price movements, U.S. household net worth appears less volatile than for most other industrialized countries during 1980–2003 (Table 3.1).

The volatility of household net worth is influenced by a variety of factors, including the degree of diversification in household portfolios. For all countries studied, the volatility of household net worth is lower than the volatility of their holdings of market-sensitive assets, in part because they also hold deposits and other assets whose principal values do not fluctuate (Table 3.1). In addition, the volatility in household holdings of market-sensitive assets stems from several factors, including the price volatility of the underlying financial and nonfinancial assets (e.g., equities and real estate, respectively), changes in the relative shares of these holdings in the overall household asset portfolio, and the degree of diversification offered by the range of assets held.[3]

Those countries and households with asset portfolios containing a wider range of assets (e.g., the United States) appear to experience larger diversification gains than countries and households with more concentrated holdings

Table. 3.1. Household Balance Sheet Volatility Measures[1]

(In percent)

	Net Worth/ Disposable Income	Market-Sensitive Assets/ Disposable Income[2]	
		Without real estate	Including real estate
1980–2003			
United States	10.6	46.4	26.0
United Kingdom	14.7	34.5	18.8
France	10.3	39.2	12.2
Japan	14.1	22.1	21.6
1998–2003			
United States	7.0	20.5	10.0
United Kingdom	5.1	29.1	7.5
Netherlands[3]	6.2	30.0	7.5
France	3.8	21.6	10.4
Germany[3]	1.5	7.0	2.5
Japan	2.5	18.3	7.1

Sources: National statistical accounts; and IMF staff estimates.
[1]Each measure is calculated as a ratio to disposable income. Volatilities of the ratios are calculated as standard deviation divided by the mean for the period.
[2]Household net worth consists of market-sensitive and nonmarket-sensitive assets. Market-sensitive assets consist of equity, bonds, mutual funds, and real estate; and nonmarket-sensitive assets consist mainly of deposits. For the United States, equity data include both direct and indirect holdings by households.
[3]For Germany, annual data are only available after 1991. For the Netherlands, annual data are only available after 1998.

(e.g., Japan). Real estate is an asset that appears sufficiently uncorrelated with equities and other financial assets in most countries in the short and medium term.[4] Consequently, adding real estate assets to holdings of market-sensitive financial assets would generally lower the volatility of total household portfolios as well as overall household net worth (compare columns 2 and 3 in Table 3.1). Compared with U.S. households' relatively large holdings of financial and nonfinancial market-sensitive assets, Japanese households have relatively concentrated holdings of real estate. However, Japanese households' large holdings of deposits have helped dampen the volatility of their net worth.

---

[3]For example, during 1998–2003, French household net worth was considerably more volatile than German household net worth because of relatively more volatile French equity and real estate prices, and relatively larger changes in the share of market-sensitive financial assets held by French, compared with German, households during that period.

[4]Some cross-country academic studies indicate that there is little short-term correlation (i.e., over a year, or even a few years) between real estate price changes and stock market returns (see Quan and Titman, 1998).

Financial Holdings

A global trend in household financial holdings over the last two decades has been the declining share of bank deposits, money market funds, and savings accounts (Figure 3.2). While it may have started at a later stage in continental European countries, such as France and Germany, the trend toward lower levels of bank deposits has been fairly pronounced there too.[5] In part, this trend may have been influenced by equity market developments during the 1990s, as the long-term trend away from bank deposits and savings accounts slowed with the equity market declines of 2000–02. Japan stands in sharp contrast to this trend, as Japanese households have not materially diversified away from bank deposits and savings accounts. The share of deposits among Japanese household total assets has been generally stable since the 1960s, and grew during the 1990s as real estate and equity prices fell.

The growth of market-sensitive holdings in the United States and Europe has favored equities over bonds.[6] This is especially the case for direct holdings of financial assets, whereas holdings of market-sensitive assets through collective investment vehicles appear more balanced between fixed-income and equity securities. In the United Kingdom, France, and, to a lesser extent, elsewhere in Europe, privatization of state-owned companies in the 1980s and 1990s contributed to the increase in direct equity holdings, as did the development of employee profit-sharing and share-ownership schemes.

There is substantial variation among countries in the distribution of household financial holdings. In Japan, the share of financial assets (20 to 30 percent of total assets) is approximately uniform across all income and age groups (Figure 3.3). In the United States, the ratio of financial assets to total assets has been between 30 and 50 percent. However, compared with Japan, the concentration and composition of net worth among U.S. households is much more skewed—the wealthiest 20 percent represent 68 percent of U.S. household net worth (with the top 1 percent holding one-third of household assets) (Figure 3.4). In the United States, the middle three income quintiles represent 29 percent of household net worth, compared with their counterparts in Japan, who represent as much as 53 percent of Japanese household net worth. Meanwhile, in the Netherlands, the share of net worth reported for the middle-income groups expanded from 44 to 58 percent between 1995 and 2004 (Figure 3.5).[7] The distribution of net worth, wealth, and financial assets is an important consideration for potential household vulnerabilities.

Housing Markets

The home is generally the largest asset in household portfolios. In most countries, nonfinancial assets (primarily housing) account for between 40 and 60 percent of total assets, with the highest proportionate shares in Germany and the United Kingdom. In Germany, low mortgage rates and varying levels of state subsidies, particularly after unification in 1990, provided strong incentives to invest in housing. In the United Kingdom, deregulation of mortgages and official incentives for tenants to buy public housing in the

---

[5]Bank deposits represented close to 60 percent of German household financial assets until the beginning of the 1980s. The deposit share moved below 48 percent at the beginning of the 1990s, and has stabilized around 33 percent since 1999. In France, savings accounts and bank deposits in 2003 represented about 30 percent of household financial assets, down from about 60 percent in the early 1980s.

[6]Nonlisted equities represent a large proportion of total equity holdings in some countries. Nonlisted equities are estimated to represent about 50 percent of all equity holdings in the United States, and more than 66 percent in France (estimates based on flow of funds and national accounts data). Many of these assets represent small businesses owned by households.

[7]However, the share of the third income quintile in total liabilities also increased to 20–25 percent in 1998–2004, and from 10–15 percent in 1993–1997. See De Nederlandsche Bank (2004).

1980s encouraged broader home ownership and, together with the more recent rise in house prices, contributed to housing's larger share of total assets. The lowest share for housing among the countries studied is reported in the United States; however, a much higher share is reported for households in the middle- and lower-income quintiles (see Figure 3.4).

Housing wealth has risen much faster than income in some countries, contributing significantly to net worth growth. House price rises have been particularly sharp in the Netherlands, the United Kingdom (at least until recently), and in parts of the United States, raising concerns about excessive valuations (Figure 3.6). In the Netherlands, house price growth averaged more than 8 percent between 1995 and 2002, second only to Ireland among OECD countries.

By contrast, housing wealth has been falling since the early 1990s in Japan, and growing by an average of 1.6 percent in Germany since 1998, although in both cases housing's share of total wealth remains high. In Germany, a more sluggish economy and a reduction in housing tax subsidies contributed to the weaker housing market. In Japan, despite price falls, the large down payment needed to buy a house leads to an older first-time buyer than in other countries, and may contribute to the relatively high share of deposits in Japan.

Increased housing wealth has been accompanied by greater mortgage debt in the Netherlands, the United Kingdom, and the United States. In all these countries, the relatively flexible mortgage markets, as well as low interest rates and the rise in house prices, have contributed to increases in mortgage debt that have outpaced gains in disposable income in recent years. In the Netherlands, where mortgage debt reached about 200 percent of disposable income, full mortgage interest deductibility may have encouraged households to utilize interest-only mortgages, which account for over 40 percent of total mortgage debt in 2004.

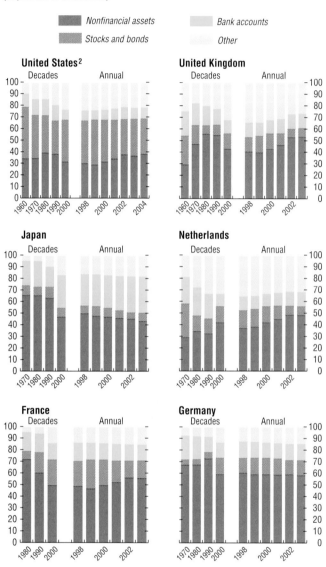

Figure 3.2. Household Sector: Total Asset Composition¹
(In percent of total assets)

Sources: U.S. Board of Governors of the Federal Reserve System; Bank of England, U.K. Office of National Statistics, National Institute of Economic and Social Research; Bank of Japan, Economic and Social Research Institute; De Nederlandsche Bank; Banque de France, INSEE; Bundesbank; and IMF staff estimates.
¹Total assets are the sum of financial assets and nonfinancial assets. Nonfinancial assets consist of mainly real estate. Other assets consist of mainly insurance and pension fund reserves.
²Data for 2004 are only available through the third quarter.

Figure 3.3. Japan: Total Asset Composition by Household Groups
(In percent)

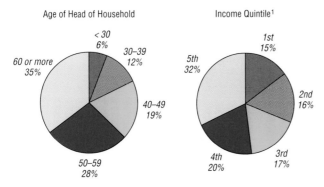

Source: Ministry of Internal Affairs and Communications, Statistics Bureau.
[1]The mean value of pre-tax income in 1999 was $27,886 for the first quintile group; $42,172 for the second; $56,262 for the third; $75,342 for the fourth; and $121,331 for the fifth.

The higher level of debt increases households' exposure to house price moves (and other asset or income changes), particularly households in their 30s or 40s who may have recently incurred high debt levels to purchase a home. In the Netherlands, more than half of homeowners aged 25–34 have a loan-to-value (LTV) ratio of above 100 percent. In the United Kingdom, the predominantly floating-rate mortgage market may make households more exposed, especially as many borrowers appear to overly focus on current debt-service costs when determining the size of their mortgage. Moreover, first-time purchasers may be more exposed to poor or even sluggish housing markets, as they may have stretched financially to buy a house in an environment of rapidly rising real estate values.

Housing has been increasingly viewed as an attractive investment, including for retirement, but such an approach includes certain risks. As previously discussed, housing provides a diversification benefit to many middle- and upper-income households, compared with a portfolio of purely financial market assets, and the risk of nominal price falls has historically been relatively limited compared with other assets. In addition, unlike many other household assets, the home also represents an important currently consumable asset, as a place to live. Nevertheless, households may be exposed in many countries to the risk of significant underperformance in the medium (or longer) term if current prices turn out to be unsustainably high.[8]

The ability to rely on housing as a source of savings or investment depends on the liquidity of the housing and mortgage markets. The flexibility of the fixed-rate, prepayable mortgage market in the United States may increase the liquidity of housing savings and invest-

---

[8]Housing risk and price movements may occur on a more global level than generally assumed. The September 2004 *World Economic Outlook* found that house price movements were highly synchronized across industrial countries, partly reflecting global interest rate movements.

ment. Meanwhile, in other countries, low liquidity in the housing market (e.g., Japan) or high transaction costs and lower flexibility in the mortgage market (e.g., France and Germany) restrict the diversification role housing may play in household savings (Table 3.2).

Pensions and Insurance

This section does not attempt to evaluate different pension systems, but analyzes their implications and the impact of ongoing reforms on the composition of financial risks transferred to the household sector. The various pension systems and reform programs reflect evolving national preferences with regard to broad economic and social challenges. In particular, while the move from defined benefit to defined contribution pension plans tends to substitute market and longevity risks for credit risk of the plan sponsor (as well as the risk of job loss or change of job), it also has an impact on other, increasingly important, features of pension plans, such as their portability. As noted, the consequences of demographic and fiscal pressures have to be dealt with under any system, though in different ways. Furthermore, a move from defined benefit to defined contribution plans may contribute to the consolidation of public and corporate finances, and to the development of local capital markets, as observed in several emerging market countries.

The degree of market risk transfer from the pension system to households varies across countries. In some countries, state pensions (Pillar I) remain a major source of retirement income for households in all income groups, and generally act to reduce the exposure of households to market volatility. This is particularly the case in many continental European countries (e.g., France, Germany, and Italy), as well as in Japan. In these countries, there has been less need for households to build up financial assets devoted to retirement during

Figure 3.4. United States: Total Asset Composition by Household Groups
(In percent)

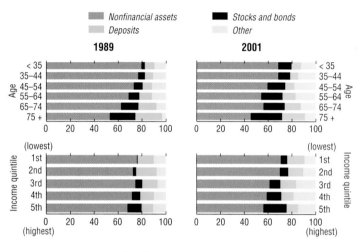

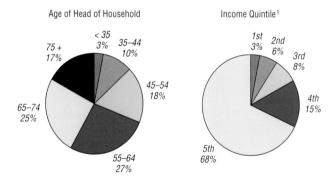

Source: Board of Governors of the Federal Reserve System.
[1]The mean value of pre-tax income in 2001 was $10,000 for the first quintile group; $24,100 for the second; $40,300 for the third; $65,200 for the fourth; and $200,350 for the fifth.

Figure 3.5. Netherlands: Distribution of Net Worth by Income Quintiles[1]

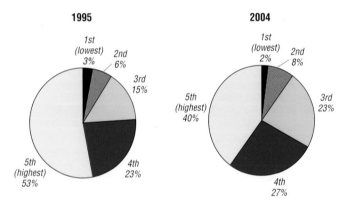

1995

1st (lowest) 3%

2nd 6%

3rd 15%

5th (highest) 53%

4th 23%

2004

1st (lowest) 2%

2nd 8%

3rd 23%

5th (highest) 40%

4th 27%

Source: De Netherlandsche Bank, *Quarterly Bulletin*, September 2004.
[1]The mean value of the 2003 net household income in euros is 6,450 for the first quintile group (lowest); 15,800 for the second; 22,300 for the third; 30,500 for the fourth; and above 35,100 for the fifth (highest).

their working lives, or to draw down savings in retirement.[9] However, such a need may grow with proposed and likely reforms of Pillar I programs in many of these countries. In some cases, such as Sweden, state pension reforms are not only designed to reduce benefit levels over time but also introduce some degree of risk sharing between the state and households by linking a portion of benefits to the performance of notional self-managed investment portfolios.[10] The Swedish reform may serve as an interesting example for countries with historically strong public sector programs or countries looking to share more risks among the public and private sectors.

In some countries, notably the United Kingdom and the United States, the composition of risks borne by households is changing as a result of the move to defined contribution schemes. In the United Kingdom, for example, active membership of open defined benefit schemes is estimated to have fallen by 60 percent since 1995, and only 15 percent of new private sector employees are members of salary-related schemes. A move to more defined contribution–based systems may address broader economic and social challenges, and this may be necessary and appro-

[9]Recently retired households are frequently described in continental European countries as the "golden generation," since they benefited from high incomes, rising asset markets, and generous pension and social benefits during their working lives. As a consequence, many of these households were not required to save for retirement, and accumulated savings frequently contributed to intergenerational transfers.

[10]An interesting feature of the new Swedish pension system is the notional defined contribution plans, under which each participant's contribution (16 percent of earnings) and future pension benefits are notionally invested, with a guaranteed rate of return equal to the national per capita real wage growth (i.e., effectively indexing benefits). A second feature of the new regime is the creation of individual defined contribution accounts, in which participants are required to pay 2.5 percent of earnings. Individuals are responsible for deciding how to invest these contributions in a menu of mutual funds. The amounts invested in these accounts represented about 12 percent of the assets of domestic mutual funds in 2004.

priate. By the same token, a shift to defined contribution schemes also exposes households more directly to market and longevity risks. The increase in exposure to longevity risk is more noticeable in countries such as the United States where most self-managed plans do not provide annuity or similar payout features.

In the Netherlands, defined benefit plans continue to cover approximately 90 percent of employees and households are therefore less exposed to market volatility. However, the Dutch pension industry is also transferring a greater amount of financial risk to Dutch households, including inflation risk, as a result of recent and ongoing reforms in the indexation of pension benefits.[11]

In some countries, a growing share of insurance products provide unit-linked investments. These products now account for as much as 40 percent of life insurance reserves in the United Kingdom, and 30 percent in the Netherlands. In other countries, however, unit-linked products still represent a small proportion of insurance holdings, and may have declined in France and Germany, as households have shifted back to guaranteed and capital protection products in recent years.

Future Costs and Obligations

Households will face additional and new risks more directly as a result of planned or anticipated reductions in public and private benefits. For example, U.K. households can be expected to provide a much larger share of pension income from their own savings than in the past.[12] In various continental European

---

[11]National accounts may mislead in this area, because the market movements in pension (and insurance) reserves do not affect households (positively or negatively) to a proportionate degree.

[12]According to the U.K. Pensions Commission (2004), to maintain existing replacement rates (and assuming no rise in the average retirement age), the share of pension income provided by funded occupational and personal pensions and other sources may need to increase from 2.2 percent of GDP to 8.4 percent (i.e., from £23 billion to £88 billion, measured at constant 2002 GDP levels).

Figure 3.6. Household Sector: Real Estate Values and Mortgage Debt

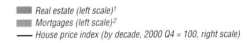

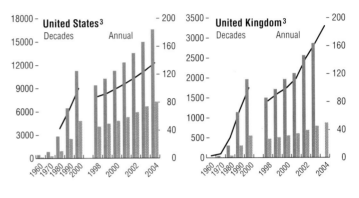

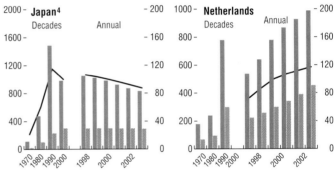

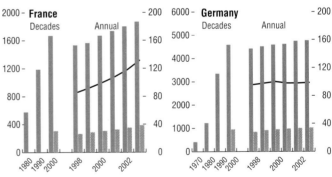

Sources: U.S. Board of Governors of the Federal Reserve, Office of Federal Housing Oversight; Bank of England, U.K. Office of the National Statistics, Nationwide Building Society; Bank of Japan, Economic and Social Research Institute, Japan Real Estate Institute; De Nederlandsche Bank; Banque de France, INSEE; Bundesbank; European Mortgage Federation; and IMF staff estimates.
[1]Real estate for United States, in billions of U.S. dollars; for United Kingdom, in billions of pounds sterling; for Japan, in trillions of yen; for Netherlands, France, and Germany, in billions of euros.
[2]Mortgages for United States, in billions of U.S. dollars; for United Kingdom, in billions of pounds sterling; for Japan, in trillions of yen; for Netherlands, France, and Germany, in billions of euros.
[3]Data for 2004 are only available through the third quarter.
[4]Residential land price index is used for house price index (based on the year-end value in each fiscal year).

countries, delaying of the legal retirement age and increases in the required years of pension contribution also change household benefits.

Looking forward, current measures of household wealth may prove inadequate and new approaches to measure household vulnerabilities, such as a "financial margin" analysis, may be increasingly useful to policymakers. As households take on more obligations and enjoy longer lives, they will need to accumulate more private savings, and develop a reasonable "financial cushion." Greater consideration of likely new household obligations may lead policymakers to question the adequacy of current savings and national account measures of wealth, particularly for middle-income and middle-aged populations. In some countries, authorities are developing additional measures, such as financial margins, which essentially provide a projected cash flow or income analysis, and may better reflect how vulnerable certain income and age groups are to proposed benefit adjustments.[13] In any case, it seems reasonable to assume that currently reported household net worth figures may be subject to greater challenges going forward.

Health care costs, which have risen well in excess of general inflation rates, may prove a significant concern for households.[14] With budgetary pressures in many industrial countries, public sector subsidies for health care and long-term care may also decline in the future. Moreover, health care costs have already become a growing share of household expenditure. For example, in France, where health care is largely provided by the government, rising health care costs have frequently led to reforms designed to rein in social security spending, and the share of health care

costs to be paid directly by French households (11 percent in 2003) is expected to increase. Over and above general increases in health care costs, the particular basket of health care goods and services consumed by the retired and elderly tend to cost much more than similar expenditures by middle-aged and younger households.

Household Investment and Risk Management Behavior

This section will discuss household balance sheet management, and related saving and investment behavior. It will focus on how saving and wealth management may be affected by changes to household risk profile (e.g., possible future reductions in social benefits and increased exposure to market risks) and review the range of new financial instruments and services being offered by financial institutions to improve household financial and risk management capabilities.

Household Behavior

While assessments of household savings adequacy need to reflect future assets and obligations described above, most available empirical studies have not taken into account the likely changes in public and private benefits. Economists have addressed the adequacy of household saving and investment using a number of different analytical frameworks, which have led to a wide range of conclusions. In the United States, several studies conclude that, on average, U.S. households appear to be accumulating sufficient wealth and/or have access to adequate pension income to avoid a significant decline in living standards

---

[13]The Sveriges Riksbank recently assessed the financial margin (i.e., post-tax income, after interest expenditure and regular living costs) of Swedish households for the years 2000 to 2002, and their ability to service their obligations when faced with unexpected shocks (e.g., a rise in interest costs and/or a decline in income; see Sveriges Riksbank, 2004).

[14]In the United States, the effects of rising health care costs on Medicare are considered by many to be a greater fiscal challenge than Social Security (see Walker, 2005).

Table 3.2. Mortgage Markets in Selected Industrialized Countries: General Characteristics

	Typical Rate Structure	Recent/Peak LTV ratios (In percent)[1]	Typical Term (Years)	Prepayment Fees	Equity Release Products	Tax Regime[2]
Denmark	Fixed	80	30	Administration fee only	Used	Partial Ded; WT; IT
France	Fixed	70/100	15	Limited to 3% of repaid principal[3]	Not used	WT; IT
Germany	Fixed	70/80	25	Lender entitled to compensation for lost income[4]	Not used	IT
Japan	Fixed	85/100	25	Lender entitled to compensation for lost income	Limited use	Limited term Ded; WT; IT
Netherlands	Fixed	100/115	10	No fees up to 10% of capital prepaid each year	Used	Ded; IT
United Kingdom	Floating	70/110	25	Usually no fees	Used	IT
United States	Fixed	80/100	30	Usually no fees	Used	Ded; IT

Sources: European Central Bank; Mercer Oliver Wyman; European Mortgage Federation; Japan, Government Housing Loan Corporation; and IMF staff estimates.

[1]Maximum loan-to-value (LTV) for eligibility to Realkreditobligationer in Denmark. Obligations Foncieres in France and Pfandbriefe in Germany are 80 percent, 60 percent, and 60 percent, respectively.

[2]Interest deductibility (Ded); Wealth tax on housing (WT); Inheritance tax on housing (IT). In most countries, capital gains are taxable. However, owner-occupiers also benefit from various degrees of tax exemptions after a number of years of occupation.

[3]Three percent of prepaid capital maximum.

[4]In the first 10 years of the loan.

upon retirement.[15] However, in most of these studies, households are assumed to benefit from existing social security, pension, and other benefits. Although social security replacement rates are expected to be reduced, few studies to date have attempted to evaluate whether households are adjusting their savings or investment patterns to meet these challenges. (See CBO, 1993, 2003; Moore and Mitchell, 1997; and Munnell, 2003).

There remains concern in some countries that households may not be adjusting their savings rates to achieve past or necessary replacement rates. Expected replacement rates from individual retirement plans may

vary greatly because of a number of factors: (1) increased job mobility may cause some workers to lose continuous access to a pension plan; (2) low participation rates in available defined contribution plans;[16] and (3) market fluctuations. For those who do participate, we should not underestimate the potential impact of down markets, particularly on individuals close to retirement age.[17] With increased exposure to market-sensitive assets, diversification and periodic portfolio review and adjustment may be more important.[18]

In the United Kingdom, the Pensions Commission Report (2004) warned that many households are significantly undersaving. The

[15]Scholz, Seshadri, and Khitatrakun (2004); and Engen, Gale, and Uccello (1999).

[16]Data from large U.S. defined contribution plan administrators show that in 2003, one-third of eligible employees did not participate in their employer's voluntary savings plan, and of those that had an employer-matching feature, 26 percent did not participate (see Ameriks, Nestor, and Utkus, 2004; and Vanguard Group, 2004).

[17]A simulation of U.S. 401k asset portfolios with, on average, a 60/40 mix of equities and bonds, indicated that a three-year bear market that reduces equity values by 25 percent would reduce replacement rates by 13.4 to 17.7 percentage points (depending on income quartile) if the decline occurred immediately before retirement, and by 2.9 to 3.7 percentage points if it occurred at the start of a worker's career. See VanDerhei and Copeland (2003).

[18]Defined contribution plan administrators report that on average the asset allocation has been reasonably balanced between equities and bonds. However, there remained significant numbers of participants with unbalanced portfolios (e.g., only fixed income or only equities, or highly concentrated positions in sponsor company stock).

Report warns that, despite high current levels of net worth, existing trends would create a severe problem of pension adequacy within 25 years. It also warns that at least 75 percent of all defined contribution plan members have contribution rates below the level likely required to provide adequate pensions. In addition, the Report indicates that nonpension financial wealth for the great majority of U.K. individuals currently may provide only a modest contribution to total retirement income. For example, the Report estimates that median nonpension financial wealth for nonretired persons 55–59 years of age would provide income equal to only 12 percent of an "adequate" replacement rate for this middle-income group (U.K. Pensions Commission Report, 2004).

In countries where public programs (e.g., health care and education) are more extensive, household saving adequacy has not been a major source of concern to date. In continental Europe and Japan, for example, retirement income has been deemed secure, with continued relatively high replacement rates offered by public (and private) pensions, and the vast majority of future expenses (e.g., medical, long-term health care, and education) are expected to be partly or fully covered by the public sector.[19] These systems do not place the onus of ensuring retirement benefits on the individual's saving and investment behavior. However, as noted previously, even in these countries, there has been increased focus on the need to encourage private savings, given budgetary pressures related to aging.

Influences on Household Decisions

Given the long-term nature of these savings and investment needs, inertia may have a large impact on household plans. This is particularly important as we move to self-directed plans. Given that the decision to enroll in a defined contribution plan is often voluntary, or less automatic than previous enrollment in a defined benefit plan, many workers do not participate in such plans. Research has also shown that "opt-out" choices for enrollment in pension plans (i.e., enrolling employees unless they actively opt out) lead to much higher participation rates than "opt-in" choices (Thaler and Benartzi, 2001). Practitioners also agree that default options are an important influence on household investment and asset allocation decisions. It is often noted by asset managers, financial advisers, and pension plan administrators that the vast majority of households exhibit extreme inertia in adjusting asset allocations as their circumstances change. In recent years, the trend toward "life-cycle" funds as the default option for many self-directed plans has accelerated, compared with previous default options such as money market funds.[20]

Some countries use tax incentives to encourage and channel savings. Tax incentives may help to overcome households' general inertia or risk aversion. A number of initiatives have been taken by governments in this area, such as IRAs and 401(k) plans for pension savings, and 529 plans for college savings in the United States. Outside of the United States, preferential tax treatment also exists for certain accounts and life insurance products (e.g., in France and Germany).[21] However, empirical evidence has been mixed on whether tax incentives help raise overall savings or merely shift existing savings. Nevertheless, even if incentives do not raise overall savings, there are likely benefits from promoting more stable and long-term savings through such vehicles (see the September 2004 GFSR).

---

[19]Börsch-Supan and Lusardi (2003). Average public sector replacement rates range from 85 percent in Germany to a relative low of 50 percent in the Netherlands. See IMF (2004b).

[20]See below for a description of life-cycle funds.

[21]For example, in France and Germany the tax benefits associated with life insurance have historically been a reason for their popularity as savings vehicles, often as conservative money market or savings accounts.

Market participants often consider tax systems to be too complicated, subject to frequent change, and thus inconsistent with efforts to develop long-term saving strategies. For example, the series of U.K. initiatives to create tax-advantaged savings products in recent years (PEPs, TESSAs, and ISAs) was noted for its detailed rules, multiple objectives, and restrictive and widely changing terms, and only modestly improved savings in the United Kingdom. A simple and stable tax environment may help long-term savings growth and encourage more advanced planning by individuals and their advisers.

In some countries, compulsory contributions to pension plans have been used as a means to build long-term savings, albeit at the cost of personal choice. In addition to Singapore's CPF, Australia has had a compulsory savings scheme since 1986.[22] In these countries, compulsory savings programs have resulted in relatively large household long-term savings; however, this may be viewed by other national authorities as representing potentially too much government involvement. Regulations may also mandate or structure asset allocations (e.g., the purchase of annuities at or after retirement or by a certain age). However, authorities need to carefully consider the balance between restricting choice and the risk that inappropriate saving or investment decisions by large numbers of households may ultimately require governments to act to meet household shortfalls.

Financial Products

As household risk profiles change, and investment and risk management challenges increase, it is important that households have access to financial tools and products to meet their investment needs. In this section, we will review a variety of products, ranging from investment and payout strategies to liability management products.

Saving and Investment Products

In recent years, the variety of saving and investment products and services available to households has improved. Financial institutions are recognizing the increasing demand from households for better risk management tools. Innovations in wholesale financial markets, including the use of derivatives, have expanded the range and delivery of financial products available to households for their long-term savings and investment needs. At the same time, asset managers, securities firms, and banks are offering more sophisticated analytical tools to retail customers, which enable them to assess their overall financial position and potential retirement needs.[23]

Governments may help to expand household investment and risk management products. Long-term and index-linked bonds may help households manage long-term savings during their working lives, and may provide a stable income in retirement, either directly or indirectly through collective investment schemes or through other products such as annuities (e.g., allowing annuity providers to better manage duration and longevity risks, as discussed in the September 2004 GFSR). Although the issuance of long-term instruments (over 20-year maturity) is limited in all mature markets relative to the size of pension fund or insurance company portfolios, there are signs that numerous governments may be considering increased long-term bond

[22]See a summary description of the CPF at http://www.cpf.gov.sg/cpf_info/goto.asp?page=overviewb.asp. Research by Australian authorities estimated that 62 percent of compulsory savings represent incremental extra savings. See Connolly and Kohler (2004).

[23]Financial institutions often segment their clients into wealth or income groups, and have generally provided individualized advice and services only to higher net worth customers, with more generic analysis provided to middle-market customers, often through online services.

issuance (including index-linked products) to meet the increasingly apparent demand.[24]

Investment Products

Mutual funds and index products are now more widely used by households. Mutual funds may be used for short-term purposes (e.g., in continental Europe, where they are frequently money market funds) or for longer-term investments (e.g., the preponderance of equity and bond funds in the United States). Innovations in the mutual fund industry have led to lower cost and more liquid investment alternatives. The growth of Exchange Traded Funds (ETFs), in particular, has been rapid in recent years. Such new products allow investors to deploy their savings to a wider range of investments, with greater diversification, liquidity, and lower fees than traditional mutual funds.

"Life-cycle" products have developed to address changing risk profiles as we age or approach targeted expenditures (e.g., education). However, such products represent a relatively small portion of the overall market for retirement savings. Life-cycle mutual funds gradually and automatically adjust asset allocations to a more conservative profile (e.g., increasing fixed-income investments) as an individual approaches retirement (or other target dates, such as college education), thereby reflecting an individual's assumed evolving risk tolerance. While the use of life-cycle products has expanded in the United States, Japan, and Europe in recent years, there may be increased scope for the inclusion of such funds among the investment (or even default) options for self-directed pension plans, and the development of a wider range of products (e.g., pace of adjust-

ment).[25] In particular, life-cycle investment schemes (including equity holdings) may have application beyond retirement dates, as individuals are expected to live longer. Indeed, as with annuitization, the full conversion of savings and investment to a fixed-income stream at the time of retirement may not be appropriate.

In some markets, there has been significant growth of structured products.[26] These products have become increasingly popular in Asia and continental Europe since the equity market downturn in 2000–02, and in response to the prolonged low interest rate environment. They offer a variety of risk/return profiles, including capital or performance guarantees, while also participating in market upswings, such as "click-funds" in the Benelux countries. However, the use of complex hybrid products, such as equity-linked and structured credit notes, may raise consumer protection issues, where households may not fully understand all the underlying risks and costs of these products.

Looking ahead, retail investment products that provide access to diversified or less correlated asset classes (e.g., hedge funds) may also grow. As noted, portfolio diversification is likely to be an important focus of household balance sheet management. Therefore, like other investors, households may increasingly seek to invest in asset classes that provide diversification benefits and uncorrelated returns. Some of these asset classes, such as hedge funds (as well as private equity or commodity funds), are generally unavailable to households today. A significantly greater household exposure to hedge funds, for example, may give renewed impetus to the debate about the regulatory framework for

---

[24]The French Trésor introduced in February 2005 a new 50-year euro-denominated bond. In the United Kingdom, the Debt Management Office announced in March 2005 that, from May 2005, it would issue 50-year conventional gilts, and that later in the year, it may also issue 50-year index-linked gilts.

[25]The U.K. authorities have required that all providers of a new government-sponsored savings product (the Child Trust Fund) offer a life-cycle approach as one of the options, to mature at age 18 of the child.

[26]These instruments typically offer guarantees of capital protection and a particular return profile, and include significant optionality.

such investment vehicles, and a stronger regulatory approach would seem appropriate for retail distribution (as opposed to institutional investor involvement).[27]

Residential real estate products are also being considered in several countries, but are still at a developmental stage. In most cases, the idea is to develop a method that allows existing homeowners (and institutions) and prospective purchasers (saving to buy) to hedge price movements. A major challenge is to develop products that would allow investors to hedge price risk as specifically as possible, based on regional or more local market indices. One interesting approach is being developed in the United States by a team of academics through a government-sponsored project to provide house price insurance in very localized areas (i.e., based on zip codes).[28] Housing-indexed products may be very useful for potential homebuyers (particularly first-time buyers), increasing their ability to save for a particular property or to invest less than the savings needed to purchase a home as they continue to save for a house. We are aware of several jurisdictions looking to possibly develop housing indices or futures, as well as more conventional Real Estate Investment Trusts (REITs) for residential property.

Payout Products

Saving and investment plans need to reflect uncertain life expectancy (i.e., longevity risk), and flexibility is needed in the conversion of savings into an annuity or other income stream. Saving and investment strategies need to consider longevity risk, either through longevity insurance provided by annuity products, or through building a greater financial margin and total savings. The shift to annuitization may need to be gradual (as with life-cycle funds), even after retirement, especially given increased life expectancy.[29] In this respect, requirements of full annuitization at retirement for defined contribution pensions, such as those in the Netherlands and (for new compulsory individual accounts) in Sweden, may be too restrictive.[30] Italy requires 50 percent annuitization at retirement, while the United Kingdom requires that at least 75 percent of pension savings be annuitized by the later age of 75 years.

The further development of annuity products depends significantly on the ability of annuity providers to hedge longevity risk. Annuity providers need to be able to manage, hedge, or insure against longevity risk, based on instruments available in the capital markets or through reinsurers (but this then becomes a circular issue, as reinsurers look to hedge these risks). Efforts are under way in the public and private sectors to increase the supply of such instruments, including the issuance of more long-term government bonds.

A potentially promising instrument is a "longevity bond," such as that developed by the European Investment Bank (see Box 3.1). The bond is intended to provide an approximate hedge to U.K. pension fund liabilities. However, the bond has a final maturity of 25 years (reflecting 90 years of age for the indexed population), demonstrating again that insurers and reinsurers remain reluctant to hedge extreme old age or this tail risk. Another, at present theoretical, alternative

---

[27]In the European Union, Hong Kong SAR, and Singapore, the marketing of hedge funds to the retail sector has raised investor protection concerns, and regulations (such as threshold limits for retail participation) have been established in a number of jurisdictions. See also the September 2004 GFSR.

[28]Case and Shiller (2003). Information on the pilot project is available via the Internet at *http://www. realliquidity.com.*

[29]See September 2004 GFSR for estimates of projected changes in life expectancy, both from time of birth and for those persons that reach 65 years of age.

[30]See Davis (2003); and Mackenzie and Schrager (2004).

Box 3.1. Longevity Bonds

The European Investment Bank (EIB), working with others and at the suggestion of the European Parliament, sought to create a capital markets instrument to help pension funds address the challenges of aging populations. The bond provides a long-term, tradable instrument that hedges longevity risk by scaling payouts according to future longevity. The United Kingdom is a logical market in which to initiate this product, since the U.K. authorities require that at least 75 percent of defined contribution or personal pensions be annuitized by age 75, and there are relatively few U.K. annuity providers.

Although the EIB is the issuer of the bond, the ultimate recipient of the longevity risk embedded in the bond is PartnerRe. The EIB will undertake a swap with BNP Paribas, with EIB receiving floating-rate sterling funding. In turn, BNP Paribas will reinsure the longevity risk with PartnerRe, leaving BNP Paribas with interest rate exposure, and PartnerRe insuring the longevity risk.

As currently structured and proposed, the bond will have a 25-year maturity, and will make annual payments related to an index, representing the number of men in England and Wales who were 65 years old at the time of the bond's issue, and who are living at each payment date. Payments on the bond will decline over its life depending on the longevity of the indexed pool (from about 9 percent to below 3 percent of the bond's initial market value, based on current actuarial estimates). There will be no separate interest or principal payments in addition to these indexed payments.

Such a bond may expand reinsurance capital available for annuity products. The risks involved in instruments based on wide population groups, such as that defined by the EIB bond, are easier for insurers to measure and manage than the risks related to specific populations of an individual pension fund or group of annuity beneficiaries that bilateral insurance deals typically involve. As such, insurers may be prepared to commit larger amounts of capital to the annuity and longevity markets.

The scope for further bond issues of this type remains uncertain at this stage, with the most significant constraints on future issuance likely to be the capacity of insurers and reinsurers to take on longevity risk, and investors' ability to price and willingness to purchase these securities.

may be the development of "macro-swaps" through which, for example, the pension fund and health care industries may swap their complementary exposures to longevity.

Some observers have noted that the only practical insurer or reinsurer of extreme old age risk may be governments. Some authorities have expressed a willingness to consider the issuance or support of longevity bonds. The Governor of the Bank of England urged the study of this possibility, given the limited availability of private longevity risk insurance in the United Kingdom, and suggested the government may have a role in sharing this risk across generations, including possibly through the issuance of longevity bonds (King, 2004). The U.K. Government said that,

while it did not envisage issuing longevity bonds in 2005–06, it may revisit the subject at a later stage, and has been seeking comment from the market (U.K. Debt Management Office, 2004). Meanwhile, the French social security refinancing agency, Caisse d'Amortissement de la Dette Sociale, has expressed possible interest in issuing a bond based on French longevity.

Liability Management Tools

Financial advisers have noted that many households appear to manage their liabilities better than their long-term savings or investment plans. The home mortgage is the largest liability for most households, and servicing it is often their largest regular expenditure.[31] Therefore, households appear to give greater consideration to liability management. In many markets, flexible refinancing practices and a fairly wide range of mortgage products have enhanced the ability of borrowers to manage their mortgage debt, adjust interest rate risk, and extract equity from home values.

Danish, U.S., and U.K. households have a significant degree of flexibility in managing their mortgage liabilities. The Danish and U.S. mortgage markets accommodate household demand for a fixed-rate, prepayable product through quite different institutional arrangements.[32] More importantly, both markets facilitate the issuance of mortgage-backed securities, allowing greater flexibility in funding and risk management, and thereby increase market capacity and product variety. The structure of the U.K. mortgage market shares many similarities with the U.S. market, and is also relatively flexible in accommodating different household preferences for repayment structures and the setting of interest rates.

Prepayment, Refinancing, and Equity Withdrawal

The commoditization of mortgage loans in Denmark provides a range of options for households to manage mortgage liabilities. For instance, Danish households have the possibility, aside from exercising their prepayment option, to buy mortgage bonds in the secondary market and to deliver them to the mortgage originator to net against their loan and reduce principal. Furthermore, the seller of a house can transfer the existing debt on the purchased property to the new owner.

In the United States, the ability of lenders and households to customize mortgage products also provides a wide range of options for managing liabilities. In addition, the deregulated market structure in the United States has led to the creation of a wide range of mortgage products with different risk characteristics, and the various stages of mortgage lending are unbundled and often conducted by different entities.

In the United Kingdom, the "Miles Review" recommended a variety of initiatives to improve the U.K. mortgage market, including the development of a longer-term fixed-rate market (Miles, 2004). The Review identified several barriers to broader and more efficient market activity, including (1) lack of access for existing customers to a lender's new mortgage products, and (2) lack of awareness of comparative information on alternative products and interest rate options. As a means to provide greater prepayment flexibility, the Review also encouraged the government to consider issuing options to provide lenders with a tool to hedge prepayments. In addition, the Review identified several obstacles to cost-effective funding of longer-term fixed-rate mortgages. These included the lack of covered bond legislation, possible higher regulatory capital weightings for fixed-rate than variable-rate mortgages, and legislative limits on the proportion of wholesale funding for building societies.

In some countries, home equity withdrawal has provided added flexibility for households. The U.S., Dutch, and U.K. markets have witnessed the development of home equity credit lines and reverse mortgages, offering households additional flexibility in converting part

[31]Other liabilities, including credit card debt, comprise a relatively small share of total household liabilities. However, increased flexibility in global credit markets has helped spur growth in these categories, especially in households in the lower-income groups.

[32]The Danish mortgage market has a relatively tight regulatory framework, intended to protect borrowers. Up to the 1990s, this had resulted in a very high level of standardization, but since then innovations in funding instruments have made available a wider range of loans to borrowers. By contrast, U.S. lenders accommodate a large variety of mortgage bond investors, while providing flexible products to borrowers. See Mercer Oliver Wyman (2003).

of their home equity into cash. Home equity lines of credit are a form of revolving credit in which the borrower's home serves as collateral. Reverse mortgages (or home equity conversion mortgages) target older homeowners and offer a variety of cash flow profiles. Payments to households are structured similar to an annuity, and require no repayment as long as the borrower uses the home as his or her principal residence. However, the use of reverse mortgages to date has been relatively limited, partly due to higher fee structures. For the lender, such products contain risks similar to an annuity, combined with risks related to preserving the value of the house and eventually selling the property (i.e., price movements and liquidity).

Broader Liability Management Tools

The prospect for new and larger household obligations resulting from reduced pension and other benefits may trigger the development of new markets. As noted, a key challenge for household financial management will be the ability to manage new and potentially significant obligations (e.g., health and long-term care, and pension-related risks) that were previously provided for by other sectors (e.g., the state or corporate plans). As these risks become better understood and their magnitude is better measured, households will likely seek new products and risk management tools to help them manage such exposures. Interestingly, it is the measurement, management, and monitoring of many of these risks that has increased the flow of risks to households and changed their risk profile. As such, if public and private sector efforts to help households manage these obligations more directly do not meet their needs, policymakers will continue to be confronted with these significant issues.

Need to Communicate, Educate, and Facilitate Advice

The long-term financial obligations and risks that households will need to manage are becoming larger and more complex. Developing and executing long-term saving and investment plans are skills that many individuals may find very difficult without expert advice and assistance. Saving for retirement is a long-term exercise for households, with a payoff that is apparent only much later, and therefore carries the risk that individuals may make significant and systematic errors over time. Furthermore, the experiences of previous generations may not provide a reliable guide, given changing benefit and pension structures, as well as available financial instruments.

There is a need for more communication by authorities of the challenges ahead, and for greater financial education for most individuals. As noted earlier, household financial behavior suggests that large numbers of individuals do not currently take a comprehensive approach to financial management, are often slow to act, and underestimate the level of savings required and the obligations and risks that they need to address in order to reach the living standards they currently expect at retirement. Surveys of households frequently show a substantial lack of knowledge about their own arrangements for retirement savings.[33] A recent study on financial literacy in France also indicated that a majority of households consider themselves ill-equipped to choose a particular investment strategy, and do not compare investment products offered by different institutions (although they do so for other financial products, such as loans), often depending on their principal banking relationship for advice (Autorité des Marchés Financiers, 2004).

---

[33]For example, 65 percent of Dutch households are unable to provide an estimate of their pension income upon retirement (De Nederlandsche Bank, 2004). In the United Kingdom, 44 percent of the population reported a basic knowledge of pensions in 2004, down from 53 percent in 2000 (U.K. Pensions Commission Report, 2004). In the United States, 47 percent of workers who have not saved at all still report themselves as confident that they will have enough money for retirement (Helman and Paladino, 2004).

Communication and education proposals require different strategies to reach different population groups and levels of sophistication. For instance, basic financial information may be provided in schools to children and young adults to create financial awareness from an early age. The need for long-term planning of retirement savings and related strategies may be particularly important for those at the beginning of their careers, and for persons approaching middle age. As individuals reach the latter half of their working lives, the focus may need to change, with a greater consideration of payout strategies (including health care and intergenerational issues).[34]

Communication

In many countries, authorities have made significant efforts to raise public awareness, but more is likely needed. Ongoing reforms to reduce the role of the state in providing pension and other benefits generally have been accompanied by actions aimed at informing households about the implications of such reforms (the same has been true, with varying degrees of success, of individual corporate pension reforms).[35] However, the public debate and awareness of these implications is often still nascent, pointing to the need for further initiatives.

Authorities in the United Kingdom have been particularly active in communicating to the public about these challenges. The U.K. Pensions Commission Report (2004) reviewed the adequacy of private pension saving and advice on policy changes, and warned that "pensioners will become poorer relative to the rest of society" unless taxes or social security contributions devoted to pensions rise, individuals save more, or employees accept longer working lives.[36] The Report has attracted wide publicity in the media, and has intensified the debate on retirement and pensions in the United Kingdom.

In continental Europe, reforms of public pension systems have typically been accompanied by government efforts to inform households about the impact of such reforms. In Sweden, a broad information campaign accompanied the introduction of the new public pension system, and subsequent surveys have shown that the share of participants who say they do not understand the system has fallen from about 30 percent in 1998 to 13 percent in 2003 (see Sundén, 2004). In France, the government will implement by 2006 a new strategy designed to make available general information on retirement savings (free publications, a "hotline," and a website), as well as more personalized information in the form of comprehensive simulations of future individual benefits.[37]

In the United States, the administration has recently begun discussions on its proposal to create personal retirement accounts, as part of a broader reform of the social security system.

[34]In the United States, for instance, 60 percent of workers aged 45–54, and 42 percent aged 55 or above, have given little or no thought to how to manage their money in retirement so as to not outlive their savings (i.e., longevity risk), and 76 percent of 45–54 year olds, and 61 percent of over–55-year-olds have given little or no thought to how to pay for long-term care or home health care costs. See Helman and Paladíno (2004).

[35]See IMF (2004a). When employees were asked what benefits they valued most, the vast majority of respondents expressed much more concern about health care and medical benefits (and a strong desire to retain such programs), relative to pension benefits.

[36]See U.K. Pensions Commission Report (2004). Two other prominent reports in the United Kingdom are the Sandler review of the U.K. market for medium- and long-term savings, and the Miles Report on the U.K. mortgage market. An overarching theme of these reports is a consideration of the appropriate structure and design of financial markets and products, in particular to provide individuals with the relevant information for them to take more control of, and responsibility for, their own financial affairs.

[37]See France, Ministère des Affaires Sociales (2003). Information on the provision of information to beneficiaries on their statutory pension rights across EU countries is available in the Report by the European Commission, Directorate-General for Employment and Social Affairs (2003).

This has already stimulated a broad debate about the balance between public and private funding of retirement savings, the distribution of the funding burden between generations, and the desirability of individuals having the option to invest and manage a portion of their social security account.

In Japan, the Central Council for Financial Services Information (CCFSI) is charged with communicating information about financial services, and coordinates its activities with the Bank of Japan (BOJ) and the Financial Services Agency (FSA). The CCFSI and BOJ also aim to communicate to the public the importance of topics such as deposit insurance and public pension reform. The CCFSI has used the BOJ's branch networks to conduct seminars on financial planning, the availability of new financial instruments, and risk management.

Education

Clearly, households remain responsible for their investment decisions. The main duty of the public sector, in turn, is to provide good regulation and supervision of the financial sector. In light of these two observations, financial education becomes all the more important to help the household sector to adequately manage their financial affairs. Governments should coordinate with the private sector in promoting such financial education.

Even though financial information may be plentiful and accessible, households often make limited use of such information. It is widely recognized by regulators, asset managers, and consumer groups that few retail investors make use of the detailed information that mutual fund sponsors are required to provide on the products they distribute.[38] In the United States, research shows that increased disclosure of financial information to consumers does not necessarily result in improved financial management in areas such as mortgages and investment—an issue increasingly explored within behavioral economics and finance (U.S. Board of Governors of the Federal Reserve System, 2002). This confirms that mere information, while important, cannot act as a substitute for greater household understanding and education.

While financial education shortcomings are not new, they become more important as households are expected to manage more directly their financial affairs. Surveys often indicate poor consumer familiarity with even basic financial issues, such as the calculation of simple interest returns.[39] Basic education in household finance and financial management historically has not been provided in schools and colleges in most countries. Moreover, in our increasingly busy lives, many adults lack the time or motivation to educate or update themselves on these issues. Alternatively, if households broadly appear unable to manage these new challenges, governments may come under growing public pressure to intervene in support of the household sector, for example, in the form of re-regulation of certain products or services, or in order to deal with waves of litigation.

Financial education seems particularly important with regard to the management of long-term savings (Häusler, 2005). Experts generally agree that the challenges for financial education (and households) are more daunting with respect to long-term savings and investment planning than with regard to debt management. The uncertainty over

---

[38]In our discussions with market practitioners, such behavior was frequently attributed to the complexity and length of this disclosure (i.e., disclosure, rather than transparency), which was attributed in part to the belief that, in some jurisdictions, such disclosure may be driven largely by legal considerations.

[39]In the United Kingdom, a survey found that only 30 percent of respondents could correctly calculate simple interest returns. See Institute of Financial Services (2004); and Financial Services Authority (2001).

returns (including the need to monitor, reevaluate, and possibly make adjustments to savings strategies), and the complexity and variety of products available are typically greater for savings and investment products than for debt products (e.g., mortgages). In addition, decisions about how much to save, investment and asset allocation strategies, and how to structure payouts during retirement are considered very difficult for most households. Accordingly, the purpose of financial education should not be to define a single approach to savings and investment (which may bring its own risks and moral hazards), but rather to equip individuals to ask informed questions and to understand the potential outcomes of their financial decisions.

There is evidence that financial education results in better financial decision-making practices, but challenges remain in identifying the most effective means to deliver educational services. In the United States, evidence has been found that financial education programs have a material impact on financial behavior (Helman and Paladíno, 2004; and Lusardi, 2004). However, there is a need to better define and coordinate strategies to strengthen financial education.[40] In particular, there may be different objectives and strategies with respect to (1) the focus of financial education programs (e.g., between topics, such as home ownership, savings accumulation, or debt reduction; and between target audiences), and (2) their delivery channels (e.g., between public and private providers, and between different media). There may also be a need to better coordinate efforts to strengthen financial education, and to evaluate the effectiveness of existing efforts. The OECD has established a Financial Education Project to develop an inventory of education programs and to report on the current state of financial literacy in member countries. The

report is expected to include a list of good practices for financial education programs (OECD, 2004).

In the United States, the Treasury in 2002 established an Office of Financial Education. This office works to coordinate the financial education efforts of other federal bodies, and more generally identifies and promotes access to financial education tools and effective education practices by a wide variety of institutions, including state, private sector, and nonprofit bodies. In France, a working group, involving representatives from the public and private sectors, was recently established by the government to (1) evaluate the financial literacy of households and existing financial education initiatives, and (2) design and implement a consistent action plan in this area. In Japan, the FSA has encouraged financial education in schools by helping to develop textbooks and other classroom materials. However, despite these efforts, the amount of public resources devoted to financial education remains quite limited (e.g., some practitioners noted that public and private spending in this area was very small relative to private sector financial advertising expenditure), and may be best leveraged through partnerships with the private sector.

The United Kingdom provides an example of coordinated initiatives to raise financial education standards in a variety of areas. In the United Kingdom, the FSA is expected to play a key coordinating role, and it has set up working groups, involving public and private sector participants, to develop proposals on improving financial capabilities across the full range of consumers' life stages and financial decisions: schools, young adults, the workplace, families, retirement, borrowing, and "generic" advice (i.e., advice that helps consumers consider how to plan finances, but does not recommend specific prod-

[40]See University of Pennsylvania (2004).

ucts).[41] The FSA also recently imposed standardized disclosure by mortgage providers of certain key facts and risks regarding mortgage borrowing, intended to complement those already required for savings products. In the United States, the Financial Literacy and Education Commission, composed of the heads of a number of federal bodies, has been established, and in August 2004 it requested public comment on the most important issues a national strategy should address, how existing resources might be employed, and how the issues may best be addressed (GPO, 2004).

The private sector, including employers, may have an important role to play within these coordinated efforts. Existing examples give an indication of the range of roles the private sector can play. In Japan, investor education is often done by banks, which take advantage of their strong relationship with depositors, and have used their branch offices to conduct seminars about new products. In the United States, many employers have supported seminars to help employees evaluate their financial needs and their investment options (and there is evidence that such seminars have a material impact on employee participation in 401(k) plans).[42]

Financial Advice

The finance industry and private sector firms are best placed to provide advice on saving and investment products and strategies. The provision of quality financial advice should progress with that of financial education. Once individuals are better equipped to ask informed questions and understand their needs, market forces may be expected to develop more financial management tools and products for households. A number of

financial institutions have already started to improve the way they operate in relation to households, realizing that it is also in their interest to help households better manage financial risks, and to provide sound advice on financial decisions and their implications.

However, there appears very little willingness on the part of households to pay for independent financial advice. To date, financial firms offering a choice between fee-based and commission-based advice have reported overwhelming consumer preference for the commission-based option. As such, financial advice (whether provided by financial intermediaries or independent advisers) is often commission or transaction based and, therefore, risks being focused on selling financial products, rather than advice. For example, we were frequently told by market participants that very often the best advice for a retail client is to reduce debt levels; however, they added, too often such advice is not given or strongly encouraged because "no one gets paid to tell a client to pay down debt."

There may be a need to strengthen the incentives for financial advisers to better support the needs of households. A relatively simple and stable tax and regulatory regime may encourage advisers to develop more tools and to provide long-term planning advice. Minimum educational standards for advisers themselves may need to be reviewed and strengthened. Several market participants spoke of practices where financial advisers have been historically paid by their employers to maximize the volume of sales, or how firms, when evaluating why customers have left their institution, frequently found client portfolios were full of "fashionable" investment products or (worse still) the "last five product launches" by the adviser's employer. Another improvement in this area may be to make commis-

---

[41]The FSA emphasizes that it sees itself as coordinating these exercises and setting standards for disclosure, rather than seeking to directly educate or, even more importantly, to advise households or individuals.

[42]See Kim, Kratzer, and Leech (2001); and Thaler and Benartzi (2001). In the United States, commercial banks also provide financial education (Consumer Bankers Association, 2004).

sions and fees more transparent. The U.K. FSA is doing this through new regulations (to be phased in by June 1, 2005), requiring advisers to provide a standardized "menu," including the costs of advice, whether provided by fees, commissions, or both.

Improving financial education is a process that will ultimately take decades to achieve, but public awareness can be increased now. All the public and private sector practitioners whom we met agreed that financial education should begin in school, and as such will filter through the population with time. But many of the current initiatives are aimed at raising broad public awareness of households' increasing need to take responsibility for their finances (e.g., U.K. Pensions Commission), and ensuring that information is provided to better enable households to understand and compare products. By raising communication and education standards in this way, a better educated consumer, capable of asking informed questions and making more informed choices, should emerge.

Concluding Observations

Households, as the shareholders of the financial system, have always been exposed to various financial and other risks. Therefore, while changes in risk management practices by institutions, often driven by regulatory and accounting standards, may not change the aggregate risk to which households are exposed in the long term, such changes frequently alter the flow of risks, and lead to changes in the risk profile of the household sector (including between different income and age groups). This final installment of our series on risk transfer has assessed the changing risk profile of the household sector, and discussed some of the associated new challenges for household investment and risk management.

Efforts to improve the collection, timeliness, and comparability of data for the household sector should be encouraged. Our review of

households has been based on available data at the aggregate and household levels. In a number of countries, it was difficult to obtain a consistent set of data for both financial and nonfinancial balance sheet items over an extended period of time. Even among countries with relatively better aggregate data, timely panel data covering households of different age and income groups is limited. As the responsibility to manage more financial risks is being shifted to households, it is increasingly important for policymakers to accurately gauge the impact of various reforms on the household sector.

As we analyzed household balance sheets for selected industrial countries, we observed various differences and trends in household exposure to market and other risks:

- *Net worth* has grown significantly relative to income in most industrialized countries during the last two or three decades, boosted in particular by capital gains on market-based assets from robust financial and real estate markets. However, planned reforms of public and private benefits mean that households will have more responsibility in managing their financial affairs, including their retirement and health care needs. Therefore, their financial position may need to be reassessed in light of these likely developments.

- In some countries, households have managed to reduce balance sheet or *net worth volatility* over the long run, despite relatively large holdings of market assets. This appears to be the case in the United States, where household balance sheets appear to have benefited from a relatively well-diversified financial portfolio. In some countries, however, a reduction in volatility from holding a diversified portfolio of market assets has been limited by events that increased the correlation between asset classes.

- Household *financial assets* over the last several decades have shifted away from bank and savings deposits to more market-sensitive assets in most countries. In part, such shifts were encouraged by equity market developments during the 1990s, and (more recently, particularly in Europe) the popularity of structured products, which may reflect institutional arrangements, and other national or regional market characteristics.

- *Housing* is the single largest asset for most households, yet real estate is a relatively less liquid asset class, with the degree of liquidity varying substantially across different countries. Interestingly, households in aggregate appear to better manage mortgage liabilities than long-term savings and investments, particularly in countries with relatively more flexible mortgage markets. While housing has always contributed to some extent to households' longer-term savings needs, there are risks in relying too heavily on such investments for retirement income. In this regard, steps to create more flexible mortgage markets should be encouraged, including the development of flexible mortgage-backed securities and derivatives markets.

- Trends in public and private *pension reform* are changing the financial positions and risk profiles of households in a number of ways. Such reforms have brought benefits and reduced some risks, but at the same time increased other risks. In particular, changes in public and private pension schemes globally have tended to increase the direct exposure of households to investment and market risks, and, more challenging, longevity risks.

- In addition to pension reform, prospective changes in *public and private benefits* (such as health care and long-term care) can be expected to devolve more responsibility to households to manage such financial implications. In order to better assess the impact of necessary reforms on the household sector, policymakers may look to develop broader, more forward-looking measures of household wealth. For example, they may try to define an appropriate financial mar-

gin measure (for income and/or savings levels) that would help to evaluate households' financial and savings cushions relative to anticipated future obligations.

Households may require new instruments to meet their saving and investment needs. Attracting savings is a key first step, and although many financial institutions are supplying households with more sophisticated analytic tools to assess their saving strategies, as well as asset allocations, more needs to be done in many countries to reach a wider range of households and to address their broader needs. However, encouraging long-term savings and investment behavior also requires consistent government policies, including relatively stable tax policies to encourage long-term strategies. To help households (and institutions) manage longer-term investments and obligations, and to facilitate the supply of annuity products, we again encourage governments to consider the issuance of long-dated, as well as index-linked, bonds to help address these longer-term and inflation-sensitive investment needs. Finally, given the relatively large concentration of housing assets in household net worth figures in many countries, some additional impetus for reverse mortgages or similar equity release products (including further analysis of the factors holding back the development of such products) may help households to more easily realize such long-term savings and to make more resources available for retirement and related obligations.

A crucial element of household saving and investment plans is the uncertainty of life expectancy, and the ability to convert long-term savings into a dependable income stream. However, annuity providers are already facing capacity constraints in some countries, related in part to their inability to hedge the longevity risks inherent in these products. A promising development is the pending issuance of longevity bonds by the European Investment Bank. More generally, governments may also consider, within their occasional role as insurer of last resort, the possible assumption of extreme old age risk (i.e., an important and costly tail risk for insurers). Indeed, such a role is already recognized in other areas where the costs or risks are deemed too great or undiversifiable for the market to effectively insure. For example, as part of the broader market for catastrophe risk, government or quasi-public bodies currently participate as insurers or reinsurers of earthquake and hurricane risks in California, Florida, Japan, Taiwan Province of China, and elsewhere (often utilizing private institutions and the capital markets to share or hedge these risks).

Governments may be well positioned to take the lead in communicating to households about their retirement challenges. Even though governments bear no responsibility for households' investment decisions, governments should coordinate with the private sector to provide financial education. In every country reviewed in our study, households appear to require more basic education about the risks and alternatives available for their financial and balance sheet management challenges. More can be done to ensure that households understand and have the basic skills and tools to manage additional and new risks. Governments and private industry have comparative advantages in addressing the different aspects necessary to educate and assist households (e.g., access to particular groups of workers, alternative channels of communication and education tools, and product and market expertise).

The incentives for financial advisers to provide long-term, impartial advice to households may need to be reexamined. The unwillingness of most individuals to pay for independent financial advice is a significant hindrance to the development of a broader advisory market. As such, there may be a need to strengthen the incentives for financial advisers to better support the needs of households, including through a relatively simple and stable tax and regulatory regime that may

encourage advisers to develop more tools and to provide long-term planning advice, combined with greater public education of the benefits of such advice and planning.

We believe it is important for policymakers to consider how policies aimed at improving financial stability are likely to influence the flow of financial risk through the financial system, and in particular the risk profile of households. During the last 20 years or so, policymakers and standard setters in many industrialized countries have successfully implemented policies designed to improve the resiliency and stability of systemically important institutions, such as banks. To differing degrees, similar policies have been or are being designed to do the same with regard to insurers and, more importantly, to public and private pension systems. In numerous countries, in response to many of the public and private actions to de-risk banks, insurers, and pensions discussed in this and previous issues of the GFSR, the financial risk profile of households is likely to be changing at this time.

Overall, there has been a transfer of financial risk over a number of years, away from the banking sector to nonbanking sectors, be they financial or the household sector. This dispersion of risk has made the financial system more resilient, not the least because the household sector is acting more as a "shock absorber of last resort." But at the same time, these new recipients of financial risks must learn how to manage the newly acquired risks. Policymakers have helped the financial system to become more resilient by providing good regulation and supervision of the financial sector. But now they also need to take the next logical step: help households to improve their financial education by obtaining quality advice and products necessary to manage their financial affairs.

References

Aizcorbe, Ana M., Arthur B. Kennickell, and Kevin B. Moore, 2003, "Recent Changes in U.S. Family

Finances: Evidence from the 1998 and 2001 Survey of Consumer Finances," *Federal Reserve Bulletin* (January), pp. 1–23.

Ameriks, John, Robert D. Nestor, and Stephen P. Utkus, 2004, "Expectations for Retirement: A Survey of Retirement Investors," Vanguard Center for Retirement Research (Valley Forge, PA: Vanguard Group, November). Available on the Internet: *http://www.vanguard.com.au.library/pdf/RL%20Retirement%20Expect%2011%2004%20P0205.pdf.*

Autorité des Marchés Financiers, 2004, press conference on L'Éducation Financière des Français TNS Sofres, Montrouge, Cedex, France, December 8. Available on the Internet: *http://www.lesechos.fr.patrimoine/document/education-financiere.pdf.*

Börsch-Supan, Axel, and Annamaria Lusardi, 2003, "Saving: A Cross-National Perspective," in *Life-Cycle Savings and Public Policy: A Cross-National Study in Six Countries,* ed. by Axel Börsch-Supan (London: Academic Press), pp. 1–32.

Case, Karl E., and Robert J. Shiller, 2003, "Is There a Bubble in the Housing Market?" *Brookings Papers on Economic Activity:* 2, Brookings Institution, pp. 299–342.

Case, Karl E., John M. Quigley, and Robert J. Shiller, 2003, "Home-buyers, Housing and the Macroeconomy," *Asset Prices and Monetary Policy* (Sydney: Reserve Bank of Australia, August).

Connolly, Ellis, and Marion Kohler, 2004, "The Impact of Superannuation on Household Saving," Research Discussion Papers RDP2004-001 (Sydney: Reserve Bank of Australia, March).

Consumer Bankers Association, 2004, "2000 Survey of Bank-Sponsored Financial Literacy Programs," *CBA ASAP Research* (April).

Davis, E. Philip, 2003, "Issues in the Regulation of Annuities Markets," Discussion Paper No. PI-0213 (London: Pensions Institute, Birkbeck College, University of London, February).

De Nederlandsche Bank, 2004, "Financial Behaviour of Dutch Households," *Quarterly Bulletin* (September), pp. 69–81.

Engen, Eric, William G. Gale, and Cori E. Uccello, 1999, "The Adequacy of Household Saving," *Brookings Papers on Economic Activity:* 2, Brookings Institution, pp. 65–165.

European Commission, Directorate-General for Employment and Social Affairs, 2003, "Adequate and Sustainable Pensions," Joint Commission/ Council Report (Brussels: European Commission March 18). Available via the Internet: *http://europa.eu.int/comm/employment_social/soc-prot/pensions/index_en.htm.*

Financial Services Authority, 2001, "Choosing a Mortgage," *Consumer Research Publications* (London, June).

France, Ministère des Affaires Sociales, 2003, *Dispositif National d'Information sur les Retraites,* Press Release (November 26).

Häusler, Gerd, 2005, "The Risks of Investor Ignorance," *Financial Times* (London), January 28.

Helman, Ruth, and Variny Paladíno, 2004, "Will Americans Ever Become Savers? The 14th Retirement Confidence Survey, 2004," Issue Brief No. 268 (Washington: Employee Benefit Research Institute, April).

Institute of Financial Services, 2004, *Say Goodbye to the Bridge,* News Release (London, August 18).

International Monetary Fund, 2004a, *Global Financial Stability Report,* World Economic and Financial Surveys (Washington, September).

———, 2004b, *World Economic Outlook* (Washington, September).

Kim, Jinhee, Constance Y. Kratzer, and Irene E. Leech, 2001, "Impacts of Workplace Financial Education on Retirement Plans," in *Proceedings of the 2001 Annual Conference of the Association for Financial Counselling and Planning Education,* ed. by Jeanne M. Hogarth,

King, Mervyn, 2004, "What Fates Impose—Facing up to Uncertainty," Speech by Governor of the Bank of England at the Eighth British Academy Annual Lecture, London, December.

Lusardi, Annamaria, 2004, *Saving and the Effectiveness of Financial Education,* Dartmouth College (January).

Mackenzie, G.A., and Allison Schrager, 2004, "Can the Private Annuity Market Provide Secure Retirement Income?" IMF Working Paper No. 04/230 (Washington: International Monetary Fund).

Mercer, Oliver Wyman, 2003, *Study on the Financial Integration of European Mortgage Markets,* Report commissioned by European Mortgage Federation (September 16).

Miles, David, 2004, "The U.K. Mortgage Market: Taking a Longer-Term View, Final Report and Recommendations" (London: Her Majesty's Treasury, March).

Moore, James F., and Olivia S. Mitchell, 1997, "Projected Retirement Wealth and Savings Adequacy in the Health and Retirement Survey," NBER Working Paper No. 6240 (Cambridge, Mass.: National Bureau of Economic Research, October).

Munnell, Alicia, 2003, "The Declining Role of Social Security," Just the Facts on Retirement Issues, No. 6 (Boston: Boston College, Center for Retirement Research, February).

OECD, 2004, "Financial Education Project," *Financial Market Trends*, No. 87 (October), pp. 223–28.

Quan, Daniel, and Sheridan Titman, 1998, "Do Real Estate Prices and Stock Prices Move Together? An International Analysis," *Real Estate Economics*, Vol. 27, No. 2, pp. 183–207.

Scholz, John Karl, Anath Seshadri, and Surachai Khitatrakun, 2004, "Are Americans Saving Optimally for Retirement?" NBER Working Paper No. 10260 (Cambridge, Mass.: National Bureau of Economic Research, January).

Sundén, Annika, 2004, "The Future of Retirement in Sweden" (Philadelphia: Pension Research Council, The Wharton School, University of Pennsylvania).

Sveriges Riksbank, 2004, *Financial Stability Report, 2004:1* and *2004:2* (Stockholm: Sveriges Riksbank).

Thaler, Richard H., and Shlomo Benartzi, 2001, "Save More Tomorrow: Using Behaviour Economics to Increase Employee Saving," Working Paper (Chicago: University of Chicago Graduate School of Business, August).

United Kingdom, Debt Management Office, 2004, "Issuance of Ultra-Long Gilt Instruments, Consultation Document" (London). Available via the Internet: *http://www.dmo.gov.uk/gilts/public/consdoc/cons021204.pdf*.

———, Her Majesty's Stationery Office, 2004, *Pensions: Challenges and Choices*, The First Report of the Pensions Commission (London). Available via the Internet: *http://www.pensionscommission.org.uk/publications/2004/annrep/appendices-all.pdf*.

United States, Board of Governors of the Federal Reserve System, 2002, *Federal Reserve Bulletin* (Washington, November).

United States, Congressional Budget Office (CBO), 1993, "Baby Boomers in Retirement: An Early Perspective" (Washington, September).

———, 2003, "Baby Boomers' Retirement Prospects: An Overview" (Washington, November).

United States, Government Printing Office (GPO), 2004, Federal Register, Vol. 69, No. 165 (August 26).

University of Pennsylvania, 2004, "Reinventing the Retirement Paradigm," Pension Research Council and Boettner Center for Pensions and Retirement Research (Philadelphia: Wharton School, August 26).

VanDerhei, Jack, and Craig Copeland, 2003, "Can America Afford Tomorrow's Retirees: Results from the EBRI-EFT Retirement Security Projection Model," Issue Brief No. 263 (Washington: Employee Benefit Research Institute, November).

Vanguard Group, 2004, *How America Saves: A Report on Vanguard Defined Contribution Plans*, Vanguard Center for Retirement Research (Valley Forge, PA: The Vanguard Group, October). Available via the Internet: *https://institutional4.vanguard.com/VGApp/iip/Research?number=10&FW_Activity=LibraryActivity&FW_Event=nextSearch&Category=Retirement_Research*.

Walker David M., 2005, "Social Security, Long-Term Challenges Warrant Early Action," Testimony Before the Special Committee on Aging, U.S. Senate (Washington: United States Government Accountability Office, February 3).

CHAPTER IV   CORPORATE FINANCE IN EMERGING MARKETS

As many emerging markets continue to consolidate balance sheets in the aftermath of crises, and growth becomes a priority, the means and obstacles to finance corporate sector activities have taken center stage in policy discussions. The September 2004 *Global Financial Stability Report* (GFSR) noted that many emerging markets had completed a deleveraging process and improved their policy framework and economic fundamentals. This has increased their resilience to future crises. To reap the rewards of these adjustments, the corporate sector in emerging markets needs to be funded by a variety of sources. Also, the incentives have to be such that they prevent the reemergence of financial vulnerabilities. This requires enhanced monitoring of potential vulnerabilities in emerging markets corporates. The fact that corporate sector bond issuance has surpassed sovereign borrowing in international markets over the past three years underscores the importance of this issue.

This chapter analyzes recent trends in corporate finance in emerging markets, institutional obstacles to more diversified and adequate funding sources for the corporate sector, and the vulnerabilities associated with the currently available sources. In particular, a selective review of the latest findings on institutional weaknesses in emerging markets suggests that, despite early steps taken in most emerging markets, important gaps remain in implementing and enforcing the now widely accepted principles of corporate governance. Also, the chapter presents new microlevel estimates of corporate sector balance sheet mismatches, shows that these mismatches continue to be a source of concern in some countries, and emphasizes the importance of a more integrated approach to assessing such vulnerabilities that accounts for interactions

between interest rate, foreign exchange, and credit risks.

The main trends in emerging markets corporate finance include an increase in corporate bond issuance and stagnation or a decline in bank lending and equity issuance. As a result, in part, of a series of policy measures, corporate bonds have become a relevant source of funding in some Asian countries, but less so in Latin America—with the exception of Mexico. In contrast, bank lending to the corporate sector and equity issuance have been on the decline, except for a recent timid recovery. Cyclical factors, including expansionary monetary policies, are underpinning this recovery, but it remains unclear to what extent structural factors may continue to constrain some of these sources of funding. In particular, some emerging markets may be starting to experience the process of bank disintermediation that several mature economies have gone through in the 1980s and 1990s, while recent efforts to improve access to equity capital may prove insufficient.

The analysis of the trends and constraints in emerging market corporate finance, as well as the associated vulnerabilities, presented in this chapter relies on a variety of micro- and macroeconomic data sources, including a new database that combines balance sheet and debt issuance data at the firm level. Corporate leverage and the use of internal sources of funding in emerging market corporates appear to be slightly higher than in mature market corporates, but these differences do not seem to be significant. Moreover, higher leverage and greater use of internal funds could be supported by higher tangibility of assets, higher profitability, or lower market-to-book values in emerging market corporates. However, the important differences are not in firm-specific factors but in institutional factors that increase the cost of equity capital and constrain access to equity markets—and, also, to some extent to long-term bond markets.

A number of institutional factors, including low transparency and weak corporate governance, are key constraints to better access to market-based sources of funding.[1] Recent assessments by international and private organizations note that, despite increasing awareness of corporate governance issues, and initial efforts by many emerging markets to correct them, implementation and enforcement problems persist. The mechanisms that protect investors against conflicts of interest between creditors and shareholders, as well as between insiders (managers and controlling shareholders) and minority shareholders, are particularly imperfect and costly in emerging markets. A growing number of recent studies demonstrate how the impact of weak internal governance practices—such as inadequate protection of minority shareholders, and lack of independent directors and/or external auditing committees—is magnified by poor external governance associated with weak contract enforcement, rule of law, and judicial systems. More recent studies emphasize the importance of disclosure that facilitates market discipline rather than public enforcement only.

Given these constraints and obstacles to adequate and diversified sources of funding, emerging market corporates rely more heavily on foreign currency and short-term debt instruments. The vulnerabilities associated with this particular composition of liabilities are well-known, but analysts and previous work at the IMF have pointed out the lack of microeconomic data on these mismatches and the limitations this imposes on conducting surveillance of the corporate sector in emerging markets. The chapter provides new estimates of these mismatches based on firm-level data, derived from a combination of sources

detailed in the Appendix. The estimates include measures of foreign currency assets and liabilities, as well as the use of hedging instruments, for a sample of Latin American countries. These mismatches are also combined with traditional financial ratios and bankruptcy risk indicators, to assess the overall level of corporate sector financial fragility.

This chapter is structured as follows. The first section presents recent trends on corporate finance in emerging markets. It is followed by a section on the main structural determinants and obstacles to a better funding mix in emerging markets. The new evidence on foreign currency and maturity mismatches, the associated risks, and vulnerability indicators is presented in the third section. The chapter concludes with a discussion of the key policy issues related to the topic.

Recent Trends in Corporate Finance

Two opposing forces have determined the evolution of emerging market corporate debt over the past decade. On the one hand, and as reported in the September 2004 GFSR, corporates engaged in a process of deleveraging in the late 1990s to correct some of the excesses that led to a string of crises during that period. On the other hand, the low interest rate environment of the early 2000s encouraged corporate borrowing as part of a global effort to come out of the deflationary environment that followed the bursting of the high-tech equity bubble in 2000. With these opposing forces as background, this section reviews major trends in the main sources of funding for the corporate sector—including domestic and international debt and equity— by comparing data from the pre-crises years 1995–97 with data from the 2000s.

Corporate debt in emerging markets, measured relative to GDP, has risen from around

---

[1]Other broad factors, such as macroeconomic and financial instability, have been discussed elsewhere (see, e.g., Mathieson and others, 2004). This chapter focuses on recent studies on emerging market institutional factors and issues that warrant further attention.

46 percent of GDP in 1995–97 to 62 percent in 2001–03 (Figure 4.1). This increase masks important regional variations. In particular, the increase is influenced, to a large extent, by the persistent growth of bank debt to GDP in China and India. Since trends in corporate borrowing in these large countries are somewhat different from the rest of the emerging markets, figures for Asia excluding China and India are included in the second panel of Figure 4.1.[2] Even with these adjustments, corporate debt in Asia continues to be above pre-crisis levels and at a level that triples that of emerging Europe and Latin America. However, emerging Europe and Latin America show totally opposite trends: while debt ratios have increased by 10 percent of GDP in Europe relative to 1995–97, Latin American corporates have experienced a decline in total corporate debt of 5–6 percent of GDP.

Trends in corporate debt can be examined from macrodata (debt-to-GDP ratios) or from microdata (individual corporate's balance sheet information).[3] While macrodata are much easier to obtain than microdata, the former could at times be misleading because they relate stocks to flows. For instance, while the macrodata may suggest that corporate leverage in Asia exceeds that of Latin America's corporates by a wide margin (Figure 4.1), microdata on individual firm debt relative to assets—a standard measure of leverage—reveal that Asian firms are not substantially more leveraged than Latin American firms (Figure 4.2). Moreover, while in 1997 Asian corporate leverage doubled the leverage in Latin America, both ratios converged to around one-third of total assets in 2003.[4]

Figure 4.1. Corporate Debt Outstanding by Instrument in Emerging Markets
(In percent of GDP)

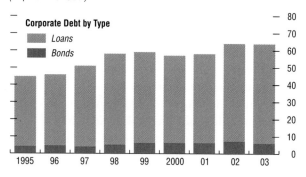
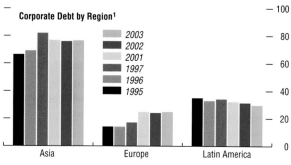
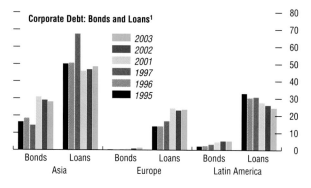

Sources: Bank for International Settlements; central banks' websites; Dealogic; Haver Analytics; Standard & Poor's EMDB database; and IMF staff estimates.
[1]Excluding China and India.

[2]The different trends in China and India will be discussed in forthcoming issues of the GFSR.
[3]A description of the data is presented in the Appendix.
[4]This may be, to some extent, because of a larger representation of small firms in the Asian sample. A low coverage of small and medium-size enterprises is a drawback of the microdata.

Balance sheet data can also be used to assess the evolution of corporate *foreign debt* exposures. A study by Ratha, Suttle, and Mohapatra (2003) suggests that Asian firms appear to have substituted domestic for external debt after 1997. However, this trend is driven mostly by Chinese and Indian firms, and the rest of the Asian firms in our sample seem to have maintained a stable ratio of foreign debt to total debt of around 27 percent in 1997–2003 (Figure 4.2). Latin American firms have gradually reduced their foreign debt ratio from 35 percent of total debt in 1997 to 26 percent in 2003.[5] More pronounced has been the drop by half in foreign debt exposure in emerging Europe in 1997–2003.

Despite the increasing importance of domestic and international bonds as a source of corporate finance, *bank lending* remains the dominant source of corporate finance for all emerging market regions (Figure 4.1). Even in Asia, where bond finance has reached almost 30 percent of GDP, bank lending dominates at around 50 percent of GDP. In Latin America, bank lending to the corporate sector was over four times the level of bond debt, while in emerging Europe, loans dwarfed the level of corporate bonds outstanding.

Bank lending to emerging market corporates has increased from 40 percent of GDP in 1995 to 60 percent in 2003 (Figure 4.3). However, excluding China and India, bank lending has contracted from 33 percent of GDP to 30 percent, with significant variations across regions. Moreover, while domestic bank lending to corporates has dropped to 23 percent of GDP in 2003 (from 27 percent in 1995), overall international bank lending has remained resilient at a stable 7 percent of GDP.

[5]This includes only corporates that participate in international capital markets (see the Appendix for definitions). Thus, it includes only international debt, but excludes foreign-currency-denominated local debt.

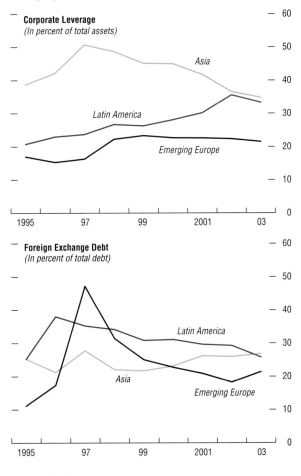

Figure 4.2. Corporate Leverage and External Debt in Emerging Markets[1]

Source: Worldscope.
[1]Excluding China and India.

Figure 4.3. Bank Credit Outstanding
(In percent of GDP)

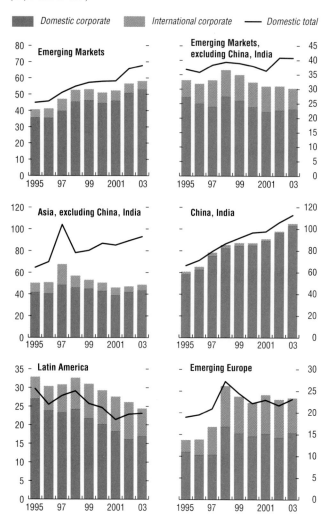

Sources: Bank for International Settlements; central banks' websites; Chilean Superintendencia de Bancos e Instituciones Financieras; and IMF staff estimates.

In Latin America, domestic bank lending to corporates has contracted the most, from 27 percent of GDP in 1995 to 17 percent in 2003, notwithstanding an increase in international lending to 8 percent of GDP in 2003 (from 6 percent in 1995). Bank credit has also declined, albeit at a more moderate pace, in Asia, because of the significant retrenchment in international lending—from 9 percent to 5 percent of GDP—that has dominated a small increase in domestic bank lending— from 41 percent to 43 percent of GDP. In emerging Europe, international and domestic bank lending increased substantially relative to the mid-1990s.

The stagnation or even contraction in bank lending to most emerging market corporates, with the exception of China and India, is a development that warrants further study, in particular an evaluation of whether this is a cyclical phenomenon, or whether emerging markets are beginning to experience the process of bank disintermediation already experienced in the mature markets. Besides cyclical forces, the decline in bank lending could be attributed to a tightening of regulations, to crowding out by the government or the household sectors, or to a process of disintermediation to the capital markets. Some of these factors are analyzed below (see Figure 4.4).

In Latin America, local banks have seen their reserves increase sharply between 1995 and 2003, a result perhaps of a tightening in regulations as well as increased risk aversion and tightened credit standards by foreign-owned banks. In contrast, Asian banks have reduced their reserves, in part because of the expansionary monetary policies in the region in the aftermath of the crisis. A persistent increase in claims on the government suggests a fair amount of crowding out in central Europe and Latin America, which contributes to low levels of intermediation. Furthermore, bank deposits have remained stagnant in Latin America, in contrast with their significant increase in Asia. However, the flattening

out of the level of deposits in Asia in 2001–03
(Figure 4.4), combined with the increase in
corporate bond markets, suggest that bank
disintermediation may be taking hold in
emerging Asia. This has been accompanied by
a sharp increase in bank lending to the household sector in that region (Figure 4.3).

The increase in corporate bond issuance in
most of the major emerging markets has compensated, to some extent, for the decline or
stagnation in corporate bank lending. This is
clearly the case in Asia and, to a lesser extent,
in Latin America. While the stock of corporate bonds in the emerging market universe
doubled to US$320 billion in 2003, the largest
share has financed Asian corporates (Figure
4.5). In contrast with their Asian counterparts,
Latin American corporates have issued a
larger share of international bonds—although
domestic bonds have also increased rapidly,
albeit from very low initial levels.

Corporate bonds have become a relevant
source of funding—that is, accounting for
more than 30 percent of total corporate
debt—in Korea, Malaysia, and Mexico,
because of the important structural changes
implemented after the crises.[6] In Korea, corporate bonds accounted for almost 50 percent
of total debt in 1998 (see Figure 4.6), in part
because in 1997 the government raised the
ceiling on corporate bond issuance from two
to four times of equity capital and eliminated
restrictions on investment in domestic bonds
by foreign investors. Malaysia's corporate
bond market is the largest among the emerging markets in relative terms (at 43 percent of
GDP) and corporate bonds have grown
steadily to become 45 percent of total debt in
2003. Among other measures, efforts to
streamline the bond issuance process and to
encourage secondary bond market activities,
as well as to relax insurance companies' portfolio limits, have contributed to such growth.

[6]The main factors behind these successful experiences will be analyzed in detail in the September 2005
GFSR.

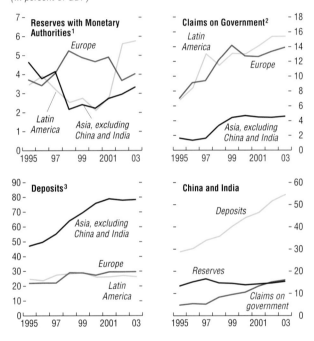

Figure 4.4. Banking Sector in Emerging Markets
(In percent of GDP)

Source: IMF, *International Financial Statistics.*
[1]Reserves include currency holdings and deposits with the monetary authorities.
[2]Claims on government include claims on central government for all countries, and
state and local for all except China, India, Korea, Thailand, Poland, and Russia.
[3]Deposits include demand deposits, time deposits, and foreign currency deposits.

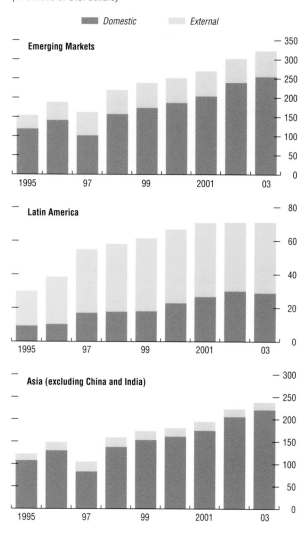

Figure 4.5. Corporate Bonds Outstanding
(In billions of U.S. dollars)

Source: Bank for International Settlements.

The growth of corporate bonds in Mexico is more recent, and they constitute 30 percent of total corporate debt. The development of a government bond yield curve that facilitated the pricing of corporate bonds and changes in the bond contracts, together with the growth of private pension funds (which were barred from investing in equities until very recently) and other institutional investors (insurance companies and mutual funds), have supported the growth of corporate bonds as a source of corporate finance.

The *overall* decline in corporate bank lending in emerging markets (exclusive of China and India) in 1995–2003, compensated only partially by an increase in domestic bond issuance, was not reciprocated by a simultaneous rebound in equity issuance. Figure 4.7 shows that equity issuance flows have experienced a sharp decline beginning in the last quarter of 2000, with only a moderate rebound in 2003. Even though emerging market issuance rose to just over a half of its 1999 level, it increased by about 32 percent between 2002 and 2003 and is estimated to have increased further in 2004. However, it remains to be seen if equity could become a reasonable source of funding for emerging market corporates.

Although some of the marked decline in emerging market equity issuance reflected factors specific to emerging markets, equity issuance in mature economies also saw a significant decline in flows since 2000. This was generally driven by market conditions—rising volatility and declining share prices—following the bursting of the high-tech equity bubble. Since the latter part of 2003, as economic and market conditions have improved, issuance activity has rebounded both in mature and in emerging equity markets.

To summarize, emerging market corporates have seen a stagnation or decline in bank lending, an increase in corporate bond issuance, and a decline in equity funds. While these trends are broadly in line with developments in the mature markets, it is unclear if the decline in overall funding (excluding China and India) is a result of reduced external financing needs or constraints on the sources of funding.[7] A complete answer to this question would require more in-depth studies at the country level. However, there may be structural differences among emerging market and mature market corporates that might call for further development of particular sources of corporate funding. Such differences are analyzed in the next section, with a view to identify constraints that may be hindering the growth of financing sources for emerging market corporates.

Structural Determinants and Obstacles

Finance matters for growth. A number of studies have established that having deep financial markets is critical for GDP growth (see Box 4.1). However, a number of features of emerging market corporates and the environment they operate in may constrain the available sources of funding to finance growth. In this section, we analyze key differences between emerging market corporates and their mature market counterparts—in particular, leverage ratios and internal versus external funding—and the main determinants of these differences, as well as constraints to achieving a better funding mix. The section shows that emerging market corporates are not that different—except for slightly higher leverage ratios and greater reliance on internal finance—from their mature market counterparts. It also highlights the fact that firms that participate in international capital markets have higher leverage and lower profitability than nonmarket participants. Finally, the section reviews institutional factors that constrain emerging market corporates' access to

[7]Throughout this chapter, external finance refers to sources external to the firm (i.e, different from internal sources of funding such as retained earnings). Financing from other jurisdictions is referred to as international debt or equity.

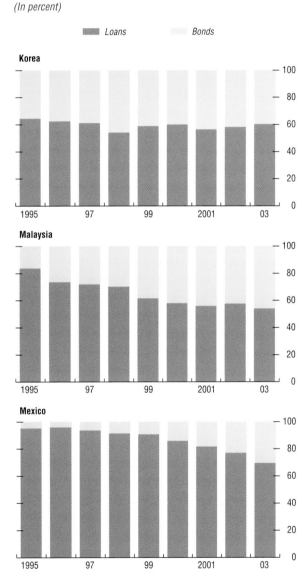

Figure 4.6. Composition of Outstanding Corporate Domestic Debt
(In percent)

Sources: Bank for International Settlements; and IMF staff estimates.

Figure 4.7. Equity Issuance
(In percent of GDP)

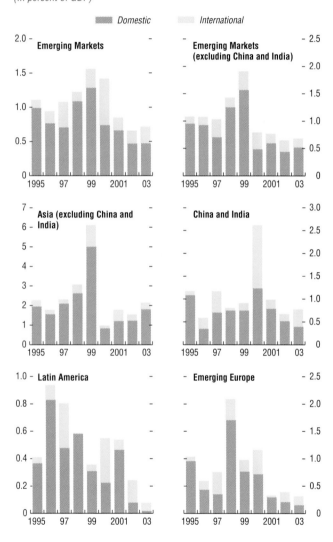

Sources: Dealogic; and IMF, *International Financial Statistics.*

equity finance—such as transparency, the rule of law and judicial efficiency, contract repudiation and bankruptcy, and concentrated ownership—focusing on problems with the implementation and enforcement of the now widely accepted principles of corporate governance.

Corporate finance theories suggest that the choice between debt and equity depends on firm-specific and institutional factors, as well as on features of the financial system in which the company operates.[8] Recent studies show that institutional factors at the country level are more important that firm-specific differences for debt-equity ratios, and that disclosing material information is critical for improving access to equity funding.

Corporate Finance and Firm-Specific Factors

Corporate *leverage,* measured as the ratio of total debt to assets, is somewhat higher in emerging markets than in the mature markets. Table 4.1 shows that the average debt ratio for emerging market corporates during 1993–2003 was 27.6 percent of assets while for the G-3 corporates, it was 23.8 percent.[9] Similarly, a study by Glen and Singh (2003) finds that corporate leverage in emerging markets during the period 1994–2002 was 56.4 percent of total assets, compared with 52.6 percent in the mature markets, although they use a sample with many more developed countries and fewer emerging markets, and they focus on median values instead of mean

---

[8]See, for instance, Myers (2001).

[9]We use weighted-average mean ratios from balance sheet information because this would be more consistent with the macrodata on aggregate debt flows. Although median ratios would be more appropriate to characterize the financial health of a "representative" firm, mean ratios are more suitable for analyzing vulnerabilities in the corporate sector as the impact of larger firms in the propagation of shocks is more significant. Also, simple means and medians yield the same patterns of corporate leverage across emerging market regions, but the differences with G-3 corporates are less clear-cut—this is, in part, because of a broader coverage in the latter group of countries.

Box 4.1. Finance and Economic Growth: A Brief Review of the Evidence

The relationship between finance and economic growth has long been a topic of interest and debate. Although there is strong evidence that a developed financial sector and a strong economy go together, the direction of the causality is debatable. While many believe that finance is an important determinant of economic growth, others argue that the development of financial systems simply responds to changing demand from economic development. Nevertheless, a large body of recent empirical research has found robust evidence that the development of financial systems contributes to economic growth. This box reviews briefly the theoretical and empirical evidence of this relationship.

An extensive economic literature focuses on the functions of financial systems and their roles in economic development.[1] By reducing costs of acquiring information, enforcing contracts, and facilitating transactions, financial systems play important roles in economic activities. Among other things, financial systems produce information about investment returns and monitor actual investments, thus reducing free riders, moral hazard, and adverse selection problems. Financial systems also help achieve a better allocation of capital by pooling and mobilizing savings toward higher-return investments. In addition, financial systems facilitate cross-section and intertemporal risk sharing among investors. In sum, financial systems facilitate a more efficient allocation of resources, influence saving and investment decisions, and thus affect the growth of economic activities.

Although theories suggest that the functions of financial systems can influence economic activities, the extent to which financial development affects economic growth remains an empirical question. A substantial body of empirical work has attempted to document this rela-

tionship at the country, industry, and firm levels. Evidence at all levels points to a positive relationship between financial development and economic growth. At the country level, evidence indicates that various measures of financial development (including financial intermediary sector's assets, liquid liabilities of financial system, domestic credit to private sectors, stock market capitalization, and bond market capitalization) are robustly and positively related to economic growth (King and Levine, 1993; Levine and Zervos, 1998; Aghion, Howitt, and Mayer-Foulkes, 2004). Other studies find a positive relationship between financial development and growth at the industry level (Rajan and Zingales, 1998). Similarly, at the firm level, researchers have consistently found that firms in countries with greater financial development are able to obtain more external funds and thus grow faster (Demirgüç-Kunt and Maksimovic, 1998; Love, 2003).

Although these studies find a strong connection between financial development and economic growth, the direction of causality is debatable. Many studies at the microlevel aim to approach this causality problem. Rajan and Zingales (1998) develop a methodology to investigate whether financial development has an influence on industrial growth by testing the hypothesis that industries that are relatively more dependent on external finance develop disproportionately faster in a country with greater financial development. Taking U.S. industries as a benchmark for the "frictionless" case where supply of funds is infinitely elastic,[2] they find that industries that are "naturally heavy users" of external finance (e.g., drugs and plastics industries) grow faster in more financially developed economies. Therefore, they conclude that financial development has a supportive influence on economic growth. In another study, Jayaratne and Strahan (1996) also find evidence supporting the argument that financial development

---

[1]The growth accounting literature suggests that capital accumulation alone does not account for much of long-run economic growth. For finance to affect growth, we need theories about how financial development influences resource allocation decisions in ways that foster productivity growth.

[2]Under such assumptions, the observed amount of funds raised would be equal to the "demand" for external funds.

Box 4.1 (concluded)

affects economic growth. Examining the liberalization of the banking sector in the United States during the early 1970s, they find that branch reform boosted bank-lending quality and had a positive influence on economic growth in states that deregulated banking.

In addition to the development of financial systems, researchers also investigate the relationship between particular structures of financial systems and economic growth.[3] Among others,

[3]See Demirgüç-Kunt and Levine (2001) and Levine (2004) for a review of the empirical results, and Allen and Gale (2001) for theoretical models

Demirgüç-Kunt and Levine (2001) find that, controlling for financial development, financial structure does not help explain economic performance. In particular, countries, industries, and firms are not found to grow faster in either market-based or bank-based economies. However, these results do not necessarily imply that institutional structure is unimportant for growth. Rather, they imply that there is no one optimal institutional structure for every economy (Levine, 2004).

comparing the structure of different financial systems.

ratios for each country group. This result is confirmed by Fan, Titman, and Twite (2004), who find a median leverage ratio for developing economies of 32 percent against 27 percent for developed countries.

More important, leverage of corporates that participate in international markets ("market participants" in Table 4.1) is higher than those that do not. Market participants have, on average, leverage ratios of 31.8 percent of assets, compared with 23.5 percent for nonmarket participants. Interestingly, market participants from Asia display higher leverage than their Latin American counterparts—with the exception of Argentina.

The evidence on *internal finance* also suggests that emerging markets rely more on internal funds than external sources of funding (Table 4.1). Internal resources, defined as cash flows generated by firm's operations divided by capital expenditures, are somewhat higher in firms in emerging markets

than in mature markets, with ratios of 2.11 and 1.97, respectively. Similarly, using data from a comprehensive survey of businesses, Beck, Demirgüç-Kunt, and Maksimovic (2002)[10] show that corporates in emerging markets, especially in Asia and emerging Europe, do use internal funds more heavily (see Figure 4.8).

Table 4.1 also includes a set of firm-level variables that were found to be correlated with leverage in corporate finance studies.[11] In particular, emerging market corporates are twice as profitable as those in the G-3 countries. Higher profitability allows the former to rely more on internal finance, but it could also reflect that they operate in riskier environments. However, market participants are less profitable than nonmarket participants, and this is consistent with the volatility of profits of the latter group (measured by the standard deviation of returns) being twice as large as the former.[12]

[10]The study uses a cross-sectional firm-level survey, conducted by the World Bank during 1995–99, with a wide coverage of small and medium-size firms (40 percent of observations; and 20 percent are from large firms).

[11]See Rajan and Zingales (1995) for a discussion of the cross-sectoral factors that appear to affect corporate leverage in the G-7 countries.

[12]This fact is also consistent with the relatively larger size of market participants. Overall, the emerging market corporates covered in these studies are not that much smaller—on average and median values—than mature market corporates (see also Glen and Singh, 2003).

Table 4.1. Structural Determinants of Corporate Leverage, 1993–2003[1]

| | Corporate Leverage Debt/Assets | | Internal Finance | Firm-Level Determinants of Corporate Leverage | | | |
| | | | | Profitability (ROA) | | | |
Country	Total	Market participants	Internal resources[4]	Total	Market participants	Asset tangibility	Market-to-book ratio[5]
Emerging Markets[2]							
Argentina	0.36	0.34	1.74	4.92	6.99	0.78	2.49
Brazil	0.23	0.25	1.22	10.67	15.07	0.80	1.30
Chile	0.30	0.34	1.86	6.71	6.45	0.80	1.95
Colombia	0.14	0.20	2.40	5.05	9.36	0.79	1.06
Mexico	0.26	0.27	1.97	7.36	7.22	0.79	2.15
Latin America	**0.26**	**0.28**	**1.84**	**6.94**	**9.02**	**0.79**	**1.79**
China	0.29	0.37	4.97	6.50	5.02	0.55	2.80
India	0.35	0.38	2.14	9.48	8.58	0.57	3.45
Korea	0.45	0.46	1.31	4.84	4.84	0.62	1.61
Malaysia	0.30	0.36	3.63	6.29	5.56	0.64	2.84
Thailand	0.49	0.53	4.67	4.99	4.22	0.68	3.02
Asia	**0.38**	**0.42**	**3.34**	**6.42**	**5.64**	**0.61**	**2.74**
Czech Republic	0.20	0.22	1.48	4.33	4.69	0.78	1.01
Hungary	0.19	0.21	1.24	9.26	7.04	0.65	1.68
Poland	0.19	0.29	1.01	10.68	6.74	0.59	2.13
Russia	0.12	0.12	0.99	8.43	8.31	0.72	0.89
Turkey	0.25	0.27	1.01	18.69	18.25	0.39	3.79
Emerging Europe	**0.19**	**0.22**	**1.14**	**10.28**	**9.00**	**0.63**	**1.90**
Emerging Markets	**0.28**	**0.31**	**2.11**	**7.88**	**7.89**	**0.68**	**2.15**
Mature Markets[3]							
United States	0.24	n.a.	2.65	3.60	n.a.	0.52	5.88
Germany	0.20	n.a.	1.52	3.88	n.a.	0.41	3.41
Japan	0.27	n.a.	1.73	2.68	n.a.	0.42	2.17
G-3	**0.24**	**n.a.**	**1.97**	**3.39**	**n.a.**	**0.45**	**3.82**

Sources: Worldscope; and Corporate Vulnerability Utility.

[1]The summary statistics presented in this table, except for debt/assets (median) and firm size, are weighted-average means of financial ratios, with firm assets used as weights. Debt/assets (median) is computed as the median leverage ratio for each country. Firm size is measured as the natural logarithm of total assets, denominated in millions of U.S. dollars, of each country's median firm. Every ratio is averaged through the period 1993–2003 for each country.

[2]The firm-level accounting data used for emerging markets' financial ratios (with the exception of "Internal Resources" and "Market-to-Book ratio") is based on the Worldscope data set, selecting the nonfinancial firms for which ratios are available. Data are checked for consistency and netted out of outliers. They cover most of the publicly traded companies in the 15 emerging markets, comprising 524 firms in Latin America, 3,213 firms in Asia, and 244 firms in emerging Europe.

[3]The indicators computed for mature markets, as well as the "Internal Resources" and "Market-to-Book" ratios for emerging markets, are extracted from the Corporate Vulnerability Utility (CVU), based on firm-level data from Worldscope and Datastream. In terms of the number of companies, the CVU covers only 60 percent of the universe of listed firms, but almost 90 percent in terms of market capitalization. For mature markets, it includes 6,941 firms in the United States, 825 firms in Germany, and 3,422 firms in Japan. For emerging markets, it covers 597 firms in Latin America, 2,936 firms in Asia, and 305 firms in emerging Europe.

[4]The internal resources index is defined as the ratio between the sum of cash flow from operations, plus decreases in inventories and receivables, plus increases in payables, over the sum of capital expenditures. This index is the complement to the Rajan and Zingales Index of External Finance, extracted from the Corporate Vulnerability Utility.

[5]The market-to-book ratio is the ratio of stock price to book value per share (computed as stockholders' book equity—common stock plus retained earnings—divided by the number of outstanding shares). This indicator is extracted from the Corporate Vulnerability Utility.

Another dimension where emerging market corporates distinguish themselves from the mature market ones is the *tangibility* of firms' assets. Emerging market corporates operate in sectors where technologies are well-known and managerial decisions are easier to monitor. Thus, the more tangible the assets, the lower the scope for informational asymmetries between insiders and outsiders, allowing for higher leverage. Table 4.1 shows that asset tangibility in emerging markets is 50 percent larger than in the G-3 countries, supporting a higher level of corporate leverage.

A low market-to-book ratio in emerging markets is associated with the difficulties in issuing equity securities. The *market-to-book* ratio, which measures the difference between investors' assessment of company shares and their book value, is almost 50 percent lower in emerging markets than in mature markets. Analysts agree that a lower market-to-book value is associated with higher corporate leverage. When the market-to-book ratio is perceived as high, firms find it advantageous to issue equity, and this has been the case more often for mature market than emerging market corporates during 1993–2003.

Even if the differences in leverage and external finance ratios between mature and emerging markets are not that significant, it is quite clear that the cost of equity capital is much higher in the latter. Estimates of the cost of equity capital (Table 4.2) highlight the differences in the risk assessment made by international investors across emerging and mature economies' corporations, which in turn reflects the reticence of investors to supply equity capital to the latter.[13] There are three different measures of the cost of capital, grouped into two categories. First, an ex ante measure of the cost of capital is based on expected earnings; the second category provides two measures of the cost of capital based on ex post returns.[14] The first ex post measure looks at the relationship between stock market performance and a public sector country risk rating, while the second is based on the country's stock market volatility relative to the United States.[15]

Figure 4.8. Internal Financing of Capital Expenditure[1]
(As percent of total financing)

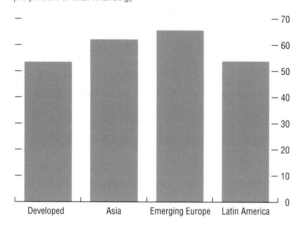

Source: IMF staff estimates based on the World Business Environment Survey (WBES), conducted by the World Bank.
[1]The region coverage is defined by the WBES.

[13]In principle, the cost of (external) capital should be a weighted average of the cost of equity and the cost of debt. Estimates of the latter are hard to obtain in a comparable basis across countries.

[14]The ex ante cost of equity capital measure is derived by substituting a firm's stock price and analyst forecasts of future earnings (taken from I/B/E/S) into an equity valuation model, similar to the dividend discount model and then backing out the internal rate of return (i.e., the risk-free rate plus the equity premium) from this model.

[15]The ex post cost of capital measures do not rely on analyst forecasts and use realized returns calculated at the country level. The first ex post measure is derived by regressing realized country-level stock index returns on the *Institutional Investor*'s country

Across almost all emerging regions the cost of capital is largely higher than that found in the United States and other mature economies.[16]

Based on the ex ante measure of the cost of equity capital, emerging market firms face a 540 basis points higher cost of capital relative to the United States (i.e., 15.6 percent versus 10.2 percent, see Table 4.2). As a result of the much higher cost of equity capital, the capital structure of firms in emerging markets in many cases is skewed away from equity and toward greater debt. A growing number of empirical studies have shown that this is due to institutional factors that put constraints on firms' access to equity capital (and, in some cases, also to bond financing), rather than resulting from the firm-specific characteristics of emerging market corporates outlined above.

Institutional Factors

A number of institutional factors, such as taxes, regulations, and the legal framework, are also important determinants of firms' financial decisions. In particular, the tax code in several countries favors debt over equity. Thus, firms have an incentive to increase leverage ratios up to the point where the expected costs of financial distress and bankruptcy equal the so-called "tax-shield" advantage of debt.

The tax treatment of interest and dividends is an important determinant of capital structure, and tends to favor higher debt-to-equity ratios. This is especially the case in classical tax systems, where interest expenses are deductible at the corporate level but dividends are not. Classical tax systems are used in most

Table 4.2. Cost of Equity Capital Estimates by Country
(In percent)

Country	Cost of Capital Measures		
	Ex ante	Ex post	
	Expected earnings	Country risk	Standard deviation
Argentina	12.8	33.1	43.0
Brazil	20.9	22.6	33.5
Chile	12.6	15.6	21.4
Colombia	. . .	22.8	18.9
Mexico	15.6	17.4	24.1
Latin America	**15.5**	**22.3**	**28.2**
China	. . .	16.5	27.5
India	14.4	20.0	18.1
Korea	14.1	16.6	20.6
Malaysia	10.7	15.4	23.3
Thailand	13.5	17.8	21.8
Asia	**13.2**	**17.2**	**22.3**
Czech Republic	. . .	15.9	19.0
Hungary	. . .	16.2	22.6
Poland	. . .	17.0	32.3
Russia	. . .	20.4	. . .
Turkey	. . .	24.6	36.2
Emerging Europe	**. . .**	**18.8**	**27.5**
Emerging Markets (15)	**14.3**	**19.5**	**26.0**
Germany	10.1	10.7	15.0
Japan	6.2	12.5	15.5
United States	10.2	10.5	12.3
G-3	**8.8**	**11.2**	**14.3**
Average Less-Developed Economies[1]	**15.6**	**19.8**	**23.7**
Average Non-U.S. Mature Economies[1]	**11.3**	**11.7**	**16.4**

Sources: Ex ante cost of capital from Hail and Leuz (2004); ex post cost of capital from Ibbotson Associates (2005).

[1]The number of countries in the less-developed markets average is 16 for ex ante cost of capital, and 23 for the ex post measures. There are 23 countries in all the non-U.S. average cost of capital measures.

emerging markets, as well as in the United States and Japan (see Fan, Titman, and Twite, 2004). Dividend relief and dividend imputation systems attempt to reduce the distortion that favors the use of debt over equity, by reducing taxes on dividends at either the indi-

---

risk rating, which itself captures various country-level risks, including political risk. The second ex post measure assigns a higher equity risk premium to those countries that display higher equity market volatility relative to U.S. equity markets.

[16]The cost of equity capital in emerging markets is also affected by the lack of liquidity on local stock exchanges. Since issues of stock market liquidity were discussed in earlier issues of the GFSR (see also Mathieson and others, 2004), this chapter focuses on transparency and governance issues in emerging markets.

Table 4.3. Bankruptcy Costs and Legal Rights, 2004

Country	Borrowers and Lenders' Legal Rights Index[1]	Contract Enforcement[2]		Bankruptcy Costs[3]	
		Time (In days)	Cost (In percentage of debt)	Time (In years)	Cost (In percent of estate)
China	2	241	25.5	2.4	18
India	4	425	43.1	10	8
Korea	6	75	5.4	1.5	4
Malaysia	8	300	20.2	2.3	18
Thailand	5	390	13.4	2.6	38
Asia	**5**	**286**	**22**	**4**	**17**
Czech Republic	6	300	9.6	9.2	18
Hungary	5	365	8.1	2	23
Poland	2	1000	8.7	1.4	18
Russia	3	330	20.3	1.5	4
Turkey	1	330	12.5	2.9	8
Eastern Europe	**3**	**465**	**12**	**3**	**14**
Argentina	3	520	15	2.8	18
Brazil[4]	2	566	15.5	10	8
Chile	4	305	10.4	5.6	18
Colombia	4	363	18.6	3	1
Mexico	2	421	20	1.8	18
Latin America	**3**	**435**	**16**	**5**	**13**
Emerging Markets	**4**	**395**	**16**	**4**	**15**
Germany	8	184	10.5	1.2	8
Japan	6	60	8.6	0.5	4
United States	7	250	7.5	3	8
Mature Markets	**7**	**165**	**9**	**2**	**7**

Source: World Bank/IFC, Doing Business database.

[1]The index measures the degree to which collateral and bankruptcy laws facilitate lending. The index ranges from 0 to 10, with higher scores indicating that collateral and bankruptcy laws are better designed to expand access to credit. This is the case when secured creditors are able to seize their collateral when a debtor enters reorganization—that is, there is no "automatic stay" or "asset freeze" imposed by the court; when secured creditors are paid first out of the proceeds from liquidating a bankrupt firm, as opposed to other parties, such as government or workers, and when management does not stay during reorganization, but instead an administrator is responsible for managing the business during reorganization.

[2]To measure the differences in contract enforcement, the evolution of a payment dispute is analyzed. In particular, the number of days from the moment the plaintiff files the lawsuit in court until the moment of actual payment, as well as the associated cost in court fees, attorney fees, and payments to accountants and advisors.

[3]The examination of bankruptcy covers the whole process leading up to filing for bankruptcy proceedings, including the petition hearing, the court's decision, and the sale of assets. The time measure captures the average time to complete the bankruptcy procedure, including delays due to legal derailment. The cost measure includes court costs as well as fees of insolvency lawyers and accountants, as a percentage of the estate value of the bankrupt business.

[4]See footnote 17 in the text.

vidual or the corporate level. Although a thorough calculation of so-called tax shields is quite involved, estimates in Beck, Demirgüç-Kunt, and Maksimovic (2002) suggest that high corporate tax rates may be one of the factors behind relatively high leverage in Asian countries.

As firms are perceived to get closer to financial distress, the increased cost deters further debt issuance. The costs of financial distress are particularly severe in emerging markets, and are a major obstacle to issuing debt

instruments. Table 4.3 shows that creditors' rights are much weaker in emerging markets, and this is reflected in contract enforcement and bankruptcy costs that, in many cases, are double of those in the mature markets. With the notable exceptions of Korea, Malaysia, and the Czech Republic, creditor rights are much lower than in the G-3 countries. Contract enforcement is estimated to add more than 10 percentage points to the cost of debt in our sample of emerging markets, except for countries in central Europe and

Korea (Table 4.3). The process of bankruptcy could take up to 10 years in Brazil and India.[17]

One of the main factors behind the reticence of investors to buy equity from emerging market corporates is the potential conflict of interest between managers and controlling shareholders (insiders) and minority shareholders—sometimes referred to as "agency costs" of insider discretion. Insiders can expropriate outside investors through higher than market salaries and perquisites, adapting investment and operations for their own benefit, or through the direct capture of assets or cash flows (referred to as "tunneling"). Investors can protect themselves against such expropriations through various mechanisms of monitoring and control, such as compensation packages that align managers' and shareholders' interests, supervision by independent directors and external committees, and the threat of takeovers.[18]

The mechanisms to protect investors against these conflicts of interests are particularly costly and imperfect in emerging markets, and analysts have stressed that this factor is important in constraining not just financing choices for emerging market corporates but also, more generally, the flow of capital from mature to emerging markets.[19] The low level of *transparency* in emerging equity markets, coupled with *weak protection of shareholders' rights* and *concentrated ownership structures,* are the main factors behind this important obstacle to achieving a better financing mix in emerging markets, in particular to financing through marketable securities. The next sections review the latest studies on these issues and present examples of successful, as well as unsuccessful, experiences in emerging markets.

Financial Transparency

There are two separate issues related to better corporate transparency and investor protection. The first refers to the accuracy and timeliness of financial statements. This in turn relates to the accounting and auditing standards adopted and enforced in a country, and the frequency with which financial statements are publicly disclosed. The second refers to the timely disclosure of material information, such as the release of detailed offering prospectuses, changes in ownership structure, and related party transactions, among other things.

It is generally recognized that emerging market accounting standards and their enforcement are weaker than in mature economies. Moreover, a study by Mitton (2002) showed that the low quality of available information was one of the main factors behind the outflow of capital during the Asian crisis. More generally, data compiled by López de Silanes (2002) show that developing countries rank on average lower than mature economies in terms of accounting standards (see Table 4.4). Although major improvements have occurred in this area over the last five years or so, in particular in countries that suffered crises, more work needs to be done.

Indeed, much of the improvement has been in the *national* accounting and auditing standards in many emerging markets, but it has not been in terms of comparability across countries. In the current globalized environment, investors seek investment opportunities all over the world and companies seek out capital at the best price almost anywhere. This creates a problem for investors in that national accounting differences can com-

---

[17]The Brazilian Congress approved a new bankruptcy regime in December 2004 that will speed up restructurings and improve investors' collection rights. Analysts have noted that the new bankruptcy system should boost confidence in corporate debt instruments (*International Finance Review*, 2004).

[18]Debt finance is also seen as a way to better align the incentives of the insiders with those of the shareholders (see Myers, 2001), because it commits insiders to invest funds wisely, rather than on projects that might garner private benefits for insiders.

[19]See, for example, Henry and Lorentzen (2003). These institutional weaknesses also constrain cross-border mergers and acquisitions; issues on FDI will be addressed in forthcoming issues of the GFSR.

Table 4.4. Investor Protection by Country

Country	Accounting Standards	Rule of Law[1]	Judicial Efficiency	Contract Repudiation	Expropriation Risk	**Country Average[2]**
Argentina	4.5	5.4	6	4.9	5.9	**5.3**
Brazil	5.4	6.3	5.8	6.3	7.6	**6.3**
Chile	5.2	7	7.3	6.8	7.5	**6.8**
Colombia	5	2.1	7.3	7	7	**5.7**
Mexico	6	5.4	6	6.6	7.3	**6.3**
Latin America	**5.2**	**5.2**	**6.5**	**6.3**	**7.1**	**6.1**
China						
India	5.7	4.2	8	6.1	7.8	**6.4**
Korea	6.2	5.4	6	8.6	8.3	**6.9**
Malaysia	7.6	6.8	9	7.4	8	**7.8**
Thailand	6.4	6.3	3.3	7.6	7.4	**6.2**
Asia	**6.5**	**5.7**	**6.6**	**7.4**	**7.9**	**6.8**
Czech Republic	. . .	. . .	. . .	. . .	. . .	. . .
Hungary	. . .	. . .	. . .	. . .	. . .	. . .
Poland	. . .	. . .	. . .	. . .	. . .	. . .
Russia	. . .	. . .	. . .	. . .	. . .	. . .
Turkey	5.1	5.2	4	6	7	**5.5**
Emerging Europe	**5.1**	**5.2**	**4**	**6**	**7**	**5.5**
Emerging Markets (15)	**5.6**	**5.4**	**5.7**	**6.6**	**7.3**	**6.1**
Germany	6.2	9.2	9	9.8	9.9	**8.8**
Japan	6.5	9	10	9.7	9.7	**9**
United States	7.1	10	10	9	10	**9.2**
G-3	**6.6**	**9.4**	**9.7**	**9.5**	**9.9**	**9**
Mean for 24 Less-Developed Countries	**3.8**	**4.7**	**6.3**	**6.1**	**6.7**	**5.5**
Mean for 25 Developed Countries	**6.4**	**9.1**	**9.1**	**9.2**	**9.5**	**8.7**

Sources: Yale University, International Institute for Corporate Governance; and staff estimates.

[1]The original source of the Rule of Law data is the *International Country Risk Guide* by the PRS Group. It is composed of two measures: the "law" subcomponent assesses the strength and impartiality of the legal system and the "order" subcomponent assesses popular observance of the law. Thus, a country can enjoy a high rating in terms of its judicial system, but a low rating if it suffers from a very high crime rate or if the law is routinely ignored without effective sanctions (for example, during widespread illegal strikes).

[2]This is a simple average of the five indicators in the previous columns.

pletely obscure their comparative assessments of various (global) investment opportunities.[20]

As a result in part of these investors' needs, and the desire to widen the investor base available to companies seeking capital, there has been an increasing push for the international convergence of accounting standards. International organizations such as IOSCO and the Financial Stability Forum (FSF) have endorsed the use of International Financial Reporting Standards (IFRS). Indeed, many small developing countries have stopped trying to develop their own national equivalent of GAAP and have instead found it easier

(cheaper) to simply adopt IFRS as their national accounting principles. Also, in a growing number of countries, the regulators allow *foreign* listed firms to report IFRS statements rather than require them to reconcile to their national GAAP (Hong Kong SAR, Japan, Malaysia, Singapore, and Thailand, among others). However, despite more flexibility for foreign listed firms, there remains a large proportion of emerging market economies that have not adopted IFRS for *domestically* listed firms, particularly in Asia and Latin America. Table 4.5 shows that national accounting standards prevail over

[20]Pacter (2003) argues that, despite the provision of reconciliation statements, foreign firms submit financial statements based on their national equivalent of generally accepted accounting principles (GAAP), making it rather difficult to compare them with U.S. firms.

international standards in most of the major emerging markets except for the central European ones.

Corporate Governance

Even under reasonable accounting and reporting standards, conflicts of interests are likely to persist because of corporate governance problems. Table 4.4 summarizes various indices of the major factors underlying investor protection, including accounting standards, rule of law, and judicial efficiency for a number of emerging market and mature economies. Emerging markets scores are in general much lower than those of mature markets, and the deficiencies are bigger in the areas of the rule of law and judicial efficiency.[21]

Early empirical studies have highlighted that the weak investor protection environment and a country's legal origin (e.g., civil versus common law) are significant obstacles to corporates' access to equity finance, and to capital market development (see La Porta and others, 1997, 1998). More recently, several studies have further demonstrated that differences in shareholder rights are associated with differences in equity valuations, firm profitability, and dividend payouts.[22] Moreover, there is also evidence that weaknesses in these factors constrain access to the international bond market.[23] Direct empirical evidence on the relationship between the cost of equity capital and a country's corporate governance environment, which has very recently been found, shows that, after controlling for macro-

Table 4.5. Use of IFRS for Domestically Listed Firms, by 2005

Country	Not Permitted	Permitted but Not Required	Required for Some	Required for All
China			x	
India	x			
Korea	x			
Malaysia	x			
Thailand	x			
Czech Republic				x[1]
Hungary				x[1]
Poland				x
Russia			x[2]	
Turkey		x		
Argentina	x			
Brazil	x			
Chile	x			
Colombia	x			
Mexico	x			

Source: Deloitte-Touche-Tohmatsu International Accounting Standards (www.iasplus.com).

Note: IFRS = International Financial Reporting Standards.

[1]EU and EEA member states are permitted to defer the application of IFRSs until 2007 (1) for companies that only have debt securities listed in a public securities market and/or (2) for companies whose securities are admitted to public trading in a nonmember state and, for that purpose, have been using internationally accepted standards other than IFRSs (such as GAAP) since a financial year that started prior to adoption of the European regulation.

[2]Requirement to use IFRSs being phased over 2004–07.

economic and firm-specific risk factors, stronger corporate governance significantly reduces a firm's cost of equity capital.[24]

Strong external corporate governance has been shown to play an important role in mitigating the effects of financial crises. During the Asian crisis, countries that had weak external corporate governance were particularly vulnerable to a sudden loss of investor confidence (Johnson and others, 2000), displaying stronger stock market declines and exchange rate depreciations than countries with strong

[21]Chile and Malaysia, two emerging markets with remarkable economic performance, score rather well on these two indicators. See Kalter and others (2004) and Meesook and others (2001) for these countries' experiences.

[22]See, for instance, La Porta and others (2002); Lombardo and Pagano (2000); Joh (2003); Klapper and Love (2004); and Doidge, Karolyi, and Stulz (2004).

[23]Investors have been found to demand higher premiums on Yankee bonds (bonds issued by non-U.S. firms in the United States) from corporates located in countries with weak legal institutions and creditor rights. Moreover, Miller and Puthenpurackal (2002) show that going from a country with a governance level such as Mexico's to a country such as the United Kingdom lowers the annual yield on an issued Yankee bond by 58 basis points.

[24]Hail and Leuz (2004) estimate the decline in the cost of equity capital to be 220 basis points when going from the 25th to the 75th percentile (improvements) of a securities regulation index that captures investor protection in that country. This is roughly half the difference between the U.S. cost of capital and the average cost across a sample of developing countries.

Table 4.6. Countries with a Code of Good Corporate Governance

Country	Existence of Code	Date	Mandatory Compliance Level
Latin America			
Argentina	n		
Brazil	y	June 2002	E
Chile	n		
Colombia	y	August 2003	
Mexico	y	January 1999	E
Asia			
China	y	January 2001	P
India	y[1]	April 1998	E
Korea	y	March 1999	E
Malaysia	y	March 2000	P
Thailand	n[2]		
Emerging Europe			
Czech Republic	y	June 2004	E
Hungary	y	February 2002	E
Poland	y	September 2002	E
Russia	y	April 2002	E
Turkey	y	June 2003	E

Sources: OECD, 2003, "White Paper on Corporate Governance in Latin America"; European Corporate Governance Institute website; and Weil, Gotshal, and Manges, 2000, "International Comparison of Corporate Governance: Guidelines and Codes of Best Practice in Developing and Emerging Markets."

Note: y = yes; n = no; E = comply or explain; P = parts of code mandated.

[1]India has incorporated directly into law many of the recommendations from various special committee reports on corporate governance.

[2]Although Thailand does not have a code for corporate governance, the Thai stock exchange does have a Code of Best Practice for Directors of Listed Companies.

governance. In this case, cross-country differences in legal systems seemed to have played an equally important role as the usual macroeconomic factors that contributed to the crisis. Although weak corporate governance likely did not trigger the Asian crisis, it seems to have made countries and firms in the region more vulnerable, exacerbating the crisis once it had begun.

In part as a result of these crises, and following recommendations from the FSF and the publication of the OECD Principles of Corporate Governance, most emerging markets have established codes of good corporate governance (see Table 4.6). The IMF and the World Bank have been assigned the key task of monitoring and evaluating countries' compliance with many of the standards proposed by the FSF (see Goldstein, 2005). The IMF–World Bank initiative on standards and codes has endorsed three "market integrity" standards—the OECD's Principles of Corporate Governance, the International Accounting Standards Board (IASB), and the International Federation of Accountants' International Standards on Auditing—and is working with UNCITRAL toward a single standard on insolvency and creditor rights (see IMF, 2003b). The World Bank assesses the observance of these standards, typically on a stand-alone basis, and the Standards and Codes are also included in the Financial Sector Assessment Programs (FSAPs). Through these mechanisms, the official sector has contributed to the dissemination and adoption of better governance practices.

Other international organizations have also contributed to raise the awareness about the importance of corporate governance in emerging markets. In particular, the Institute of International Finance (IIF) has also published a set of guidelines on corporate governance and has conducted assessments in seven emerging markets—Brazil, China, Korea, Mexico, Poland, Russia, and South Africa. They describe, in broad terms, South Africa, Korea, and Mexico as having a relatively high level of corporate governance, with Poland somewhere in between these three and the other three countries in terms of ranking.[25] Separately, the IIF (2005) notes that India's equity market in recent years has benefited from the recognition that its corporate governance and transparency standards are superior to those in most emerging markets, a leading factor supporting the recent growth of primary equity markets in India.

[25]The IIF's revised corporate governance guidelines were published in May 2003 and are available via the Internet at www.iif.com—together with the country assessments.

Although many emerging markets have adopted corporate governance principles and rules that are not substantially different from the OECD principles, in many jurisdictions corporate governance practices often fall short in terms of implementation or enforcement. For instance, several FSAP assessments have found that the disclosure requirements for related-party transactions were too weak and have recommended broadening the definition of related parties. Also, a recent FSAP assessment of corporate governance in Korea highlighted the need for more effective enforcement of the legislative changes that have been put in place since the Asian crisis. The fact that good corporate governance practices have not taken hold in the Korean corporate sector illustrates the minority shareholders' lack of success in forcing corporations to adhere to good governance standards.[26] Moreover, the Asian Corporate Governance Association (ACGA) has noted that, with the exceptions of Singapore and Taiwan Province of China, it is not easy for minority shareholders to remove a director convicted of fraud or other serious corporate crime (see Allen, 2004).

In analyzing the issue of enforcement, recent studies have shown that specific regulations that support "private enforcement" or market discipline tend to be more effective than those that support "public enforcement," over and above the effect stemming from the legal institutions of a country.[27] Public enforcement refers to market supervision by the securities regulator and its investigative powers. Private enforcement refers to measures that make it easier for investors to make informed decisions and to take remedial action when deceived—including laws and regulations stipulating various disclosure requirements, such as details on director compensation and the firm's ownership structure, and disclosure of related party transactions—as well as where the burden of proof is placed in securities civil suits.[28] Empirically, a particularly important aspect of market discipline is the level of material information disclosure requirements in a country.[29]

Corporate governance measures that improve investor protection facilitate issuance by increasing the investor base, but compliance with the measures may be burdensome for small corporates and increase the cost of issuance. This is a difficult trade-off that the authorities and market participants have to assess in each country, and there are examples of the tensions in both mature and emerging markets. For instance, a number of European firms have been considering delisting from U.S. stock exchanges as a result of the costs associated with Sarbanes-Oxley provisions. Also, in 2002, the Hong Kong stock exchange (HKEx) had to back away from proposals to introduce quarterly reporting and increase the number of independent directors on companies' boards. Some respondents to the HKEx proposal noted that quarterly reporting

[26]Specifically, there have been some cases in which executive directors convicted and imprisoned for fraudulent offenses against their firms have been reappointed to the same firm by its board of directors (see *Euromoney*, 2004).

[27]For example, La Porta, López de Silanes, and Shleifer (2003) find that, when measures of private and public enforcement are used, civil law is not an important determinant of equity market development, contrary to the findings of previous studies. Fan, Titman, and Twite (2004) also found that, after controlling for corruption, the legal system per se, that is, whether common or civil law, plays a somewhat less important role than previously believed. Rajan and Zingales (2003b) also argue that the main impediment is not the legal system but interest groups that create barriers to access finance and impede the deepening of financial markets.

[28]In the least investor-friendly regimes, the burden of proof falls on the investors, who must show that the corporation was grossly negligent or fraudulent, while at the other extreme, it is the firm that must prove that they did what was necessary (due diligence) to stay within the law.

[29]Hail and Leuz (2004) report that extensive disclosure requirements significantly reduce the cost of equity capital for firms. By going up from the 25th to the 75th percentile of the disclosure requirements index (i.e., moving up to better disclosure), the average cost of equity capital declines by 90 basis points.

would sharply increase the companies' cost and lead investors to focus too much on short-term profits, while a shortage of "quality" director candidates would also make the second requirement rather costly. In the end, the HKEx left the rules unchanged but incorporated the proposals into the exchange's nonmandatory code of best practice.

Besides disclosure and the associated market discipline, there are other private sector initiatives that enhance private enforcement mechanisms for protecting minority shareholders' rights, are likely to prove quicker to implement, and are perhaps more effective than government initiatives. For example, binding arbitration dispute settlement procedures, such as the one put forward by the Brazilian stock exchange (Bovespa), would allow corporate governance enforcement mechanism to overcome weaknesses in the judicial system of some emerging markets.[30]

One of the first things that many jurisdictions have sought to improve is the structure and responsibility of the board of directors of a corporation. Many have put in place rules that mandate a minimum number of independent directors, but recent research has shown that there is a negative relation between firm performance and the number of outside directors, which seems to result from a firm's willingness to add directors without any regard to their expertise or qualifications. In particular, the ACGA has noted that, of the 10 large Asian markets that have a national code of best practice based on international standards, only India, Malaysia, the Philippines, and Taiwan Province of China have a truly robust definition of what constitutes an independent director (Allen, 2004). However, firms perform better when there exist various board committees (particularly audit committees), when directors from financial institu-

tions sit on the board, and when there is a minimum number of outside directors that sit on the audit committee (Erickson and others, 2003). Thus, there is an important role for the staff of financial and auditing institutions in providing guidance on the boards of nonfinancial corporations.

The introduction of "voluntary" codes of (good) corporate governance across many emerging markets, developed by public-, private-, and academic-sector groups or the local stock exchanges is another example of private sector interests enhancing the corporate governance environment. In most emerging markets, the codes are adopted by corporations, on a "comply or explain" basis. By having to note publicly which aspects of the code they do not comply with, the corporations subject themselves to market discipline and greater disclosure. In some jurisdictions, compliance with parts of the code is mandatory. For example, in June 2003, the Chinese securities commission enforced the strict compliance with their code's requirement that one-third of a corporation's board of directors be independent. This was done after the securities commission found widespread disregard for this important aspect of the code. A relatively straightforward way to further enhance the corporate governance in emerging markets would be for the authorities to mandate adherence to all or parts of their country's code.

Finally, individual firms can themselves be proactive and voluntarily institute higher governance standards in their corporate charter. In many cases firms have done so in response to active efforts by institutional investors. Examples of this are Cemex in Mexico, and Ultrapar and CCR in Brazil, whose securities have been rewarded by early actions to improve several aspects of corporate governance (see O'Brian, 2003). Institutional

---

[30]Other improvements in the Bovespa include the introduction of three new listing levels—Levels 1 and 2, and the Novo Mercado—that carry more stringent corporate governance standards than do basic listings, including issue-only voting stock, offer full tag-along rights, maintain a free float of 25 percent, and disclose quarterly its financial statements on a consolidated basis using either IFRS or U.S. GAAP (see IIF, 2004; and IMF, 2003a).

investors, both local and international, have played an increasingly active role in developing better corporate governance standards, in particular in Latin America. There are several examples in Latin America of local institutional investors who held minority voting stakes in firms and were "frozen out" of many mergers and acquisition transactions, receiving little of the profits from the sale of the firms to new entities. Local institutional investors played an important role in prodding a series of legislative and private initiatives in these countries in the late 1990s and early 2000s (Jordan and Lubrano, 2002). Some foreign institutional investors have also singled out the practice of family members issuing nonvoting shares to raise capital while retaining control as the main problem in corporate governance in Latin America, and have campaigned actively to change it.

Concentrated Ownership

A particularly detrimental effect on an emerging market firm's valuation and its ability to access capital markets result from a high degree of concentrated ownership where insiders possess control rights in excess of their proportional ownership (cash flow rights) and are able to extract private benefits from this control via tunneling or opaque related-party transactions that siphon off firm value at the expense of those shareholders that hold a minority of voting or control rights. The separation of cash flow rights and voting rights can be achieved through cross-

holdings or pyramid structures in which one firm is controlled by another firm, which may itself be controlled by some other entity and so forth. Alternatively, this can be achieved via dual-class shareholding structures in which insiders (managers or controlling families) hold shares with superior (to their ownership or cash-flow) voting rights. Several studies have documented that outside investors discount strongly the shares of firms with severe agency problems that stem from concentrated control—over and above other weaknesses in external governance levels.[31]

Concentrated ownership and poor corporate governance tend to also constrain the supply of equity capital to emerging markets. Specifically, there is evidence that firms with insiders who have sufficient control rights to allow them to expropriate other investors attract significantly less U.S. equity flows, and that the impact of weak internal governance is magnified in countries with poor external governance (see Lins and Warnock, 2004).[32]

Many would argue that outside the United Kingdom and the United States, concentrated ownership is commonplace in mature economies, and wonder why emerging market policymakers should be concerned about controlling family or pyramidal corporate structures. However, Table 4.7 shows how, across emerging markets, private benefits of control, as measured by the control premium, are in general much higher than in mature markets.[33] Across 18 emerging markets, the average control premium is roughly 19 percent, while for developed economies the average

[31]See, for example, Claessens and others (2002). A large number of studies documents the importance of both tunneling and private benefits of control in countries whose large corporate sectors are dominated by pyramidal and other business groups (see Morck, Wolfenzon, and Yeung, 2004).

[32]In particular, Korean chaebol firms with concentrated ownership experienced a larger drop in stock value than other firms during the crisis. However, Korean firms that had unaffiliated (to insiders) foreign block ownership or a U.S. ADR listing experienced smaller share price declines during the crisis (Baek, Kang, and Park, 2004). Cumulative stock returns of roughly 800 firms across East Asia for which insiders had high levels of control rights but few cash flow rights were found to be 10 to 20 percent lower than those of other firms during the Asian crisis (Lemmon and Lins, 2003).

[33]These data are derived by comparing the price of block share transactions that results in a change of control of a firm with the market value of the stock the day before the transaction's announcement. This difference provides a measure of the control premium.

Table 4.7. Estimates of Average Firm-Level Private Benefits of Control Across Countries

Country	Control Premium
Argentina	18.30
Brazil	65.50
Chile	16.00
Colombia	28.20
Mexico	34.80
Latin America	**32.60**
China	. . .
India	. . .
Korea	12.80
Malaysia	9.00
Thailand	11.10
Asia	**10.97**
Czech Republic	56.30
Hungary	. . .
Poland	4.50
Russia	. . .
Turkey	36.40
Emerging Europe	**32.40**
Emerging Markets (15)	**22.90**
Germany	3.80
Japan	−3.20
United States	3.70
G-3	**1.40**
Average of 18 Less-Developed Markets	**19.20**
Average of 20 Mature Markets	**5.70**

Source: Dyck and Zingales, 2004, Table 3.
Note: Data based on 1990–2000 sample of transactions.

level is 6 percent. This data suggest that, without the mitigating external corporate governance mechanisms that are typically found in mature economies, controlling shareholders find it substantially easier to expropriate private benefits from emerging market corporations.[34]

Unfortunately, concentrated ownership is one of the most pervasive problems in emerging market corporate governance and one that is difficult to solve. Morck, Wolfenzon, and Yeung (2004) argue that concentrated corporate ownership structures are hard to dismantle because of the political power they confer on their controlling shareholders, and

thus are quite persistent. Indeed, Krueger (2002), Rajan and Zingales (2003b), and others argue that politically connected controlling shareholders of large business groups may deliberately impede the development of institutions that permit low-cost market transactions so as to preserve the status quo. Moreover, this might retard economic development in many low-income countries. In addition, these controlling shareholders tend to become entrenched in the financial and political landscape of the country, perpetuating the problem.

Financial System Design

Banks are the dominant source of debt financing in emerging markets, and although there are several reasons for this dominance, banks are likely to complement and reinforce the development of securities markets. Indeed, overcoming the institutional constraints discussed so far is likely to help develop both banks and markets as complementary sources of funding for the corporate sector.

Analysts have suggested that in several European countries and Japan, the market power of banks had impeded the development of securities markets until the late 1980s.[35] Banks can do this by controlling access to distribution networks, or by encouraging regulations that increase the cost of issuance and underwriting of securities. In Japan, for instance, until 1987 the issuance conditions of corporate bonds were determined by a "Bond Committee," controlled by the major commercial banks. The bond issuance conditions were unfavorable to the development of the corporate bond market and involved the use of collateral, high management fees, and quantitative limits related to the company's equity.

---

[34]Dyck and Zingales (2004) find that a one standard deviation increase in an index measuring accounting standards reduces control premiums by 9 percent and a one standard deviation increase in law enforcement decreases the value by 7 percent.

[35]Schinasi and Smith (1998); and Rajan and Zingales (2003a).

However, the last two decades have witnessed an expansion of securities markets everywhere (Rajan and Zingales, 2003a). Moreover, the recent growth of corporate bond markets in the EU and Canada demonstrate that banks and markets can grow in tandem and actually support and complement each other. In Canada, corporations have increasingly become dependent on market-based financing over the 1980s and 1990s as banking legislation changes allowed banks to become increasingly involved in financial market activities such as underwriting and brokerages services (Calmès, 2004). In particular, loan financing by Canadian nonfinancial corporations declined from 40–50 percent of total funding in the early 1980s to 20 percent in 2004, as bond and equity financing increased.

In emerging markets, growth of bank corporate lending and local securities markets seem to have largely moved together—except perhaps for some cyclical episodes. Figure 4.9 presents a scattered plot of bond and stock market capitalization versus bank lending to corporates that also suggests a positive association on a cross-section basis. Although countries may not deepen both sources of funding in a monotonic way, there does not seem to be a negative association between them. Moreover, in cases such as Korea and Malaysia, measures to improve the institutional framework together with the recapitalization of the banks have contributed to the joint growth of both sources of funding.

Similarly, the rapid growth of institutional investors has been highly supportive of market-based sources of funding. As noted in IMF (2004a), the growth of local institutional investors, and the increased participation of global institutional investors, have contributed to the development of local securities and derivatives markets. Although this impact has been mostly felt in government bond markets, corporate bond markets have started to also share the positive influence of institutional investors and their need for long-term securities.

Figure 4.9. Outstanding Bank Loans and Securities
(In percent of GDP)

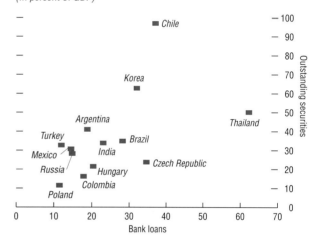

Sources: Dealogic; IMF, *International Financial Statistics*; and IMF staff estimates.

115

Vulnerabilities Associated with the Level and Composition of Corporate Finance

In response to the constraints and obstacles to adequate and diversified sources of funding discussed above, as well as to the risks of macroeconomic instability, emerging market corporates tend to rely more heavily on foreign currency and short-term debt instruments. As with the sovereign, this particular composition of liabilities in the corporate sector leads to vulnerabilities that suggest that lower leverage ratios than in the mature markets may be desirable.[36] This section analyzes this issue for emerging market corporates, provides new evidence on the persistence and severity of currency and maturity mismatches, and discusses different approaches toward monitoring these vulnerabilities.

Corporate Sector Currency and Maturity Mismatches

It is generally acknowledged that aggregate balance sheet mismatches pose serious problems for policymakers. Both currency and maturity mismatches can exacerbate the impact of exogenous shocks in emerging markets, increase the severity of crises, and slow down the postcrisis adjustment. Although aggregate mismatches seem to have lessened in recent years (Goldstein and Turner, 2004), corporate sector balance sheet mismatches remain at high levels.

Many analysts have argued that excessive short-term debt, liability dollarization, and the use of foreign jurisdictions are endogenous ways of coping with systemic risks and financial underdevelopment prevalent in emerging markets.[37] Indeed, weaknesses in macroeconomic policies and financial market frictions contribute to higher instability of the operating environment in emerging markets compared with mature markets, complicate financial contracting, and limit the available sources of funding for local firms. First, the "original sin" problem prevents both emerging market sovereigns and corporates from issuing domestic currency debt abroad.[38] Second, the relative underdevelopment of local capital markets often prevents local firms from issuing domestic debt in long tenors or effectively hedging their currency and duration risk exposures through financial derivatives. Third, weak institutions and corporate governance problems limit firms' access to equity financing. Thus, an emerging market firm that is unable to obtain long-term funding locally faces a trade-off between financing long-term investments with short-term local currency liabilities, which creates a *maturity mismatch*, or borrowing long-term in foreign currency, which creates a *currency mismatch*.

The precise measurement of the corporate sector balance sheet mismatches in emerging markets is complicated by the fact that the microlevel data on the currency composition of debt are difficult to come by. The firm-level data used in this study come from two sources: the *Emerging Markets Corporate database* (IMF) and the *IADB Corporate Balance Sheet database*, which are described in detail in the Appendix. In the following discussion, the estimated outstanding stocks of the foreign-currency-denominated bonds and syndicated loans will be used as proxies for corporates' foreign debt stocks.[39] To examine the characteristics of the foreign debt issuers, each country sam-

---

[36]This argument has been forcefully made for the sovereign sector in Reinhart, Rogoff, and Savastano (2003).

[37]See, for example, Caballero and Krishnamurthy (2003); and de la Torre and Schmukler (2004).

[38]"Original sin" refers to the inability of emerging markets to borrow abroad in their own local currencies, which forces them to issue in foreign currencies to capture foreign savings and exposes them to foreign currency risk.

[39]This methodology follows the approach used in the recent World Bank study (Ratha, Suttle, and Mohapatra, 2003) and is described in the Appendix. Its main limitation is that the foreign debt estimates do not include the nontraded portion of the foreign currency liabilities (i.e., foreign bank loans) as well as the dollar-linked bonds issued locally, and therefore represent lower-bound estimates of the firms' foreign debt.

ple is split into two groups: *market participants,* that is, those firms that have issued foreign-currency-denominated debt in international capital markets, and *nonparticipants.*

The examination of the debt structures of market participants and nonparticipants reveals some interesting patterns. First, nonparticipants are on average more dependent on short-term financing than market participants (see Table 4.8).[40] This seems plausible because those firms that do not borrow from international capital markets are more likely to rely primarily on bank loans and local currency bonds of shorter maturities. Second, the "foreign debt-to-total debt" ratios of market participants appear to be higher than their "short-term debt-to-total debt" ratios in most emerging markets, with very few exceptions.[41] The latter is in line with other studies that note the dominance of dollar contracts over short-duration contracts in Latin America.[42] Third, a relatively sharp decline in the share of foreign debt in total debt is often associated with an increase (albeit temporary) in the share of short-term debt in total debt. This supports the view that both short-term debt and dollar debt can be viewed as alternative mechanisms for coping with a highly volatile environment in emerging markets. It also suggests that it is not possible to obtain an accurate assessment of the corporate sector financial fragility without considering interest rate and exchange rate risk exposures jointly, and not in isolation.

A higher ratio of foreign to total debt is a necessary, but not sufficient, condition for a currency mismatch. To assess the scale of currency mismatches in the nonfinancial sector of an emerging market country, one of the following two approaches could be used: first, the *direct* approach based on accounting data, which amounts to measuring the net foreign currency stock exposure (as the difference between dollar assets and dollar liabilities), and comparing it with an estimate of expected foreign currency earnings. However, this approach is difficult to implement given that information on the currency composition of asset holdings and cash flows of the nonfinancial firms is generally not available. Second, one can gauge the severity of the currency mismatches *indirectly,* by looking at the statistical relationship between foreign currency-to-total debt ratios, and profitability indicators, controlling for other factors that affect corporate earnings. The notion is that the companies that have "unmatched" dollar liabilities should suffer disproportionately more from currency devaluations than those companies that are not exposed to a currency mismatch.[43]

Empirical studies on the balance sheet effects of exchange rate fluctuations on the profitability and investment of firms with dollar debt, that is, those that follow the indirect approach, suggest that vulnerabilities vary substantially across countries and regions. In particular, most studies that focused on Latin American countries found that exchange rate fluctuations had a strong negative balance sheet effect on the level of investment of firms with dollar debt.[44] In contrast, the microlevel studies of the Asian emerging market countries seem to suggest that the balance sheet effect was not as significant as pointed out by early accounts of the

---

[40]The results described above are illustrated in Table 4.8 using the sample averages. However, these results are robust to the changes in the sample period.

[41]In addition, the analysis of the IADB data set confirms that the dollarization of short-term liabilities has always been higher in Latin America than the dollarization of long-term liabilities, especially during 1996–2000.

[42]See, for example, de la Torre and Schmukler (2004).

[43]For example, in the case of exporters, a currency devaluation would have two effects: the competitive effect (raise the expected value of the future export receipts) and the balance sheet effect (increase the local currency value of foreign liabilities and diminish the firms' borrowing capacity).

[44]See Galindo, Panizza, and Schiantarelli (2003) for an overview of these studies.

Table 4.8. Corporate Debt Structures[1]

	Short-Term Debt in Percent of Total Debt			FX Debt in Percent of Total Debt
	Market participants	Nonparticipants		Market participants
Argentina	43.1	60.7	Argentina	51.4
Brazil	23.5	47.9	Brazil	11.1
Chile	21.8	32.8	Chile	34.9
China	48.5	61.9	China	21.3
Colombia	31.3	43.6	Colombia	53.9
Czech Republic	23.9	56.9	Czech Republic	20.4
Hungary	33.0	49.8	Hungary	
India	28.8	34.0	India	20.9
Korea	46.0	57.7	Korea	12.2
Malaysia	35.8	60.0	Malaysia	29.8
Mexico	27.4	35.1	Mexico	16.5
Poland	37.7	63.1	Poland	22.0
Russia	42.7	64.4	Russia	46.8
Thailand	36.5	42.9	Thailand	30.8
Turkey	55.3	65.5	Turkey	12.8
Latin America	29.4	44.0	Latin America	33.6
Asia	39.1	51.3	Asia	23.0
India and China	38.7	48.0	India and China	21.1
Europe	38.5	59.9	Europe	20.4
All Emerging Market Countries	35.7	51.7	All Emerging Market Countries	25.7

	Current Ratio			Quick Ratio	
	Market participants	Nonparticipants		Market participants	Nonparticipants
Argentina	0.8	1.6	Argentina	0.6	1.1
Brazil	1.2	1.3	Brazil	1.0	1.0
Chile[2]	1.4	2.5	Chile[2]	1.0	1.9
China	1.4	1.6	China	0.9	1.1
Colombia[2]	1.9	1.6	Colombia[2]	1.4	1.0
Czech Republic[2]	0.9	1.6	Czech Republic[2]	0.7	1.1
Hungary[2]	1.7	1.7	Hungary[2]	1.1	1.2
India	1.4	1.6	India	0.8	1.0
Korea	0.9	1.1	Korea (South)	0.6	0.8
Malaysia	1.2	1.7	Malaysia	0.9	1.3
Mexico	1.4	2.2	Mexico	1.0	1.5
Poland	1.0	2.2	Poland	0.7	1.4
Russia[2]	1.4	3.0	Russia[2]	1.1	2.3
Thailand	1.3	1.5	Thailand	0.7	1.1
Turkey	1.4	1.7	Turkey[2]	1.0	1.2
Latin America	1.3	1.9	Latin America	1.0	1.3
Asia	1.2	1.5	Asia	0.8	1.1
India and China	1.4	1.6	India and China	0.9	1.1
Europe	1.3	2.1	Europe	0.9	1.4
All Emerging Market Countries	1.3	1.8	All Emerging Market Countries	0.9	1.3

Sources: Worldscope; Dealogic; and IMF staff estimates.
[1]Individual country ratios are value weighted (by firm's total assets). Regional ratios are equal-weighted averages of country ratios. Note on the small sample bias: the average sample size of market participants for 1993–2003 in the Czech Republic, Poland, Turkey, Hungary, and Colombia is less than 10.
[2]Indicates that the difference between market participants and nonparticipants is not statistically significant.

crises.[45] Luengnaruemitchai (2003), for instance, finds that firms with more foreign currency debt increase their investment relative to other firms following the currency

[45]This result may be because of a relatively large share of tradable firms in the sample that had natural foreign exchange hedges. For instance, Malaysian firms in the tradable sector had a ratio of foreign exchange debt to total

depreciation. This result, however, is based on a relatively small sample of the largest publicly traded nonfinancial firms from eight East Asian countries. Also, Allayannis, Brown, and Klapper (2003) find no evidence indicating that unhedged foreign currency debt was associated with significantly worse performance during the Asian crisis.

Using a large data set of the nonfinancial firms from 21 emerging market countries, Ratha, Suttle, and Mohapatra (2003) found that emerging market firms that borrowed abroad during 1992–2001 had lower profit rates (despite lower average cost of credit) than those firms that never borrowed from international capital markets (nonpartici-pants). Moreover, it turned out that foreign borrowing was associated with a larger decline in profitability per unit increase in leverage. Their interpretation of this result is that at high debt levels, the losses from currency depreciations tend to outweigh the benefits of the lower cost of foreign borrowing. Our analysis confirms the findings of Ratha, Suttle, and Mohapatra (2003), that is, market partici-pants (on average) do not appear to be more profitable than nonparticipants.

The use of the direct approach toward measuring the firm's foreign exchange exposure would require information on the currency composition of assets, liabilities, cash flows as well as off-balance-sheet positions, which is rarely available. The analysis of the currency composition of assets and liabilities for a subset of Latin American countries based on the IADB data reveals that the share of dollar assets in total assets (asset dollarization) tends to be much smaller than the share of dollar liabilities in total liabilities (liability dollarization) (see Figure 4.10). This could, in

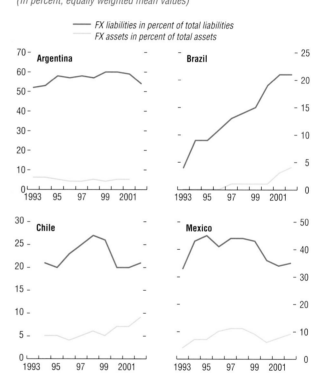

Figure 4.10. Dollarization of Assets and Liabilities in the Nontradable Sector in Latin America
(In percent; equally weighted mean values)

Sources: Inter-American Development Bank database; and IMF staff estimates.

---

liabilities of just 10 percent, while their share of earnings in foreign currency was about 14 percent; in contrast, Indonesian corporates in the nontradable sector had about 35 percent of their liabilities in foreign currency with only 9 percent of earnings in foreign currency, and were hit much harder by the devaluation.

principle, mean that in some cases dollar liabilities could be used as sufficient statistic of the firm's net (stock) dollar exposure (dollar liabilities minus dollar assets). In other cases, however, it is the information on off-balance-sheet derivatives positions that may substantially alter the perception about the overall risk profile of a firm and therefore turn out to be critical for its vulnerability assessment. This issue is particularly important in countries such as Brazil that have experienced a significant growth in foreign exchange rate derivatives trading in recent years. In this regard, Box 4.2 provides new firm-level evidence on the extent and nature of hedging activities of the Brazilian corporate sector during 1996–2002, largely drawn from Kamil (2005). This evidence confirms that the switch to floating exchange rate regimes eliminates the perception of implicit exchange rate guarantees, forcing firms to internalize currency risk and demand hedging instruments.

To gauge the scale of maturity mismatches (and the associated risks) in the corporate sector of an emerging market country, it is not sufficient to look at the ratio of short-term to total debt. A more thorough balance sheet approach should consider standard measures of corporate liquidity, such as the current and quick ratios.[46] A relatively low liquidity ratio indicates that a company may not be able to reduce its current assets for cash in order to meet maturing obligations and, therefore, may be forced to roll over its debt to avoid insolvency. Table 4.8 shows that the liquidity indicators of market participants tend to be lower than those of nonparticipants in all countries and during all time periods. Given that nonparticipants also tend to have relatively higher short-term debt-to-total debt ratios, this means that nonparticipants generally address the potential risks stemming from maturity mismatches by hold-

ing a larger proportion of liquid assets. This is in line with the results of a recent study (Bleakley and Cowan, 2004) that shows that while East Asian firms indeed tended to have more short-term debt than Latin American companies, their short-term liabilities were generally matched with larger holdings of liquid assets.

Overall, despite improvements in some countries, the level of currency and maturity mismatches remains relatively stable over the past 10 years. The short-term debt-to-total debt ratios have been either stable or declining in recent years in most emerging markets, with the exception of Argentina and Hungary. Based on the IADB data, the average firm-level liability dollarization has been either stable or declining moderately in Latin America, with the exception of Brazil, where the level is lower than other countries and is likely to have declined since 2002.

It should be noted, however, that most simple stand-alone measures of balance sheet mismatches do not provide an accurate assessment of the associated risks. First, using precrisis levels of the relevant indicators as the "critical levels" may not always be appropriate. Second, most simple measures of currency and maturity mismatches do not take into account the interaction between interest rate and exchange rate risk factors. This interaction can be captured either through their historical correlations or with a theoretical model reflecting key features of the monetary and exchange rate regime of a particular country. Third, none of these measures takes into account the exchange rate and interest rate volatilities that are critical in assessing any market risk exposure. Fourth, none of these measures gives an indication of the extent to which an increase (decline) in certain balance sheet mismatches may contribute to the deterioration (improvement) of the overall financial health of the

[46]Current ratio is the ratio of current assets to current liabilities; quick ratio is a more conservative measure of liquidity that differs from the current ratio only in that the numerator is reduced by the value of inventories.

corporate sector. All of the above suggest that a more integrated approach, which takes into account the interaction between interest rate, foreign exchange, and credit risks, would be more effective in detecting corporate sector vulnerabilities.

Assessing Corporate Credit Risk

Two approaches to assessing the overall financial health of a company are commonly used by practitioners: traditional financial ratios analysis, based on the accounting information, and the contingent claims approach, which combines the balance sheet data and the market prices of the publicly traded securities of a firm. The financial ratios approach consists in selecting several key financial ratios that are then drawn together in one score, which provides a snapshot of the firm's financial health, for example, the Altman's Z-score. The contingent claims approach uses the well-known Black-Scholes-Merton (BSM) methodology for calculating the probability of default.[47]

Based on an analysis of the average Z-scores for the entire sample of firms, the bankruptcy (credit) risk of market participants does not appear to be significantly lower than that of nonparticipants. This suggests that the ability to borrow abroad is not necessarily associated with higher credit quality. In addition, Figure 4.11 presents the median Altman's Z-scores[48]

---

[47]The BSM method is based on the assumption that the equity value of a firm can be viewed as a European call option on the firm's assets, with the debt value as the strike price. The "distance to default" can therefore be calculated using the standard option pricing equations and interpreted as the number of standard deviations of asset growth by which the market value of assets exceeds its liabilities. Examples on the usefulness of the distance-to-default measure are provided in IMF, 2004b, Chapter 4.

[48]Altman's Z-scores for emerging markets (see Altman, 2000) are weighted averages of the following accounting ratios: working capital/total assets, retained earnings/total assets, earnings before interest and taxes/total assets, and market value equity/book value of total liabilities. A score close to zero indicates that a company is close to bankruptcy/default.

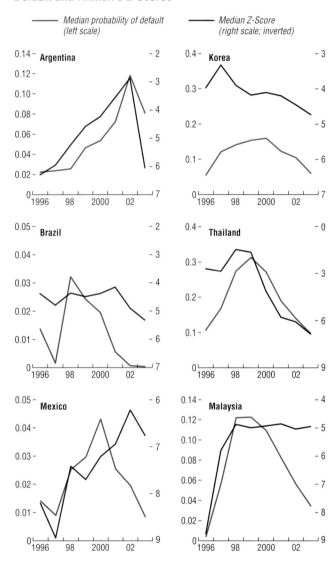

Figure 4.11. Bankruptcy Risk Indicators: Probability of Default and Altman's Z-Scores[1]

Sources: Datastream; Dealogic; Worldscope; and IMF staff estimates.
[1]The bankruptcy indicators presented in the chart are based on the constant samples of firms from the Emerging Market Corporate database (IMF). Only those firms that had sufficiently liquid (actively traded) shares throughout the entire sample period (1993–2003) were included in the sample. For Latin American countries, the average sample size is 16 firms; for Asian countries, the average sample size is 120 firms.

Box 4.2. New Firm-Level Evidence on Hedging Activities in the Nonfinancial Sector in Latin America

Derivatives markets in Latin America are dominated by interest rate and foreign exchange products, which are typically used by local entities to hedge risks associated with raising funds, both domestically and abroad. The most traded instruments in each country tend to be the ones that "match" the hedging needs of local firms, their prevalent capital structures, as well as the key features of local debt markets. For instance, *foreign exchange swaps* are commonly used when the foreign exchange exposure horizon is longer than a year, as in the case of bank loans or corporate bonds. By contrast, *forward contracts* are the preferred hedging instruments when foreign exchange exposure is short term. The latter is often the case in trade financing, where contracts are typically settled in less than a year.

In Colombia, currency forwards account for the bulk of derivatives trading. Most of the derivatives activity has traditionally concentrated in the financial sector, since liability dollarization in Colombia's corporate sector has been extremely low, averaging 5 percent during 1994–2002. However, foreign currency hedging by nonfinancial firms has been increasing in importance in recent years. Consistent with the fact that trade credits make up the bulk of foreign currency liabilities of Colombian firms (Echeverry and others, 2003), almost 90 percent of currency hedging is done through forward contracts (Kamil, 2005). Similarly, in Chile, the main hedging instruments are forwards for short-term foreign exchange rate protection and

currency swaps for longer-term foreign exchange protection, with the former accounting for almost 86 percent of all foreign currency contracts (Cowan, Hansen, and Herrera, 2004). In contrast, the most commonly used instruments to hedge foreign currency exposures in Brazil are currency swaps. This is because the demand for a currency hedge has been primarily driven by firms that issue dollar-denominated or dollar-linked debt. The firm-level evidence presented in the table below confirms that currency swaps constitute over 95 percent of all hedging instruments used by Brazilian firms.

The table below reports key summary statistics on the extent and nature of financial hedging by the Brazilian nonfinancial sector using a sample of 620 companies. This analysis is based on a unique database of derivatives positions compiled from the information contained in the footnotes to annual financial statements (Kamil, 2005). The key "stylized facts" derived from the analysis are as follows:

1. The fraction of firms using some form of financial hedge (swaps, forwards, and/or options) has increased steadily since 1996, reaching 19 percent of the firms in the sample in 2002. This trend becomes most noticeable after 1999, following the floatation of the real.

2. The fraction of net exchange rate exposure (dollar liabilities minus dollar assets) of the average firm, which was hedged via any type of financial derivatives, has increased steadily and reached 14 percent in 2002.

Financial Hedging by Nonfinancial Firms in Brazil, Balanced Sample: 1996–2002
(In percent of total)

| | Fraction of Firms That Use Financial Derivatives | Notional Value of Derivative Position over Net Stock of Dollar Liabilities | | Fraction of Market Participants That Use Financial Derivatives | Use of FX Derivatives by Hedgers by Type of Instrument | | |
		All firms	Market participants		SWAP	FORWARD	OPTION
1996	0	0	0	0	0	0	0
1997	4	3	1	8	88	0	6
1998	6	4	5	11	92	4	4
1999	6	5	8	13	90	6	3
2000	9	6	5	23	98	5	5
2001	12	10	12	25	96	2	2
2002	19	14	20	28	96	4	2

Source: Kamil (2005).

3. Among the companies with outstanding dollar debt in every year, the fraction of those using currency derivatives has risen sharply as well. By contrast, the fraction of firms that have derivatives exposures but no dollar liabilities has remained extremely low. The significant differences in derivative positions across dollar debtors and nondebtors suggest that currency derivatives were unlikely to have been used for speculative purposes.

Evidence presented in the table confirms the widely held, but seldom proven, notion that the switch to a floating exchange rate regime eliminates the perception of implicit exchange rate insurance and forces firms to internalize the exchange rate risk. This is also consistent with the argument that growth in derivatives activity takes off whenever an increase in the exchange rate volatility is sufficient to induce local entities to seek protection against it. Interestingly, in Brazil, it was the government who was the primary provider of currency hedges to the private sector through the issuance of the foreign exchange rate–linked domestic debt throughout 1999–2003.

Finally, both anecdotal and empirical evidence presented in the table suggest that Brazilian firms, which had access to international financial markets ("market participants"), were also active users of interest rate and/or foreign exchange swaps. Market participants would typically find it cheaper to issue dollar-denominated debt abroad and then swap it into Brazilian reals than to issue the real denominated debt locally. Thus, given the strong positive association between foreign debt and the use of foreign currency hedging instruments, one could expect that a sharp decline in the supply of hedge would induce Brazilian firms to reduce their borrowing from

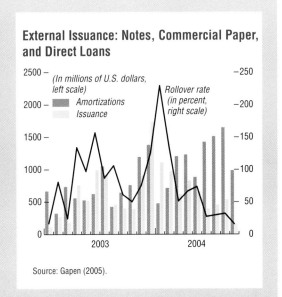

External Issuance: Notes, Commercial Paper, and Direct Loans

(In millions of U.S. dollars, left scale)
■ Amortizations
□ Issuance

Rollover rate *(in percent, right scale)*

Source: Gapen (2005).

abroad. This has indeed been confirmed by recent events. Starting in June 2003, the rollover rate on the government foreign currency–linked debt has been reduced dramatically, from an average of 42 percent in the second half of 2003 to only 7 percent during the first nine months of 2004. As a result, the stock of foreign currency–linked domestic debt and swaps fell from $68 billion at end-May 2003 to $33 billion in September 2004, reducing the supply of foreign currency hedge and pushing up its cost. Higher hedging costs increased the overall cost of borrowing from abroad and contributed to lower rollover rate on foreign debt by Brazilian firms (see the figure), forcing some of them to look for domestic sources of funding. As a result, the corporate issuance in local bond markets rose to over $3 billion during the first nine months of 2004, compared with less than $2 billion in 2003 (see Gapen, 2005).

and probabilities of default for (balanced) subsamples of firms from Argentina, Brazil, Korea, Malaysia, Mexico, and Thailand. Both measures show an overall improvement in the credit quality of the nonfinancial firms in all countries (with the exception of Argentina) since 2000.

Combining the currency mismatch indicators and bankruptcy risk measures allows the examination of the relationship between changes in currency mismatches and changes in the financial health of the corporate sector. Focusing on the nontradable firms in

Latin America (using the IADB database), Figure 4.12 shows two currency mismatch indicators—"total dollar liabilities to net sales" and "short-term dollar liabilities to net sales" ratios—together with a measure of bankruptcy risk (Altman's Z-score).[49] Given that the nontradable firms tend to be most vulnerable to currency depreciations when exposed to currency mismatches, one would expect to see at least some degree of comovement between the mismatch ratios and the Z-scores. Figure 4.12 does indeed suggest that an increase (decline) in a currency mismatch may be associated with a deterioration (improvement) of the corporate credit quality for countries with relatively high liability dollarization, but not for countries where liability dollarization is relatively low.

How well do these measures reflect the overall credit risk of the corporate sector in a particular country? Clearly, simply averaging the risk indicators by country or by industry segment does not take into account possible correlations of bankruptcy risk measures across firms, which may amplify the impact of a small number of corporate failures on the entire sector. In addition, these measures do not take into account the impact of macroeconomic factors on corporate sector vulnerability indicators as some risks for the corporate sector may be of systemic nature and, therefore, nondiversifiable (see Duffie and Wang, 2004). These factors also call for a more integrated assessment of corporate sector vulnerabilities.

Policy Issues

This chapter discussed both structural and surveillance issues related to the corporate

---

Figure 4.12. Foreign Currency Mismatch in the Nontradable Sector in Latin America

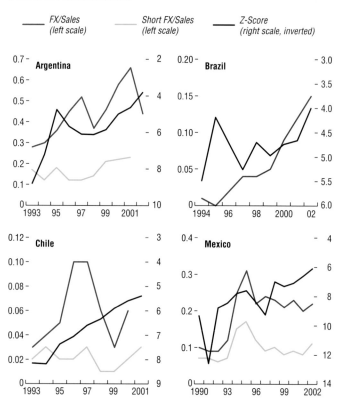

Sources: Inter-American Development Bank database; and IMF staff estimates.

---

[49]These ratios could be considered as reasonably good proxies of currency mismatches in the nontradable sector, as net sales are mostly in local currency. However, they are subject to similar criticisms as the standard macroeconomic external vulnerability indicators, that is, foreign debt-to-GDP and short-term foreign debt-to-GDP ratios. For a more detailed discussion of this issue, see Goldstein and Turner (2004).

sector in emerging markets. Policy issues related to both these aspects are discussed in the next section.

Structural Issues

The corporate sector is the main driver of economic growth, and studies reviewed in this chapter indicate that overall financial development contributes significantly to growth. At the same time, there is no evidence that market-based systems, or bank-based systems, are associated with better economic performance. Although there is agreement that bank-based systems are prevalent when firms and markets are small, transparency and disclosure is low, and the rule of law and judicial efficiency are weak, and many emerging markets have some of these features, financing with market securities has been growing in most emerging markets, and may be desirable for financial stability reasons as well.[50] Rather than promote one system over the other, it is quite clear that emerging markets should improve a number of institutional features that constrain the development of both bank-based and market-based sources of funding for the corporate sector. Indeed, a recent study (Singh and others, 2005) notes that in the context of the resolution of banking crises, several Latin American countries have strengthened the broader institutional framework that will also allow capital markets to grow.[51] Similar reforms were undertaken, to varying degrees, by Asian emerging markets in the wake of the Asian crisis and by European emerging markets in the road to accession to the EU.[52]

Access to external finance depends on factors such as accounting and disclosure, contract enforcement and the cost of financial distress, and the rule of law and judicial effi-

ciency. Many emerging markets have made some progress in these areas, in part aided by the Reports on Observance of Standards and Codes (ROSCs) and FSAPs undertaken by the IMF and the World Bank. However, a lot more needs to be done for securities markets to become a relevant source of funding for the corporate sector, in particular in the areas of implementation and enforcement. Moreover, these policy efforts may not have the benefit of the globalization trends of the 1990s or the catalytic role of crises, thus requiring additional efforts on the part of the authorities. The studies and experiences reviewed in this chapter suggest the following specific measures and lessons to improve the institutional framework in emerging markets:

- *Adoption of international accounting rules.* A number of emerging markets have improved their accounting rules, but efforts to converge to international standards appear to be much slower. Of the medium-size emerging markets, only countries in central Europe have adopted (or are in the process of adopting) IFRS. As demonstrated by the number of firms that cross-list in more investor-friendly markets, countries have to make important efforts in this area to keep the market liquidity at home and facilitate equity issuance in the local market.

- *Require better disclosure of material information and frequent and timely reporting of financial statements.* Emphasis on better disclosure requirements seems to be the most effective governance mechanism. This facilitates market discipline (rather than public regulator enforcement) that is less dependent on the quality of the judicial system of the country than public enforcement. It has been shown to significantly reduce the cost of equity capital for firms.

---

[50]See Mathieson and others (2004) for a discussion of policies aimed at the development of local securities and derivatives markets.
[51]This includes improvements in accounting standards (Mexico and Venezuela), disclosure requirements (Mexico), rotation on external auditors (Brazil and Mexico), and reform of the legal and regulatory framework for bankruptcy (Argentina, Brazil, and Mexico).
[52] See, for instance, Capulong and others (2000); and Feldman and others (2002).

- *However, compliance with enhanced disclosure could be very costly for small corporates.* This is a difficult trade-off that the authorities and market participants have to assess in each country; a gradual approach in consultation with market participants is advisable.
- *Broaden the definition of related party transactions and independent directors, and strengthen minority shareholders' rights to remove directors convicted of fraud or other corporate crimes.* Although many emerging markets have adopted codes of corporate governance that are not substantially different from the OECD principles, in many jurisdictions corporate governance practices often fall short in terms of implementation or enforcement. The three issues above have been signaled as the key weaknesses in implementation and enforcement of the codes.
- *Prioritize the role of auditing committees.* Firms perform better when there exist various board committees (particularly audit committees), when directors from financial institutions sit on the board, and when there is a minimum number of outside directors that sit on the audit committees.
- *Mandate adherence to parts of a country's voluntary code of governance when there is widespread disregard of the code.* This should only be done after consultation with market participants and when there are clear disincentives to adopt the code in a voluntary fashion.
- *Encourage institutional investors to take an active role in corporate governance.* Rapidly growing institutional investors in emerging markets have a vested interest in improved corporate governance and have proven to be effective enforcers in several countries.
- *Promote private sector initiatives that are likely to prove quicker and perhaps more effective than government initiatives.* These could include the use of stock exchanges' binding arbitra-

tion dispute settlement procedures. Such initiatives provide an effective corporate governance enforcement mechanism.
- *Good compliance with a number of corporate governance principles may compensate for the potential problems associated with concentrated ownership.* Although a country's legal or social norms might lead to concentrated control structures in its corporate sector, it need not lead to more private benefits of control if other factors (outside those typically thought as supporting good external governance), such as high ethical standards, independent media coverage, a high degree of market competition, and an effective tax system, are in place.[53]

Finally, particular care should be exercised when adopting policy measures oriented to develop local securities markets or to maximize fiscal revenues that could have long-lasting (negative) effects on ownership concentration, as shown by the experience of Brazil. Efforts to increase the number of firms listed in the stock exchange, while preserving the original owners' control with the allowance of two-thirds of nonvoting shares, led to a structure of shares that permitted control of a company with less than 17 percent of total equity capital. Also, the removal of tag-along rights for minority voting shareholders in order to maximize the revenues from privatization further aggravated this problem. The Brazilian authorities and the stock exchange have made tremendous efforts to reverse these distortions since the mid-1990s and it has been an uphill battle (see IMF, 2003a; and IIF, 2004).

Surveillance Issues

Our analysis shows that emerging market corporates still have a substantial degree of maturity and currency mismatches on their

---

[53]The case of Sweden is often put forward as an example of this. Although Sweden is renowned for its widespread use of dual class share structures (thus ensuring concentrated control rights), it is also renowned for a high level of legal enforcement, low corruption level, and high rate of tax compliance. As such Sweden displays a relatively low level of private benefits of control.

balance sheets. Although these mismatches may not be a concern in the current external environment of low interest rates and appreciating emerging market currencies, they may become a source of financial instability once external conditions become less benign. Since dollarization in emerging markets is often a response to systemic risks and institutional weaknesses, the first best policy measures should be aimed at addressing the underlying problems. In particular, many analysts emphasize the importance of strengthening institutions that promote monetary credibility and fiscal soundness, implementing specific measures of prudential supervision for the banking system (such as special reserves against dollar loans to local currency earning borrowers; see Gulde and others, 2004), as well as developing local financial markets. Policies to achieve the objective of developing local financial markets, including establishing benchmarks, improving market infrastructure, and increasing the role of institutional and foreign investors, were discussed in IMF (2003a).

A systematic assessment of corporate sector vulnerabilities should, therefore, become an integral part of an early warning system of crisis prevention, particularly for emerging market countries. Recent work by the IMF staff on the use of the balance sheet approach (BSA) to detect vulnerabilities in emerging markets has focused on a sector-by-sector analysis and proposed a number of aggregate mismatch indicators for each of the key economic sectors: public sector, financial private sector, and nonfinancial private sector.[54] The staff notes, however, that while data for the first two sectors are often readily available, the nonfinancial private sector data are harder to obtain and, therefore, may have to be derived as a residual. These arguments call for a greater use of the microlevel data, such as the data used in this chapter, for the analysis of corpo-

rate sector vulnerabilities in emerging market countries.

Specifically, the analysis of the debt-related corporate sector vulnerabilities presented in this chapter suggests that

- debt structures may be as important sources of vulnerabilities as debt levels;
- foreign currency asset holdings of emerging market corporates (at least in Latin America) are fairly small compared with foreign liabilities, which implies that mismatch measures based on the currency composition of liabilities could be a good approximation;
- firm-level accounting data should be supplemented (whenever possible) with the information contained in the prices of tradable securities, which is available at higher frequency and is more forward-looking than the balance sheet data;
- firms' exposures to market risk factors (such as exchange rates and interest rates) should be considered jointly, with the associated vulnerability measure reflecting the interaction between these factors; the analysis of vulnerabilities that relies on the historical volatilities of exchange rates, interest rates, and commodity prices should be supplemented with stress testing;
- to integrate these corporate sector vulnerability indicators into the macrofinancial risk assessment of an emerging market, two approaches have proven useful: first, Early Warning Models, which explicitly include one or more corporate sector vulnerability indicators as additional explanatory variables; and, second, macrofinancial models (e.g., Moody's MfRisk Model), which allow an estimation of the risks of default and evaluate risk transfers across the aggregate balance sheets of the corporate, financial, and public sectors.[55] The choice between these two approaches will ultimately depend on data availability as well as on

[54]See Allen and others (2002).
[55]See Gray (2004).

the specific objectives of the vulnerability exercise; and

- finally, a complete assessment of the corporate sector should encompass not just quantitative indicators but also the qualitative information from corporate governance indicators. For instance, leaving aside the well-known vulnerability of short-term liabilities, Korean firms had, in general, good financial ratios (for instance, in terms of profitability, see Joh, 2003) in the wake of the crisis of 1997. However, analysts (for instance, Johnson and others, 2000) have stressed that corporate governance problems had a major role in the propagation and depth of the crisis. Prevention of such crisis in other countries would require monitoring of more qualitative information about potential governance problems.

Appendix

To track the trends in corporate finance in our sample of emerging market countries, we used both macroeconomic and microeconomic information.

Macroeconomic Data Sources

(1) Domestic bank lending data to the private sector and to the nonfinancial private sector from *DX Windows* and *monetary authorities.*

(2) Reserves held by deposit money banks (including currency holdings and deposits with the monetary authorities); claims on government; and demand, time, and foreign currency deposits from the IMF's *International Financial Statistics* (IFS).

(3) International bank lending data from consolidated claims to nonfinancial private sector, and corporate bonds outstanding, from the Bank of International Settlements (BIS).

(4) International bonds syndicated loans and equity from the IMF's *BEL system,* which is based on the information provided by Dealogic Bondware and Loanware.[56]

(5) Domestic equity issuance from *IFC.*

Microeconomic Data Sources

The firm-level data used in this study come from two sources: the *Emerging Markets Corporate database* (IMF) and the *IADB Corporate Balance Sheet database.*

The Emerging Markets Corporate database has been constructed by IMF staff, following the approach used in Ratha, Suttle, and Mohapatra (2003). It builds upon the balance sheet data from Worldscope and is augmented by including the estimated outstanding foreign currency debt stocks for those companies that issued debt in international capital markets during 1990–2003.[57] For each issuer, the outstanding foreign debt series is constructed by summing up all debt issues (syndicated loans and bonds) beginning in 1990, and netting out debt that matured or was paid off during the period, using the IMF's BEL system. The Emerging Markets Corporate database spans 1990 to 2003 and covers most of the publicly traded nonfinancial firms from 15 emerging market countries (see Table 4.9). The final dataset was checked for accounting consistency and outliers, and revised accordingly.

The main advantage of the Emerging Markets Corporate database (compared with

---

[56]Dealogic is a primary information provider on individual syndicated credit facilities and securities. Information is available on the characteristics of the loans and bonds (that is, amount, currency of denomination, maturity, and pricing) and of the borrowers (that is, name, nationality, and business sector).

[57]As in Ratha, Suttle, and Mohapatra (2003), this method ignores outstanding debt issued before 1990. However, because private debt flows to emerging markets were small in the aftermath of the debt crisis of the 1980s, this does not affect the results presented here.

Table 4.9. Nonfinancial Private Sector Firms: Sample Size for 2002

	Emerging Markets Corporate Database			IADB Database Total
	Total	Market Participants	Non-participants	
Argentina	62	16	46	66
Brazil	234	23	211	240
Chile	142	13	129	228
China	1,262	35	1,227	n.a.
Colombia	22	2	20	121
Czech Republic	29	3	26	n.a.
Hungary	31	4	27	n.a.
India	321	63	258	n.a.
Korea	668	99	569	n.a.
Malaysia	662	32	630	n.a.
Mexico	95	22	73	120
Poland	70	4	66	n.a.
Russia	32	11	21	n.a.
Thailand	270	40	230	n.a.
Turkey	149	7	142	n.a.

Source: IMF staff.

Worldscope or Economatica) is that it introduces the distinction between market participants (that is, firms that issued debt in the international capital markets during 1990–2003) and nonparticipants for a wide range of emerging market countries. In addition, the constructed firm-level series of outstanding debt issued in the international capital markets can be used as a first order approximation of the firms' foreign currency debt stocks.

The second source of microlevel information, referred to as the *IADB database*, provides annual accounting and other relevant firm-specific information for approximately 2,000 nonfinancial firms from 10 Latin American countries for 1990–2002.[58] The thrust of the information was collected from annual reports and corporate filings from local stock markets and financial statements from credit registries, regulatory agencies, and/or trade chambers in each country.[59] In addition to basic accounting data, the database also contains other firm-specific information that provides a picture of its production mix and export orientation; access to international financial markets; ownership structure; and multinational affiliation and a history of the main corporate events, including mergers, acquisitions, and privatizations.[60] Table 4.9 provides the number of firm observations per country and year.

The IADB database has several unique features. First, it contains firm-level accounting information on the currency composition of assets and liabilities, the maturity profile of domestic- and foreign-currency-denominated debt and the fraction of exports in total sales. Second, for each country in the sample, the database provides information on both publicly traded and nontraded firms.[61] Third, adding information on international bond and loan issuance (from Dealogic) to the IADB database allows us to jointly consider three key dimensions of the firm's financing choice: currency of denomination (foreign vs. local currency), maturity (short-term vs. long-term), and jurisdiction (domestic vs. foreign).

References

Aghion, Philippe, Peter Howitt, and David Mayer-Foulkes, 2004, "The Effect of Financial Development on Convergence: Theory and Evidence,"

---

[58]The sample includes companies from Argentina, Bolivia, Brazil, Chile, Colombia, Costa Rica, Mexico, Peru, Uruguay, and Venezuela. Five of these countries (Bolivia, Costa Rica, Peru, Uruguay, and Venezuela) are not included in the Worldscope database.

[59]This database builds upon—and substantially expands—the outcome of a Red de Centros Project coordinated by the Inter-American Development Bank. For details, see Galindo, Panizza, and Schiantarelli (2003).

[60]Kamil (2004) provides a detailed account of sources, and method of construction and definition of variables, including several checks performed to ensure that variables' definitions were uniform across countries and that firm-level accounting information was accurate within countries, comparable across economies, and consistent across time.

[61]Most commercial databases—including Worldscope—consist of publicly traded companies, so that smaller and government-owned firms remain typically underrepresented.

NBER Working Paper No. 10358 (Cambridge, Mass.: National Bureau of Economic Research).

Allayannis, George, Gregory W. Brown, and Leora F. Klapper, 2003, "Capital Structure and Financial Risk: Evidence from Foreign Debt Use in East Asia," *The Journal of Finance*, Vol. 58, No. 6, pp. 2667–710.

Allen, Franklin, and Douglas Gale, 2001, *Comparing Financial Systems* (Cambridge, Mass.: MIT Press).

Allen, Jamie, 2004, "Weak Rules Hinder Corporate Governance Reform in Asia," *International Financial Law Review* (November).

Allen, Mark, Christoph B. Rosenberg, Christian Keller, Brad Setser, and Nouriel Roubini, 2002, "A Balance Sheet Approach to Financial Crisis," IMF Working Paper 02/210 (Washington: International Monetary Fund).

Altman E., 2000, "Predicting Financial Distress of Companies: Revisiting the Z-Scores and ZETA Models" (unpublished; New York: New York University).

Baek, Jae-Seung, Jun-Koo Kang, and Kyung Suh Park, 2004, "Corporate Governance and Firm Value: Evidence from the Korean Financial Crisis," *Journal of Financial Economics*, Vol. 71, No. 2, pp. 265–313.

Beck Thorsten, Asli Demirgüç-Kunt, and Vojislav Maksimovic, 2002, "Financing Patterns Around the World: The Role of Institutions," Policy Research Working Paper No. 2905 (Washington: World Bank).

Bleakley, Hoyt, and Kevin Cowan, 2004, "Maturity Mismatch and Financial Crises: Evidence from Emerging Market Corporations," Working Paper No. 2004–16 (San Diego: University of California).

Caballero, Ricardo J., and Arvind Krishnamurthy, 2003, "Excessive Dollar Debt: Financial Development and Underinsurance," *The Journal of Finance*, Vol. 58, No. 2, pp. 867–94.

Calmès, Christian, 2004, "Regulatory Changes and Financial Structure: The Case of Canada," Working Paper No. 2004–26 (Ottawa: Bank of Canada).

Capulong, Ma Virginita, David Edwards, David Webb, and Juzhong Zhuang, 2000, "Recent Corporate Governance Reforms in the Five Affected Countries," in *Corporate Governance and Finance in East Asia: A Study of Indonesia, Republic of Korea, Malaysia, Philippines, and Thailand, Consolidated Report*, Vol. 1 (Manila: Asian Development Bank), pp. 61–72.

Claessens, Stijn, Simeon Djankov, Joseph P.H. Fan, and Larry H.P. Lang, 2002, "Disentangling the Incentive and Entrenchment Effects of Large Shareholdings," *The Journal of Finance*, Vol. 57, No. 6, pp. 2741–71.

Cowan, Kevin, Erwin Hansen, and Luis Oscar Herrera, 2004, "Currency Mismatches, Balance Sheet Effects and Hedging in Chilean Non-Financial Corporations," paper prepared for the Eighth Annual Conference of the Central Bank of Chile, "External Vulnerability and Policies for Prevention," Santiago, Chile.

de la Torre, Augusto, and Sergio Schmukler, 2004, "Coping with Risk Through Mismatches: Domestic and International Financial Contracts for Emerging Economies," Policy Research Working Paper No. 3212 (Washington: World Bank, February).

Demirgüç-Kunt, Asli, and Ross Levine, 2001, *Financial Structure and Economic Growth: A Cross-Country Comparison of Banks, Markets, and Development* (Cambridge, Mass.: MIT Press).

Demirgüç-Kunt, Asli, and Vojislav Maksimovic, 1998, "Law, Finance, and Firm Growth," *The Journal of Finance*, Vol. 53, No. 6, pp. 2107–37.

Doidge, Craig, G. Andrew Karolyi, and René Stulz, 2004, "Why Do Countries Matter So Much for Corporate Governance?" Working Paper No. 50 (Brussels: European Corporate Governance Institute).

Duffie, Darrel, and Ke Wang, 2004, "Multi-Period Corporate Failure Prediction with Stochastic Covariates," NBER Working Paper No. 10743 (Cambridge, Mass.: National Bureau of Economic Research).

Dyck, Alexander, and Luigi Zingales, 2004, "Private Benefits of Control: An International Comparison," *The Journal of Finance*, Vol. 59, No. 2, pp. 537–600.

Echeverry, Juan Carlos, Leopoldo Fergusson, Roberto Steiner, and Camila Aguilar, 2003, "Dollar Debt in Colombian Firms: Are Sinners Punished During Devaluations?" *Emerging Markets Review*, Vol. 4, No. 4, pp. 417–49.

Erickson, John, Yun Park, Joe Reising, and Hyun-Han Shin, 2003, "Board of Directors as an Endogenously Determined Institution and Firm Value: The Canadian Evidence," paper presented at the 3rd Asia Corporate Governance Conference Program, Seoul, Korea, May.

Euromoney, 2004, "Trouble at the Chaebol," December, Vol. 35, No. 428, pp. 24–25.

Fan, Joseph, Sheridan Titman, and Garry Twite, 2004, "An International Comparison of Capital Structure and Debt Maturity Choices" (unpublished; Austin: University of Texas).

Feldman, Robert A., C. Maxwell Watson, and a staff team, 2002, *Into the EU: Policy Frameworks in Central Europe* (Washington: International Monetary Fund).

Galindo, Arturo, Ugo Panizza, and Fabio Schiantarelli, 2003, "Debt Composition and Balance Sheet Effects of Currency Depreciations: A Summary of the Micro-Evidence," *Emerging Markets Review*, Vol. 4, No. 4, pp. 330–39.

Gapen, Michael, 2005, "Balance Sheet Developments and Trends in Corporate Sector Financing in Brazil" (unpublished; Washington: International Monetary Fund).

Glen, Jack, and Ajit Singh, 2003, "Capital Structure, Rates of Return, and Financing Corporate Growth: Comparing Developed and Emerging Markets, 1994–2000" in *The Future of Domestic Capital Markets in Developing Countries*, World Bank/IMF/Brookings Emerging Market Series, ed. by Robert Litan, Michael Pomerleano, and V. Sundararajan (Washington: Brookings Institution Press).

Goldstein, Morris, and Philip Turner, 2004, *Controlling Currency Mismatches in Emerging Markets* (Washington: Institute for International Economics).

Gray, Dale, 2004, "Modeling Sovereign Default Risk and Country Risk Using Moody's MfRisk Framework" (unpublished; Washington: International Monetary Fund).

Gulde, Anne-Marie, David Hoelscher, Alain Ize, David Marston, and Gianni De Nicolo, 2004, *Financial Stability in Dollarized Economies*, Occasional Paper No. 230 (Washington: International Monetary Fund).

Hail, Luzi, and Christian Leuz, 2004, "International Differences in the Cost of Equity Capital: Do Legal Institutions and Securities Regulation Matter?" Working Paper No. 15 (Brussels: European Corporate Governance Institute).

Henry, Peter Blair, and Peter Lombard Lorentzen, 2003, "Domestic Capital Market Reform and Access to Global Finance: Making Markets Work," in *The Future of Domestic Capital Markets in Developing Countries*, Bank/IMF/Brookings Emerging Markets Series, ed. By Robert Litan,

Michael Pomerleano, and V. Sundararajan World (Washington: Brookings Institution Press).

Ibbotson Associates, 2005, "Ibbotson's International Cost of Capital Report" (Chicago: Ibbotson Associates).

International Finance Review (IFR), 2004, "Brazil Overhauls Bankruptcy Law," No. 1564 (December 18), p. 65.

Institute of International Finance, 2004, "Corporate Governance in Brazil, An Investor Perspective," Task Force Report, June (IIF Equity Advisory Group).

———, 2005, "Capital Flows to Emerging Market Economies" (January).

International Monetary Fund, 2003a, *Global Financial Stability Report*, World Economic and Financial Surveys (Washington, March).

———, 2003b, "International Standards: Strengthening Surveillance, Domestic Institutions, and International Markets" (unpublished; Washington: International Monetary Fund). Available via the Internet: *www.imf.org/external/np/pdr/sac/2003/030503s/.htm*.

———, 2004a, *Global Financial Stability Report*, World Economic and Financial Surveys (Washington, April).

———, 2004b, *Global Financial Stability Report*, World Economic and Financial Surveys (Washington, September).

Jayaratne, Jith, and Philip E. Strahan, 1996, "The Finance-Growth Nexus: Evidence from Bank Branch Deregulation," *Quarterly Journal of Economics*, Vol. 111, No. 3, pp. 639–70.

Joh, Sung Wook, 2003, "The Korean Economic Crisis and Corporate Governance System," in *Governance, Regulation, and Privatization in the Asia-Pacific Region*, ed. by Takatoshi Ito and Anne O. Krueger (Chicago: University of Chicago Press), pp. 129–57.

Johnson, Simon, Peter Boone, Alasdair Breach, and Eric Freidman, 2000, "Corporate Governance in the Asian Financial Crisis," *Journal of Financial Economics*, Vol. 58, No. 1–2, pp. 141–86.

Jordan, Cally, and Michel Lubrano, 2002, "How Effective Are Capital Markets in Exerting Governance on Corporations," in *Financial Sector Governance: The Roles of the Public and Private Sectors*, World Bank/IMF/Brookings Emerging Markets Series, ed. by Robert E. Litan, Michael Pomerleano, and V. Sundararajan (Washington: Brooking Institution Press).

Kalter, Eliot, Steven Phillips, Marco A. Espinosa-Vega, Rodolfo Luzio, Mauricio Villafuerte, and Manmohan Singh, 2004, *Chile: Institutions and Policies Underpinning Stability and Growth*, Occasional Paper No. 231 (Washington: International Monetary Fund).

Kamil, Herman, 2004, "A New Database on Currency Composition and Maturity Structure of Firms' Balance Sheets in Latin America: 1990–2002" (unpublished; Washington: Inter-American Development Bank). Available via the Internet: *www.iadb.org/res/files/databases/ Cowan–Kamil.pdf*.

———, 2005, "Does Moving to a Floating Exchange Rate Regime Reduce Balance Sheet Mismatches? New Firm-Level Evidence for Latin America" (unpublished; Ann Arbor: University of Michigan).

King, Robert G., and Ross Levine, 1993, "Finance and Growth: Schumpeter Might Be Right," *Quarterly Journal of Economics*, Vol. 108, No. 3, pp. 717–37.

Klapper, Leora F., and Inessa Love, 2004, "Corporate Governance, Investor Protection, and Performance in Emerging Markets," *Journal of Corporate Finance*, Vol. 10, No. 5, pp. 659–775.

Krueger, Anne, 2002, "Why Crony Capitalism Is Bad for Growth," in *Crony Capitalism and Economic Growth in Latin America*, ed. by Stephen Haber (San Francisco: Hoover Press).

La Porta, Rafael, Florencio López de Silanes, and Andrei Shleifer, 2003, "What Works in Securities Law?" NBER Working Paper No. 9882 (Cambridge, Mass.: National Bureau of Economic Research).

———, and Robert Vishny, 1997, "Legal Determinants of External Finance," *The Journal of Finance*, Vol. 52, No. 3, pp. 1131–50.

———, 1998, "Law and Finance," *The Journal of Political Economy*, Vol. 106, No. 6, pp. 1113–55.

———, 2002, "Investor Protection and Corporate Valuation," *The Journal of Finance*, Vol. 57, No. 3, pp. 1147–70.

Lemmon, Michael L., and Karl V. Lins, 2003, "Ownership Structure, Corporate Governance, and Firm Value: Evidence from the East Asian Financial Crisis," *The Journal of Finance*, Vol. 58, No. 4, pp. 1445–68.

Levine, Ross, 2004, "Finance and Growth: Theory and Evidence," NBER Working Paper No. 10766

(Cambridge, Mass.: National Bureau of Economic Research).

———, and Sara Zervos, 1998, "Stock Markets, Banks, and Economic Growth," *American Economic Review*, Vol. 88, No. 3, pp. 537–58.

Lins, Karl, and Francis Warnock, 2004, "Corporate Governance and the Shareholder Base," International Finance Discussion Papers No. 816 (Washington: Board of Governors of the Federal Reserve System).

Lombardo, Davide, and Marco Pagano, 2000, "Legal Determinants of the Return on Equity," CSEF Working Paper No. 24, (Salerno: Dipartimento de Scienze Economiche, Universitá degli Estudi di Salerno, November).

López de Silanes, Florencio, 2002, "The Politics of Legal Reform," *Economia*, Vol. 2 (spring), pp. 91–152.

Love, Inessa, 2003, "Financial Development and Financing Constraints: International Evidence from the Structural Investment Model," *The Review of Financial Studies*, Vol. 16, No. 3, pp. 765–91.

Luengnaruemitchai, Pipat, 2003, "The Asian Crisis and the Mystery of the Missing Balance Sheet Effect" (unpublished; Berkeley: University of California, Department of Economics).

Mathieson, Donald J., Jorge E. Roldos, Ramana Ramaswamy, and Anna Ilyina, 2004, *Emerging Local Securities and Derivatives Markets*, World Economic and Financial Surveys (Washington: International Monetary Fund).

Meesook, Kanitta, Il Houng Lee, Olin Liu, Yougesh Khatri, Natalia Tamirisa, Michael Moore, and Mark H. Krysl, 2001, *Malaysia: From Crisis to Recovery*, Occasional Paper 207 (Washington: International Monetary Fund).

Miller, Darius P., and John J. Puthenpurackal, 2002, "The Costs, Wealth Effects, and Determinants of International Capital Raising: Evidence from Public Yankee Bonds," *Journal of Financial Intermediation*, Vol. 11, No. 4 (October), pp. 455–85.

Mitton, Todd, 2002, "A Cross-Firm Analysis of the Impact of Corporate Governance on the East Asian Financial Crisis," *Journal of Financial Economics*, Vol. 64, No. 2, pp. 215–41.

Morck, Randall, Daniel Wolfenzon, and Bernard Yeung, 2004, "Corporate Governance, Economic Entrenchment, and Growth," NBER Working Paper No. 10692 (Cambridge, Mass.: National Bureau of Economic Research).

Myers, Stewart, 2001, "Capital Structure," *Journal of Economic Perspectives*, Vol. 15, No. 2, pp. 81–102.

O'Brian, Maria, 2003, "On the Outside Looking In," *Latin Finance*, pp. 57–60 (September).

Pacter, Paul, 2003, "International Financial Reporting Standards," in *Handbook of International Finance and Accounting*, 3rd ed., ed. by Frederick D.S. Choi (New York: Wiley).

Rajan, Raghuram G., and Luigi Zingales, 1995, "What Do We Know About Capital Structure? Some Evidence from International Data," *The Journal of Finance*, Vol. 50, No. 5, pp. 1421–60.

———, 1998, "Financial Dependence and Growth," *American Economic Review*, Vol. 88, No. 3, pp. 559–86.

———, 2003a, "Banks and Markets: The Changing Character of European Finance," NBER Working Paper No. 9595 (Cambridge, Mass.: National Bureau of Economic Research).

———, 2003b, *Saving Capitalism from the Capitalists: Unleashing the Power of Financial Markets to Create Wealth and Spread Opportunity* (New York: Crown Business).

———, 2003c, "The Great Reversals: The Politics of Financial Development in the Twentieth Century," *Journal of Financial Economics*, Vol. 69, No. 1, pp. 5–50.

Ratha, Dilip, Philip Suttle, and Sanket Mohapatra, 2003, "Corporate Financing Patterns and Performance in Emerging Markets," in *The Future of Domestic Capital Markets in Developing Countries*, WB/IMF/Brookings Emerging Markets Series, ed. by Robert R. Litan, Michael Pomerleano, and V. Sundararajan (Washington: Brookings Institution Press).

Reinhart, Carmen M., Kenneth S. Rogoff, and Miguel A. Savastano, 2003, "Debt Intolerance," in *Brookings Papers on Economic Activity: 1*, ed. by William Brainard and George Perry, pp. 1–74.

Schinasi, Garry J., and R. Todd Smith, 1998, "Fixed-Income Markets in the United States, Europe, and Japan: Some Lessons for Emerging Markets," IMF Working Paper 98/173 (Washington: International Monetary Fund).

Singh, Anoop, Agnès Belaish, Charles Collyns, Paula De Masi, Reva Krieger, Guy Meredith, and Robert Rennhack, 2005, *Stabilization and Reform in Latin America: A Macroeconomic Perspective on the Experience Since the Early 1990s*, Occasional Paper No. 238 (Washington: International Monetary Fund).

GLOSSARY

401(k)	U.S. tax-deferred retirement plan that allows workers to contribute a percentage of their pre-tax salary for investment in stocks, bonds, or other securities. The employer may match all or part of employees' contributions.
Accrued benefit	Amount of accumulated pension benefits of a pension plan member.
Accumulated benefit obligation (ABO)	Present value of pension benefits promised by a company to its employees, at a particular date and based on current salaries.
Actuarial gain/loss	An actuarial gain (loss) appears when actual experience is more (less) favorable than the actuary's estimate.
Annuity	A contract that provides an income for a specified period of time, such as a number of years or for life.
Asset/liability management (ALM)	The management of assets to ensure that liabilities are sufficiently covered by suitable assets at all times.
Balance sheet mismatch	A balance sheet is a financial statement showing a company's assets, liabilities, and equity on a given date. Typically, a mismatch in a balance sheet implies that the maturities of the liabilities differ (are typically shorter) from those of the assets and/or that some liabilities are denominated in a foreign currency while the assets are not.
Banking soundness	The financial health of a single bank or of a country's banking system.
Beneficiary	Individual who is entitled to a pension benefit (including the pension plan member and dependants).
Book reserve scheme (also known as *Direktzusage*)	In Germany, accounting system whereby the actuarial value of future pension benefits appears as a liability, but is not offset by any specific provision on the sponsor company's balance sheet.
Brady bonds	Bonds issued by emerging market countries as part of a restructuring of defaulted commercial bank loans. These bonds are named after former U.S. Treasury Secretary Nicholas Brady and the first bonds were issued in March of 1990.
Carry trade	A leveraged transaction in which borrowed funds are used to buy a security whose yield is expected to exceed the cost of the borrowed funds.
Cash securitization	The creation of securities from a pool of pre-existing assets and receivables that are placed under the legal control of investors through a special intermediary created for this purpose. This compares with a "synthetic" securitization where the generic securities are created out of derivative instruments.

Collective action clause	A clause in bond contracts that includes provisions allowing a qualified majority of lenders to amend key financial terms of the debt contract and bind a minority to accept these new terms.
Corporate governance	The governing relationships between all the stakeholders in a company—including the shareholders, directors, and management—as defined by the corporate charter, bylaws, formal policy, and rule of law.
Credit default swap	A financial contract under which an agent buys protection against credit risk for a periodic fee in return for a payment by the protection seller contingent on the occurrence of a credit/default event.
Credit risk	The risk that a counterparty to the insurer is unable or unwilling to meet its obligations causing a financial loss to the insurer.
Credit spreads	The spread between sovereign benchmark securities and other debt securities that are comparable in all respects except for credit quality (e.g., the difference between yields on U.S. Treasuries and those on single A-rated corporate bonds of a certain term to maturity).
Defined benefit plan	Pension plan in which benefits are determined by such factors as salary history and duration of employment. The sponsor company is responsible for the investment risk and portfolio management.
Defined contribution plan	Pension plan in which benefits are determined by returns on the plan's investments. Beneficiaries bear the investment risk.
Dependency ratio	Ratio of pensioners to those of working age in a given population.
Derivatives	Financial contracts whose value derives from underlying securities prices, interest rates, foreign exchange rates, market indexes, or commodity prices.
Dollarization	The widespread domestic use of another country's currency (typically the U.S. dollar) to perform the standard functions of money—that of a unit of account, medium of exchange, and store of value.
EMBI	The acronym for the J.P. Morgan *Emerging Market Bond Index* that tracks the total returns for traded external debt instruments in the emerging markets.
Emerging markets	Developing countries' financial markets that are less than fully developed, but are nonetheless broadly accessible to foreign investors.
Foreign direct investment	The acquisition abroad (i.e., outside the home country) of physical assets, such as plant and equipment, or of a controlling stake (usually greater than 10 percent of shareholdings).
Forward price-earnings ratio	The multiple of future expected earnings at which a stock sells. It is calculated by dividing the current stock price (adjusted for stock splits) by the estimated earnings per share for a future period (typically the next 12 months).

Funded pension plan	Pension plan that has accumulated dedicated assets to pay for the pension benefits.
Funding gap	The difference between the discounted value of accumulating future pension obligations and the present value of investment assets.
Funding ratio	Ratio of the amount of assets accumulated by a defined benefit pension plan to the sum of promised benefits.
Hedge funds	Investment pools, typically organized as private partnerships and often resident offshore for tax and regulatory purposes. These funds face few restrictions on their portfolios and transactions. Consequently, they are free to use a variety of investment techniques—including short positions, transactions in derivatives, and leverage—to raise returns and cushion risk.
Hedging	Offsetting an existing risk exposure by taking an opposite position in the same or a similar risk, for example, by buying derivatives contracts.
Hybrid pension plan	Retirement plan that has characteristics typical of both defined benefit and defined contribution plans.
Individual Retirement Account (IRA)	In the United States, tax-deferred retirement plan permitting all individuals to set aside a fraction of their wages (additional contributions are possible on a nondeductible basis).
Interest rate swaps	An agreement between counterparties to exchange periodic interest payments on some predetermined dollar principal, which is called the notional principal amount. For example, one party will make fixed-rate and receive variable-rate interest payments.
Intermediation	The process of transferring funds from the ultimate source to the ultimate user. A financial institution, such as a bank, intermediates credit when it obtains money from depositors and relends it to borrowers.
Investment-grade issues (Subinvestment-grade issues)	A bond that is assigned a rating in the top four categories by commercial credit rating agencies. S&P classifies investment-grade bonds as BBB or higher, and Moody's classifies investment-grade bonds as Baa or higher. (Subinvestment-grade bond issues are rated bonds that are below investment grade.)
Leverage	The proportion of debt to equity. Leverage can be built up by borrowing (on-balance-sheet leverage, commonly measured by debt-to-equity ratios) or by using off-balance-sheet transactions.
Lump sum payment	Withdrawal of accumulated benefits all at once, as opposed to in regular installments.
Mark-to-market	The valuation of a position or portfolio by reference to the most recent price at which a financial instrument can be bought or sold

in normal volumes. The mark-to-market value might equal the current market value—as opposed to historic accounting or book value—or the present value of expected future cash flows.

Nonperforming loans	Loans that are in default or close to being in default (i.e., typically past due for 90 days or more).
Occupational pension scheme	Pension plan set up and managed by a sponsor company for the benefit of its employees.
Offshore instruments	Securities issued outside of national boundaries.
Overfunded plan	Defined benefit pension plan in which assets accumulated are greater than the sum of promised benefits.
Pillar I	National pension systems are typically represented as a "multi-pillar" structure with the sources of retirement income derived from a mixture of government, employment, and individual savings. Pillar I refers to state-based retirement income, often a combination of universal entitlement and an earnings-related component. See Chapter III of the September 2004 GFSR for further details. (Note: Another classification scheme used in pension studies, particularly for emerging markets, was first developed at the World Bank. It describes Pillar 1 as "non-contributory state pensions," Pillar 2 as "mandatory contributory," and Pillar 3 as "voluntary contributory".)
Pillar II	Occupational pension funds, increasingly funded, organized at the workplace (e.g., defined benefit, defined contribution, and hybrid schemes).
Pillar III	Private saving plans and products for individuals, often tax advantaged.
Pair-wise correlations	A statistical measure of the degree to which the movements of two variables (e.g., asset returns) are related.
Pay-as-you-go basis (PAYG)	Arrangement under which benefits are paid out of revenue over each period, and no funding is made for future liabilities.
Pension benefit	Benefit paid to a participant (beneficiary) in a pension plan.
Pension contribution	Payment made to a pension plan by the sponsor company or by plan participants.
Primary market	The market where a newly issued security is first offered/sold to the public.
Private pension plan	Pension plan where a private entity receives pension contributions and administers the payment of pension benefits.
Projected benefit obligation (PBO)	Present value of pension benefits promised by a company to its employees at a particular date, and including assumption about future salary increases (i.e., assuming that the plan will not terminate in the foreseeable future).

Public pension plan	Pension plan where the general government administers the payment of pension benefits (e.g., Social Security and similar schemes).
Put (call) option	A financial contract that gives the buyer the right, but not the obligation, to sell (buy) a financial instrument at a set price on or before a given date.
Reinsurance	Insurance placed by an underwriter in another company to cut down the amount of the risk assumed under the original insurance.
Risk aversion	The degree to which an investor who, when faced with two investments with the same expected return but different risk, prefers the one with the lower risk. That is, it measures an investor's aversion to uncertain outcomes or payoffs.
Secondary markets	Markets in which securities are traded after they are initially offered/sold in the primary market.
Solvency	Narrowly defined as the ability of an insurer to meet its obligations (liabilities) at any time. In order to set a practicable definition, it is necessary to clarify the type of claims covered by the assets, e.g., already written business (run-off basis, break-up basis), or would future new business (going-concern basis) also to be considered. In addition, questions regarding the volume and the nature of an insurance company's business, the appropriate time horizon to be adopted, and setting an acceptable probability of becoming insolvent are taken into consideration in assessing a company's solvency.
Sponsor company	Company that designs, negotiates, and normally helps to administer an occupational plan for its employees and members.
Spread	See "credit spreads" above (the word credit is sometimes omitted). Other definitions include (1) the gap between bid and ask prices of a financial instrument; (2) the difference between the price at which an underwriter buys an issue from the issuer and the price at which the underwriter sells it to the public.
Syndicated loans	Large loans made jointly by a group of banks to one borrower. Usually, one lead bank takes a small percentage of the loan and partitions (syndicates) the rest to other banks.
Tail events	The occurrence of large or extreme security price movements that, in terms of their probability of occurring, lie within the tail region of the distribution of possible price movements.
Trustee	Private entity (person or organization) with a duty to receive, manage and disburse the assets of a plan.
Underfunded plan	Defined benefit pension plan in which assets accumulated are smaller than the sum of promised benefits.

Unfunded benefit liability	Amount of promised pension benefits that exceeds a plan's assets.
Vesting	Right of an employee, on termination of employment, to obtain part or all of his accrued benefits.
With-profits policies	The insurance company guarantees to pay an agreed amount at a specific time in the future, and may increase this guaranteed amount through bonus payments. In effect, the policy holders are participating in the profits of the life insurance company.
Yield curve	A chart that plots the yield to maturity at a specific point in time for debt securities having equal credit risk but different maturity dates.

The following remarks by the Acting Chair were made at the conclusion of the Executive Board's discussion of the Global Financial Stability Report *on March 18, 2005.*

Executive Directors welcomed the further strengthening of the financial system in the past six months, supported by solid global economic growth and continued improvements in balance sheets of the corporate, financial, and household sectors in many countries. They also welcomed ongoing improvements in the fundamentals of many emerging market countries. Prospects for continued financial stability are underpinned by the still favorable outlook for the world economy, and by the growing sophistication in financial markets that has helped spread risk. Nonetheless, Directors noted that currently low long-term interest rates and credit spreads could mask underlying vulnerabilities and pose risks of market reversals, especially for less credit-worthy sovereigns and corporations. While these risks are generally expected to be manageable given the strength of financial institutions, Directors stressed the need for continued vigilant monitoring and timely policy measures.

Global Financial Market Surveillance

Directors noted that markets have remained orderly through the ongoing interest rate tightening cycle in mature markets, facilitated by the increasingly transparent communication strategies of major central banks. Still abundant global liquidity and improving credit quality have kept mature market bond yields and financial market volatility low. Other factors that have contributed to relatively low long-term bond yields include expectations that inflation will remain under control, low corporate demand for net credit, and growing demand for long-term bonds by pension funds and life insurance companies. More generally, low short-term interest rates have encouraged investors to use leverage and move out along the risk spectrum in their quest for yield, buoying asset valuations and compressing credit spreads.

Directors noted that the corporate balance sheet improvements in mature markets and the quest for yield have encouraged investors to increase their exposure to credit risk. This has contributed to falling corporate bond spreads, and possibly to reduced investor discrimination. Directors noted the growth of credit derivatives markets, which facilitate the trading and hedging of credit risks. At the same time, many Directors acknowledged that the derivatives markets' expansion may expose some investors to the possibility of leveraged losses, which could be amplified by potential liquidity problems. Furthermore, risk management models designed to deal with these new and more complex financial instruments may have yet to be put to a significant live test. Several Directors also called for increased disclosure and continued monitoring of hedge fund activities. Directors appreciated the GFSR's continued attention to developments in energy markets, and supported its call for more timely and reliable data on global demand and supply conditions.

Directors observed that, along with improvements in many emerging market countries' fundamentals, abundant liquidity and quest for yield have been driving factors in recent developments in emerging financial markets.

Spreads on emerging market debt have narrowed to near record lows and investors' appetite for emerging market financial assets has grown considerably. Ongoing, healthy market developments include the expansion of the investor base for emerging markets to include a more diverse universe of long-term investors; the increasing diversification of investor portfolios into local emerging markets; the extension of local government yield curves in a number of countries; and the inclusion of more local currency sovereign bonds in major benchmark global bond indices.

Directors generally expected financing prospects for emerging markets to remain solid, underpinned by benign financial market conditions and further improvements in the credit quality of emerging market borrowers. Most emerging market sovereign borrowers have used this period well, undertaking substantial prefinancing of their external financing needs, conducting debt management operations to improve the resilience of their balance sheets, and, in a couple of instances, issuing local currency bonds in global markets. Directors also welcomed broad-based improvements in the financial health of the domestic banking sector in emerging market countries, while encouraging authorities to continue structural reforms aimed at increasing their resiliency to potential shocks.

Turning to risks in the current environment, Directors noted that the long period of high liquidity and low volatility may have led to a sense of complacency on the part of some investors, and that compression of inflation and risk premia leaves little room for error in terms of asset valuations. Against this backdrop, the risk that long-term market rates might rise abruptly requires continued vigilance. While no single event may trigger such a rise, most Directors highlighted concerns about the possibility of a combination or correlation of events, noting the potential risks of a disorderly adjustment of global imbalances, possibly associated with a diversification of

international investors away from dollar holdings, as well as the possibility of an unanticipated increase in inflation, particularly related to oil and other commodity prices.

Directors considered a number of steps to enhance global financial stability and mitigate potential risks. In particular, they reiterated their call for cooperative efforts and credible policy measures to enhance the market's confidence that global imbalances will be reduced in an orderly manner. At a microeconomic level, supervisors and regulators should be vigilant to the risk profile of financial intermediaries, and their exposure to abrupt market price shocks. Emerging market country authorities should continue to adopt prudent macroeconomic policies that reduce financing needs, while taking advantage of the current benign conditions to fulfill their external financing requirements, improve the structure of their debt, and press ahead with efforts to develop local financial markets. In addition, structural reforms to enhance growth prospects remain a critical avenue for reducing debt-to-GDP ratios to more manageable levels.

Household Balance Sheets

Directors welcomed the staff's study on the changing risk profile of the household sector resulting from the transfer, reallocation, and improved management of financial risks by banks, insurance companies, and pension funds. While households always have been the ultimate bearers of financial risks, through a variety of channels, these risks traditionally have been intermediated by governments and private financial and nonfinancial institutions. Directors supported the view that policies designed to improve the financial stability of systemically or otherwise important institutions should also consider the consequent flow of risks to households and their ability to absorb or manage such risks.

Directors observed that trends in the evolution of household balance sheets in different jurisdictions have benefited households in various ways, including through a significant growth in net worth relative to income, boosted by capital gains. At the same time, the shift away from bank and savings deposits to more market-sensitive assets has also exposed them to greater market risk. Directors considered that planned reforms of public and private retirement benefits may imply that households will have even more responsibility going forward in managing their financial affairs. Such reforms have brought benefits, such as the portability of defined contribution or hybrid pension plans. While they have reduced some risks, these reforms have also increased the direct exposure of households to investment and market risks, and possibly more challenging, longevity risk.

Directors observed that as more households rely primarily on defined contribution and other self-directed pension plans, there may be scope for incentives to educate households, and thereby increase their ability to manage these risks and to obtain better financial advice. These measures could also include developing new instruments to help households realize more easily long-term savings and make resources available for retirement. Several Directors highlighted the role of consistent government policies, including stable tax policies, in encouraging long-term savings strategies. A crucial element of household saving and investment planning is the uncertainty of life expectancy, and the ability to convert long-term savings into a dependable income stream. Directors suggested, in this context, that the issuance of long-dated, index-linked, and longevity bonds could facilitate the management of longer-term investments and obligations and the supply of annuity products.

Directors generally saw a role for governments in developing communication strategies to inform households about their retirement challenges, and in coordinating with the private sector to provide financial education. They welcomed the initiatives undertaken by organizations such as the

OECD and several national authorities to foster the financial education of households. Directors noted the importance of increased efforts to improve the collection, timeliness, and comparability of data on the household sector for assessing the flow of financial risk through the financial system, and in particular the risk profile of households. More generally, they looked forward to keeping the systemic and policy implications of the flow of risks to households under review.

Corporate Finance in Emerging Markets

Directors welcomed the detailed study on corporate finance in emerging markets. They observed that it is unclear whether the decline in domestic bank lending to corporations (outside China and India) is a result of reduced external financing needs or constraints on the sources of funding. Nevertheless, Directors called for continued efforts by emerging markets to improve their institutional frameworks to facilitate corporates' access to equity finance on appropriate terms. Directors saw a need to narrow gaps in the implementation and enforcement of widely accepted principles of corporate governance, disclosure and transparency, while recognizing the need to take into account country-specific legal and institutional circumstances as well as the stage of market development. Several Directors saw merit in integrating the analysis and discussion on corporate finance and bank disintermediation across mature and emerging markets, as common trends are likely in an integrated global economy.

Directors recognized the importance of assessing corporate sector financial fragilities, given the increased importance of corporates relative to sovereigns in international markets and the potential risks should market conditions become less benign. They underscored the desirability of an integrated approach to corporate sector vulnerability that would account for interactions between interest rate, foreign exchange and credit risks, as well as linkages with the financial and government sectors. While the effort to develop new databases was welcomed, some Directors nevertheless cautioned that care should be taken in drawing inferences from dated and incomplete data. Some Directors encouraged the development of hedging instruments to address exposures to foreign currency risk, and also noted the important role of financial intermediaries, and their regulators, in monitoring balance sheet mismatches in the corporate sector.

STATISTICAL APPENDIX

This statistical appendix presents data on financial developments in key financial centers and emerging markets. It is designed to complement the analysis in the text by providing additional data that describe key aspects of financial market developments. These data are derived from a number of sources external to the IMF, including banks, commercial data providers, and official sources, and are presented for information purposes only; the IMF does not, however, guarantee the accuracy of the data from external sources.

Presenting financial market data in one location and in a fixed set of tables and charts, in this and future issues of the GFSR, is intended to give the reader an overview of developments in global financial markets. Unless otherwise noted, the statistical appendix reflects information available up to February 16, 2005.

Mirroring the structure of the chapters of the report, the appendix presents data separately for key financial centers and emerging market countries. Specifically, it is organized into three sections:

- Figures 1–14 and Tables 1–9 contain information on market developments in key financial centers. This includes data on global capital flows, and on markets for foreign exchange, bonds, equities, and derivatives, as well as sectoral balance sheet data for the United States, Japan, and Europe.
- Figures 15 and 16, and Tables 10–21 present information on financial developments in emerging markets, including data on equity, foreign exchange, and bond markets, as well as data on emerging market financing flows.
- Tables 22–28 report key financial soundness indicators for selected countries, including bank profitability, asset quality, and capital adequacy.

List of Tables and Figures

Key Financial Centers

Figures

Tables

Emerging Markets

Figures

Tables

Financial Soundness Indicators

Figure 1. Global Capital Flows: Sources and Uses of Global Capital in 2003

Countries That Export Capital[1]

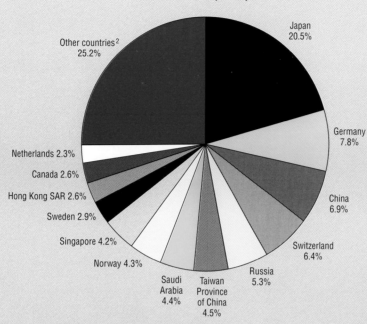

Japan
20.5%

Other countries[2]
25.2%

Germany
7.8%

China
6.9%

Netherlands 2.3%

Canada 2.6%

Hong Kong SAR 2.6%

Switzerland
6.4%

Sweden 2.9%

Singapore 4.2%

Russia
5.3%

Norway 4.3%

Saudi
Arabia
4.4%

Taiwan
Province
of China
4.5%

Countries That Import Capital[3]

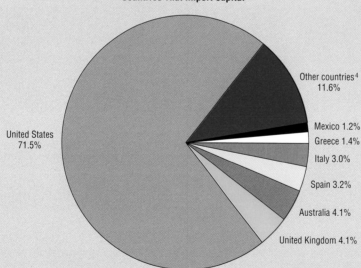

Other countries[4]
11.6%

United States
71.5%

Mexico 1.2%

Greece 1.4%

Italy 3.0%

Spain 3.2%

Australia 4.1%

United Kingdom 4.1%

Source: International Monetary Fund, *World Economic Outlook* database as of March 11, 2005.
[1]As measured by countries' current account surplus (assuming errors and omissions are part of the capital and financial accounts).
[2]Other countries include all countries with shares of total surplus less than 2.3 percent.
[3]As measured by countries' current account deficit (assuming errors and omissions are part of the capital and financial accounts).
[4]Other countries include all countries with shares of total deficit less than 1.2 percent.

Figure 2. Exchange Rates: Selected Major Industrial Countries

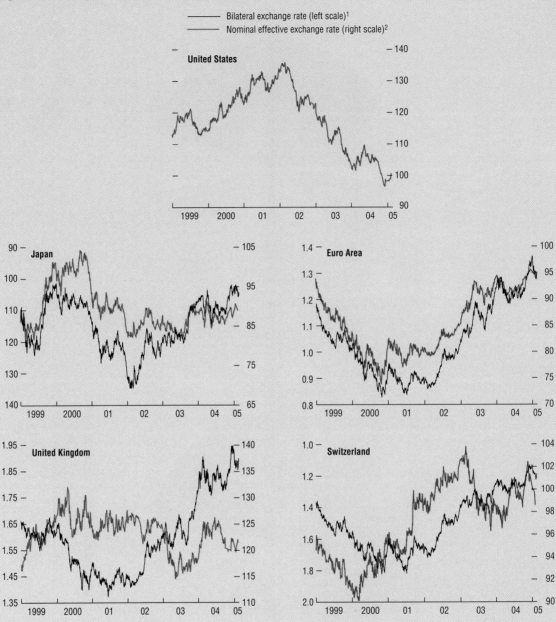

——— Bilateral exchange rate (left scale)[1]
——— Nominal effective exchange rate (right scale)[2]

Sources: Bloomberg L.P.; and the IMF Competitive Indicators System.
Note: In each panel, the effective and bilateral exchange rates are scaled so that an upward movement implies an appreciation of the respective local currency.
[1]Local currency units per U.S. dollar except for the euro area and the United Kingdom, for which data are shown as U.S. dollars per local currency.
[2]1995 = 100; constructed using 1989–91 trade weights.

Figure 3. United States: Yields on Corporate and Treasury Bonds
(Weekly data)

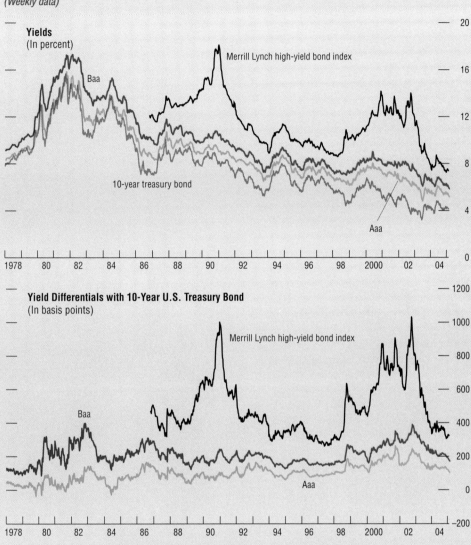

Sources: Bloomberg L.P.; and Merrill Lynch.

Figure 4. Selected Spreads
(In basis points)

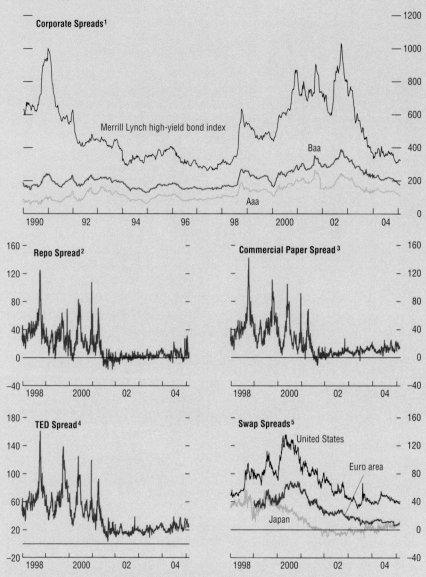

Sources: Bloomberg L.P.; and Merrill Lynch.
[1]Spread over 10-year U.S. treasury bond; weekly data.
[2]Spread between yields on three-month U.S. treasury repo and on three-month U.S. treasury bill.
[3]Spread between yields on 90-day investment-grade commercial paper and on three-month U.S. treasury bill.
[4]Spread between three-month U.S. dollar LIBOR and yield on three-month U.S. treasury bill.
[5]Spread over 10-year government bond.

Figure 5. Nonfinancial Corporate Credit Spreads
(In basis points)

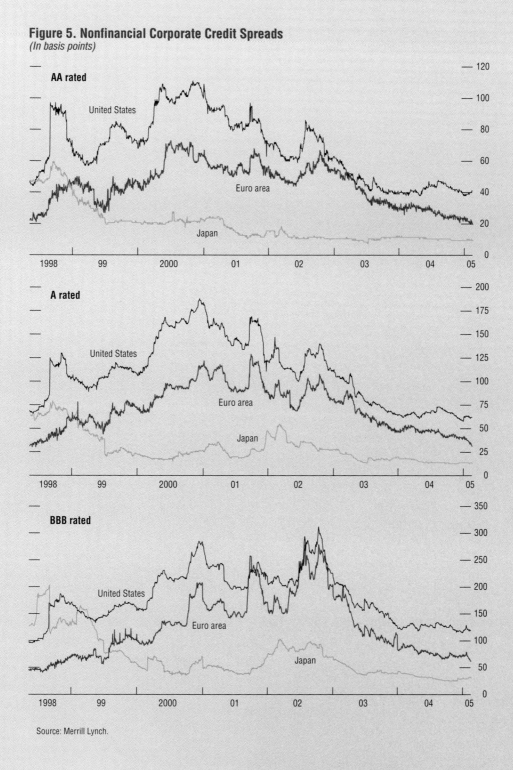

Source: Merrill Lynch.

Figure 6. Equity Markets: Price Indexes
(January 1, 1990 = 100; weekly data)

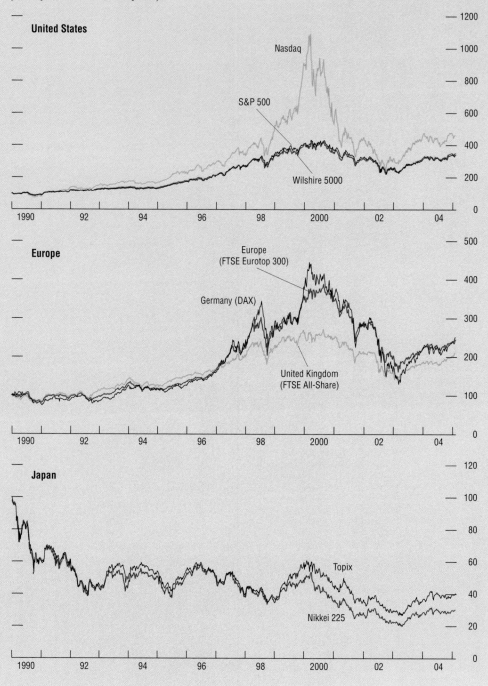

Source: Datastream.

Figure 7. Implied and Historical Volatility in Equity Markets

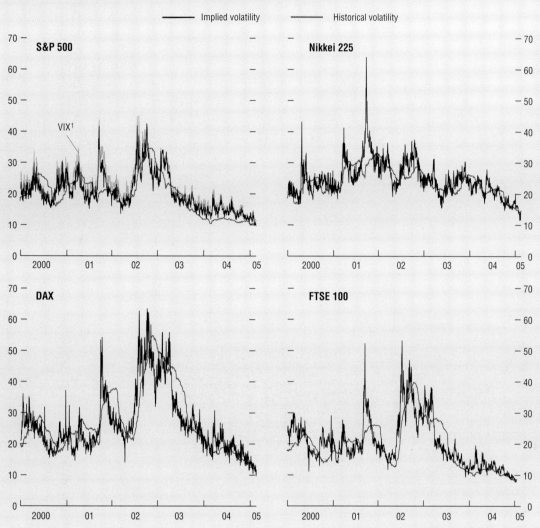

Sources: Bloomberg L.P.; and IMF staff estimates.
Note: Implied volatility is a measure of the equity price variability implied by the market prices of call options on equity futures. Historical volatility is calculated as a rolling 100-day annualized standard deviation of equity price changes. Volatilities are expressed in percent rate of change.
[1]VIX is the Chicago Board Options Exchange's volatility index. This index is calculated by taking a weighted average of implied volatility for the eight S&P 500 calls and puts.

Figure 8. Historical Volatility of Government Bond Yields and Bond Returns for Selected Countries[1]

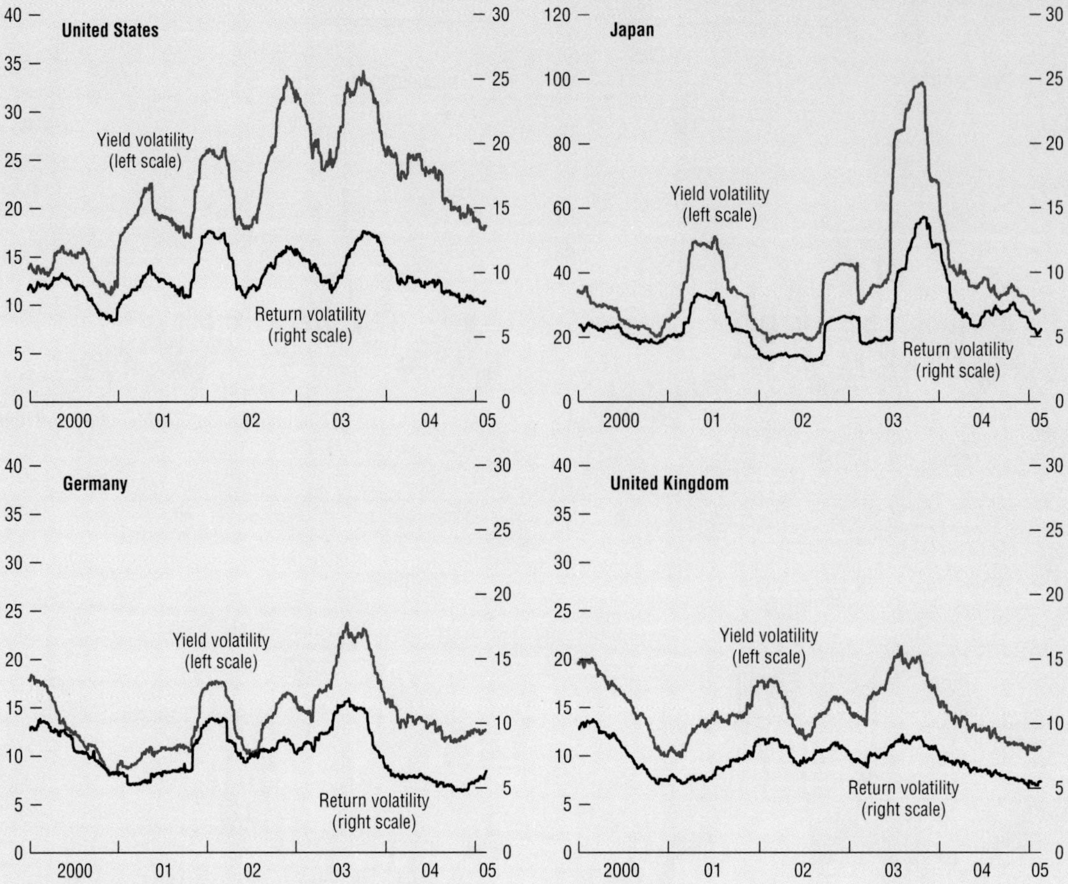

Sources: Bloomberg L.P.; and Datastream.
[1]Volatility calculated as a rolling 100-day annualized standard deviation of changes in yield and returns on 10-year government bonds. Returns are based on 10-plus year government bond indexes.

Figure 9. Twelve-Month Forward Price/Earnings Ratios

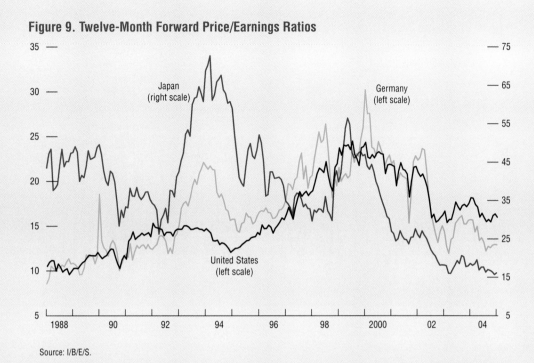

Source: I/B/E/S.

Figure 10. Flows into U.S.-Based Equity Funds

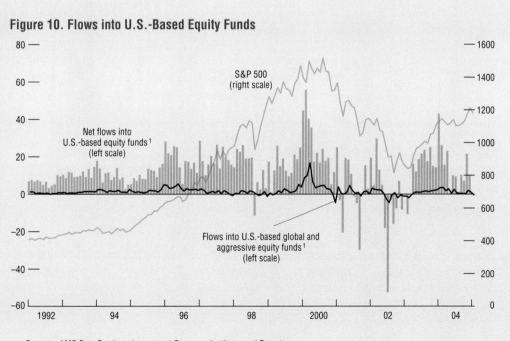

Sources: AMG Data Services; Investment Company Institute; and Datastream.
[1]In billions of U.S. dollars.

Figure 11. United States: Corporate Bond Market

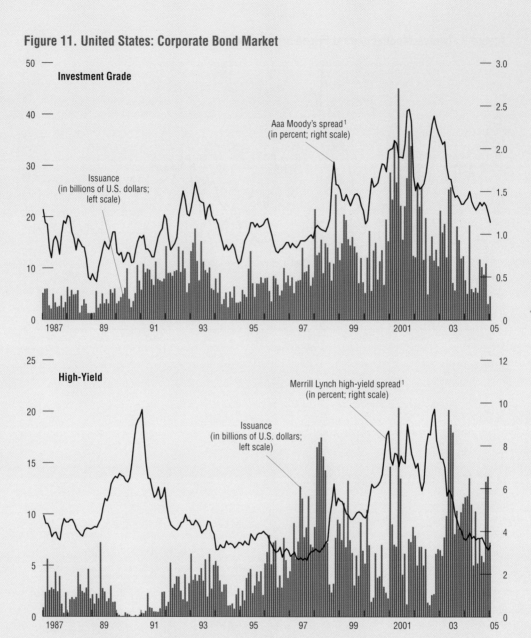

Sources: Board of Governors of the Federal Reserve System; and Bloomberg L.P.
[1]Spread against yield on 10-year U.S. government bonds.

Figure 12. Europe: Corporate Bond Market[1]

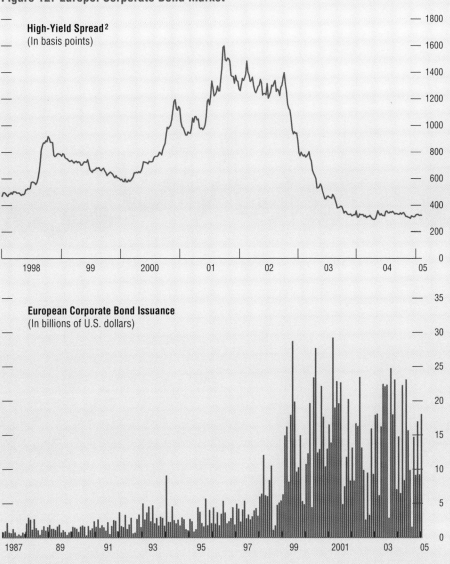

High-Yield Spread[2]
(In basis points)

European Corporate Bond Issuance
(In billions of U.S. dollars)

Sources: Bondware; and Datastream.
[1]Nonfinancial corporate bonds.
[2]Spread between yields on a Merrill Lynch High-Yield European Issuers Index bond and a 10-year German government benchmark bond.

Figure 13. United States: Commercial Paper Market[1]

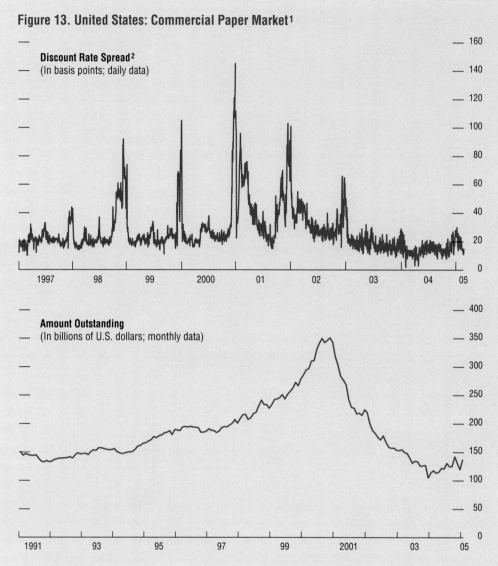

Discount Rate Spread[2]
(In basis points; daily data)

Amount Outstanding
(In billions of U.S. dollars; monthly data)

Source: Board of Governors of the Federal Reserve System.
[1]Nonfinancial commercial paper.
[2]Difference between 30-day A2/P2 and AA commercial paper.

Figure 14. United States: Asset-Backed Securities

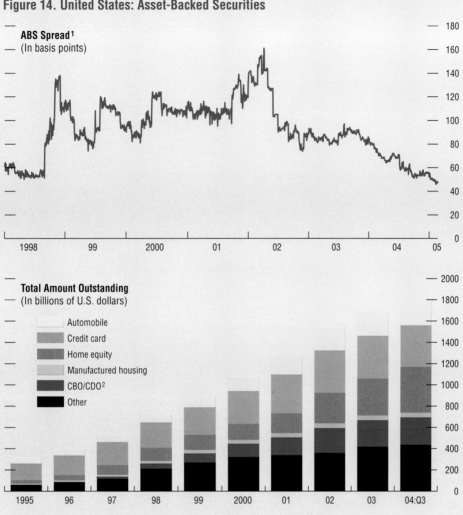

Sources: Merrill Lynch; Datastream; and the Bond Market Association.
[1]Merrill Lynch AAA Asset-Backed Master Index (fixed rate) option-adjusted spread.
[2]Collateralized bond/debt obligations.

Table 1. Global Capital Flows: Inflows and Outflows[1]
(In billions of U.S. dollars)

	Inflows										
	1993	1994	1995	1996	1997	1998	1999	2000	2001	2002	2003
United States											
Direct investment	51.4	46.1	57.8	86.5	105.6	179.0	289.4	321.3	167.0	72.4	39.9
Portfolio investment	111.0	139.4	210.4	332.8	333.1	187.6	285.6	436.6	428.3	427.9	544.5
Other investment	119.7	120.5	170.4	131.8	268.1	57.0	165.2	289.0	187.5	268.0	244.8
Reserve assets	n.a.	n.a.	n.a.	n.a.	n.a.	n.a.	n.a.	n.a.	n.a.	n.a.	n.a.
Total capital flows	282.1	306.0	438.6	551.1	706.8	423.6	740.2	1,046.9	782.9	768.2	829.2
Canada											
Direct investment	4.7	8.2	9.3	9.6	11.5	22.7	24.8	66.1	27.5	20.9	6.3
Portfolio investment	41.4	17.2	18.4	13.7	11.7	16.6	2.7	10.3	24.6	13.4	13.2
Other investment	−6.7	16.0	−3.9	15.7	28.0	5.4	−10.8	0.8	7.5	5.0	10.9
Reserve assets	n.a.	n.a.	n.a.	n.a.	n.a.	n.a.	n.a.	n.a.	n.a.	n.a.	n.a.
Total capital flows	39.4	41.4	23.9	39.1	51.2	44.8	16.6	77.2	59.7	39.3	30.3
Japan											
Direct investment	0.1	0.9	0.0	0.2	3.2	3.3	12.3	8.2	6.2	9.1	6.2
Portfolio investment	−6.1	64.5	59.8	66.8	79.2	56.1	126.9	47.4	60.5	−20.0	81.2
Other investment	−32.7	−5.6	97.3	31.1	68.0	−93.3	−265.1	−10.2	−17.6	26.6	34.1
Reserve assets	n.a.	n.a.	n.a.	n.a.	n.a.	n.a.	n.a.	n.a.	n.a.	n.a.	n.a.
Total capital flows	−38.7	59.8	157.1	98.1	150.4	−34.0	−125.9	45.4	49.1	15.7	121.5
United Kingdom											
Direct investment	16.5	10.7	21.7	27.4	37.4	74.7	89.5	122.2	53.8	25.5	20.7
Portfolio investment	43.6	47.0	58.8	68.0	43.5	35.2	183.9	255.6	69.6	76.6	153.6
Other investment	191.4	−10.8	106.2	254.4	328.5	103.9	83.6	423.2	333.2	111.4	416.7
Reserve assets	n.a.	n.a.	n.a.	n.a.	n.a.	n.a.	n.a.	n.a.	n.a.	n.a.	n.a.
Total capital flows	251.6	46.9	186.7	349.7	409.4	213.7	357.1	801.0	456.6	213.5	591.0
Euro area[2]											
Direct investment	...	...	...	...	...	...	209.7	404.8	182.5	138.2	117.9
Portfolio investment	...	...	...	...	...	...	282.9	270.7	311.3	273.7	342.7
Other investment	...	...	...	...	...	...	208.3	337.2	241.1	62.6	185.3
Reserve assets	n.a.	n.a.	n.a.	n.a.	n.a.	n.a.	n.a.	n.a.	n.a.	n.a.	n.a.
Total capital flows	...	...	...	...	...	...	700.8	1,012.7	734.8	474.6	645.9
Emerging Markets and Developing Countries[2]											
Direct investment	71.4	96.0	123.9	142.9	184.6	183.6	207.0	211.7	224.1	168.7	177.0
Portfolio investment	94.7	93.7	38.0	113.8	88.3	35.2	113.8	75.4	−8.0	−21.4	49.2
Other investment	40.7	17.7	139.8	85.1	169.0	−99.5	−64.8	5.1	−42.7	35.2	121.2
Reserve assets	n.a.	n.a.	n.a.	n.a.	n.a.	n.a.	n.a.	n.a.	n.a.	n.a.	n.a.
Total capital flows	206.8	207.4	301.7	341.8	441.9	119.3	256.0	292.2	173.4	182.5	347.4

Sources: International Monetary Fund, *World Economic Outlook* database as of March 11, 2005, and *International Financial Statistics*.

[1]The total net capital flows are the sum of direct investment, portfolio investment, other investment flows, and reserve assets. "Other investment" includes bank loans and deposits.

[2]This aggregate comprises the group of Other Emerging Market and Developing Countries defined in the World Economic Outlook, together with Hong Kong SAR, Israel, Korea, Singapore, and Taiwan Province of China.

					Outflows					
1993	1994	1995	1996	1997	1998	1999	2000	2001	2002	2003
−84.0	−80.2	−98.8	−91.9	−104.8	−142.6	−224.9	−159.2	−142.4	−134.8	−173.8
−146.2	−63.2	−122.4	−149.3	−116.9	−124.2	−116.2	−121.9	−84.6	15.9	−72.3
31.0	−40.9	−121.4	−178.9	−262.8	−74.2	−171.2	−288.4	−134.9	−75.4	−38.8
−1.4	5.3	−9.7	6.7	−1.0	−6.7	8.7	−0.3	−4.9	−3.7	1.5
−200.5	−178.9	−352.3	−413.4	−485.5	−347.8	−503.7	−569.8	−366.8	−198.0	−283.4
−5.7	−9.3	−11.5	−13.1	−23.1	−34.1	−17.3	−44.5	−36.2	−26.5	−22.2
−13.8	−6.6	−5.3	−14.2	−8.6	−15.1	−15.6	−43.0	−24.4	−15.9	−9.1
−0.4	−20.4	−8.3	−21.1	−16.2	9.4	10.2	−4.2	−10.5	−8.5	−20.6
−0.9	0.4	−2.7	−5.5	2.4	−5.0	−5.9	−3.7	−2.2	0.2	3.3
−20.8	−35.9	−27.9	−53.9	−45.4	−44.8	−28.5	−95.4	−73.3	−50.7	−48.7
−13.8	−18.1	−22.5	−23.4	−26.1	−24.6	−22.3	−31.5	−38.5	−32.0	−28.8
−63.7	−92.0	−86.0	−100.6	−47.1	−95.2	−154.4	−83.4	−106.8	−85.9	−176.3
15.1	−35.1	−102.2	5.2	−192.0	37.9	266.3	−4.1	46.6	36.4	149.9
−27.5	−25.3	−58.6	−35.1	−6.6	6.2	−76.3	−49.0	−40.5	−46.1	−187.2
−90.0	−170.4	−269.4	−154.0	−271.6	−75.8	13.4	−168.0	−139.2	−127.7	−242.3
−27.3	−34.9	−45.3	−34.8	−62.4	−122.1	−201.6	−245.4	−59.7	−49.5	−65.4
−133.6	31.5	−61.7	−93.1	−85.1	−53.2	−34.2	−97.1	−124.7	1.2	−58.3
−68.5	−42.4	−74.9	−217.8	−276.0	−29.8	−92.8	−417.5	−254.7	−150.5	−436.1
−1.3	−1.5	0.9	0.7	3.9	0.3	1.0	−5.3	4.5	0.6	2.6
−230.5	−47.4	−181.0	−345.1	−419.6	−204.9	−327.5	−765.3	−434.6	−198.1	−557.3
...	...	...	...	...	...	−338.2	−404.9	−283.1	−141.9	−133.9
...	...	...	...	...	...	−330.5	−385.2	−252.8	−162.6	−321.8
...	...	...	...	...	...	−31.0	−166.2	−244.0	−224.2	−265.7
...	...	...	...	...	...	11.6	16.2	16.5	−2.6	35.1
...	...	...	...	...	...	−688.1	−940.1	−763.3	−531.3	−686.4
−17.1	−15.6	−23.6	−28.2	−37.3	−24.2	−34.0	−36.9	−33.8	−25.6	−27.5
3.4	−12.1	−13.0	−34.8	−46.2	7.6	−38.3	−87.8	−92.9	−69.6	−111.5
−23.7	−64.9	−48.9	−91.0	−138.6	32.0	−79.4	−149.2	11.4	−8.6	−127.5
−65.5	−67.4	−129.9	−91.5	−105.2	−36.8	−94.1	−120.5	−114.1	−197.3	−370.3
−103.0	−160.0	−215.3	−245.6	−327.3	−21.5	−245.8	−394.4	−229.5	−301.0	−636.8

Table 2. Global Capital Flows: Amounts Outstanding and Net Issues of International Debt Securities by Currency of Issue and Announced International Syndicated Credit Facilities by Nationality of Borrower
(In billions of U.S. dollars)

	1997	1998	1999	2000	2001	2002	2003	2004 Q1	2004 Q2	2004 Q3
Amounts outstanding of international debt securities by currency of issue										
U.S. dollar	1,432.9	1,832.6	2,357.3	2,907.9	3,610.4	4,045.9	4,494.9	4,653.4	4,708.9	4,765.4
Japanese yen	444.4	462.6	497.5	452.5	411.5	433.3	488.4	508.3	504.2	501.3
Pound sterling	266.7	322.4	391.1	452.7	506.0	618.6	778.6	831.5	858.9	883.2
Canadian dollar	67.2	55.5	56.4	51.5	47.5	51.5	79.3	84.5	86.0	98.4
Swedish krona	4.1	7.5	7.2	7.7	8.2	11.1	15.8	15.4	16.3	17.6
Swiss franc	138.5	153.5	135.5	132.0	123.6	159.1	195.6	194.3	199.8	205.7
Euro[1]	848.6	1,133.6	1,451.1	1,768.7	2,288.5	3,282.8	4,834.3	4,931.8	5,126.9	5,431.1
Other	78.8	84.3	98.5	97.3	110.3	152.3	217.2	236.1	238.5	254.8
Total	3,281.2	4,052.0	4,994.6	5,870.3	7,106.0	8,754.6	11,104.1	11,455.3	11,739.5	12,157.5
Net issues of international debt securities by currency of issue										
U.S. dollar	320.3	399.7	525.2	550.5	702.5	435.4	448.9	158.5	55.4	56.5
Japanese yen	34.0	−33.0	−23.5	10.9	18.6	−17.5	3.8	6.6	14.7	7.1
Pound sterling	46.4	53.9	77.8	92.2	65.5	52.3	86.0	31.1	37.6	26.9
Canadian dollar	−6.2	−7.5	−2.3	−2.8	−1.1	3.6	15.6	6.2	3.3	7.3
Swedish krona	−0.4	3.6	0.1	1.2	1.4	1.1	2.0	0.4	0.8	0.8
Swiss franc	−1.6	6.3	4.0	−0.2	−5.2	8.0	15.8	4.8	2.0	5.5
Euro[1]	130.2	214.6	506.9	423.7	624.0	494.7	786.4	259.4	221.2	193.9
Other	23.2	8.9	14.7	9.0	19.0	31.1	38.4	19.0	12.5	9.1
Total	545.9	646.5	1,102.9	1,084.5	1,424.7	1,008.7	1,396.9	486.0	347.5	307.1
Announced international syndicated credit facilities by nationality of borrower										
All countries	1,080.6	905.3	1,025.2	1,450.0	1,381.4	1,296.9	1,241.4	264.2	523.4	430.3
Industrial countries	903.6	819.4	959.6	1,313.8	1,269.2	1,197.8	1,129.6	235.9	486.6	384.7
Of which:										
United States	606.7	575.1	622.6	792.4	844.8	735.0	609.2	132.3	325.5	206.0
Japan	6.1	11.4	15.4	17.5	23.8	19.5	18.2	10.3	4.4	8.6
Germany	23.6	15.5	34.0	42.4	35.8	85.2	97.1	12.0	27.8	14.1
France	38.7	19.8	33.7	72.9	50.1	63.9	65.8	17.8	29.7	66.3
Italy	10.1	6.0	16.1	34.9	36.0	22.9	45.3	8.1	4.2	6.1
United Kingdom	101.3	79.8	109.0	131.1	105.7	110.0	104.0	25.2	28.4	28.9
Canada	37.6	41.4	22.8	37.8	38.6	34.9	28.4	3.5	11.2	5.2

Source: Bank for International Settlements.
[1]For 1997–98, the euro includes euro area currencies.

Table 3. Selected Indicators on the Size of the Capital Markets, 2003
(In billions of U.S. dollars unless noted otherwise)

	GDP	Total Reserves Minus Gold[1]	Stock Market Capitalization	Debt Securities Public	Debt Securities Private	Debt Securities Total	Bank Assets[2]	Bonds, Equities, and Bank Assets[3]	Bonds, Equities, and Bank Assets[3] (In percent of GDP)
World	36,319.7	3,155.9	31,202.3	19,993.6	31,311.1	51,304.7	47,834.3	130,341.3	358.9
European Union	10,530.5	285.3	7,754.0	6,242.6	10,433.4	16,676.0	22,361.1	46,791.1	444.3
Euro area	8,216.0	186.6	4,882.8	5,444.2	7,958.7	13,402.9	16,570.8	35,050.4	426.6
North America	11,876.4	111.1	15,154.7	5,631.3	16,063.2	21,694.5	7,160.2	44,009.4	370.6
Canada	872.3	36.2	888.7	607.5	372.4	979.9	1,323.9	3,192.5	366.0
United States	11,004.1	74.9	14,266.0	5,023.8	15,690.8	20,714.6	5,836.3	40,816.9	370.9
Japan	4,299.6	663.3	4,904.6	5,835.1	2,252.6	8,087.7	7,239.9	20,232.3	470.6
Memorandum items:									
EU countries									
Austria	253.3	8.5	56.5	165.0	204.9	369.9	334.6	761.0	300.5
Belgium	304.9	11.0	170.7	379.1	316.6	695.7	1,213.3	2,079.7	682.1
Denmark	212.4	37.1	118.2	115.5	314.7	430.2	526.6	1,075.0	506.2
Finland	162.1	10.5	170.3	110.7	69.9	180.6	193.9	544.8	336.1
France	1,762.6	30.2	1,237.6	1,045.8	1,545.2	2,591.0	4,498.6	8,327.2	472.4
Germany	2,406.6	50.7	1,079.0	1,165.0	2,864.7	4,029.7	3,508.6	8,617.3	358.1
Greece	173.1	4.4	103.8	225.3	21.3	246.6	225.3	575.7	332.6
Ireland	152.4	4.1	85.1	39.2	136.8	176.0	706.1	967.2	634.6
Italy	1,471.1	30.4	614.8	1,498.4	1,116.9	2,615.3	2,195.2	5,425.4	368.8
Luxembourg	27.1	0.3	37.3	0.0	38.5	38.5	662.4	738.2	2,725.2
Netherlands	513.7	11.0	539.0	257.8	909.5	1,167.3	1,857.3	3,563.6	693.7
Portugal	146.9	5.9	62.4	106.8	120.5	227.3	179.6	469.3	319.4
Spain	842.2	19.8	726.2	451.1	613.9	1,065.0	1,189.7	2,981.0	354.0
Sweden	302.3	19.7	293.0	169.2	268.1	437.3	352.3	1,082.7	358.2
United Kingdom	1,799.8	41.9	2,460.1	513.7	1,891.9	2,405.6	4,717.4	9,583.1	532.4
Emerging market countries[4]	8,456.7	1,937.1	3,947.3	1,949.5	1,119.3	3,068.8	8,074.7	15,090.8	178.4
Of which:									
Asia	3,917.8	1,248.6	2,942.8	843.8	837.2	1,681.0	5,648.3	10,272.1	262.2
Latin America	1,742.6	195.7	608.1	635.3	202.1	837.4	904.4	2,349.8	134.8
Middle East	823.8	149.5	96.4	10.1	12.7	22.8	648.1	767.3	93.1
Africa	561.5	91.9	168.3	71.6	26.3	97.9	400.6	666.7	118.7
Europe	1,410.9	251.5	131.8	388.7	41.0	429.7	473.4	1,034.9	73.3

Sources: World Federation of Exchanges; Bank for International Settlements; International Monetary Fund, *International Financial Statistics* (IFS) and World Economic Outlook database as of March 11, 2005; and ©2003 Bureau van Dijk Electronic Publishing-Bankscope.
[1]Data are from the IFS. For the United Kingdom, excludes the assets of the Bank of England.
[2]Assets of commercial banks.
[3]Sum of the stock market capitalization, debt securities, and bank assets.
[4]This aggregate comprises the group of Other Emerging Market and Developing Countries defined in the World Economic Outlook, together with Hong Kong SAR, Israel, Korea, Singapore, and Taiwan Province of China.

Table 4. Global Over-the-Counter Derivatives Markets: Notional Amounts and Gross Market Values of Outstanding Contracts[1]

(In billions of U.S. dollars)

	Notional Amounts					Gross Market Values				
	End-June 2002	End-Dec. 2002	End-June 2003	End-Dec. 2003	End-June 2004	End-June 2002	End-Dec. 2002	End-June 2003	End-Dec. 2003	End-June 2004
Total	**127,509**	**141,665**	**169,658**	**197,167**	**220,058**	**4,450**	**6,360**	**7,896**	**6,987**	**6,395**
Foreign exchange	18,068	18,448	22,071	24,475	26,997	1,052	881	996	1,301	867
Outright forwards and forex swaps	10,426	10,719	12,332	12,387	13,926	615	468	476	607	308
Currency swaps	4,215	4,503	5,159	6,371	7,033	340	337	419	557	442
Options	3,427	3,226	4,580	5,717	6,038	97	76	101	136	116
Interest rate[2]	**89,955**	**101,658**	**121,799**	**141,991**	**164,626**	**2,467**	**4,266**	**5,459**	**4,328**	**3,951**
Forward rate agreements	9,146	8,792	10,271	10,769	13,144	19	22	20	19	29
Swaps	68,234	79,120	94,583	111,209	127,570	2,213	3,864	5,004	3,918	3,562
Options	12,575	13,746	16,946	20,012	23,912	235	381	434	391	360
Equity-linked	**2,214**	**2,309**	**2,799**	**3,787**	**4,521**	**243**	**255**	**260**	**274**	**294**
Forwards and swaps	386	364	488	601	691	62	61	67	57	63
Options	1,828	1,944	2,311	3,186	3,829	181	194	193	217	231
Commodity[3]	**777**	**923**	**1,040**	**1,406**	**1,270**	**79**	**86**	**100**	**128**	**166**
Gold	279	315	304	344	318	28	28	12	39	45
Other	498	608	736	1,062	952	51	58	88	88	121
Forwards and swaps	290	402	458	420	503	...	...	...	...	...
Options	208	206	279	642	449	...	...	...	...	...
Other	**16,496**	**18,328**	**21,949**	**25,508**	**22,644**	**609**	**871**	**1,081**	**957**	**1,116**
Memorandum items:										
Gross credit exposure[4]	n.a.	n.a.	n.a.	n.a.	n.a.	1,317	1,511	1,750	1,969	1,478
Exchange-traded derivatives	18,068	18,448	22,071	24,475	26,997	...	...	...	...	...

Source: Bank for International Settlements.

[1]All figures are adjusted for double-counting. Notional amounts outstanding have been adjusted by halving positions vis-à-vis other reporting dealers. Gross market values have been calculated as the sum of the total gross positive market value of contracts and the absolute value of the gross negative market value of contracts with nonreporting counterparties.

[2]Single-currency contracts only.

[3]Adjustments for double-counting are estimated.

[4]Gross market values after taking into account legally enforceable bilateral netting agreements.

Table 5. Global Over-the-Counter Derivatives Markets: Notional Amounts and Gross Market Values of Outstanding Contracts by Counterparty, Remaining Maturity, and Currency[1]
(In billions of U.S. dollars)

	Notional Amounts					Gross Market Values				
	End-June 2002	End-Dec. 2002	End-June 2003	End-Dec. 2003	End-June 2004	End-June 2002	End-Dec. 2002	End-June 2003	End-Dec. 2003	End-June 2004
Total	**127,509**	**141,665**	**169,658**	**197,167**	**220,058**	**4,450**	**6,360**	**7,896**	**6,987**	**6,395**
Foreign exchange	**18,068**	**18,448**	**22,071**	**24,475**	**26,997**	**1,052**	**881**	**996**	**1,301**	**867**
By counterparty										
With other reporting dealers	6,602	6,842	7,954	8,660	10,796	372	285	284	395	247
With other financial institutions	7,210	7,597	8,948	9,450	10,113	421	377	427	535	352
With nonfinancial customers	4,256	4,009	5,168	6,365	6,088	259	220	286	370	267
By remaining maturity										
Up to one year[2]	14,401	14,522	17,543	18,840	21,252	...	...	...	...	...
One to five years[2]	2,537	2,719	3,128	3,901	3,912	...	...	...	...	...
Over five years[2]	1,130	1,208	1,399	1,734	1,834	...	...	...	...	...
By major currency										
U.S. dollar[3]	15,973	16,500	19,401	21,429	24,551	948	813	891	1,212	808
Euro[3]	7,297	7,794	9,879	10,145	10,312	445	429	526	665	380
Japanese yen[3]	4,454	4,791	4,907	5,500	6,516	254	189	165	217	178
Pound sterling[3]	2,522	2,462	3,093	4,286	4,614	112	98	114	179	130
Other[3]	5,890	5,349	6,862	7,590	8,001	345	233	296	329	238
Interest rate[4]	**89,955**	**101,658**	**121,799**	**141,991**	**164,626**	**2,467**	**4,266**	**5,459**	**4,328**	**3,951**
By counterparty										
With other reporting dealers	43,340	46,722	53,622	63,579	72,550	1,081	1,848	2,266	1,872	1,606
With other financial institutions	36,310	43,607	53,133	57,564	70,219	1,025	1,845	2,482	1,768	1,707
With nonfinancial customers	10,304	11,328	15,044	20,847	21,857	361	573	710	687	638
By remaining maturity										
Up to one year[2]	33,674	36,938	44,927	46,474	57,157	...	...	...	...	...
One to five years[2]	34,437	40,137	46,646	58,914	66,093	...	...	...	...	...
Over five years[2]	21,844	24,583	30,226	36,603	41,376	...	...	...	...	...
By major currency										
U.S. dollar	32,178	34,399	40,110	46,178	57,827	1,127	1,917	2,286	1,734	1,464
Euro	30,671	38,429	50,000	55,793	63,006	710	1,499	2,178	1,730	1,774
Japanese yen	13,433	14,650	15,270	19,526	21,103	326	378	405	358	324
Pound sterling	6,978	7,442	8,322	9,884	11,867	151	252	315	228	188
Other	6,695	6,738	8,097	10,610	10,823	153	220	275	278	201
Equity-linked	**2,214**	**2,309**	**2,799**	**3,787**	**4,521**	**243**	**255**	**260**	**274**	**294**
Commodity[5]	**777**	**923**	**1,040**	**1,406**	**1,270**	**79**	**86**	**100**	**128**	**166**
Other	**16,496**	**18,328**	**21,949**	**25,508**	**22,644**	**609**	**871**	**1,081**	**957**	**1,116**

Source: Bank for International Settlements.
[1]All figures are adjusted for double-counting. Notional amounts outstanding have been adjusted by halving positions vis-à-vis other reporting dealers. Gross market values have been calculated as the sum of the total gross positive market value of contracts and the absolute value of the gross negative market value of contracts with nonreporting counterparties.
[2]Residual maturity.
[3]Counting both currency sides of each foreign exchange transaction means that the currency breakdown sums to twice the aggregate.
[4]Single-currency contracts only.
[5]Adjustments for double-counting are estimated.

Table 6. Exchange-Traded Derivative Financial Instruments: Notional Principal Amounts Outstanding and Annual Turnover

	1988	1989	1990	1991	1992	1993	1994	1995	1996
	(In billions of U.S. dollars)								
Notional principal amounts outstanding									
Interest rate futures	895.4	1,201.0	1,454.8	2,157.4	2,913.1	4,960.4	5,807.6	5,876.2	5,979.0
Interest rate options	279.0	386.0	595.4	1,069.6	1,383.8	2,361.4	2,623.2	2,741.8	3,277.8
Currency futures	12.1	16.0	17.0	18.3	26.5	34.7	40.4	33.8	37.7
Currency options	48.0	50.2	56.5	62.9	71.6	75.9	55.7	120.4	133.4
Stock market index futures	27.0	41.1	69.1	76.0	79.8	110.0	127.7	172.2	195.9
Stock market index options	42.7	70.2	93.6	136.8	163.1	231.6	242.7	337.7	394.5
Total	1,304.1	1,764.5	2,286.4	3,521.0	4,637.9	7,774.1	8,897.2	9,282.1	10,018.1
North America	951.2	1,153.5	1,264.4	2,152.8	2,698.1	4,359.9	4,823.5	4,852.3	4,841.2
Europe	177.4	250.9	461.4	710.7	1,114.4	1,777.9	1,831.8	2,241.3	2,828.1
Asia-Pacific	175.5	360.1	560.5	657.0	823.5	1,606.0	2,171.8	1,990.2	2,154.0
Other	0.0	0.0	0.1	0.5	1.9	30.3	70.1	198.3	194.8
	(In millions of contracts traded)								
Annual turnover									
Interest rate futures	156.4	201.0	219.1	230.9	330.1	427.0	628.5	561.0	612.2
Interest rate options	30.5	39.5	52.0	50.8	64.8	82.9	116.6	225.5	151.1
Currency futures	22.5	28.2	29.7	30.0	31.3	39.0	69.8	99.6	73.6
Currency options	18.2	20.7	18.9	22.9	23.4	23.7	21.3	23.3	26.3
Stock market index futures	29.6	30.1	39.4	54.6	52.0	71.2	109.0	114.8	93.9
Stock market index options	79.1	101.7	119.1	121.4	133.9	144.1	197.6	187.3	172.3
Total	336.3	421.2	478.2	510.4	635.6	787.9	1,142.9	1,211.6	1,129.3
North America	252.3	288.0	312.3	302.6	341.4	382.4	513.5	455.0	428.4
Europe	40.8	64.3	83.0	110.5	185.1	263.4	398.1	354.7	391.8
Asia-Pacific	34.3	63.6	79.1	85.8	82.9	98.5	131.7	126.4	115.9
Other	8.9	5.3	3.8	11.5	26.2	43.6	99.6	275.5	193.2

Source: Bank for International Settlements.

	1997	1998	1999	2000	2001	2002	2003	2004 Q1	2004 Q2	2004 Q3
	(In billions of U.S. dollars)									
	7,586.7	8,031.4	7,924.8	7,907.8	9,269.5	9,955.6	13,123.8	16,231.5	19,150.6	17,024.8
	3,639.9	4,623.5	3,755.5	4,734.2	12,492.8	11,759.5	20,793.8	26,283.2	30,234.4	28,335.0
	42.3	31.7	36.7	74.4	65.6	47.0	80.1	75.2	65.7	84.1
	118.6	49.2	22.4	21.4	27.4	27.4	37.9	47.0	32.3	37.2
	210.9	291.5	340.3	371.5	333.9	325.5	501.9	549.2	537.4	552.9
	808.7	907.4	1,510.2	1,148.3	1,574.9	1,700.8	2,202.3	2,689.9	2,781.5	2,958.1
	12,407.1	13,934.7	13,589.9	14,257.7	23,764.1	23,815.7	36,739.8	45,875.9	52,802.0	48,992.1
	6,347.9	7,355.1	6,930.6	8,167.9	16,203.2	13,693.8	19,504.0	23,736.7	31,061.1	27,897.6
	3,587.4	4,397.1	4,008.5	4,197.4	6,141.3	8,800.4	15,406.1	19,862.0	19,302.1	18,509.2
	2,235.7	1,882.5	2,401.3	1,606.2	1,308.5	1,192.4	1,613.1	2,076.6	2,239.9	2,370.3
	236.1	300.0	249.5	286.2	111.1	129.1	216.6	200.6	198.9	215.0
	(In millions of contracts traded)									
	701.6	760.0	672.7	781.2	1,057.5	1,152.0	1,576.8	454.6	495.7	484.5
	116.7	129.6	117.9	107.6	199.6	240.3	302.2	92.4	99.0	89.8
	73.5	54.6	37.2	43.6	49.1	42.7	58.7	18.7	19.0	20.5
	21.1	12.1	6.8	7.1	10.5	16.1	14.3	3.6	3.2	2.7
	115.9	178.0	204.8	225.2	337.1	530.2	725.7	207.9	200.7	188.1
	178.2	195.1	322.5	481.4	1,148.2	2,235.4	3,233.9	731.5	851.0	666.8
	1,207.2	1,329.4	1,361.9	1,646.1	2,802.0	4,216.8	5,911.7	1,508.6	1,668.5	1,452.4
	463.6	530.2	463.0	461.3	675.7	912.2	1,279.7	366.3	428.1	430.0
	482.8	525.9	604.5	718.5	957.8	1,074.8	1,346.4	389.0	353.1	330.5
	126.8	170.9	207.8	331.3	985.1	2,073.1	3,099.6	685.4	823.8	628.3
	134.0	102.4	86.6	135.0	183.4	156.7	186.0	67.9	63.5	63.6

Table 7. United States: Sectoral Balance Sheets
(In percent)

	1997	1998	1999	2000	2001	2002	2003
Corporate sector							
Debt/net worth	51.1	51.3	51.1	49.0	52.1	51.6	49.7
Short-term debt/total debt	40.5	40.3	38.9	39.4	33.7	30.5	27.4
Interest burden[1]	11.0	12.6	13.4	15.8	17.7	15.7	13.2
Household sector							
Net worth/assets	85.4	85.7	86.1	85.0	83.8	82.0	82.3
Equity/total assets	29.7	31.5	35.1	31.0	26.6	20.8	24.1
Equity/financial assets	42.8	45.0	49.4	45.3	40.4	33.3	38.0
Home mortgage debt/total assets	9.5	9.4	9.1	9.8	10.7	12.2	12.3
Consumer credit/total assets	3.4	3.3	3.2	3.5	3.8	4.1	3.8
Total debt/financial assets	21.0	20.5	19.5	21.9	24.6	28.8	27.8
Debt service burden[2]	12.1	12.1	12.3	12.6	13.1	13.3	13.2
Banking sector[3]							
Credit quality							
Nonperforming loans[4]/total loans	1.0	1.0	1.0	1.1	1.4	1.5	1.2
Net loan losses/average total loans	0.7	0.7	0.6	0.7	1.0	1.1	0.9
Loan-loss reserve/total loans	1.8	1.8	1.7	1.7	1.9	1.9	1.8
Net charge-offs/total loans	0.6	0.7	0.6	0.7	1.0	1.1	0.9
Capital ratios							
Total risk-based capital	12.2	12.2	12.2	12.1	12.7	12.8	12.8
Tier 1 risk-based capital	9.6	9.5	9.5	9.4	9.9	10.0	10.1
Equity capital/total assets	8.3	8.5	8.4	8.5	9.1	9.2	9.1
Core capital (leverage ratio)	7.6	7.5	7.8	7.7	7.8	7.9	7.9
Profitability measures							
Return on average assets (ROA)	1.3	1.3	1.3	1.2	1.2	1.4	1.4
Return on average equity (ROE)	15.6	14.8	15.7	14.8	14.2	14.9	15.2
Net interest margin	4.3	4.0	4.0	3.9	3.9	4.1	3.7
Efficiency ratio[5]	59.2	61.0	58.7	58.4	57.7	55.8	56.5

Sources: Board of Governors of the Federal Reserve System, *Flow of Funds;* Department of Commerce, Bureau of Economic Analysis; Federal Deposit Insurance Corporation; and Federal Reserve Bank of St. Louis.

[1]Ratio of net interest payments to pre-tax income.
[2]Ratio of debt payments to disposable personal income.
[3]FDIC-insured commercial banks.
[4]Loans past due 90+ days and nonaccrual.
[5]Noninterest expense less amortization of intangible assets as a percent of net interest income plus noninterest income.

Table 8. Japan: Sectoral Balance Sheets[1]
(In percent)

	FY1997	FY1998	FY1999	FY2000	FY2001	FY2002	FY2003
Corporate sector							
Debt/shareholders' equity (book value)	207.9	189.3	182.5	156.8	156.0	146.1	121.3
Short-term debt/total debt	41.8	39.0	39.4	37.7	36.8	39.0	37.8
Interest burden[2]	39.1	46.5	36.3	28.4	32.3	27.8	22.0
Debt/operating profits	1,498.5	1,813.8	1,472.1	1,229.3	1,480.0	1,370.0	1,079.2
Memorandum items:							
Total debt/GDP[3]	106.7	106.9	108.3	102.1	100.5	99.4	89.5
Household sector							
Net worth/assets	85.3	85.1	85.5	85.3	85.1	85.1	...
Equity	4.3	3.1	5.6	4.9	4.5	5.0	...
Real estate	40.0	39.5	37.6	36.7	35.5	34.1	...
Interest burden[4]	5.5	5.3	5.0	5.1	5.0	4.9	4.7
Memorandum items:							
Debt/equity	345.2	477.6	259.4	299.5	333.4	298.5	...
Debt/real estate	36.7	37.8	38.6	40.0	41.9	43.7	...
Debt/net disposable income	126.1	127.0	126.7	128.5	130.3	127.5	...
Debt/net worth	17.2	17.6	17.0	17.2	17.5	17.6	...
Equity/net worth	5.0	3.7	6.5	5.7	5.2	5.9	...
Real estate/net worth	46.9	46.5	43.9	43.0	41.7	40.1	...
Total debt/GDP[3]	75.9	77.4	77.7	76.4	77.1	76.5	...
Banking sector							
Credit quality							
Nonperforming loans[5]/total loans	5.4	6.2	5.9	6.3	8.4	7.4	5.8
Capital ratio							
Stockholders' equity/assets	2.8	4.4	4.8	4.6	3.9	3.3	3.9
Profitability measures							
Return on equity (ROE)[6]	−20.4	−12.5	2.6	−0.5	−14.3	−19.5	−2.7

Sources: Ministry of Finance, *Financial Statements of Corporations by Industries*; Cabinet Office, Economic and Social Research Institute, *Annual Report on National Accounts*; Japanese Bankers Association, *Financial Statements of All Banks*; and Financial Services Agency, *The Status of Nonperforming Loans*.

[1]Data are for fiscal years beginning April 1.
[2]Interest payments as a percent of operating profits.
[3]Revised due to the change in GDP figures.
[4]Interest payments as a percent of disposable income.
[5]From FY1998 onward, nonperforming loans are based on figures reported under the Financial Reconstruction Law. Up to FY1997, they are based on loans reported by banks for risk management purposes.
[6]Net income as a percentage of stockholders' equity (no adjustment for preferred stocks, etc.).

Table 9. Europe: Sectoral Balance Sheets[1]
(In percent)

	1997	1998	1999	2000	2001	2002	2003
Corporate sector							
Debt/equity[2]	85.3	83.6	84.8	82.7	83.8	84.3	81.9
Short-term debt/total debt	38.1	37.3	37.7	39.9	38.9	37.1	37.4
Interest burden[3]	17.2	16.8	17.1	18.9	19.8	19.1	18.6
Debt/operating profits	263.6	258.8	288.1	315.2	322.2	336.6	326.2
Memorandum items:							
Financial assets/equity	1.7	1.8	2.1	2.0	1.9	1.6	1.6
Liquid assets/short-term debt	94.5	92.9	89.6	85.7	88.8	93.1	90.3
Household sector							
Net worth/assets	85.4	85.3	85.7	85.4	84.7	84.4	84.4
Equity/net worth	14.8	15.9	18.6	17.5	16.6	13.1	12.7
Equity/net financial assets	37.6	39.5	43.9	43.3	43.0	37.4	36.3
Interest burden[4]	6.4	6.7	6.4	6.6	6.3	6.2	6.1
Memorandum items:							
Nonfinancial assets/net worth	59.5	58.9	56.8	58.7	60.9	65.0	64.9
Debt/net financial assets	45.4	44.0	41.5	43.0	45.4	51.1	50.2
Debt/income	89.5	91.8	94.7	95.5	95.6	99.6	102.8
Banking sector[5]							
Credit quality							
Nonperforming loans/total loans	5.0	6.1	5.6	3.5	3.4	3.7	3.7
Loan-loss reserve/nonperforming loans	74.7	76.5	72.0	78.5	81.1	76.9	76.1
Loan-loss reserve/total loans	2.1	2.7	2.7	2.8	2.7	2.9	2.8
Loan-loss provisions/total operating income[6]	13.2	11.7	9.1	7.4	10.0	13.1	11.1
Capital ratios							
Total risk-based capital	10.7	10.6	10.5	11.0	11.2	11.4	. . .
Tier 1 risk-based capital	7.2	7.0	7.2	7.7	7.7	8.1	. . .
Equity capital/total assets	3.7	3.9	3.8	4.1	4.0	4.0	4.1
Capital funds/liabilities	6.1	6.3	6.2	6.6	6.5	6.6	6.6
Profitability measures							
Return on assets, or ROA (after tax)	0.4	0.4	0.5	0.7	0.4	0.3	0.4
Return on equity, or ROE (after tax)	9.7	11.2	11.7	17.6	10.3	8.2	9.4
Net interest margin	1.9	1.7	1.4	1.5	1.5	1.6	1.6
Efficiency ratio[7]	69.5	68.4	68.6	68.9	70.3	71.0	66.9

Sources: ©2003 Bureau van Dijk Electronic Publishing-Bankscope; ECB *Monthly Bulletin*; and IMF staff estimates.
[1]GDP-weighted average for France, Germany, and the United Kingdom, unless otherwise noted.
[2]Corporate equity adjusted for changes in asset valuation.
[3]Interest payments as a percent of gross operating profits.
[4]Interest payments as a percent of disposable income.
[5]Fifty largest European banks. Data availability may restrict coverage to less than 50 banks for specific indicators.
[6]Includes the write-off of goodwill in foreign subsidiaries by banks with exposure to Argentina.
[7]Cost-to-income ratio.

Figure 15. Emerging Market Volatility Measures

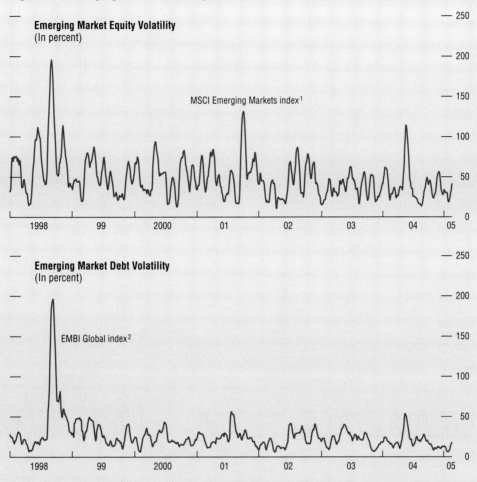

Emerging Market Equity Volatility
(In percent)

MSCI Emerging Markets index[1]

Emerging Market Debt Volatility
(In percent)

EMBI Global index[2]

Sources: For "Emerging Market Equity Volatility," Morgan Stanley Capital International (MSCI); and IMF staff estimates. For "Emerging Market Debt Volatility," J.P. Morgan Chase & Co.; and IMF staff estimates.
[1]Data utilize the Emerging Markets index in U.S. dollars to calculate 30-day rolling volatilities.
[2]Data utilize the EMBI Global total return index in U.S. dollars to calculate 30-day rolling volatilities.

Figure 16. Emerging Market Debt Cross-Correlation Measures

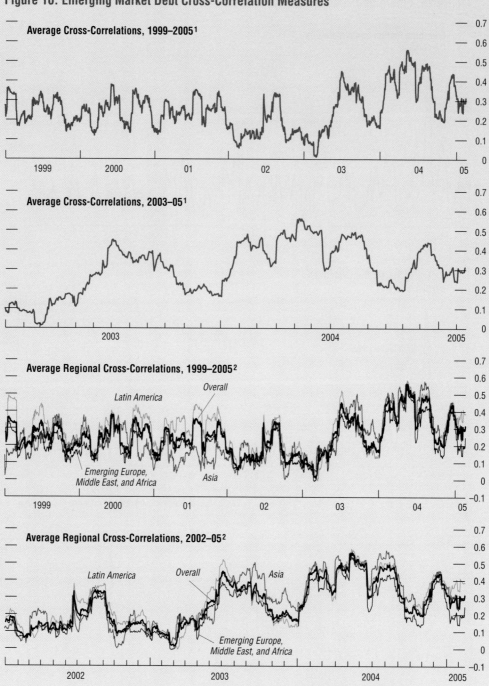

Average Cross-Correlations, 1999–2005[1]

Average Cross-Correlations, 2003–05[1]

Average Regional Cross-Correlations, 1999–2005[2]

Latin America

Overall

Emerging Europe, Middle East, and Africa

Asia

Average Regional Cross-Correlations, 2002–05[2]

Latin America

Overall

Asia

Emerging Europe, Middle East, and Africa

Sources: J.P. Morgan Chase & Co.; and IMF staff estimates.
[1]Thirty-day moving simple average across all pair-wise return correlations of 20 constituents included in the EMBI Global.
[2]Simple average of all pair-wise correlations of all markets in a given region with all other bond markets, regardless of region.

Table 10. Equity Market Indices

	Year to Date (as of 2/16/05)	2004 End of Period				End of Period					12-Month High	12-Month Low	All-Time High[1]	All-Time Low[1]
		Q1	Q2	Q3	Q4	2000	2001	2002	2003	2004				
World	**1,169.7**	**1,059.2**	**1,062.5**	**1,047.9**	**1,169.3**	**1,221.3**	**1,003.5**	**792.2**	**1,036.3**	**1,169.3**	**1,170.0**	**997.0**	**1,448.8**	**423.1**
Emerging Markets														
Emerging Markets Free	**562.5**	**482.1**	**432.2**	**464.2**	**542.2**	**333.8**	**317.4**	**292.1**	**442.8**	**542.2**	**542.3**	**395.9**	**587.1**	**175.3**
EMF Latin America	**1,555.4**	**1,169.5**	**1,062.4**	**1,238.3**	**1,483.6**	**915.6**	**876.2**	**658.9**	**1,100.9**	**1,483.6**	**1,483.6**	**942.2**	**1,569.6**	**185.6**
Argentina	1,328.0	1,034.6	847.8	1,073.7	1,163.0	1,232.7	959.6	470.3	933.6	1,163.0	1,163.2	758.4	2,052.2	152.6
Brazil	1,103.9	786.9	686.4	862.9	1,046.6	763.2	597.1	395.4	802.0	1,046.6	1,047.3	584.1	1,306.4	84.1
Chile	975.9	779.6	762.0	870.5	997.3	604.7	568.7	445.5	800.6	997.3	997.3	705.7	1,119.6	183.0
Colombia	252.7	152.8	145.8	184.6	245.0	42.1	57.7	68.3	108.6	245.0	251.3	127.6	255.4	41.2
Mexico	2,871.7	2,241.1	2,114.1	2,222.4	2,715.6	1,464.9	1,698.2	1,442.8	1,873.1	2,715.6	2,730.3	1,930.1	2,890.0	308.9
Peru	350.8	364.7	308.8	340.5	343.4	125.0	144.1	182.7	344.1	343.4	364.7	275.6	364.7	73.5
Venezuela	138.6	123.0	131.7	149.4	151.0	106.1	95.4	77.7	103.8	151.0	166.4	105.5	278.4	56.1
EMF Asia	**242.4**	**222.1**	**195.0**	**203.2**	**231.6**	**143.6**	**149.7**	**140.4**	**206.4**	**231.6**	**234.9**	**178.4**	**433.0**	**104.1**
China	25.7	24.7	22.5	24.1	25.3	22.8	16.8	14.1	25.5	25.3	27.1	19.0	136.9	12.9
India	273.1	230.8	201.6	232.1	273.1	173.4	141.2	148.8	246.2	273.1	276.9	184.9	323.9	77.7
Indonesia	1,420.3	892.4	927.3	1,060.5	1,324.0	456.4	437.2	519.6	831.1	1,324.0	1,386.9	839.9	1,420.3	280.0
Korea	279.7	276.1	237.3	245.9	256.4	125.6	190.4	184.7	246.0	256.4	292.9	215.7	292.9	59.5
Malaysia	342.4	342.6	306.5	316.8	335.9	245.2	250.7	244.0	300.4	335.9	348.3	293.5	465.7	88.3
Pakistan	263.6	200.7	192.4	188.2	211.7	99.1	67.4	146.0	188.2	211.7	242.4	177.3	263.6	54.4
Philippines	433.4	296.1	331.8	364.7	381.1	352.6	292.2	210.1	303.7	381.1	421.9	287.6	917.3	132.6
Taiwan Province of China	258.5	277.0	248.3	243.8	257.7	222.2	255.6	189.5	259.1	257.7	300.6	224.3	483.5	103.9
Thailand	287.7	240.8	245.3	247.4	263.9	102.5	107.5	130.2	280.5	263.9	279.1	217.9	669.4	72.0
EMF Europe, Middle East, and Africa	**225.2**	**185.6**	**171.8**	**185.3**	**222.7**	**. . .**	**103.5**	**108.4**	**163.9**	**222.7**	**223.8**	**157.5**	**225.2**	**80.8**
Czech Republic	266.3	191.1	178.4	197.3	234.8	107.6	97.5	116.2	152.9	234.8	255.5	160.1	266.3	62.8
Egypt	690.1	282.6	284.2	422.1	505.3	154.9	101.9	97.4	234.6	505.3	689.8	258.7	704.4	89.9
Hungary	1,253.0	782.7	812.9	888.9	1,057.0	582.9	507.9	535.5	646.9	1,057.0	1,119.2	682.6	1,253.0	77.1
Israel	165.7	156.5	167.5	139.0	167.4	196.0	132.7	90.8	141.4	167.4	167.5	135.2	236.2	67.6
Jordan	413.3	250.2	252.5	284.0	379.2	116.1	149.5	153.5	238.3	379.2	439.0	239.8	439.0	103.1
Morocco	188.3	188.3	189.4	190.6	189.1	198.9	180.1	138.5	171.4	189.1	197.2	158.5	302.1	99.6
Poland	1,502.2	1,251.6	1,218.3	1,264.7	1,419.3	1,307.9	891.9	861.0	1,118.3	1,419.3	1,425.0	1,142.5	1,792.9	99.6
Russia	506.6	596.7	470.5	508.7	479.9	155.2	237.8	270.7	461.1	479.9	626.8	408.2	626.8	30.6
South Africa	356.8	302.7	278.9	327.8	352.4	244.8	309.3	272.7	296.8	352.4	356.0	269.5	356.8	99.7
Turkey	463,719	336,724	303,284	369,472	425,008	163,012	234,490	169,900	319,808	425,008	458,546	265,612	474,160	426
EMF sectors														
Energy	367.9	324.4	277.8	324.5	349.0	148.5	162.1	163.1	287.4	349.0	349.0	265.9	367.9	81.7
Materials	271.9	253.1	222.3	262.0	265.0	140.8	173.9	182.8	250.1	265.0	271.7	207.6	271.9	98.5
Industrials	132.8	107.2	99.2	106.8	128.0	73.4	63.8	61.8	98.9	128.0	129.5	87.6	276.8	52.6
Consumer discretionary	299.8	250.9	218.7	241.9	292.3	126.0	130.6	138.8	233.8	292.3	295.1	199.6	299.8	74.1
Consumer staple	150.6	124.4	117.1	126.4	147.0	103.1	94.6	88.2	118.6	147.0	147.1	109.6	151.1	80.4
Health care	277.8	286.6	291.6	251.4	290.8	173.9	146.5	169.8	272.5	290.8	300.7	243.0	300.7	83.3
Financials	195.6	151.0	138.8	149.5	187.9	112.6	107.7	98.6	138.8	187.9	188.6	124.7	196.2	74.6
Information technology	173.0	174.5	149.5	141.6	161.5	130.9	134.2	103.9	149.6	161.5	187.3	130.8	300.0	73.1
Telecommunications	134.7	108.9	104.1	106.9	131.6	113.8	91.9	72.7	100.8	131.6	133.0	92.4	211.5	62.9
Utilities	153.8	127.7	114.3	132.4	149.8	95.7	91.5	72.4	127.2	149.8	149.9	106.8	247.8	63.1

Table 10 *(continued)*

	Year to Date (as of 2/16/05)	Period on Period Percent Change									12-Month High	12-Month Low	All-Time High[1]	All-Time Low[1]
		2004 End of Period				End of Period								
		Q1	Q2	Q3	Q4	2000	2001	2002	2003	2004				
World	—	**2.2**	**0.3**	**−1.4**	**11.6**	**−14.1**	**−17.8**	**−21.1**	**30.8**	**12.8**	...	...	...	...
Emerging Markets														
Emerging Markets Free	3.7	8.9	−10.3	7.4	16.8	−31.8	−4.9	−8.0	51.6	22.4	...	...	...	...
EMF Latin America	4.8	6.2	−9.2	16.6	19.8	−18.4	−4.3	−24.8	67.1	34.8	...	...	...	...
Argentina	14.2	10.8	−18.1	26.7	8.3	−26.1	−22.2	−51.0	98.5	24.6	...	...	...	...
Brazil	5.5	−1.9	−12.8	25.7	21.3	−14.2	−21.8	−33.8	102.9	30.5	...	...	...	...
Chile	−2.1	−2.6	−2.2	14.2	14.6	−17.0	−6.0	−21.7	79.7	24.6	...	...	...	...
Colombia	3.1	40.7	−4.5	26.6	32.7	−41.2	37.1	18.3	59.0	125.7	...	...	...	...
Mexico	5.8	19.7	−5.7	5.1	22.2	−21.5	15.9	−15.0	29.8	45.0	...	...	...	...
Peru	2.1	6.0	−15.3	10.3	0.9	−26.7	15.3	26.8	88.4	−0.2	...	...	...	...
Venezuela	−8.2	18.5	7.0	13.5	1.1	0.8	−10.0	−18.6	33.6	45.4	...	...	...	...
EMF Asia	4.6	7.6	−12.2	4.2	14.0	−42.5	4.2	−6.2	47.1	12.2	...	...	...	...
China	1.6	−3.0	−9.1	7.3	5.1	−32.0	−26.0	−16.0	80.3	−0.7	...	...	...	...
India	—	−6.3	−12.6	15.1	17.7	−17.2	−18.6	5.3	65.5	11.0	...	...	...	...
Indonesia	7.3	7.4	3.9	14.4	24.8	−49.3	−4.2	18.9	60.0	59.3	...	...	...	...
Korea	9.1	12.2	−14.1	3.6	4.3	−44.6	51.6	−3.0	33.2	4.2	...	...	...	...
Malaysia	1.9	14.0	−10.5	3.4	6.0	−17.3	2.3	−2.7	23.1	11.8	...	...	...	...
Pakistan	24.5	6.6	−4.1	−2.2	12.5	−4.3	−32.0	116.7	28.9	12.5	...	...	...	...
Philippines	13.7	−2.5	12.1	9.9	4.5	−32.1	−17.1	−28.1	44.5	25.5	...	...	...	...
Taiwan Province of China	0.3	6.9	−10.4	−1.8	5.7	−42.3	15.0	−25.8	36.7	−0.6	...	...	...	...
Thailand	9.0	−14.1	1.9	0.9	6.7	−50.0	4.9	21.1	115.4	−5.9	...	...	...	...
EMF Europe, Middle East, and Africa	1.1	13.2	−7.4	7.8	20.2	...	...	4.7	51.2	35.8	...	...	...	...
Czech Republic	13.4	25.0	−6.6	10.6	19.0	5.5	−9.4	19.2	31.6	53.6	...	...	...	...
Egypt	36.6	20.5	0.5	48.5	19.7	−38.4	−34.2	−4.4	140.8	115.4	...	...	...	...
Hungary	18.5	21.0	3.9	9.3	18.9	−19.6	−12.9	5.4	20.8	63.4	...	...	...	...
Israel	−1.0	10.7	7.0	−17.0	20.4	24.7	−32.3	−31.6	55.7	18.4	...	...	...	...
Jordan	9.0	5.0	0.9	12.5	33.5	−24.7	28.8	2.6	55.3	59.1	...	...	...	...
Morocco	−0.5	9.8	0.6	0.6	−0.8	−20.2	−9.5	−23.1	23.8	10.4	...	...	...	...
Poland	5.8	11.9	−2.7	3.8	12.2	−4.8	−31.8	−3.5	29.9	26.9	...	...	...	...
Russia	5.6	29.4	−21.2	8.1	−5.7	−30.4	53.2	13.9	70.3	4.1	...	...	...	...
South Africa	1.3	2.0	−7.9	17.5	7.5	−1.2	26.3	−11.8	8.8	18.7	...	...	...	...
Turkey	9.1	5.3	−9.9	21.8	15.0	−33.5	43.8	−27.5	88.2	32.9	...	...	...	...
EMF sectors														
Energy	5.4	12.9	−14.4	16.8	7.6	−24.7	9.2	0.6	76.2	21.4	...	...	...	...
Materials	2.6	1.2	−12.2	17.9	1.2	−21.0	23.5	5.2	36.8	6.0	...	...	...	...
Industrials	3.8	8.4	−7.4	7.7	19.8	−41.7	−13.1	−3.2	60.1	29.5	...	...	...	...
Consumer discretionary	2.6	7.3	−12.8	10.6	20.8	−41.6	3.6	6.3	68.4	25.0	...	...	...	...
Consumer staple	2.4	4.9	−5.8	7.9	16.3	−20.2	−8.2	−6.7	34.4	24.0	...	...	...	...
Health care	−4.5	5.2	1.7	−13.8	15.7	0.7	−15.8	15.9	60.5	6.7	...	...	...	...
Financials	4.1	8.8	−8.1	7.7	25.7	−24.3	−4.3	−8.4	40.7	35.4	...	...	...	...
Information technology	7.1	16.7	−14.3	−5.3	14.0	−44.9	2.6	−22.6	43.9	8.0	...	...	...	...
Telecommunications	2.4	8.0	−4.4	2.7	23.1	−31.1	−19.2	−20.9	38.7	30.5	...	...	...	...
Utilities	2.7	0.4	−10.5	15.8	13.2	−25.0	−4.4	−20.9	75.7	17.8	...	...	...	...

Table 10 *(concluded)*

	Year to Date (as of 2/16/05)	2004 End of Period				End of Period					12-Month High	12-Month Low	All-Time High[1]	All-Time Low[1]
		Q1	Q2	Q3	Q4	2000	2001	2002	2003	2004				
Developed Markets														
Australia	823.1	680.5	700.6	725.2	797.9	640.1	690.8	604.4	655.5	797.9	639.6	539.9	712.9	250.2
Austria	197.5	141.1	150.7	156.9	185.3	96.9	94.6	91.8	118.0	185.3	105.4	79.7	105.4	96.2
Belgium	82.9	63.6	66.3	72.2	77.9	85.8	78.6	55.3	60.1	77.9	65.0	38.1	53.9	51.2
Canada	1,185.9	1,062.0	1,058.7	1,072.3	1,139.3	1,156.4	965.8	818.3	1,019.7	1,139.3	886.4	705.8	1,511.4	338.3
Denmark	2,254.7	1,909.4	2,011.5	2,092.1	2,115.9	2,333.3	2,060.1	1,448.8	1,772.7	2,115.9	1,752.8	1,245.8	2,776.6	556.5
Finland	99.4	113.1	91.6	88.1	93.9	267.5	171.8	100.3	97.4	93.9	126.0	78.8	383.1	78.8
France	105.7	95.3	98.0	96.0	100.6	152.0	123.1	81.3	93.2	100.6	95.3	63.4	178.6	63.4
Germany	81.1	73.0	75.4	72.6	79.2	124.0	100.1	56.0	74.6	79.2	78.4	42.9	163.6	41.4
Greece	90.3	67.0	68.5	68.7	83.3	106.1	76.8	46.8	63.6	83.3	61.9	38.2	197.2	38.2
Hong Kong SAR	7,494.2	6,747.8	6,349.0	6,956.4	7,668.5	7,690.1	6,058.0	4,808.4	6,341.3	7,668.5	5,553.6	4,305.4	10,165.3	1,995.5
Ireland	91.8	71.0	76.4	78.4	85.2	92.1	93.1	56.8	65.9	85.2	67.1	51.9	107.3	51.9
Italy	97.3	79.8	83.1	83.1	93.2	119.9	91.2	69.6	78.1	93.2	78.4	58.7	132.1	58.7
Japan	702.4	709.2	714.6	665.9	699.1	808.2	650.3	524.3	637.3	699.1	628.7	462.1	1,655.3	462.1
Netherlands	74.4	67.4	69.2	65.2	69.3	124.5	100.4	66.0	68.4	69.3	80.9	47.4	134.9	47.4
New Zealand	129.9	112.8	115.6	119.9	127.0	83.9	94.2	90.0	107.6	127.0	101.4	86.6	141.0	56.7
Norway	1,811.9	1,407.3	1,475.8	1,603.2	1,690.3	1,458.0	1,278.4	898.3	1,240.9	1,690.3	1,116.3	762.2	1,599.1	455.9
Portugal	79.0	74.1	72.7	72.7	74.7	97.9	79.5	57.0	66.1	74.7	64.6	48.1	123.1	48.1
Singapore	1,193.7	1,048.3	1,041.3	1,110.7	1,148.1	1,173.4	936.8	764.9	1,005.1	1,148.1	922.1	687.3	1,624.2	508.2
Spain	109.6	92.0	92.8	91.7	104.3	107.7	99.0	69.9	89.6	104.3	81.9	61.1	133.7	27.4
Sweden	5,953.5	5,238.6	5,385.2	5,451.9	5,785.4	7,735.0	6,178.8	3,517.4	4,675.2	5,785.4	4,173.8	2,914.9	12,250.4	787.2
Switzerland	771.0	734.4	735.8	717.5	747.1	1,017.0	813.4	603.2	714.3	747.1	716.9	481.4	1,032.8	158.1
United Kingdom	1,525.6	1,321.9	1,349.4	1,376.6	1,453.0	1,841.4	1,586.2	1,179.2	1,348.7	1,453.0	1,336.7	986.4	1,974.2	585.4
United States	1,135.2	1,055.9	1,068.9	1,044.5	1,137.4	1,249.9	1,084.5	824.6	1,045.4	1,137.4	950.4	726.5	1,493.0	273.7

	Period on Period Percent Change									
Developed Markets										
Australia	3.2	3.8	3.0	3.5	10.0	3.7	7.9	−12.5	8.5	21.7
Austria	6.6	19.6	6.8	4.1	18.1	−7.6	−2.4	−3.0	28.5	57.0
Belgium	6.4	5.8	4.3	8.8	7.9	−13.1	−8.3	−29.7	8.7	29.5
Canada	4.1	4.1	−0.3	1.3	6.3	8.1	−16.5	−15.3	24.6	11.7
Denmark	6.6	7.7	5.3	4.0	1.1	9.9	−11.7	−29.7	22.4	19.4
Finland	5.9	16.2	−19.1	−3.8	6.5	−8.9	−35.8	−41.6	−2.9	−3.6
France	5.1	2.3	2.9	−2.0	4.7	1.4	−19.0	−34.0	14.6	7.9
Germany	2.5	−2.2	3.4	−3.8	9.1	−10.8	−19.3	−44.0	33.2	6.1
Greece	8.5	5.4	2.2	0.4	21.2	−38.6	−27.6	−39.1	35.8	31.1
Hong Kong SAR	−2.3	6.4	−5.9	9.6	10.2	−16.7	−21.2	−20.6	31.9	20.9
Ireland	7.9	7.7	7.5	2.6	8.6	−8.5	1.1	−39.0	16.0	29.2
Italy	4.4	2.3	4.0	—	12.1	3.9	−24.0	−23.6	12.2	19.3
Japan	0.5	11.3	0.8	−6.8	5.0	−20.3	−19.5	−19.4	21.6	9.7
Netherlands	7.5	−1.5	2.8	−5.8	6.2	1.0	−19.4	−34.3	3.6	1.3
New Zealand	2.3	4.8	2.5	3.8	5.9	−24.9	12.2	−4.4	19.6	18.0
Norway	7.2	13.4	4.9	8.6	5.4	7.1	−12.3	−29.7	38.1	36.2
Portugal	5.7	12.1	−1.9	—	2.7	−6.2	−18.8	−28.3	15.9	13.1
Singapore	4.0	4.3	−0.7	6.7	3.4	−25.7	−20.2	−18.4	31.4	14.2
Spain	5.0	2.6	0.8	−1.1	13.8	−11.2	−8.0	−29.5	28.3	16.4
Sweden	2.9	12.1	2.8	1.2	6.1	−13.8	−20.1	−43.1	32.9	23.7
Switzerland	3.2	2.8	0.2	−2.5	4.1	6.2	−20.0	−25.8	18.4	4.6
United Kingdom	5.0	−2.0	2.1	2.0	5.5	−6.7	−13.9	−25.7	14.4	7.7
United States	−0.2	1.0	1.2	−2.3	8.9	−13.6	−13.2	−24.0	26.8	8.8

Source: Data are provided by Morgan Stanley Capital International. Regional and sectoral compositions conform to Morgan Stanley Capital International definitions.
[1]From 1990 or initiation of the index.

Table 11. Foreign Exchange Rates

(Units per U.S. dollar)

	Year to Date (as of 2/16/05)	2004 End of Period				End of Period					12-Month High	12-Month Low	All-Time High[1]	All-Time Low[1]
		Q1	Q2	Q3	Q4	2000	2001	2002	2003	2004				
Emerging Markets														
Latin America														
Argentina	2.89	2.86	2.96	2.98	2.97	1.00	1.00	3.36	2.93	2.97	2.81	3.06	0.98	3.86
Brazil	2.58	2.90	3.09	2.86	2.66	1.95	2.31	3.54	2.89	2.66	2.61	3.21	0.00	3.95
Chile	568.30	612.40	636.00	610.75	555.75	573.85	661.25	720.25	592.75	555.75	555.75	650.30	295.18	759.75
Colombia	2,333.00	2,679.55	2,693.20	2,618.90	2,354.75	2,236.00	2,277.50	2,867.00	2,780.00	2,354.75	2,311.00	2,774.70	689.21	2,980.00
Mexico	11.15	11.13	11.49	11.38	11.15	9.62	9.16	10.37	11.23	11.15	10.90	11.67	2.68	11.67
Peru	3.26	3.46	3.47	3.34	3.28	3.53	3.44	3.51	3.46	3.28	3.26	3.50	1.28	3.65
Venezuela	1,918.00	1,917.60	1,917.60	1,917.60	1,918.00	699.51	757.50	1,388.80	1,598.00	1,918.00	1,598.00	1,918.00	45.00	1,921.80
Asia														
China	8.28	8.28	8.28	8.28	8.28	8.28	8.28	8.28	8.28	8.28	8.28	8.28	4.73	8.80
India	43.77	43.60	46.06	45.95	43.46	46.68	48.25	47.98	45.63	43.46	43.46	46.47	16.92	49.05
Indonesia	9,290.00	8,564.00	9,400.00	9,155.00	9,270.00	9,675.00	10,400.00	8,950.00	8,420.00	9,270.00	8,388.00	9,440.00	1,977.00	16,650.00
Korea	1,027.03	1,147.27	1,155.45	1,151.85	1,035.10	1,265.00	1,313.50	1,185.70	1,192.10	1,035.10	1,023.80	1,188.25	683.50	1,962.50
Malaysia	3.80	3.80	3.80	3.80	3.80	3.80	3.80	3.80	3.80	3.80	3.80	3.80	2.44	4.71
Pakistan	59.40	57.39	58.08	59.19	59.43	57.60	59.90	58.25	57.25	59.43	57.18	61.33	21.18	64.35
Philippines	55.05	56.20	56.12	56.28	56.23	50.00	51.60	53.60	55.54	56.23	55.08	56.46	23.10	56.46
Taiwan Province of China	31.60	33.02	33.78	33.98	31.74	33.08	34.95	34.64	33.96	31.74	31.74	34.20	24.48	35.19
Thailand	38.54	39.29	40.93	41.40	38.92	43.38	44.21	43.11	39.62	38.92	38.41	41.65	23.15	55.50
Europe, Middle East, and Africa														
Czech Republic	23.10	26.67	26.17	25.37	22.42	37.28	35.60	30.07	25.71	22.42	22.34	27.66	22.34	42.17
Egypt	5.82	6.20	6.19	6.24	6.09	3.89	4.58	4.62	6.17	6.09	5.84	6.25	3.29	6.25
Hungary	187.12	201.68	205.61	198.21	181.02	282.34	274.81	224.48	208.70	181.02	180.05	216.93	90.20	317.56
Israel	4.36	4.53	4.50	4.48	4.32	4.04	4.40	4.74	4.39	4.32	4.32	4.63	1.96	5.01
Jordan	0.71	0.71	0.71	0.71	0.71	0.71	0.71	0.71	0.71	0.71	0.71	0.71	0.64	0.72
Morocco	11.23	9.18	10.73	10.56	11.09	10.56	11.59	10.18	8.80	11.09	10.10	11.13	7.75	11.28
Poland	3.06	3.86	3.69	3.51	3.01	4.13	3.96	3.83	3.73	3.01	2.98	4.05	1.72	4.71
Russia	28.00	28.52	29.07	29.22	27.72	28.16	30.51	31.96	29.24	27.72	27.72	29.28	0.98	31.96
South Africa	5.98	6.29	6.14	6.45	5.67	7.58	11.96	8.57	6.68	5.67	5.62	7.04	2.50	12.45
Turkey	1.31	1.31	1.48	1.51	1.34	0.67	1.45	1.66	1.41	1.34	1.31	1.56	0.01	1.77
Developed Markets														
Australia[2]	0.78	0.77	0.70	0.73	0.78	0.56	0.51	0.56	0.75	0.78	0.80	0.68	0.84	0.48
Canada	1.24	1.31	1.33	1.26	1.20	1.50	1.59	1.57	1.30	1.20	1.18	1.40	1.12	1.61
Denmark	5.71	6.05	6.09	5.98	5.49	7.92	8.35	7.08	5.91	5.49	5.45	6.29	5.34	9.00
Euro[2]	1.30	1.23	1.22	1.24	1.36	0.94	0.89	1.05	1.26	1.36	1.36	1.18	1.36	0.83
Hong Kong SAR	7.80	7.79	7.80	7.80	7.77	7.80	7.80	7.80	7.76	7.77	7.77	7.80	7.70	7.82
Japan	105.42	104.22	108.77	110.05	102.63	114.41	131.66	118.79	107.22	102.63	102.05	114.51	80.63	159.90
New Zealand[2]	0.71	0.67	0.64	0.68	0.72	0.44	0.42	0.52	0.66	0.72	0.72	0.60	0.72	0.39
Norway	6.42	6.84	6.93	6.71	6.08	8.80	8.96	6.94	6.67	6.08	6.05	7.13	5.51	9.58
Singapore	1.64	1.67	1.72	1.68	1.63	1.73	1.85	1.73	1.70	1.63	1.63	1.73	1.39	1.91
Sweden	6.97	7.54	7.51	7.27	6.66	9.42	10.48	8.69	7.19	6.66	6.60	7.74	5.09	11.03
Switzerland	1.19	1.27	1.25	1.25	1.14	1.61	1.66	1.38	1.24	1.14	1.13	1.31	1.12	1.82
United Kingdom[2]	1.89	1.85	1.82	1.81	1.92	1.49	1.45	1.61	1.79	1.92	1.95	1.76	2.01	1.37

Table 11 (concluded)

	Year to Date (as of 2/16/05)	Period on Period Percent Change									12-Month High	12-Month Low	All-Time High[1]	All-Time Low[1]
		2004 End of Period				End of Period								
		Q1	Q2	Q3	Q4	2000	2001	2002	2003	2004				
Emerging Markets														
Latin America														
Argentina	2.8	2.6	−3.4	−0.8	0.3	0.2	−0.2	−70.2	14.7	−1.4	...	...	...	...
Brazil	3.0	−0.1	−6.1	7.8	7.7	−7.7	−15.6	−34.7	22.4	8.9	...	...	...	...
Chile	−2.2	−3.2	−3.7	4.1	9.9	−7.8	−13.2	−8.2	21.5	6.7	...	...	...	...
Colombia	0.9	3.7	−0.5	2.8	11.2	−16.3	−1.8	−20.6	3.1	18.1	...	...	...	...
Mexico	—	0.9	−3.1	0.9	2.1	−1.2	5.1	−11.7	−7.6	0.7	...	...	...	...
Peru	0.6	0.1	−0.3	3.9	1.8	−0.5	2.4	−2.0	1.5	5.6	...	...	...	...
Venezuela	—	−16.7	—	—	—	−7.3	−7.7	−45.5	−13.1	−16.7	...	...	...	...
Asia														
China	—	—	—	—	—	—	—	—	—	—	...	...	...	...
India	−0.7	4.6	−5.3	0.2	5.7	−6.7	−3.3	0.6	5.2	5.0	...	...	...	...
Indonesia	−0.2	−1.7	−8.9	2.7	−1.2	−26.6	−7.0	16.2	6.3	−9.2	...	...	...	...
Korea	0.8	3.9	−0.7	0.3	11.3	−9.9	−3.7	10.8	−0.5	15.2	...	...	...	...
Malaysia	—	—	—	—	—	—	—	—	—	—	...	...	...	...
Pakistan	0.1	−0.2	−1.2	−1.9	−0.4	−10.1	−3.8	2.8	1.7	−3.7	...	...	...	...
Philippines	2.1	−1.2	0.1	−0.3	0.1	−19.5	−3.1	−3.7	−3.5	−1.2	...	...	...	...
Taiwan Province of China	0.5	2.8	−2.2	−0.6	7.1	−5.1	−5.3	0.9	2.0	7.0	...	...	...	...
Thailand	1.0	0.8	−4.0	−1.1	6.4	−13.6	−1.9	2.6	8.8	1.8	...	...	...	...
Europe, Middle East, and Africa														
Czech Republic	−2.9	−3.6	1.9	3.1	13.2	−3.9	4.7	18.4	16.9	14.7	...	...	...	...
Egypt	4.6	−0.5	0.1	−0.7	2.4	−11.5	−15.1	−0.9	−25.1	1.3	...	...	...	...
Hungary	−3.3	3.5	−1.9	3.7	9.5	−10.6	2.7	22.4	7.6	15.3	...	...	...	...
Israel	−0.9	−3.0	0.6	0.4	3.6	2.7	−8.1	−7.3	8.0	1.6	...	...	...	...
Jordan	—	−0.1	0.1	—	0.0	−0.3	0.2	−0.1	0.1	—	...	...	...	...
Morocco	−1.2	−4.2	−14.4	1.6	−4.8	−4.6	−8.9	13.9	15.7	−20.7	...	...	...	...
Poland	−1.6	−3.3	4.7	5.0	16.6	0.4	4.2	3.5	2.6	24.0	...	...	...	...
Russia	−1.0	2.5	−1.9	−0.5	5.4	−2.2	−7.7	−4.5	9.3	5.5	...	...	...	...
South Africa	−5.2	6.2	2.5	−4.9	13.9	−18.8	−36.6	39.6	28.2	18.0	...	...	...	...
Turkey	2.3	7.0	−11.4	−1.4	12.1	−18.6	−53.9	−12.4	17.7	4.7	...	...	...	...
Developed Markets														
Australia	0.5	2.0	−8.8	4.1	7.2	−14.9	−8.8	10.2	33.9	3.8	...	...	...	...
Canada	−2.8	−0.9	−1.8	5.7	4.9	−3.5	−5.9	1.3	21.2	7.9	...	...	...	...
Denmark	−4.0	−2.2	−0.8	1.8	9.1	−6.7	−5.1	17.9	19.8	7.8	...	...	...	...
Euro	−3.9	−2.2	−0.9	1.9	9.0	−6.3	−5.6	18.0	20.0	7.6	...	...	...	...
Hong Kong SAR	−0.3	−0.4	−0.1	—	0.3	−0.3	—	0.0	0.4	−0.1	...	...	...	...
Japan	−2.6	2.9	−4.2	−1.2	7.2	−10.4	−13.1	10.8	10.8	4.5	...	...	...	...
New Zealand	−0.7	2.0	−4.8	6.5	6.0	−14.9	−6.1	25.9	25.0	9.5	...	...	...	...
Norway	−5.3	−2.6	−1.2	3.3	10.3	−8.9	−1.8	29.2	4.1	9.6	...	...	...	...
Singapore	−0.6	1.5	−2.5	2.0	3.2	−4.0	−6.0	6.4	2.1	4.2	...	...	...	...
Sweden	−4.5	−4.6	0.3	3.3	9.2	−9.5	−10.2	20.6	20.9	8.0	...	...	...	...
Switzerland	−4.0	−2.1	1.4	0.2	9.3	−1.3	−3.0	20.0	11.7	8.7	...	...	...	...
United Kingdom	−1.7	3.4	−1.4	−0.5	5.9	−7.7	−2.6	10.7	10.9	7.4	...	...	...	...

Source: Bloomberg L.P.

[1]High value indicates value of greatest appreciation against the U.S. dollar; low value indicates value of greatest depreciation against the U.S. dollar. "All Time" refers to the period since 1990 or initiation of the currency.

[2]U.S. dollars per unit.

Table 12. Emerging Market Bond Index: EMBI Global Total Returns Index

	Year to Date (as of 2/16/05)	2004 End of Period				End of Period					12-Month High	12-Month Low	All-Time High[1]	All-Time Low[1]
		Q1	Q2	Q3	Q4	2000	2001	2002	2003	2004				
EMBI Global	**321**	**292**	**276**	**301**	**316**	**196**	**199**	**225**	**283**	**316**	**318**	**260**	**323**	**63**
Latin America														
Argentina	80	74	70	74	81	183	61	57	67	81	81	67	194	47
Brazil	449	387	364	418	446	222	238	230	390	446	446	331	451	68
Chile	173	168	164	170	172	116	129	150	162	172	173	159	174	98
Colombia	228	216	199	216	228	115	149	169	201	228	228	184	228	70
Dominican Republic	134	97	85	112	126	. . .	102	117	99	126	135	83	137	83
Ecuador	596	523	437	519	562	177	241	230	464	562	591	387	604	61
El Salvador	126	119	111	119	123	. . .	. . .	98	110	123	124	109	127	95
Mexico	315	299	282	300	308	192	219	254	284	308	312	269	318	58
Panama	521	475	449	478	511	300	353	395	452	511	513	418	522	56
Peru	483	440	408	452	485	244	307	341	431	485	486	376	487	52
Uruguay	134	106	94	116	129	. . .	105	62	97	129	130	87	134	38
Venezuela	480	398	390	451	484	224	236	281	393	484	485	357	485	59
Asia														
China	255	249	240	249	253	179	203	230	241	253	254	233	257	98
Malaysia	209	200	191	203	207	133	150	175	194	207	209	186	211	64
Philippines	292	265	262	276	280	157	201	230	261	280	289	250	294	81
Thailand	189	188	184	188	188	138	153	174	184	188	189	182	189	75
Europe, Middle East, and Africa														
Bulgaria	641	594	592	616	630	372	468	525	578	630	636	569	644	80
Côte d'Ivoire	65	65	56	65	65	42	54	43	58	65	73	54	100	29
Egypt	151	145	142	147	150	. . .	103	122	140	150	151	140	151	87
Hungary	144	144	142	144	144	111	122	137	142	144	144	142	144	97
Lebanon	196	184	185	192	195	122	130	148	177	195	196	178	196	99
Morocco	270	264	265	268	268	199	222	237	262	268	270	262	270	73
Nigeria	671	618	595	638	656	267	364	376	586	656	661	574	671	66
Pakistan	107	160	100	105	107	. . .	122	160	160	107	160	96	160	91
Poland	320	306	292	309	312	221	245	280	290	312	318	282	323	71
Russia	492	446	417	441	475	164	256	348	426	475	484	392	496	26
South Africa	327	312	298	315	323	190	220	271	297	323	327	285	328	99
Tunisia	141	134	127	135	138	. . .	. . .	112	127	138	139	122	141	98
Turkey	311	290	261	294	307	144	176	213	279	307	308	242	312	91
Ukraine	321	295	281	294	310	127	199	241	289	310	318	265	321	100
Latin	289	259	244	271	285	202	177	189	252	285	286	228	290	62
Non-Latin	383	355	337	359	374	186	240	291	342	374	379	321	385	72

Table 12 *(concluded)*

	Year to Date (as of 2/16/05)	Period on Period Percent Change									12-Month High	12-Month Low	All-Time High[1]	All-Time Low[1]
		2004 End of Period				End of Period								
		Q1	Q2	Q3	Q4	2000	2001	2002	2003	2004				
EMBI Global	**16.3**	**3.4**	**−5.5**	**9.0**	**4.9**	**14.4**	**1.4**	**13.1**	**25.7**	**11.7**	...	...	...	...
Latin America														
Argentina	14.8	9.2	−4.9	5.0	9.8	7.8	−66.9	−6.4	19.1	19.8	...	...	...	...
Brazil	23.3	−0.9	−5.8	14.9	6.7	13.0	7.3	−3.6	69.8	14.3	...	...	...	...
Chile	5.7	3.5	−2.6	3.7	1.3	12.2	11.7	15.8	8.3	6.0	...	...	...	...
Colombia	14.3	7.1	−7.6	8.5	5.3	3.0	29.5	13.3	19.4	13.2	...	...	...	...
Dominican Republic	57.2	−2.0	−11.9	31.7	11.8	...	...	13.9	−15.3	27.2	...	...	...	...
Ecuador	36.3	12.9	−16.4	18.7	8.2	53.9	36.1	−4.7	101.5	21.1	...	...	...	...
El Salvador	13.1	7.9	−6.3	6.6	3.4	...	...	...	11.9	11.5	...	...	...	...
Mexico	11.8	5.3	−5.6	6.4	2.7	17.5	14.3	16.1	11.6	8.6	...	...	...	...
Panama	16.0	5.2	−5.5	6.4	6.8	8.3	17.6	11.9	14.4	13.0	...	...	...	...
Peru	18.2	2.0	−7.1	10.7	7.4	0.2	26.2	10.8	26.6	12.6	...	...	...	...
Uruguay	42.9	10.2	−11.9	24.2	11.2	...	...	−40.6	55.6	34.0	...	...	...	...
Venezuela	23.1	1.4	−2.1	15.6	7.3	16.0	5.6	18.9	39.9	23.2	...	...	...	...
Asia														
China	6.3	3.3	−3.6	4.0	1.4	12.1	13.3	13.6	4.5	5.1	...	...	...	...
Malaysia	9.0	3.2	−4.5	5.9	2.1	11.6	12.9	16.9	10.7	6.6	...	...	...	...
Philippines	11.2	1.4	−0.9	5.2	1.3	−2.9	27.6	14.6	13.4	7.1	...	...	...	...
Thailand	2.5	2.2	−2.2	1.9	0.2	14.3	11.3	13.5	5.9	2.0	...	...	...	...
Europe, Middle East, and Africa														
Bulgaria	8.2	2.6	−0.3	4.0	2.2	5.1	25.7	12.2	10.2	8.9	...	...	...	...
Côte d'Ivoire	16.7	12.9	−14.3	16.7	—	−20.2	30.5	−20.7	34.8	12.9	...	...	...	...
Egypt	6.3	3.8	−2.2	3.2	1.9	...	...	18.5	14.4	6.8	...	...	...	...
Hungary	1.6	1.4	−1.5	1.5	−0.1	9.8	10.4	12.3	3.7	1.2	...	...	...	...
Lebanon	5.6	3.8	0.8	3.8	1.3	8.9	6.2	14.1	19.5	9.9	...	...	...	...
Morocco	2.2	0.7	0.4	1.1	0.1	5.5	11.1	7.2	10.2	2.4	...	...	...	...
Nigeria	12.6	5.4	−3.6	7.2	2.8	5.3	36.3	3.3	55.8	11.9	...	...	...	...
Pakistan	7.4	—	−37.7	5.0	1.9	...	...	31.3	−0.2	−33.3	...	...	...	...
Poland	9.7	5.4	−4.5	5.9	1.0	15.9	10.6	14.2	3.7	7.5	...	...	...	...
Russia	17.9	4.7	−6.5	5.8	7.6	54.9	55.8	35.9	22.4	11.5	...	...	...	...
South Africa	9.6	4.9	−4.4	5.5	2.8	8.5	16.2	22.9	9.6	8.8	...	...	...	...
Tunisia	10.8	5.1	−4.7	5.8	2.7	...	...	...	13.3	8.7	...	...	...	...
Turkey	19.2	4.2	−10.1	12.7	4.3	1.1	22.5	21.1	30.8	10.0	...	...	...	...
Ukraine	14.3	2.2	−5.0	4.8	5.3	...	57.1	21.0	19.8	7.2	...	...	...	...
Latin	18.3	3.1	−5.9	10.9	5.4	12.5	−12.4	6.8	33.0	13.4	...	...	...	...
Non-Latin	13.5	3.8	−5.0	6.5	4.1	18.2	28.8	21.0	17.7	9.2	...	...	...	...

Sources: J.P. Morgan Chase & Co.; and IMF staff estimates.
[1]From 1990 or initiation of the index.

Table 13. Emerging Market Bond Index: EMBI Global Yield Spreads

	Year to Date (as of 2/16/05)	2004 End of Period				End of Period					12-Month High	12-Month Low	All-Time High[1]	All-Time Low[1]
		Q1	Q2	Q3	Q4	2000	2001	2002	2003	2004				
EMBI Global	**345**	**414**	**482**	**409**	**347**	**735**	**728**	**725**	**403**	**347**	**549**	**335**	**1,631**	**335**
Latin America														
Argentina	4,831	4,840	5,087	5,389	4,527	770	5,363	6,342	5,485	4,527	5,762	4,401	7,222	381
Brazil	398	554	646	466	376	748	864	1,460	459	376	801	372	2,451	372
Chile	58	91	83	78	64	220	175	176	90	64	113	60	260	58
Colombia	355	379	483	407	332	755	508	633	427	332	599	327	1,076	261
Dominican Republic	687	1,338	1,730	1,079	824	. . .	446	499	1,141	824	1,750	663	1,750	304
Ecuador	638	701	952	778	690	1,415	1,233	1,801	799	690	1,081	643	4,764	626
El Salvador	250	255	274	276	245	. . .	. . .	411	284	245	299	217	434	217
Mexico	165	184	218	189	174	391	306	329	201	174	255	165	1,149	165
Panama	273	334	365	351	274	501	404	446	324	274	433	274	769	273
Peru	263	355	450	340	239	687	521	609	325	239	552	234	1,061	234
Uruguay	376	576	710	497	388	. . .	284	1,228	636	388	768	378	1,982	251
Venezuela	451	647	643	490	403	958	1,130	1,131	586	403	752	388	2,658	388
Asia														
China	53	65	67	75	57	160	99	84	58	57	80	55	364	39
Malaysia	79	113	129	104	78	237	207	212	100	78	148	76	1,141	76
Philippines	417	480	448	456	457	644	466	522	415	457	508	409	993	300
Thailand	34	69	76	64	61	173	132	128	67	61	98	44	951	34
Europe, Middle East, and Africa														
Bulgaria	66	165	137	115	77	772	433	291	177	77	205	72	1,679	66
Côte d'Ivoire	3,210	2,798	3,273	2,955	3,121	2,443	2,418	3,195	3,013	3,121	3,408	2,544	3,408	582
Egypt	72	133	130	127	101	. . .	360	325	131	101	156	79	646	72
Hungary	25	29	44	10	32	136	93	52	28	32	57	-4	196	-29
Lebanon	320	400	346	332	334	338	645	776	421	334	435	297	1,082	111
Morocco	180	164	168	165	170	584	518	390	160	170	208	131	1,606	128
Nigeria	482	504	591	491	457	1,807	1,103	1,946	499	457	634	389	2,937	389
Pakistan	218	289	313	270	233	. . .	1,115	271	. . .	233	348	229	2,225	0
Poland	42	72	72	64	69	241	195	185	76	69	88	43	410	17
Russia	191	256	304	298	213	1,172	669	478	257	213	360	205	7,063	190
South Africa	97	135	168	143	102	418	319	250	152	102	209	87	757	87
Tunisia	70	132	144	115	91	. . .	. . .	273	146	91	192	79	394	70
Turkey	263	316	465	323	264	803	702	696	309	264	550	252	1,196	252
Ukraine	194	294	358	333	255	1,953	940	671	258	255	430	208	2,314	194
Latin	423	531	600	492	415	702	888	981	518	415	686	403	1,532	401
Non-Latin	222	257	316	289	239	791	523	444	248	239	357	230	1,812	222

Table 13 *(concluded)*

	Year to Date (as of 2/16/04)	Period on Period Spread Change									12-Month High	12-Month Low	All-Time High[1]	All-Time Low[1]
		2004 End of Period				End of Period								
		Q1	Q2	Q3	Q4	2000	2001	2002	2003	2004				
EMBI Global	**−2**	**11**	**68**	**−73**	**−62**	**−16**	**−7**	**−3**	**−322**	**−56**	...	...	...	...
Latin America														
Argentina	304	−645	247	302	−862	237	4,593	979	−857	−958	...	...	...	...
Brazil	22	95	92	−180	−90	110	116	596	−1,001	−83	...	...	...	...
Chile	−6	1	−8	−5	−14	81	−45	1	−86	−26	...	...	...	...
Colombia	23	−48	104	−76	−75	339	−247	125	−206	−95	...	...	...	...
Dominican Republic	−137	197	392	−651	−255	...	...	53	642	−317	...	...	...	...
Ecuador	−52	−98	251	−174	−88	−1,938	−182	568	−1,002	−109	...	...	...	...
El Salvador	5	−29	19	2	−31	...	...	...	−127	−39	...	...	...	...
Mexico	−9	−17	34	−29	−15	30	−85	23	−128	−27	...	...	...	...
Panama	−1	10	31	−14	−77	91	−97	42	−122	−50	...	...	...	...
Peru	24	30	95	−110	−101	244	−166	88	−284	−86	...	...	...	...
Uruguay	−12	−60	134	−213	−109	...	...	944	−592	−248	...	...	...	...
Venezuela	48	61	−4	−153	−87	90	172	1	−545	−183	...	...	...	...
Asia														
China	−4	7	2	8	−18	35	−61	−15	−26	−1	...	...	...	...
Malaysia	1	13	16	−25	−26	65	−30	5	−112	−22	...	...	...	...
Philippines	−40	65	−32	8	1	334	−178	56	−107	42	...	...	...	...
Thailand	−27	2	7	−12	−3	9	−41	−4	−61	−6	...	...	...	...
Europe, Middle East, and Africa														
Bulgaria	−11	−12	−28	−22	−38	146	−339	−142	−114	−100	...	...	...	...
Côte d'Ivoire	89	−215	475	−318	166	1,051	−25	777	−182	108	...	...	...	...
Egypt	−29	2	−3	−3	−26	...	...	−35	−194	−30	...	...	...	...
Hungary	−7	1	15	−34	22	19	−43	−41	−24	4	...	...	...	...
Lebanon	−14	−21	−54	−14	2	119	307	131	−355	−87	...	...	...	...
Morocco	10	4	4	−3	5	204	−66	−128	−230	10	...	...	...	...
Nigeria	25	5	87	−100	−34	770	−704	843	−1,447	−42	...	...	...	...
Pakistan	−15	0	24	−43	−37	...	...	−844	18	−56	...	...	...	...
Poland	−27	−4	0	−8	5	29	−46	−10	−109	−7	...	...	...	...
Russia	−22	−1	48	−6	−85	−1,260	−503	−191	−221	−44	...	...	...	...
South Africa	−5	−17	33	−25	−41	141	−99	−69	−98	−50	...	...	...	...
Tunisia	−21	−14	12	−29	−24	...	...	...	−127	−55	...	...	...	...
Turkey	−1	7	149	−142	−59	360	−101	−6	−387	−45	...	...	...	...
Ukraine	−61	36	64	−25	−78	...	−1,013	−269	−413	−3	...	...	...	...
Latin	8	13	69	−108	−77	104	186	93	−463	−103	...	...	...	...
Non-Latin	−17	9	59	−27	−50	−222	−268	−79	−196	−9	...	...	...	...

Sources: J.P. Morgan Chase & Co.; and IMF staff estimates.
[1]From 1990 or initiation of the index.

Table 14. Total Emerging Market Financing
(In millions of U.S. dollars)

	1999	2000	2001	2002	2003	2004	2004 Q1	Q2	Q3	Q4
Total	**163,569.6**	**216,402.7**	**162,137.7**	**147,395.6**	**199,265.6**	**280,294.7**	**69,878.1**	**62,983.4**	**69,341.8**	**78,090.3**
Africa	**4,707.2**	**9,382.8**	**6,992.3**	**7,019.0**	**12,306.3**	**12,111.9**	**2,383.3**	**2,228.1**	**5,440.1**	**2,059.8**
Algeria	...	...	50.0	150.0	75.0	271.7	...	165.8	105.9	...
Angola	...	...	455.0	350.0	1,542.0	2,900.0	550.0	...	2,350.0	...
Botswana	...	...	22.5	...	...	...	...	...	...	...
Cameroon	...	...	53.8	...	100.0	...	...	...	...	...
Chad	...	...	400.0	...	...	...	...	...	...	...
Congo, Dem. Rep. of	...	20.8	...	...	...	...	...	...	...	...
Côte d'Ivoire	179.0	...	15.0	...	...	100.0	...	...	100.0	...
Gabon	...	...	...	...	...	22.0	...	...	...	22.0
Ghana	30.0	320.0	300.0	420.0	650.0	875.0	...	...	875.0	...
Guinea	...	...	...	...	...	70.0	...	...	70.0	...
Kenya	...	7.5	80.2	...	134.0	...	...	...	...	...
Malawi	...	...	...	...	...	4.8	...	4.8	...	...
Mali	...	...	...	150.4	287.6	288.9	...	...	...	288.9
Mauritius	160.0	...	...	...	...	...	...	...	...	...
Morocco	322.2	56.4	136.1	...	474.7	800.9	...	...	...	800.9
Mozambique	...	...	200.0	...	35.5	...	...	...	...	...
Namibia	...	...	...	...	35.0	...	...	...	...	...
Niger	...	...	...	...	27.0	...	...	...	...	...
Nigeria	90.0	...	100.0	960.0	593.0	250.0	30.0	...	220.0	...
Senegal	...	...	...	40.0	...	...	...	...	...	...
Seychelles	...	50.0	...	150.0	...	80.0	80.0	...	...	...
South Africa	3,423.4	8,698.8	4,646.7	4,058.1	7,837.4	5,413.3	1,179.3	2,027.6	1,679.2	527.1
Tanzania	...	135.0	...	...	...	...	...	...	...	...
Tunisia	352.6	94.3	533.0	740.5	485.2	924.4	544.0	30.0	...	349.9
Zambia	...	...	...	...	30.0	...	...	...	...	...
Zimbabwe	150.0	...	...	...	...	...	...	...	...	...
Asia	**55,958.6**	**85,881.0**	**67,483.4**	**67,201.3**	**87,968.3**	**121,327.0**	**33,116.2**	**29,714.1**	**25,538.2**	**32,958.5**
Brunei	...	...	...	129.0	...	...	...	...	...	...
China	3,461.8	23,063.4	5,567.3	8,891.6	13,589.8	22,996.4	7,727.1	7,017.0	3,287.4	4,965.3
Hong Kong SAR	11,488.3	21,046.4	18,307.3	12,602.1	9,055.7	13,767.4	1,953.0	2,026.9	3,025.4	6,762.2
India	2,376.2	2,224.2	2,382.2	1,380.8	4,094.1	13,590.9	4,460.0	2,282.0	3,253.9	3,594.9
Indonesia	1,465.3	1,283.1	964.9	974.0	5,109.9	3,696.9	2,253.0	95.1	175.0	1,173.8
Korea	13,542.3	14,230.4	17,021.0	14,693.5	17,237.0	23,843.0	5,650.0	5,997.3	6,549.3	5,646.5
Lao P.D.R.	...	...	...	71.4	...	210.0	...	70.0	...	140.0
Macao SAR	...	29.5	...	...	...	382.0	...	...	382.0	...
Malaysia	5,177.2	4,506.4	4,432.4	5,597.3	5,729.2	7,770.2	834.3	3,525.5	1,361.1	2,049.2
Marshall Islands	...	...	...	34.7	...	...	...	...	...	...
Pakistan	...	...	182.5	289.1	9.3	840.0	500.0	340.0	...	...
Papua New Guinea	232.4	...	...	...	153.7	...	...	...	...	...
Philippines	7,181.7	5,021.9	3,658.8	5,458.1	5,453.5	6,188.8	2,220.0	1,756.7	2,024.1	188.0
Singapore	4,338.7	6,079.7	10,383.6	3,810.0	6,792.7	8,619.2	1,340.4	1,108.1	3,126.8	3,043.5
Sri Lanka	23.0	100.0	105.0	...	186.0	135.0	...	35.0	...	100.0
Taiwan Province of China	4,019.9	6,703.5	3,794.0	10,959.3	18,149.3	15,215.9	5,124.2	4,380.5	1,714.5	3,996.7
Thailand	2,551.7	1,572.5	684.4	1,927.0	2,357.2	3,957.3	1,054.2	1,080.0	524.7	1,298.4
Vietnam	100.0	20.0	...	383.5	51.0	114.0	...	...	114.0	...
Europe	**26,191.5**	**37,021.7**	**22,787.7**	**29,566.9**	**47,854.8**	**72,521.7**	**14,523.5**	**15,384.7**	**19,363.8**	**23,249.4**
Azerbaijan	77.2	...	16.0	...	...	1,065.4	997.0	10.2	41.0	17.2
Belarus	...	...	...	...	36.0	21.4	...	...	...	21.4
Bulgaria	53.9	8.9	242.3	1,260.8	381.3	859.5	...	540.5	29.5	289.4
Croatia	1,504.9	1,498.7	1,766.0	1,425.4	2,026.0	2,330.1	373.0	724.8	926.6	306.0
Cyprus	288.5	86.3	633.0	547.9	648.2	1,174.0	...	...	1,174.0	...
Czech Republic	540.3	127.1	564.6	453.4	4,349.5	2,904.1	...	2,185.8	124.5	593.9
Estonia	289.2	412.7	202.1	292.6	507.7	1,093.7	...	164.1	...	929.6
Georgia	...	...	...	...	6.0	...	...	...	...	...
Gibraltar	65.0	80.0	...	...	...	...	...	...	...	...
Hungary	3,471.2	1,308.8	1,364.7	1,040.2	3,774.8	10,831.4	1,833.0	1,983.0	3,541.3	3,473.6
Kazakhstan	417.0	429.6	573.5	743.5	1,535.0	3,354.0	239.2	219.0	1,047.8	1,848.0

Table 14 *(concluded)*

	1999	2000	2001	2002	2003	2004	2004 Q1	Q2	Q3	Q4
Europe *(continued)*										
Kyrgyz Republic	...	...	...	95.0	...	...	...	...	...	...
Latvia	288.9	23.0	212.1	74.6	70.7	889.3	494.0	84.3	145.0	166.6
Lithuania	959.7	683.8	247.3	374.3	431.7	898.2	754.0	...	71.5	72.5
Macedonia	...	...	...	...	47.6	92.7	10.3	...	...	82.5
Malta	57.0	...	85.0	...	114.7	392.7	150.0	242.7	...	...
Moldova	40.0	...	...	...	...	7.0	...	...	2.0	5.0
Poland	3,780.7	5,252.9	4,836.6	5,913.2	7,818.1	4,909.6	3,523.8	591.2	24.4	770.1
Romania	176.0	594.4	1,347.2	1,442.2	1,828.2	846.9	1,094.7	281.5	203.8	116.9
Russia	166.8	3,950.7	3,200.1	8,496.0	12,081.2	21,284.6	984.4	4,991.4	5,496.9	8,961.8
Slovak Republic	994.7	1,466.7	219.9	143.1	940.6	1,329.0	...	1,235.3	30.5	63.3
Slovenia	687.7	672.7	827.2	309.3	394.8	1,391.8	76.2	606.7	653.6	55.3
Turkey	11,900.0	20,385.4	6,405.1	6,376.0	9,413.0	14,210.0	3,294.0	1,504.2	4,006.7	5,404.9
Ukraine	290.7	...	15.0	514.0	1,400.0	2,606.9	700.0	10.0	1,840.0	56.9
Uzbekistan	142.0	40.0	30.0	46.0	38.7	28.0	...	10.0	3.6	14.3
Middle East	**15,387.4**	**14,999.7**	**11,020.3**	**10,685.4**	**8,368.1**	**21,324.0**	**5,444.9**	**6,086.8**	**3,092.0**	**6,700.2**
Bahrain	361.1	1,391.0	207.0	665.0	1,800.0	1,517.0	...	...	442.0	1,075.0
Egypt	1,533.7	919.4	2,545.0	670.0	155.0	1,158.7	200.0	737.7	...	221.0
Iran, I.R. of	692.0	757.7	887.0	2,666.4	700.0	1,942.7	179.3	1,497.6	39.9	225.9
Israel	3,719.0	2,908.5	1,602.6	344.4	750.0	3,514.0	758.1	1,264.7	341.1	1,150.1
Jordan	...	60.0	...	80.9	...	199.4	...	...	...	199.4
Kuwait	147.5	250.0	770.0	750.0	365.0	1,482.5	300.0		157.5	1,025.0
Lebanon	1,421.4	1,752.4	3,300.0	990.0	160.0	3,263.5		1,268.0	620.5	1,375.0
Libya	...	50.0	...	...	...	...	...	...	...	...
Oman	356.8	685.0	...	2,332.0	907.8	1,328.6	98.6	600.0	175.0	455.0
Qatar	2,000.0	1,980.0	913.0	1,536.7	880.8	2,042.7	1,125.0	719.0	...	198.7
Saudi Arabia	4,374.8	2,200.9	275.0	280.0	569.5	2,134.0	718.0	...	816.0	600.0
United Arab Emirates	781.0	2,045.0	520.7	370.0	2,080.0	2,741.0	2,066.0	...	500.0	175.0
Latin America	**61,324.9**	**69,117.6**	**53,854.0**	**32,923.0**	**42,768.1**	**53,010.1**	**14,410.3**	**9,569.7**	**15,907.7**	**13,122.4**
Argentina	17,844.4	16,648.5	3,423.9	824.2	160.0	1,890.8	1,165.0	205.4	...	520.0
Bolivia	...	...	20.0	90.0	...	191.0	...	...	...	191.0
Brazil	12,951.9	23,238.2	19,532.9	10,925.6	12,001.2	15,197.7	4,679.8	3,080.6	4,821.5	2,615.8
Chile	8,031.7	5,782.5	3,935.3	2,959.6	4,699.0	6,549.4	1,375.0	403.8	1,585.9	3,184.7
Colombia	3,555.8	3,093.2	4,895.0	2,096.0	1,911.3	1,543.8	500.0	...	500.0	543.8
Costa Rica	300.0	250.0	400.0	250.0	490.0	310.0	310.0	...	...	...
Dominican Republic	...	74.0	531.1	258.0	670.4	140.5	31.0	8.5	101.0	...
Ecuador	73.0	...	910.0	10.0	...	...	...	...	...	...
El Salvador	316.5	160.0	488.5	1,251.5	381.0	467.0	...	...	427.0	40.0
Grenada	...	...	...	100.0	...	...	...	...	...	...
Guadeloupe	...	...	...	17.4	...	...	...	...	...	...
Guatemala	222.0	505.0	325.0	44.0	300.0	439.3	59.3	...	330.0	50.0
Jamaica	...	421.0	726.5	345.0	49.6	903.2	248.0	151.3	317.8	186.2
Mexico	14,099.5	15,313.4	13,823.5	10,040.6	16,992.3	18,771.8	4,635.4	4,085.1	6,040.6	4,011.0
Nicaragua	...	...	...	...	...	22.0	22.0	...	...	...
Paraguay	55.0	...	70.0	...	...	...	...	...	...	...
Peru	1,618.4	465.4	137.5	1,993.0	1,375.0	1,530.7	90.0	635.0	...	805.7
St. Lucia	...	...	...	...	20.0	...	...	...	...	...
Trinidad and Tobago	230.0	301.0	70.0	303.0	46.0	415.0	...	...	115.0	200.0
Uruguay	465.0	602.1	1,147.4	400.0	...	...	100.0	...	...	...
Venezuela	1,561.7	2,263.3	3,417.5	1,015.0	3,672.5	4,399.1	1,125.0	1,000.0	1,500.0	774.1

Source: Data provided by the Bond, Equity and Loan database of the International Monetary Fund sourced from Capital Data.

Table 15. Emerging Market Bond Issuance
(In millions of U.S. dollars)

	1999	2000	2001	2002	2003	2004	2004 Q1	Q2		Q4
Developing Countries	**82,359.4**	**80,475.4**	**89,036.9**	**61,647.4**	**97,388.2**	**131,519.1**	**24,601.4**	**24,732.5**	**38,3..**	**26,859.7**
Africa	**2,345.5**	**1,485.8**	**2,109.6**	**2,161.1**	**5,511.9**	**2,495.4**	**1,180.0**	**1,100.0**	**214.7**	...
Mauritius	160.0	...	...	...	...	...	...	...	...	
Morocco	151.5	...	...	...	464.9	...	...	...	...	...
South Africa	1,804.7	1,485.8	1,647.7	1,511.1	4,690.0	1,950.9	636.0	1,100.0	214.7	...
Tunisia	229.3	...	462.0	650.0	357.0	544.5	544.0	...	...	
Asia	**23,424.7**	**24,501.4**	**35,869.2**	**22,532.7**	**35,778.8**	**52,085.8**	**14,414.0**	**11,341.4**	**13,922.0**	**12,408.3**
China	1,060.0	1,770.7	2,341.9	602.8	2,034.2	4,775.3	39.0		2,642.8	2,093.8
Hong Kong SAR	7,124.8	7,058.9	10,458.6	1,951.6	2,625.6	3,912.4	981.0	190.0	1,575.6	1,165.7
India	100.0	100.0	99.3	153.0	450.0	4,377.1	888.0	975.0	814.0	1,700.0
Indonesia	...	...	125.0	375.0	609.0	1,363.5	1,300.0	25.3		38.2
Korea	4,905.8	7,653.0	7,756.3	6,705.5	11,531.3	16,965.5	5,130.0	4,111.7	3,490.5	4,233.4
Malaysia	2,062.4	1,419.7	2,150.0	1,880.0	962.5	2,514.5	325.0	1,650.0	125.0	414.5
Pakistan	...	...	...	...	...	500.0	500.0	...	...	
Philippines	4,751.2	2,467.3	1,842.4	4,773.8	3,799.6	4,458.1	2,150.0	650.0	1,658.1	...
Singapore	2,147.1	2,333.8	8,664.7	562.1	4,336.8	4,552.6	302.0	523.4	2,616.8	1,110.1
Sri Lanka	...	...	...	...	...	100.0	...	...	...	100.0
Taiwan Province of China	475.0	1,698.0	2,152.4	5,480.8	9,129.7	7,166.7	2,799.0	2,216.1	599.0	1,552.7
Thailand	798.4	...	278.6	48.0	300.0	1,400.0	...	1,000.0	400.0	...
Europe	**13,872.8**	**14,202.5**	**11,558.6**	**14,997.0**	**24,411.4**	**35,201.9**	**10,358.0**	**7,403.7**	**10,898.0**	**6,541.8**
Bulgaria	53.9	...	223.4	1,247.8	...	...	...	...	...	...
Croatia	601.2	858.0	934.0	847.5	983.6	1,651.0	373.0	724.8	553.5	...
Cyprus	288.5	...	480.5	479.8	648.2	1,174.0	...	...	1,174.0	
Czech Republic	421.7	...	50.7	428.4	3,168.4	2,538.6	...	2,011.4	124.5	402.8
Estonia	84.9	335.7	65.5	292.6	323.3	964.8	...	35.2		929.6
Hungary	2,410.5	540.8	1,247.8	70.5	2,211.4	8,134.0	1,239.0	1,350.4	3,541.3	2,002.8
Kazakhstan	300.0	350.0	250.0	209.0	100.0	1,325.0	100.0	100.0	200.0	925.0
Latvia	236.7	...	180.8	...	...	536.1	494.0	36.0	...	6.6
Lithuania	531.5	376.2	222.4	355.6	431.7	815.7	754.0	...	61.5	...
Poland	1,652.6	1,553.5	2,773.7	2,679.9	4,301.2	3,502.4	3,080.0	422.2	...	...
Romania	...	259.5	908.6	1,062.2	813.6	...	850.0	...	...	
Russia	...	75.0	1,352.7	3,391.5	4,005.0	5,104.9	...	775.0	1,904.9	1,575.0
Slovak Republic	800.2	978.3	219.9	143.1	861.3	1,198.8	...	1,198.8	...	...
Slovenia	439.1	384.7	490.0	30.2	...	...	...	...	...	
Turkey	5,761.2	8,490.8	2,158.7	3,259.8	5,253.8	5,941.5	2,768.0	750.0	1,723.2	700.0
Ukraine	290.7	...	...	499.0	1,310.0	2,315.0	700.0	...	1,615.0	...
Middle East	**4,409.8**	**4,670.6**	**5,920.7**	**3,706.6**	**1,860.0**	**8,785.5**	**2,710.0**	**2,518.0**	**620.5**	**2,937.0**
Bahrain	209.1	188.5	...	325.0	750.0	42.0	...	...	...	42.0
Egypt	100.0	...	1,500.0	...	...	...	...	...	...	...
Iran, I.R. of	...	...	...	986.3	...	...	...	...	...	...
Israel	1,679.2	1,329.7	1,120.7	344.4	750.0	2,520.0	645.0	1,000.0	...	875.0
Jordan	...	...	...	80.9	...	145.0	...	...	...	145.0
Kuwait	...	...	...	750.0	200.0	500.0	...	...	...	500.0
Lebanon	1,421.4	1,752.4	3,300.0	990.0	160.0	3,263.5	...	1,268.0	620.5	1,375.0
Oman	...	...	...	...	...	250.0	...	250.0	...	...
Qatar	1,000.0	1,400.0	...	...	...	665.0	665.0	...	...	...
United Arab Emirates	...	...	...	230.0	...	1,400.0	1,400.0	...	...	...
Latin America	**38,306.7**	**35,615.2**	**33,578.8**	**18,250.0**	**31,215.5**	**32,950.6**	**11,359.0**	**6,203.0**	**8,267.4**	**7,121.2**
Argentina	14,182.8	13,024.8	1,500.5	...	100.0	1,115.4	915.0	100.0	...	100.0
Brazil	8,585.8	11,382.1	12,238.8	6,375.5	10,709.9	9,123.4	2,955.0	1,329.7	3,083.1	1,755.5
Chile	1,763.8	679.7	1,536.0	1,728.9	2,900.0	2,350.0	1,150.0		...	1,200.0
Colombia	1,675.6	1,547.2	4,263.3	1,000.0	1,765.0	1,543.8	500.0	...	500.0	543.8
Costa Rica	300.0	250.0	250.0	250.0	490.0	310.0	310.0	...	...	...
Dominican Republic	...	...	500.0	...	600.0	...	...	...	...	
El Salvador	150.0	50.0	353.5	1,251.5	348.5	286.5	...	...	286.5	...
Grenada	...	...	...	100.0	...	...	...	...	...	
Guatemala	...	...	325.0	...	300.0	380.0	50.0	...	330.0	...
Jamaica	...	421.0	690.7	300.0	...	806.9	248.0	125.0	247.8	186.2
Mexico	9,854.0	7,078.4	9,231.7	4,914.1	9,082.1	11,369.0	4,131.0	3,148.3	2,320.0	1,770.0
Peru	...	...	...	1,930.0	1,250.0	1,305.7	...	500.0	...	805.7
Trinidad and Tobago	230.0	250.0	...	...	...	100.0	...	...	...	...
Uruguay	350.0	442.6	1,106.1	400.0	...	...	100.0	...	...	...
Venezuela	1,214.7	489.4	1,583.2	...	3,670.0	4,260.0	1,000.0	1,000.0	1,500.0	760.0

Source: Data provided by the Bond, Equity and Loan database of the International Monetary Fund sourced from Capital Data.

Table 16. Emerging Market Equity Issuance
(In millions of U.S. dollars)

	1999	2000	2001	2002	2003	2004	2004 Q1	2004 Q2	2004 Q3	2004 Q4
Developing Countries	**23,187.4**	**41,772.8**	**11,245.9**	**16,359.4**	**28,295.7**	**43,449.8**	**13,093.9**	**10,374.8**	**5,566.7**	**14,414.4**
Africa	**658.7**	**103.3**	**150.9**	**340.5**	**977.4**	**2,547.2**	**223.3**	**927.6**	**564.5**	**831.9**
Côte d'Ivoire	...	...	...	...	...	100.0	...	...	100.0	...
Morocco	...	56.4	6.8	...	...	800.9	...	...	...	800.9
South Africa	658.7	46.9	144.1	340.5	977.4	1,615.3	223.3	927.6	464.5	...
Sudan	...	...	...	...	...	31.0	...	...	...	31.0
Asia	**18,271.8**	**31,567.7**	**9,591.5**	**12,411.4**	**24,679.6**	**32,990.3**	**11,885.9**	**7,999.5**	**4,079.0**	**9,025.9**
China	1,477.4	20,239.7	2,810.4	2,546.0	6,413.2	13,256.5	6,151.1	5,370.6	213.6	1,521.3
Hong Kong SAR	3,370.0	3,088.6	297.1	2,857.7	3,480.1	5,152.6	857.4	582.9	584.5	3,127.9
India	874.4	916.7	467.2	264.8	1,299.7	3,937.6	2,566.0	...	683.4	688.1
Indonesia	522.2	28.2	347.2	281.0	1,008.4	500.9	338.0	19.8	...	143.1
Korea	6,590.6	784.8	3,676.4	1,553.7	1,222.6	3,223.3	94.4	937.3	2,191.6	...
Macao SAR	...	29.5	...	...	...	...	...	...	...	...
Malaysia	...	...	15.4	891.2	618.2	529.8	104.3	11.2	283.1	131.2
Papua New Guinea	232.4	...	...	...	153.7	...	...	...	...	...
Philippines	221.7	194.6	...	11.3	...	18.0	...	...	...	18.0
Singapore	1,725.6	2,202.2	625.8	891.6	1,168.7	1,996.9	493.4	145.2	24.2	1,334.1
Taiwan Province of China	2,500.4	3,951.5	1,126.6	3,057.9	8,276.3	3,350.0	1,062.9	932.5	98.6	1,256.0
Thailand	757.3	132.0	225.3	56.3	1,038.7	1,024.8	218.5	...	...	806.2
Europe	**1,411.6**	**3,339.8**	**259.4**	**1,612.4**	**1,811.3**	**5,261.2**	**848.1**	**419.4**	**88.7**	**3,905.0**
Croatia	...	...	22.3	...	...	...	...	...	...	...
Czech Republic	...	...	...	...	824.6	174.4	...	174.4	...	...
Estonia	190.3	...	...	...	...	...	...	...	...	...
Hungary	529.2	19.1	...	...	13.2	884.7	349.7	...	...	535.0
Latvia	...	...	...	22.7	...	...	...	...	...	...
Lithuania	...	150.5	...	...	...	...	...	...	...	...
Poland	636.3	358.9	...	217.3	604.9	841.4	...	107.4	...	734.1
Russia	55.8	387.7	237.1	1,301.0	368.7	2,674.4	237.4	28.5	...	2,408.5
Turkey	...	2,423.8	...	71.4	...	686.3	261.0	109.2	88.7	227.4
Middle East	**2,084.0**	**1,618.1**	**86.8**	**...**	**...**	**788.5**	**136.6**	**264.7**	**221.1**	**166.1**
Egypt	89.2	319.4	...	...	...	141.0	...	...	...	141.0
Israel	1,994.8	1,298.7	86.8	...	...	624.0	113.1	264.7	221.1	25.1
Oman	...	...	...	...	...	23.6	23.6	...	...	...
Latin America	**761.3**	**5,143.9**	**1,157.2**	**1,995.0**	**827.4**	**1,862.5**	**...**	**763.7**	**613.4**	**485.4**
Argentina	349.6	393.1	34.4	...	...	105.4	...	105.4	...	...
Brazil	161.4	3,102.5	1,122.9	1,148.5	287.4	1,455.4	...	517.5	452.5	485.4
Chile	...	...	...	...	...	160.9	...	...	160.9	...
Dominican Republic	...	74.0	...	...	...	...	...	...	...	...
Mexico	162.0	1,574.3	...	846.6	540.0	140.8	...	140.8	...	...
Peru	88.4	...	...	...	...	...	...	...	...	...

Source: Data provided by the Bond, Equity and Loan database of the International Monetary Fund sourced from Capital Data.

Table 17. Emerging Market Loan Syndication
(In millions of U.S. dollars)

	1999	2000	2001	2002	2003	2004	2004 Q1	2004 Q2	2004 Q3	2004 Q4
Total	**58,022.8**	**94,154.5**	**61,854.9**	**69,388.9**	**80,840.8**	**105,325.8**	**22,863.2**	**23,478.7**	**17,850.9**	**18,195.3**
Africa	**1,703.0**	**7,793.7**	**4,731.8**	**4,517.4**	**5,817.1**	**7,069.4**	**980.0**	**200.6**	**4,660.9**	**1,227.9**
Algeria	...	...	50.0	150.0	75.0	271.7	...	165.8	105.9	...
Angola	...	...	455.0	350.0	1,542.0	2,900.0	550.0	...	2,350.0	...
Botswana	...	...	22.5	...	...	...	...	...	...	...
Cameroon	...	...	53.8	...	100.0	...	...	...	...	...
Chad	...	...	400.0	...	...	...	...	...	...	...
Congo, Dem. Rep. of	...	20.8	...	...	...	...	...	...	...	...
Côte d'Ivoire	179.0	...	15.0	...	...	...	...	...	...	...
Djibouti	...	...	...	...	...	40.0	...	...	...	40.0
Ethiopia	...	...	...	...	...	40.0	...	...	40.0	...
Gabon	...	...	...	...	...	22.0	...	...	...	22.0
Ghana	30.0	320.0	300.0	420.0	650.0	875.0	...	...	875.0	...
Guinea	...	...	...	...	...	70.0	...	...	70.0	...
Kenya	...	7.5	80.2	...	134.0	...	...	...	...	...
Malawi	...	...	...	...	...	4.8	...	4.8	...	...
Mali	...	...	...	150.4	287.6	288.9	...	...	...	288.9
Morocco	170.6	...	129.3	...	9.8	...	...	...	...	...
Mozambique	...	...	200.0	...	35.5	...	...	...	...	...
Namibia	...	...	...	...	35.0	...	...	...	...	...
Niger	...	...	...	...	27.0	...	...	...	...	...
Nigeria	90.0	...	100.0	960.0	593.0	250.0	30.0	...	220.0	...
Senegal	...	...	...	40.0	...	...	...	...	...	...
Seychelles	...	50.0	...	150.0	...	80.0	80.0	...	...	...
South Africa	960.0	7,166.1	2,855.0	2,206.5	2,170.0	1,847.1	320.0	...	1,000.0	527.1
Tanzania	...	135.0	...	...	...	...	...	...	...	...
Tunisia	123.4	94.3	71.0	90.5	128.2	379.9	...	30.0	...	349.9
Zambia	...	...	...	...	30.0	...	...	...	...	...
Zimbabwe	150.0	...	...	...	...	...	...	...	...	...
Asia	**14,262.0**	**29,812.0**	**22,022.7**	**32,257.3**	**27,509.9**	**36,250.9**	**6,816.2**	**10,373.2**	**7,537.2**	**11,524.3**
Brunei	...	...	...	129.0	...	...	...	...	...	...
China	924.4	1,053.1	415.0	5,742.8	5,142.4	4,964.6	1,537.0	1,646.4	431.0	1,350.2
Hong Kong SAR	993.5	10,898.9	7,551.6	7,792.9	2,950.0	4,702.4	114.6	1,254.1	865.2	2,468.6
India	1,401.8	1,207.6	1,815.7	963.1	2,344.4	5,276.3	1,006.0	1,307.0	1,756.5	1,206.8
Indonesia	943.1	1,254.9	492.6	318.0	3,492.5	1,832.4	615.0	50.0	175.0	992.4
Korea	2,046.0	5,792.6	5,588.2	6,434.3	4,483.0	3,654.1	425.6	948.3	867.1	1,413.1
Lao P.D.R.	...	...	...	71.4	...	210.0	...	70.0	...	140.0
Macao SAR	...	...	...	...	...	382.0	...	...	382.0	...
Malaysia	3,114.8	3,086.7	2,267.0	2,826.1	4,148.6	4,725.8	405.0	1,864.3	953.0	1,503.5
Marshall Islands	...	...	...	34.7	...	...	...	...	...	...
Pakistan	...	...	182.5	289.1	9.3	340.0	...	340.0	...	...
Philippines	2,208.9	2,360.0	1,816.4	673.0	1,653.8	1,712.8	70.0	1,106.7	366.0	170.1
Singapore	466.0	1,543.7	1,093.2	2,356.3	1,287.2	2,069.7	545.0	439.5	485.8	599.4
Sri Lanka	23.0	100.0	105.0	...	186.0	35.0	...	35.0	...	...
Taiwan Province of China	1,044.5	1,054.0	515.0	2,420.5	743.3	4,699.2	1,262.3	1,232.0	1,016.9	1,188.0
Thailand	996.0	1,440.5	180.5	1,822.7	1,018.5	1,532.6	835.7	80.0	124.7	492.2
Vietnam	100.0	20.0	...	383.5	51.0	114.0	...	...	114.0	...
Europe	**10,907.1**	**19,479.3**	**10,969.7**	**12,957.5**	**21,632.1**	**32,058.6**	**3,317.4**	**7,561.5**	**8,377.1**	**12,802.6**
Azerbaijan	77.2	...	16.0	...	...	1,065.4	997.0	10.2	41.0	17.2
Belarus	...	...	...	...	36.0	21.4	...	...	...	21.4
Bulgaria	...	8.9	18.9	13.0	381.3	859.5	...	540.5	29.5	289.4
Croatia	903.6	640.7	809.8	577.8	1,042.5	679.1	...	...	373.1	306.0
Cyprus	...	86.3	152.5	68.1	...	...	...	...	...	...
Czech Republic	118.6	127.1	513.9	25.0	356.5	191.1	...	...	...	191.1
Estonia	14.0	77.0	136.6	...	184.3	128.9	...	128.9	...	...
Georgia ·	...	...	...	...	6.0	...	...	...	...	...
Gibraltar	65.0	80.0	...	...	...	...	...	...	...	...
Hungary	531.6	748.9	116.9	969.7	1,550.2	1,812.7	244.3	632.6	...	935.8
Kazakhstan	117.0	79.6	323.5	534.5	1,435.0	2,029.0	139.2	119.0	847.8	923.0
Kyrgyz Republic	...	...	...	95.0	...	...	...	...	...	...

Table 17 (concluded)

	1999	2000	2001	2002	2003	2004	2004			
							Q1	Q2	Q3	Q4
Europe (continued)										
Latvia	52.2	23.0	31.3	51.9	70.7	353.2	...	48.3	145.0	160.0
Lithuania	428.2	157.2	24.9	18.8	...	82.5	...	...	10.0	72.5
Macedonia	...	...	...	...	47.6	92.7	10.3	...	...	82.5
Malta	57.0	...	85.0	...	114.7	392.7	150.0	242.7	...	...
Moldova	40.0	...	...	...	...	7.0	...	...	2.0	5.0
Poland	1,491.9	3,340.5	2,062.9	3,016.0	2,912.1	565.8	443.8	61.6	24.4	36.0
Romania	176.0	334.9	438.6	380.0	1,014.6	846.9	244.7	281.5	203.8	116.9
Russia	111.0	3,488.1	1,610.3	3,803.5	7,707.5	13,505.3	747.0	4,187.9	3,592.0	4,978.3
Slovak Republic	194.5	488.3	...	...	79.3	130.3	...	36.5	30.5	63.3
Slovenia	248.6	288.0	337.2	279.0	394.8	1,391.8	76.2	606.7	653.6	55.3
Tajikistan	...	...	...	...	...	1.2	...	...	1.2	...
Turkey	6,138.8	9,470.9	4,246.4	3,044.8	4,159.2	7,582.3	265.0	645.0	2,194.7	4,477.6
Ukraine	...	...	15.0	15.0	90.0	291.9	...	10.0	225.0	56.9
Uzbekistan	142.0	40.0	30.0	46.0	38.7	28.0	...	10.0	3.6	14.3
Middle East	**8,893.7**	**8,711.0**	**5,012.7**	**6,978.8**	**6,508.1**	**11,750.0**	**2,598.3**	**3,304.2**	**2,250.4**	**3,597.1**
Bahrain	152.0	1,202.5	207.0	340.0	1,050.0	1,475.0	...	...	442.0	1,033.0
Egypt	1,344.5	600.0	1,045.0	670.0	155.0	1,017.7	200.0	737.7	...	80.0
Iran, I.R. of	692.0	757.7	887.0	1,680.1	700.0	1,942.7	179.3	1,497.6	39.9	225.9
Israel	45.0	280.0	395.0	...	...	370.0	...	...	120.0	250.0
Jordan	...	60.0	...	...	...	54.4	...	...	...	54.4
Kuwait	147.5	250.0	770.0	...	165.0	982.5	300.0	...	157.5	525.0
Libya	...	50.0	...	...	...	...	...	...	...	...
Oman	356.8	685.0	...	2,332.0	907.8	1,055.0	75.0	350.0	175.0	455.0
Qatar	1,000.0	580.0	913.0	1,536.7	880.8	1,377.7	460.0	719.0	...	198.7
Saudi Arabia	4,374.8	2,200.9	275.0	280.0	569.5	2,134.0	718.0	...	816.0	600.0
United Arab Emirates	781.0	2,045.0	520.7	140.0	2,080.0	1,341.0	666.0	...	500.0	175.0
Latin America	**22,257.0**	**28,358.5**	**19,118.0**	**12,677.9**	**10,725.2**	**18,197.0**	**3,051.3**	**2,603.0**	**7,026.9**	**5,515.8**
Argentina	3,312.1	3,230.6	1,889.0	824.2	60.0	670.0	250.0	...	...	420.0
Bolivia	...	...	20.0	90.0	...	191.0	...	...	...	191.0
Brazil	4,204.7	8,753.6	6,171.3	3,401.7	1,003.9	4,618.9	1,724.8	1,233.4	1,285.9	374.9
Chile	6,267.9	5,102.8	2,399.3	1,230.7	1,799.0	4,038.5	225.0	403.8	1,425.0	1,984.7
Colombia	1,880.2	1,546.0	631.7	1,096.0	146.3	...	...	...	...	...
Costa Rica	...	...	150.0	...	...	...	...	...	...	...
Cuba	...	...	...	...	...	69.8	69.8	...	...	...
Dominican Republic	...	...	31.1	258.0	70.4	140.5	31.0	8.5	101.0	...
Ecuador	73.0	...	910.0	10.0	...	...	...	...	...	...
El Salvador	166.5	110.0	135.0	...	32.5	180.5	...	...	140.5	40.0
Guadeloupe	...	...	...	17.4	...	...	...	...	...	...
Guatemala	222.0	505.0	...	44.0	...	59.3	9.3	...	...	50.0
Honduras	...	...	...	...	...	169.0	...	...	169.0	...
Jamaica	...	...	35.8	45.0	49.6	96.3	...	26.3	70.0	...
Mexico	4,083.6	6,660.7	4,591.8	4,280.0	7,370.2	7,262.0	504.4	796.0	3,720.6	2,241.1
Nicaragua	...	...	...	...	...	22.0	22.0	...	...	...
Paraguay	55.0	...	70.0	...	...	...	...	...	...	...
Peru	1,530.0	465.4	137.5	63.0	125.0	225.0	90.0	135.0	...	...
St. Lucia	...	...	...	...	20.0	...	...	...	...	...
Trinidad and Tobago	...	51.0	70.0	303.0	46.0	315.0	...	...	115.0	200.0
Uruguay	115.0	159.5	41.3	...	...	...	...	...	...	...
Venezuela	347.0	1,773.9	1,834.3	1,015.0	2.5	139.1	125.0	...	...	14.1

Source: Data provided by the Bond, Equity and Loan database of the International Monetary Fund sourced from Capital Data.

Table 18. Equity Valuation Measures: Dividend-Yield Ratios

	1999	2000	2001	2002	2003	2004	2004			
							Q1	Q2	Q3	Q4
Argentina	3.29	4.62	5.16	3.42	1.08	1.00	0.98	1.37	1.08	1.00
Brazil	2.95	3.18	4.93	5.51	3.46	4.43	3.27	3.78	5.02	4.43
Chile	1.88	2.33	2.31	2.76	1.76	3.01	1.96	1.99	1.89	3.01
China	3.14	0.95	1.95	2.41	2.19	2.26	2.26	2.44	2.39	2.26
Colombia	6.78	11.12	5.63	4.78	3.92	2.52	3.06	3.24	2.79	2.52
Czech Republic	1.36	0.95	2.28	2.36	6.85	4.29	7.35	8.36	5.08	4.29
Egypt	3.92	5.75	6.48	7.53	4.69	1.98	4.23	3.57	2.34	1.98
Hong Kong SAR	2.31	2.58	3.25	3.85	2.82	2.74	2.84	3.08	3.00	2.74
Hungary	1.14	1.46	1.30	1.40	0.94	1.95	0.78	2.52	2.30	1.95
India	1.25	1.59	2.03	1.81	1.47	1.53	1.61	2.04	1.79	1.53
Indonesia	0.91	3.05	3.65	4.17	3.83	3.23	3.66	3.83	3.54	3.23
Israel	1.87	2.26	2.24	1.47	1.10	1.43	1.01	0.88	1.30	1.43
Jordan	4.24	4.54	3.51	3.77	2.36	1.57	2.25	2.27	1.91	1.57
Korea	0.81	2.05	1.54	1.38	1.82	2.40	1.88	2.10	2.50	2.40
Malaysia	1.15	1.70	1.87	2.04	2.38	2.22	1.92	2.24	2.28	2.22
Mexico	1.27	1.63	1.98	2.30	1.83	1.87	1.66	2.18	2.14	1.87
Morocco	2.49	3.59	3.97	4.84	4.18	3.61	3.79	3.83	3.54	3.61
Pakistan	4.00	5.12	16.01	10.95	8.63	7.04	8.20	7.01	7.46	7.04
Peru	2.86	3.38	3.16	2.37	1.75	3.28	1.70	2.43	2.58	3.28
Philippines	1.08	1.44	1.43	1.97	1.43	1.65	1.53	1.50	1.61	1.65
Poland	0.70	0.68	1.87	1.84	1.28	1.28	1.14	1.41	1.72	1.28
Russia	0.14	0.92	1.11	1.87	2.38	3.12	2.00	2.68	2.50	3.12
Singapore	0.86	1.40	1.80	2.27	2.03	2.25	1.98	2.25	2.29	2.25
South Africa	2.09	2.75	3.47	3.83	3.22	2.63	2.93	3.29	2.74	2.63
Sri Lanka	3.22	5.59	4.79	3.35	2.51	2.63	2.27	2.58	2.62	2.63
Taiwan Province of China	0.97	1.71	1.42	1.60	1.86	2.95	1.73	2.24	3.13	2.95
Thailand	0.70	2.13	2.02	2.48	1.69	3.03	2.43	2.88	3.12	3.03
Turkey	0.76	1.91	1.15	1.35	0.89	1.93	1.44	2.80	2.22	1.93
Venezuela	5.80	5.05	3.89	2.38	3.68	5.75	3.03	8.64	5.98	5.75
Emerging Markets	1.52	2.09	2.30	2.43	2.25	2.61	2.16	2.55	2.74	2.61
EM Asia	1.01	1.71	1.73	1.81	1.96	2.48	1.97	2.30	2.59	2.48
EM Latin America	2.28	2.69	3.37	3.64	2.61	3.30	2.43	2.95	3.56	3.30
EM Europe and Middle East	1.16	1.84	1.69	1.71	1.81	2.15	1.75	2.22	2.17	2.15
ACWI Free	1.27	1.46	1.72	2.25	1.99	2.08	2.03	2.05	2.15	2.08

Data are from Morgan Stanley Capital International. The countries above include the 27 constituents of the Emerging Markets index as well as Hong Kong SAR and Singapore. Regional breakdowns conform to Morgan Stanley Capital International conventions. All indices reflect investible opportunities for global investors by taking into account restrictions on foreign ownership. The indices attempt to achieve an 85 percent representation of freely floating stocks.

Table 19. Equity Valuation Measures: Price-to-Book Ratios

	1999	2000	2001	2002	2003	2004	2004 Q1	Q2	Q3	Q4
Argentina	1.47	1.04	0.86	1.20	1.79	2.242	2.00	1.65	2.16	2.24
Brazil	1.24	1.18	1.11	1.24	1.81	1.841	1.79	1.61	1.82	1.84
Chile	1.69	1.49	1.39	1.15	1.55	1.781	1.33	1.56	1.67	1.78
China	0.69	2.75	1.88	1.30	2.16	1.979	2.13	1.85	1.88	1.98
Colombia	0.71	0.49	0.53	1.18	1.34	1.921	1.81	1.74	1.64	1.92
Czech Republic	0.80	1.00	0.81	0.84	1.06	1.644	1.30	1.16	1.35	1.64
Egypt	3.57	2.32	1.39	1.05	2.17	3.887	2.67	2.32	3.38	3.89
Hong Kong SAR	2.27	1.67	1.38	1.10	1.47	1.712	1.56	1.45	1.56	1.71
Hungary	3.35	2.33	2.03	1.91	1.97	2.621	2.28	2.29	2.43	2.62
India	3.55	2.71	2.13	2.15	3.79	3.631	3.53	3.07	3.13	3.63
Indonesia	2.41	1.03	2.72	2.23	2.26	3.096	2.42	2.37	2.50	3.10
Israel	2.53	3.04	2.22	1.74	2.46	2.624	2.75	2.77	2.23	2.62
Jordan	1.03	1.02	1.38	1.26	1.98	3.01	2.08	2.49	2.31	3.01
Korea	1.42	0.82	1.33	1.21	1.52	1.364	1.71	1.39	1.38	1.36
Malaysia	1.98	1.59	1.76	1.54	1.85	1.949	2.11	1.85	1.86	1.95
Mexico	2.31	1.91	1.99	1.77	2.20	2.575	2.49	2.31	2.38	2.58
Morocco	3.53	2.56	1.79	1.40	1.50	2.421	1.64	1.85	1.91	2.42
Pakistan	1.48	1.41	0.88	2.04	2.31	2.392	2.41	2.30	2.15	2.39
Peru	1.92	1.13	1.29	1.84	2.77	2.284	3.01	2.35	2.39	2.28
Philippines	1.64	1.27	1.11	0.85	1.40	1.61	1.36	1.48	1.56	1.61
Poland	2.12	2.10	1.33	1.37	1.72	2.105	1.92	1.83	1.82	2.11
Russia	2.41	0.90	1.27	1.22	1.33	1.108	1.64	1.35	1.39	1.11
Singapore	2.56	2.05	1.63	1.26	1.62	1.697	1.67	1.58	1.65	1.70
South Africa	2.75	2.68	1.81	1.72	1.95	2.43	1.96	1.81	2.01	2.43
Sri Lanka	1.00	0.60	0.83	1.22	1.52	1.433	1.57	1.69	1.45	1.43
Taiwan Province of China	3.46	1.87	1.98	1.53	2.10	1.875	2.25	1.90	1.82	1.88
Thailand	2.04	1.51	1.68	1.83	2.94	2.41	2.49	2.42	2.34	2.41
Turkey	9.21	2.72	3.80	1.76	2.02	1.922	2.06	1.54	1.66	1.92
Venezuela	0.63	0.67	0.48	0.87	1.41	1.633	1.78	1.58	1.65	1.63
Emerging Markets	2.12	1.64	1.59	1.45	1.90	1.911	2.01	1.78	1.82	1.91
EM Asia	2.09	1.53	1.68	1.41	1.95	1.806	2.06	1.75	1.75	1.81
EM Latin America	1.57	1.36	1.35	1.44	1.90	2.047	1.95	1.82	1.97	2.05
EM Europe and Middle East	3.41	2.15	1.70	1.42	1.67	1.776	1.95	1.78	1.72	1.78
ACWI Free	4.23	3.46	2.67	2.07	2.46	2.455	2.48	2.44	2.34	2.46

Data are from Morgan Stanley Capital International. The countries above include the 27 constituents of the Emerging Markets index as well as Hong Kong SAR and Singapore. Regional breakdowns conform to Morgan Stanley Capital International conventions. All indices reflect investible opportunities for global investors by taking into account restrictions on foreign ownership. The indices attempt to achieve an 85 percent representation of freely floating stocks.

Table 20. Equity Valuation Measures: Price-Earnings Ratios

| | 1999 | 2000 | 2001 | 2002 | 2003 | 2004 | 2004 | | | |
							Q1	Q2	Q3	Q4
Argentina	24.82	20.69	19.13	−12.86	13.72	47.24	18.25	27.81	244.47	47.24
Brazil	18.64	12.83	8.49	11.23	10.34	10.80	9.99	9.05	9.89	10.80
Chile	46.40	31.96	18.02	17.16	30.81	23.06	22.26	23.37	25.04	23.06
China	14.97	40.60	14.09	12.14	17.11	13.83	17.09	15.16	13.15	13.83
Colombia	20.30	−103.44	64.91	9.55	8.94	17.67	12.12	11.80	10.56	17.67
Czech Republic	−42.04	16.49	9.21	10.40	12.49	26.64	16.91	22.38	18.18	26.64
Egypt	16.54	9.35	6.28	7.33	10.90	14.23	13.23	10.51	13.88	14.23
Hong Kong SAR	30.81	7.64	20.47	14.91	20.00	19.90	21.83	21.37	19.50	19.90
Hungary	18.50	14.82	19.34	10.06	13.11	11.26	13.23	12.14	11.89	11.26
India	22.84	15.61	13.84	13.56	18.96	17.65	17.62	14.52	15.63	17.65
Indonesia	−48.73	18.68	8.37	7.14	10.37	12.91	11.06	10.75	11.14	12.91
Israel	25.51	23.88	228.84	−46.62	34.05	20.11	32.58	41.55	17.36	20.11
Jordan	13.51	−107.11	15.10	12.39	21.38	32.50	22.45	28.39	25.04	32.50
Korea	23.24	8.12	15.23	11.44	13.93	8.24	15.26	12.56	9.09	8.24
Malaysia	−8.41	20.63	22.62	13.21	16.33	16.05	18.98	15.80	15.55	16.05
Mexico	14.64	13.78	14.23	14.07	15.70	15.02	17.32	14.29	15.66	15.02
Morocco	18.65	9.30	10.77	9.87	22.46	15.55	24.79	22.85	26.69	15.55
Pakistan	17.60	8.39	4.53	8.07	8.68	9.45	9.46	9.18	8.76	9.45
Peru	18.46	15.44	14.08	20.42	26.45	11.88	30.59	20.52	17.69	11.88
Philippines	142.83	−35.06	43.72	18.21	20.18	14.87	19.09	17.79	14.35	14.87
Poland	22.33	14.30	18.32	−261.14	19.50	13.27	25.13	15.75	12.58	13.27
Russia	−126.43	5.69	5.03	7.33	11.13	8.19	12.47	8.92	9.59	8.19
Singapore	41.18	18.94	16.53	21.07	21.38	14.33	19.93	15.51	14.00	14.33
South Africa	18.73	14.87	11.30	10.50	12.75	14.97	13.78	13.22	14.38	14.97
Sri Lanka	7.59	4.24	8.53	14.35	12.69	11.03	11.95	12.99	10.53	11.03
Taiwan Province of China	38.26	14.06	21.08	73.13	25.70	12.40	27.76	16.76	12.76	12.40
Thailand	−8.94	−14.61	16.67	15.52	15.24	11.49	13.23	12.38	11.33	11.49
Turkey	38.60	11.77	25.51	101.33	11.01	13.61	9.95	8.32	11.85	13.61
Venezuela	17.68	21.76	18.43	13.43	24.40	12.44	26.55	19.33	14.91	12.44
Emerging Markets	27.17	14.85	13.99	13.95	15.03	12.15	15.75	13.48	12.22	12.15
EM Asia	40.98	15.47	16.73	14.85	16.72	11.23	17.52	14.08	11.47	11.23
EM Latin America	18.28	14.93	11.67	13.84	13.18	13.10	13.30	11.91	12.82	13.10
EM Europe and Middle East	37.25	14.05	13.10	16.27	14.65	12.64	15.56	13.78	12.31	12.64
ACWI Free	35.70	25.44	26.76	23.18	21.94	17.94	20.77	19.36	17.41	17.94

Data are from Morgan Stanley Capital International. The countries above include the 27 constituents of the Emerging Markets index as well as Hong Kong SAR and Singapore. Regional breakdowns conform to Morgan Stanley Capital International conventions. All indices reflect investible opportunities for global investors by taking into account restrictions on foreign ownership. The indices attempt to achieve an 85 percent representation of freely floating stocks.

Table 21. United States: Mutual Fund Flows
(In millions of U.S. dollars)

	1999	2000	2001	2002	2003	2004	2004 Q1	Q2	Q3	Q4
Asia Pacific (ex-Japan)	151.7	−1,207.9	−496.2	−43.0	1,510.8	1,574.3	1,068.2	−404.5	−42.1	952.7
Corporate high yield	−510.1	−6,162.3	5,938.3	8,082.4	20,261.9	−3,259.3	−1,601.7	−3,807.3	1,490.4	659.4
Corporate investment grade	7,136.3	4,253.7	21,692.0	32,688.3	16,660.2	3,339.1	3,095.3	−1,560.5	1,677.9	126.4
Emerging markets debt	18.4	−499.9	−447.7	449.7	889.0	211.4	325.2	−243.6	99.9	29.9
Emerging markets equity	23.5	−349.9	−1,662.7	−330.7	4,672.7	5,815.8	3,112.0	−895.2	105.9	3,493.1
European equity	−1,664.9	620.9	−1,790.8	−1,044.8	−947.4	873.2	374.2	−96.9	−118.7	714.5
Global equity	4,673.2	12,626.7	−3,005.5	−5,152.1	−1,995.4	8,373.4	2,574.7	1,609.2	1,453.7	2,735.7
Growth-Aggressive	15,247.5	46,610.3	17,882.8	5,611.6	11,464.9	9,915.4	6,022.1	4,081.0	−356.3	168.5
International and global debt	−1,581.6	−3,272.2	−1,602.2	−823.0	3,225.0	5,143.4	2,159.0	221.2	724.0	2,039.3
International equity	2,998.5	13,322.4	−4,488.2	4,240.0	14,650.8	35,441.1	14,256.4	5,285.1	4,211.2	11,688.6
Japanese equity	731.0	−830.6	−269.8	−82.0	1,863.3	3,313.7	1,541.4	1,314.6	422.7	35.1
Latin American equity	−120.9	−94.6	−146.7	32.7	185.7	65.3	−39.7	−53.0	−1.6	159.7

Data are provided by AMG Data Services and cover net flows of U.S.-based mutual funds. Fund categories are distinguished by a primary investment objective that signifies an investment of 65 percent or more of a fund's assets. Primary sector data are mutually exclusive, but emerging and regional sectors are all subsets of international equity.

Table 22. Bank Regulatory Capital to Risk-Weighted Assets
(In percent)

	2000	2001	2002	2003	2004	Latest
Latin America						
Argentina[1]	10.4	13.2	13.9	12.1	11.2	September
Bolivia	13.4	14.6	16.1	15.3	15.0	October
Brazil	14.3	15.3	16.7	18.9	18.3	September
Chile	13.3	12.7	14.0	14.1	13.3	September
Colombia	12.2	12.4	12.1	12.4	12.8	November
Costa Rica	16.7	15.1	15.8	16.5	. . .	
Dominican Republic	12.1	11.8	12.0	11.4	10.5	September
Ecuador[2]	13.1	13.5	14.4	14.9	14.9	April
Mexico	13.8	14.7	15.5	14.2	14.6	September
Nicaragua	14.3	16.4	18.0	14.2	15.7	June
Paraguay[3]	17.2	16.2	17.9	20.1	23.8	September
Peru	12.9	13.4	12.5	13.3	14.1	September
Venezuela	. . .	. . .	. . .	. . .	. . .	
Emerging Europe						
Bulgaria	35.6	31.1	25.2	22.0	17.1	September
Croatia	21.3	18.5	17.2	15.7	14.7	September
Czech Republic	14.8	15.4	14.3	14.5	13.6	June
Estonia	13.2	14.4	15.3	14.5	13.4	December
Hungary	13.7	13.9	13.0	11.8	11.5	March
Israel[4]	9.2	9.4	9.9	10.3	. . .	September
Latvia	14.0	14.2	13.1	11.7	12.1	June
Lithuania	16.3	15.7	14.8	13.2	12.8	October
Moldova	48.6	43.1	36.4	31.8	31.9	September
Poland	12.9	15.1	13.8	13.7	15.7	June
Russia	19.0	20.3	19.1	19.1	17.4	September
Slovak Republic	12.5	19.8	21.3	21.6	20.5	September
Slovenia	13.5	11.9	11.9	11.5	. . .	
Turkey	9.3	20.8	25.1	30.9	26.5	December
Ukraine	15.5	20.7	18.0	15.2	16.8	December
Western Europe						
Austria	13.3	13.7	13.3	14.4	14.0	April
Belgium	11.9	12.9	13.1	12.8	. . .	
Finland[5]	11.6	10.5	11.7	18.9	19.1	June
France	11.9	12.1	12.3	12.6	. . .	
Germany	11.7	12.0	12.7	12.9	. . .	
Greece	13.6	12.5	10.6	12.0	. . .	
Iceland	9.8	11.4	12.2	12.3	13.1	June
Ireland	10.7	10.6	12.3	13.9	. . .	
Italy	10.1	10.4	11.2	11.4	. . .	
Luxembourg	13.1	13.7	15.0	17.1	17.4	June
Netherlands[6]	10.6	10.8	11.1	11.2	. . .	
Norway	12.1	12.6	12.2	12.4	11.8	September
Portugal	9.2	9.5	9.8	10.0	10.3	June
Spain	12.4	12.9	12.5	12.5	12.1	June
Sweden	9.9	10.0	10.1	10.1	10.0	March
Switzerland	12.7	11.8	12.1	11.2	. . .	
United Kingdom	13.0	13.2	12.2	12.4	. . .	
Asia						
Bangladesh	6.7	6.7	7.5	8.4	. . .	
China[7]	13.5	12.3	11.2	. . .	. . .	
Hong Kong SAR	17.8	16.5	15.7	15.3	15.9	September
India	11.1	11.4	11.9	12.9	13.4	June
Indonesia[8]	21.6	18.2	20.1	22.3	22.4	September
Korea	10.5	10.8	10.5	10.5	10.9	June
Malaysia	12.5	13.0	13.2	13.8	13.7	October
Philippines[9]	. . .	14.5	15.5	16.0	. . .	
Singapore	19.6	18.1	16.9	17.9	15.5	December
Thailand	11.3	13.3	13.0	13.4	11.7	June

Table 22 *(concluded)*

	2000	2001	2002	2003	2004	Latest
Middle East and Central Asia						
Azerbaijan	...	...	...	14.7	20.9	June
Egypt	10.2	10.2	9.9	11.0	11.1	June
Jordan[10]	19.4	17.4	16.7	15.9	...	
Kuwait	22.2	22.0	19.7	18.4	...	June
Kyrgyz Republic	30.5	52.2	36.4	35.3	27.7	July
Lebanon	16.9	18.0	19.4	22.3	...	
Morocco	12.8	12.6	12.2	9.6	...	
Oman	16.5	15.6	16.9	...	...	
Pakistan[11]	11.4	11.3	12.6	11.1	11.6	September
Saudi Arabia	21.0	20.3	21.3	19.4	17.5	March
Tunisia	13.3	10.6	9.8	9.3	9.3	December
United Arab Emirates	20.2	20.0	18.9	18.2	...	
Sub-Saharan Africa						
Ghana	11.6	14.7	13.4	9.3	...	
Guinea	...	11.6	24.1	20.6	...	
Kenya	17.6	17.3	17.0	17.3	16.5	June
Mauritius	12.3	13.0	13.0	14.3	...	
Nigeria	17.5	16.2	18.1	17.8	...	
Senegal	...	...	...	11.5	12.7	March
Sierra Leone	24.6	29.4	48.4	39.8	37.1	December
South Africa	14.5	11.4	12.6	12.2	12.7	April
Tanzania	9.6	9.6	8.6	...	...	
Uganda	20.5	23.1	20.7	16.7	20.6	December
Zimbabwe	44.0	44.5	30.6	16.2	...	
Other						
Australia	9.8	10.5	9.9	10.1	10.6	September
Canada	11.9	12.3	12.4	12.6	13.5	June
Japan[12]	11.7	10.8	9.4	11.1	11.2	September
United States[13]	12.4	12.9	13.0	13.0	13.2	September

Sources: National authorities; and IMF staff estimates.

[1]Includes banks and nonbank financial companies.

[2]Capital in balance sheet at the end of the year net of profits to risk-weighted assets.

[3]Private banks.

[4]Ratio for the five largest banking groups.

[5]All Finnish banks, including the Nordea Bank Finland Group. Due to frequent restructuring within the Nordea group, the data are not directly comparable over time.

[6]Ratio for the large and complex financial institutions.

[7]Ratio for the state commercial banks.

[8]Ratio for the top 16 banks.

[9]Based on the new regulatory framework.

[10]For 2003, the calculations include market risk, which reduced the capital adequacy ratio by 2 percentage points.

[11]The data refer to commercial banks only, excluding specialized banks.

[12]Ratio for the major banks.

[13]Includes all FDIC-insured commercial banks and savings associations.

Table 23. Bank Capital to Assets
(In percent)

	2000	2001	2002	2003	2004	Latest
Latin America						
Argentina	. . .	. . .	. . .	. . .	. . .	
Bolivia	9.8	10.5	11.9	12.1	11.9	October
Brazil	12.1	13.6	13.5	16.2	16.0	November
Chile	7.5	7.2	7.2	7.3	6.9	November
Colombia	10.1	9.4	9.3	9.8	10.0	September
Costa Rica	10.8	12.9	12.6	13.6	13.4	March
Dominican Republic	9.4	10.0	10.7	7.8	7.4	March
Ecuador	12.9	8.8	10.3	10.2	10.4	September
Mexico	9.6	9.4	11.1	11.4	11.5	September
Nicaragua	. . .	. . .	. . .	. . .	. . .	
Paraguay	12.4	12.1	10.9	10.0	10.0	March
Peru	9.1	9.8	10.1	9.3	10.1	August
Venezuela	13.0	14.1	15.9	14.3	13.2	September
Emerging Europe						
Bulgaria	15.3	13.5	13.3	13.2	12.0	September
Croatia	11.9	9.3	9.5	9.0	8.7	June
Czech Republic	5.4	5.2	5.2	5.7	5.7	September
Estonia	12.6	13.3	12.1	11.3	9.8	December
Hungary	9.8	9.5	10.0	9.8	. . .	
Israel	7.3	7.7	6.5	7.2	7.3	October
Latvia	8.5	9.1	8.8	8.6	8.2	November
Lithuania	9.2	9.4	9.9	9.8	. . .	
Moldova	30.6	27.5	23.0	21.1	20.2	September
Poland	7.1	8.0	8.7	8.2	8.2	June
Russia	12.1	14.4	14.0	14.6	13.4	November
Slovak Republic	4.6	6.3	6.8	7.7	7.2	August
Slovenia	10.1	8.8	8.4	8.4	8.2	March
Turkey	6.1	9.6	11.6	13.6	14.0	November
Ukraine	16.2	15.6	14.9	12.3	13.1	December
Western Europe						
Austria	5.2	5.1	5.6	5.8	6.0	December
Belgium	4.6	4.4	4.7	4.3	4.1	December
Finland	6.3	10.2	10.1	9.6	8.2	December
France	6.7	6.7	6.8	6.7	6.5	December
Germany	4.2	4.3	4.5	4.5	4.3	November
Greece	8.9	9.2	9.4	7.6	7.9	December
Iceland	6.2	6.5	7.2	7.1	7.1	June
Ireland	6.5	5.9	5.5	5.2	4.9	December
Italy	6.7	6.7	6.5	6.5	. . .	
Luxembourg	3.9	3.9	3.7	3.8	. . .	
Netherlands	5.1	4.8	4.7	4.3	3.9	December
Norway	7.0	6.8	6.3	6.0	5.9	March
Portugal	5.8	5.6	5.7	5.9	5.9	March
Spain	7.3	7.2	7.0	7.0	. . .	
Sweden	5.3	5.6	5.2	5.2	. . .	
Switzerland	5.8	5.5	5.4	5.3	. . .	
United Kingdom[1]	6.5	6.6	6.7	6.8	. . .	
Asia						
Bangladesh	3.5	3.5	4.1	3.2	2.7	May
China[2]	5.3	5.1	4.6	4.3	4.1	March
Hong Kong SAR	9.0	9.8	10.7	11.5	12.3	November
India	5.7	5.3	5.5	5.7	5.9	March
Indonesia	6.0	5.3	7.1	8.7	. . .	
Korea	3.8	4.1	4.0	4.1	. . .	
Malaysia	8.5	8.5	8.7	8.5	8.1	December
Philippines	13.6	13.6	13.4	13.1	12.8	June
Singapore	10.0	10.0	11.0	11.0	. . .	
Thailand[3]	7.5	8.9	8.9	9.6	8.5	June

Table 23 *(concluded)*

	2000	2001	2002	2003	2004	Latest
Middle East and Central Asia						
Azerbaijan	. . .	19.5	19.8	15.6	14.7	June
Egypt	5.6	5.2	4.8	5.3	4.8	June
Jordan	7.0	6.6	6.2	6.4	. . .	
Kuwait	11.5	11.2	10.4	10.8	. . .	
Kyrgyz Republic	20.5	31.5	27.7	. . .	. . .	June
Lebanon	6.4	6.2	6.4	6.1	5.8	November
Morocco	9.2	9.3	8.9	8.2	8.7	November
Oman	13.0	12.6	12.5	. . .	. . .	
Pakistan[4]	4.9	4.6	6.1	6.0	6.2	September
Saudi Arabia	9.7	9.9	10.2	10.8	. . .	
Tunisia	. . .	. . .	. . .	. . .	. . .	
United Arab Emirates	. . .	. . .	. . .	. . .	. . .	
Sub-Saharan Africa						
Ghana	11.8	12.5	12.0	12.0	12.4	July
Guinea	. . .	. . .	. . .	. . .	. . .	
Kenya	12.9	13.3	11.6	11.8	11.4	June
Mauritius	7.8	8.4	9.0	9.4	. . .	
Nigeria	7.4	7.5	10.4	8.6	. . .	
Senegal	. . .	. . .	. . .	. . .	. . .	
Sierra Leone	18.5	20.0	18.0	20.3	11.6	December
South Africa	8.7	7.8	8.2	7.0	6.9	March
Tanzania	9.6	9.6	8.6	. . .	. . .	
Uganda	9.8	10.0	9.5	9.9	. . .	
Zimbabwe	9.4	9.3	9.5	7.6	9.8	September
Other						
Australia[3]	6.9	7.1	6.3	5.8	5.2	June
Canada	4.7	4.6	4.6	4.7	4.3	November
Japan	4.6	3.8	3.3	3.9	3.9	September
United States[5]	8.5	9.0	9.2	9.2	10.1	September

Sources: National authorities; and IMF staff estimates.
[1]Data for U.K. large commercial banks (exclusive of mortgage banks and other banks).
[2]Ratio for the state commercial banks. 2004 data do not reflect recapitalization of the first two banks.
[3]Tier 1 capital to total assets.
[4]The data refer to commercial banks only, excluding specialized banks.
[5]Includes all FDIC-insured commercial banks and savings associations.

Table 24. Bank Nonperforming Loans to Total Loans
(In percent)

	2000	2001	2002	2003	2004	Latest
Latin America						
Argentina[1]	16.0	19.1	35.6	33.6	32.0	September
Bolivia	10.3	14.4	17.7	17.1	16.0	November
Brazil***	8.4	5.7	5.3	4.4	3.8	September
Chile	1.7	1.6	1.8	1.6	1.4	September
Colombia	11.0	9.7	8.7	6.8	6.7	March
Costa Rica	3.5	2.4	3.2	1.7	. . .	
Dominican Republic	2.6	2.6	4.9	8.9	8.9	September
Ecuador	31.0	27.8	8.4	7.9	8.3	September
Mexico	5.8	5.1	4.6	3.2	2.7	September
Nicaragua	5.2	9.3	12.6	12.7	10.5	August
Paraguay[2]	12.0	12.3	14.7	15.0	9.9	September
Peru	9.8	9.0	7.6	5.8	4.6	September
Venezuela	6.6	7.0	9.2	7.7	4.4	September
Emerging Europe						
Bulgaria[3]	17.3	13.1	8.6	7.3	6.7	September
Croatia***	9.5	7.3	5.9	5.1	4.6	September
Czech Republic	19.9	13.7	10.6	4.9	4.5	June
Estonia	1.0	1.3	0.8	0.4	0.3	December
Hungary	3.0	2.7	2.9	2.6	2.7	March
Israel[4]	6.7	8.1	9.9	10.3	. . .	September
Latvia	4.6	2.8	2.0	1.4	1.4	June
Lithuania**	11.3	8.3	6.5	3.0	2.1	October
Moldova	20.6	10.4	7.7	6.2	6.5	September
Poland**	15.5	18.6	22.0	22.2	18.1	June
Russia[5]	7.7	6.2	5.6	5.0	15.0	September
Slovak Republic[6]	13.7	12.3	9.2	6.4	5.4	August
Slovenia	6.5	7.0	7.0	6.5	. . .	
Turkey	11.1	25.2	17.6	11.5	6.1	December
Ukraine[7]	29.6	25.1	21.9	28.3	28.0	September
Western Europe						
Austria	1.9	1.3	1.3	. . .	. . .	
Belgium	2.7	2.9	2.9	3.4	. . .	June
Finland	0.6	0.6	0.5	0.4	0.4	June
France	5.0	5.0	5.0	4.8	. . .	
Germany	5.1	4.9	5.0	4.8	. . .	
Greece	12.3	9.2	8.1	8.4	. . .	
Iceland[8]	1.5	2.0	2.6	2.1	1.7	June
Ireland	1.0	1.0	1.0	0.9	. . .	
Italy	5.7	4.7	4.5	4.7	. . .	
Luxembourg[9]	0.5	0.4	0.4	0.3	0.3	June
Netherlands[10]	1.8	1.8	2.3	2.1	. . .	
Norway	1.3	1.4	2.0	1.7	1.3	September
Portugal	2.2	2.1	2.3	2.4	2.2	June
Spain	1.2	1.2	1.1	1.0	0.8	June
Sweden	1.6	1.5	1.2	1.2	1.2	March
Switzerland	3.8	4.1	3.6	3.6	. . .	
United Kingdom	2.5	2.6	2.6	2.2	. . .	
Asia						
Bangladesh	34.9	31.5	28.0	22.1	. . .	
China[11]	22.4	29.8	25.5	17.9	. . .	
Hong Kong SAR	7.3	6.5	5.0	3.9	2.7	September
India	12.8	11.4	10.4	8.8	6.6	June
Indonesia[12]	34.4	28.6	22.1	17.9	14.9	September
Korea	8.9	3.3	2.4	2.7	2.4	September
Malaysia	15.4	17.8	15.8	13.9	12.6	October
Philippines[13]	. . .	. . .	26.4	26.1	26.2	June
Singapore	3.4	3.6	3.4	3.2	2.9	December
Thailand	17.7	10.5	15.7	12.9	12.4	June

Table 24 *(concluded)*

	2000	2001	2002	2003	2004	Latest
Middle East and Central Asia						
Azerbaijan	...	28.0	21.5	23.0	18.7	June
Egypt	13.6	15.6	16.9	20.2	24.2	June
Jordan	18.4	19.3	21.0	19.9	...	
Kuwait	19.2	10.3	7.8	7.0	...	June
Kyrgyz Republic	30.9	13.4	13.3	11.2	8.0	July
Lebanon[14]	7.8	10.0	12.4	12.8	12.2	May
Morocco	17.5	16.8	17.2	18.1	...	
Oman	7.5	10.6	11.9	12.8	...	
Pakistan[15]	19.5	19.6	17.7	13.7	11.0	September
Saudi Arabia	10.4	10.1	9.2	5.4	...	
Tunisia	21.6	19.2	20.9	24.0	23.8	December
United Arab Emirates	12.7	15.7	15.3	14.3	...	
Sub-Saharan Africa						
Ghana	11.9	19.6	22.7	18.3	...	
Guinea	25.0	27.7	25.7	28.0	...	
Kenya	33.3	30.1	29.8	25.6	22.9	June
Mauritius	7.7	8.0	8.6	9.6	...	
Nigeria	22.6	19.7	21.4	19.8	...	
Senegal	...	...	...	13.3	14.7	March
Sierra Leone	37.9	29.1	17.1	9.9	14.3	December
South Africa	...	3.2	2.9	2.4	2.2	April
Tanzania	17.3	12.0	9.2	...	...	
Uganda****	9.8	6.5	3.0	7.2	2.6	December
Zimbabwe	19.6	11.4	4.2	4.7	...	
Other						
Australia	0.5	0.7	0.6	0.4	0.3	June
Canada	1.3	1.5	1.6	1.4	1.0	June
Japan[16]	5.3	8.4	7.2	5.2	4.7	September
United States[17]	1.1	1.3	1.4	1.1	0.9	September

Sources: National authorities; and IMF staff estimates.

[1]Includes banks and nonbank financial companies.

[2]Private banks.

[3]Loans in categories "watch," "substandard," "doubtful," "loss."

[4]Ratio for the five largest banking groups.

[5]In 2004 the ratio includes substandard loans.

[6]Without KB.

[7]The increase in nonperforming loans (NPLs) in 2003 reflects a revision in the official definition.

[8]NPLs net of specific provisions and excluding appropriated assets.

[9]Value adjustments on credit to total gross credit.

[10]Simple average of the impaired loan ratios of the three largest banks.

[11]State commercial banks.

[12]Compromised assets include reported NPLs, restructured loans classified as pass or special mention, and foreclosed real estate and equities. The denominator includes foreclosed real estate and surrendered equities.

[13]NPLs plus "real and other properties owned or acquired."

[14]Problem loans net of provisions and unearned interest.

[15]The data refer to commercial banks only, excluding specialized banks.

[16]Ratio for the major banks.

[17]Includes all FDIC-insured commercial banks and savings associations.

(**)30-day NPL classification.

(***)60-day NPL classification.

(****)180-day NPL classification.

Table 25. Bank Provisions to Nonperforming Loans
(In percent)

	2000	2001	2002	2003	2004	Latest
Latin America						
Argentina	61.1	66.4	73.8	78.4	80.0	September
Bolivia	61.2	63.9	63.3	72.4	77.0	November
Brazil	82.1	126.1	143.5	165.6	183.2	September
Chile	145.5	146.5	128.1	130.9	147.5	September
Colombia	56.6	77.5	86.5	98.1	100.9	March
Costa Rica	100.8	113.2	102.6	145.9	. . .	
Dominican Republic	121.6	112.3	64.9	65.0	. . .	
Ecuador	104.0	102.2	131.4	127.3	101.7	September
Mexico	115.3	123.8	138.1	167.1	197.1	September
Nicaragua	5.7	3.5	5.4	4.6	4.7	June
Paraguay[1]	39.2	39.8	50.3	59.2	60.5	September
Peru	104.3	114.2	133.2	141.1	154.7	September
Venezuela	93.6	92.4	97.9	103.7	113.1	September
Emerging Europe						
Bulgaria	65.9	61.7	65.0	52.8	49.1	September
Croatia	79.9	71.8	68.1	60.8	61.4	September
Czech Republic	46.8	60.3	77.5	77.1	76.8	March
Estonia	. . .	. . .	. . .	. . .	. . .	
Hungary	56.4	57.7	51.3	47.7	. . .	
Israel	55.8	57.1	54.7	53.8	. . .	
Latvia	74.1	80.4	95.5	98.5	89.2	June
Lithuania	34.6	34.2	18.6	21.6	. . .	
Moldova	. . .	. . .	. . .	. . .	. . .	
Poland	40.5	42.6	46.7	47.3	58.0	June
Russia	102.6	108.1	112.5	118.0	35.3	September
Slovak Republic[2]	75.1	79.7	86.1	88.3	89.1	August
Slovenia[3]	101.0	100.5	102.0	101.5	. . .	
Turkey	63.1	48.9	64.2	88.5	88.6	December
Ukraine	38.4	39.2	39.6	22.7	20.7	September
Western Europe						
Austria	. . .	. . .	. . .	. . .	. . .	
Belgium	57.0	57.0	51.8	46.3	. . .	June
Finland	. . .	. . .	. . .	. . .	. . .	
France	60.8	59.9	58.3	58.4		
Germany	. . .	. . .	. . .	. . .	. . .	
Greece	36.8	43.3	46.9	49.9	. . .	
Iceland	52.5	46.8	43.7	. . .	. . .	
Ireland	106.1	110.8	108.7	97.0	. . .	
Italy	48.6	50.0	53.6	55.1	. . .	
Luxembourg	. . .	. . .	. . .	. . .	. . .	
Netherlands[4]	73.7	73.3	55.0	59.6	. . .	
Norway[5]	37.8	30.6	35.7	34.2	. . .	
Portugal	66.7	66.8	62.8	72.6	. . .	
Spain[6]	134.9	160.4	183.2	209.7	266.2	June
Sweden	60.0	64.9	73.8	. . .	. . .	
Switzerland	. . .	. . .	. . .	. . .	. . .	
United Kingdom	65.0	69.5	72.3	. . .	. . .	
Asia						
Bangladesh	59.1	60.5	55.8	40.3	. . .	
China[7]	4.7	5.2	5.3	. . .	. . .	
Hong Kong SAR	. . .	. . .	. . .	. . .	. . .	
India	. . .	. . .	. . .	. . .	. . .	
Indonesia[8]	36.1	35.5	35.9	43.4	42.9	June
Korea	. . .	. . .	. . .	. . .	. . .	
Malaysia	41.0	37.7	38.1	38.9	39.4	October
Philippines[9]	28.6	29.6	30.1	30.9	30.6	June
Singapore[10]	. . .	60.1	61.2	64.9	72.8	September
Thailand	47.2	54.9	61.8	72.8	69.0	February

Table 25 *(concluded)*

	2000	2001	2002	2003	2004	Latest
Middle East and Central Asia						
Azerbaijan	. . .	. . .	. . .	. . .	. . .	
Egypt	73.5	69.4	67.5	62.3	57.0	June
Jordan	34.6	36.4	36.7	38.9	. . .	
Kuwait	50.1	53.7	64.3	72.4	. . .	June
Kyrgyz Republic	. . .	47.1	51.2	46.9	57.6	July
Lebanon	72.5	69.3	68.2	71.4	. . .	
Morocco	45.7	53.0	57.1	66.5	. . .	
Oman	71.9	68.5	79.7	. . .	. . .	
Pakistan[11]	53.9	53.2	58.2	64.7	70.2	September
Saudi Arabia	99.0	107.0	110.4	136.0	. . .	
Tunisia	49.2	47.4	43.9	43.1	45.9	December
United Arab Emirates	. . .	. . .	. . .	. . .	. . .	
Sub-Saharan Africa						
Ghana	58.6	46.4	63.6	64.4	. . .	
Guinea	83.2	87.6	88.5	83.7	. . .	
Kenya	. . .	. . .	. . .	. . .	. . .	
Mauritius	. . .	. . .	. . .	. . .	. . .	
Nigeria	49.7	73.6	60.9	. . .	. . .	
Senegal	. . .	. . .	. . .	75.3	70.4	March
Sierra Leone	95.0	108.6	119.6	92.7	43.1	December
South Africa	44.0	46.0	54.2	66.1	67.1	April
Tanzania	. . .	. . .	. . .	. . .	. . .	
Uganda	. . .	. . .	. . .	. . .	. . .	
Zimbabwe	44.4	28.3	52.8	70.1	. . .	
Other						
Australia[12]	132.1	107.1	109.8	138.3	150.8	June
Canada[13]	42.8	44.0	41.1	43.5	49.9	November
Japan	35.5	31.8	36.1	43.6	43.9	September
United States[14]	146.4	128.8	123.7	140.4	165.4	September

Source: National authorities; and IMF staff estimates.
[1]Private banks.
[2]Without KB.
[3]Actual provisioning as a percentage of required provisioning.
[4]Ratio for the three largest banks.
[5]Loan-loss provision ratio for enterprise loans.
[6]Includes general provisions.
[7]State commercial banks.
[8]Loan-loss reserve to compromised assets.
[9]Nonperforming assets coverage ratio.
[10]Total cumulative provisions to total NPLs.
[11]The data refer to commercial banks only, excluding specialized banks.
[12]Includes general provisions.
[13]Specific provisions only.
[14]Includes all FDIC-insured commercial banks and savings associations.

Table 26. Bank Return on Assets
(In percent)

	2000	2001	2002	2003	2004	Latest
Latin America						
Argentina[1]	0.3	−0.2	−10.3	−2.6	−0.9	September
Bolivia	−0.9	−0.4	0.1	0.3	−0.1	October
Brazil	1.0	0.2	1.9	1.6	1.5	September
Chile	1.0	1.3	1.1	1.3	1.3	September
Colombia[2]	−0.2	1.9	2.8	3.7	5.5	March
Costa Rica[3]	1.5	1.7	1.8	2.1	. . .	
Dominican Republic	1.6	1.9	2.3	0.0	0.3	May
Ecuador	−2.8	−6.6	1.5	1.5	2.1	September
Mexico	0.9	0.8	−1.1	1.7	1.1	September
Nicaragua	1.9	1.8	1.8	2.1	2.9	June
Paraguay	1.4	2.2	1.0	0.4	1.7	September
Peru	0.3	0.4	0.8	1.1	1.1	September
Venezuela	2.8	2.8	5.3	6.2	5.8	September
Emerging Europe						
Bulgaria	3.1	2.9	2.1	2.4	2.3	September
Croatia	1.3	0.7	1.3	1.4	1.5	September
Czech Republic	0.7	0.7	1.2	1.2	1.2	March
Estonia	1.2	2.7	1.6	1.7	1.6	March
Hungary	1.3	1.4	1.4	1.5	2.3	March
Israel[4]	0.5	0.3	0.1	0.4	. . .	September
Latvia	2.0	1.5	1.5	1.4	1.6	June
Lithuania	0.5	−0.1	1.0	1.4	. . .	
Moldova[5]	7.4	4.3	4.3	4.5	3.9	September
Poland	1.1	1.0	0.5	0.5	1.5	June
Russia	0.9	2.4	2.6	2.6	3.1	September
Slovak Republic	0.5	1.0	1.2	1.2	1.0	September
Slovenia	1.1	0.5	1.1	1.0	. . .	
Turkey	−3.0	−6.1	1.4	2.5	1.7	December
Ukraine	−0.1	1.2	1.2	1.0	1.1	December
Western Europe						
Austria	0.4	0.5	0.3	0.4	. . .	
Belgium	0.6	0.4	0.4	0.4	. . .	
Finland	1.2	0.7	0.5	0.7	1.0	June
France	0.5	0.5	0.5	0.4	. . .	
Germany[6]	0.2	0.1	0.1	−0.1	. . .	
Greece	1.4	1.0	0.5	0.6	. . .	
Iceland	0.7	0.8	1.1	1.3	2.5	June
Ireland	1.2	0.9	1.0	0.9	. . .	
Italy	0.8	0.6	0.5	0.5	. . .	
Luxembourg	0.5	0.5	0.4	0.5	. . .	
Netherlands[7]	0.8	0.6	0.5	0.6	. . .	
Norway[3]	1.4	0.9	0.6	0.7	1.1	September
Portugal	0.9	0.8	0.7	0.8	0.8	June
Spain	1.0	1.0	0.9	0.9	1.0	June
Sweden[8]	0.9	0.8	0.6	0.7	. . .	
Switzerland[3]	1.1	0.6	0.5	0.7	. . .	
United Kingdom[3]	0.9	0.5	0.9	0.5	. . .	
Asia						
Bangladesh	0.0	0.7	0.5	0.5	. . .	
China[9]	0.1	0.1	0.1	. . .	. . .	
Hong Kong SAR	0.8	0.8	0.8	0.8	. . .	
India[3]	0.7	0.5	0.8	1.0	1.2	June
Indonesia[10]	0.3	0.6	1.4	1.6	2.8	September
Korea[3]	−0.5	0.8	0.6	0.1	0.9	June
Malaysia	1.4	1.0	1.3	1.4	1.5	June
Philippines	0.4	0.4	0.8	1.1	1.1	June
Singapore	1.3	0.8	0.8	0.9	1.4	December
Thailand	−0.2	1.5	0.2	0.7	1.5	June

Table 26 *(concluded)*

	2000	2001	2002	2003	2004	Latest
Middle East and Central Asia						
Azerbaijan	. . .	0.5	1.5	1.8	1.3	June
Egypt	0.9	0.8	0.7	0.5	0.5	June
Jordan	0.3	0.7	0.5	0.7	. . .	
Kuwait	2.0	2.0	1.8	2.0	. . .	March
Kyrgyz Republic	−1.1	1.4	1.1	1.3	2.0	July
Lebanon	0.7	0.5	0.6	0.7	. . .	
Morocco	0.7	0.9	0.3	0.6	. . .	
Oman	1.3	0.1	1.4	. . .	. . .	
Pakistan[11]	−0.01	−0.01	0.8	1.2	1.2	September
Saudi Arabia	2.0	2.1	2.1	2.2	2.7	June
Tunisia	1.2	1.1	0.7	0.6	. . .	
United Arab Emirates	1.8	2.6	2.2	2.3	. . .	
Sub-Saharan Africa						
Ghana[3]	9.7	8.7	6.8	6.4	. . .	
Guinea	. . .	. . .	. . .	. . .	. . .	
Kenya[3]	0.5	1.6	1.0	2.3	2.1	June
Mauritius[3]	2.3	2.2	2.3	2.3	. . .	
Nigeria	4.0	3.3	2.4	1.7	. . .	
Senegal	. . .	. . .	. . .	. . .	. . .	
Sierra Leone	15.9	11.9	10.4	10.7	8.4	December
South Africa[3]	1.4	1.0	0.8	1.1	1.4	April
Tanzania	1.3	1.2	1.3	. . .	. . .	
Uganda	4.4	4.4	2.7	3.3	4.5	December
Zimbabwe	6.0	5.1	4.0	6.7	. . .	
Other						
Australia	1.3	1.0	1.2	1.1	. . .	
Canada	0.7	0.7	0.4	0.7	0.8	September
Japan[3]	0.1	−0.7	−0.6	0.1	0.3	September
United States[12]	1.10	1.10	1.30	1.4	1.3	September

Sources: National authorities; and IMF staff estimates.
[1]Includes banks and nonbank financial companies.
[2]Operating margin to assets.
[3]Before tax.
[4]Data for the five largest banking groups.
[5]Gross profits as percent of assets.
[6]The 2003 figure is for large banks only.
[7]Ratio for the large and complex financial institutions.
[8]Ratio for the four largest financial groups.
[9]State commercial banks.
[10]Ratio for the top 16 banks.
[11]The data refer to commercial banks only, excluding specialized banks.
[12]Includes all FDIC-insured commercial banks and savings associations.

Table 27. Bank Return on Equity
(In percent)

	2000	2001	2002	2003	2004	Latest
Latin America						
Argentina[1]	3.1	−1.5	−74.0	−20.8	−8.5	September
Bolivia	−9.5	−4.3	0.7	2.8	−0.3	October
Brazil	11.3	2.4	20.8	16.4	16.3	September
Chile	12.7	17.7	14.4	16.7	17.7	September
Colombia	−20.7	1.1	9.6	17.0	23.2	June
Costa Rica[2]	16.3	18.7	17.1	19.5	. . .	
Dominican Republic	26.1	21.7	21.0	−0.5	15.4	September
Ecuador	−21.3	−36.0	15.3	12.7	19.7	September
Mexico	10.4	8.6	−10.4	14.2	9.9	September
Nicaragua	27.1	28.7	23.9	29.2	37.5	June
Paraguay	12.4	21.2	9.0	4.5	16.4	September
Peru	3.1	4.5	8.4	10.8	10.7	September
Venezuela	23.1	20.3	35.6	44.0	43.6	September
Emerging Europe						
Bulgaria	20.3	20.2	14.9	22.7	22.2	September
Croatia	10.4	6.5	13.7	15.6	17.7	June
Czech Republic	13.1	16.6	27.4	23.8	23.0	June
Estonia	8.0	20.7	11.9	14.2	13.8	March
Hungary	13.4	17.6	16.2	19.3	27.8	March
Israel[3]	11.7	5.9	2.8	7.6	. . .	September
Latvia	18.6	19.0	16.4	16.7	20.0	March
Lithuania	5.0	−1.2	9.8	13.5	. . .	
Moldova	25.0	14.3	16.7	20.3	18.2	September
Poland	14.5	12.8	5.2	5.4	18.5	June
Russia	8.0	19.4	18.0	17.8	22.0	September
Slovak Republic	11.2	15.4	17.1	14.9	11.9	August
Slovenia	11.4	4.8	13.3	12.6	. . .	
Turkey	−43.7	−57.5	11.2	15.8	11.3	December
Ukraine	−0.5	7.5	8.0	7.6	8.4	December
Western Europe						
Austria	9.4	9.8	5.4	7.2	. . .	
Belgium	20.4	13.7	11.8	13.6	. . .	
Finland	22.4	13.5	10.7	10.1	12.4	June
France	9.7	9.6	9.1	8.6	. . .	
Germany	6.1	4.6	2.9	−1.5	. . .	
Greece	15.4	12.4	6.8	8.9	. . .	
Iceland	10.7	13.5	18.1	22.1	41.9	June
Ireland	22.0	16.0	18.0	17.8	. . .	
Italy	11.2	8.6	7.1	7.3	. . .	
Luxembourg	36.7	40.7	36.4	34.9	. . .	
Netherlands[2,4]	19.6	14.3	12.8	16.9	. . .	
Norway[2]	19.2	13.0	9.2	12.0	. . .	
Portugal	15.1	14.9	11.7	13.9	13.3	June
Spain	18.5	16.5	14.6	16.6	. . .	
Sweden	15.7	13.0	10.1	12.3	. . .	
Switzerland[2]	18.6	11.8	9.5	13.5	. . .	
United Kingdom[2]	13.5	7.7	12.0*	14.0*	. . .	
Asia						
Bangladesh	0.3	15.9	11.6	9.8	. . .	
China	. . .	. . .	. . .	. . .	. . .	
Hong Kong SAR	13.5	13.9	13.3	13.5	. . .	
India	12.8	10.4	11.9	13.1	. . .	March
Indonesia	19.6	13.4	22.7	22.1	. . .	
Korea[2]	−9.7	16.9	14.4	2.8	19.7	June
Malaysia	19.3	13.1	16.3	17.1	17.5	June
Philippines	2.6	3.2	5.8	8.5	8.3	June
Singapore	. . .	9.7	7.6	10.1	10.5	September
Thailand	−4.8	32.8	4.2	10.5	20.5	June

Table 27 (concluded)

	2000	2001	2002	2003	2004	Latest
Middle East and Central Asia						
Azerbaijan	. . .	2.8	7.6	11.8	9.2	June
Egypt	16.1	13.7	12.4	8.8	9.8	June
Jordan	4.4	10.9	8.7	10.2	. . .	
Kuwait	17.6	18.2	17.4	18.2	. . .	March
Kyrgyz Republic	−5.3	5.1	5.1	8.0	12.4	July
Lebanon	11.1	9.1	9.4	10.4	. . .	
Morocco	8.1	10.2	1.9	6.8	. . .	
Oman	12.0	1.2	14.3	. . .	. . .	
Pakistan[5]	−0.3	−0.3	14.3	20.5	19.9	September
Saudi Arabia	37.9	42.1	43.0	48.7	61.4	June
Tunisia	13.7	14.0	8.0	7.6	5.4	December
United Arab Emirates	14.9	16.7	15.6	16.4	. . .	
Sub-Saharan Africa						
Ghana	65.7	49.7	36.9	54.0	. . .	
Guinea	. . .	. . .	. . .	. . .	. . .	
Kenya[2]	4.9	15.7	10.9	23.2	22.7	June
Mauritius[2]	22.1	20.6	22.0	21.4	. . .	
Nigeria	. . .	43.7	28.1	19.8	. . .	
Senegal	. . .	. . .	. . .	22.1	22.1	March
Sierra Leone	56.7	39.9	33.3	33.0	29.6	December
South Africa	12.0	9.1	6.0	12.1	17.7	April
Tanzania	20.5	21.4	17.6	. . .	. . .	
Uganda	53.1	45.8	33.5	. . .	. . .	
Zimbabwe	43.2	42.7	57.7	114.8	. . .	
Other						
Australia	19.4	15.6	18.2	19.4	20.3	June
Canada[6]	15.3	13.9	9.4	14.9	17.6	September
Japan[7]	−0.5	−14.3	−19.5	−2.7	2.7	September
United States[8]	13.5	13.0	14.1	15.0	13.5	September

Sources: National authorities; and IMF staff estimates.

[1]Includes banks and nonbank financial companies.
[2]Before tax.
[3]Ratio for the five largest financial groups.
[4]Ratio for the large and complex financial institutions.
[5]The data refer to commercial banks only, excluding specialized banks.
[6]Ratio for the six largest commercial banks.
[7]After tax.
[8]Includes all FDIC-insured commercial banks and savings associations.
(*) After-tax ROE for the U.K. banks for 2002 and 2003.

Table 28. Moody's Weighted Average Bank Financial Strength Index[1]

	Financial Strength Index				Financial Strength Index		
	Dec. 2002	Dec. 2003	Dec. 2004		Dec. 2002	Dec. 2003	Dec. 2004
Asia				**Western Europe** (continued)			
China	10.0	10.0	10.0	Luxembourg	68.3	66.7	63.9
Hong Kong SAR	62.3	62.3	62.3	Netherlands	84.2	84.2	84.2
India	27.5	27.5	24.2	Norway	65.0	67.5	67.5
Indonesia	3.0	3.0	7.3	Portugal	64.2	64.2	64.2
Korea	16.7	18.3	18.3	Spain	75.0	76.7	76.7
Malaysia	31.7	33.3	35.2	Sweden	73.0	75.0	78.0
Philippines	20.4	20.4	19.2	Switzerland	72.1	72.1	73.0
Singapore	74.7	74.7	74.7	United Kingdom	83.8	83.3	83.3
Thailand	15.8	15.8	15.8				
				Latin America			
Emerging Europe				Argentina	0.0	0.0	0.0
Bulgaria	16.7	20.8	20.8	Bolivia	8.3	2.1	0.0
Croatia	33.3	33.3	33.3	Brazil	25.0	24.3	24.3
Czech Republic	32.5	33.9	41.0	Chile	52.5	56.5	57.8
Estonia	46.7	46.7	46.7	Colombia	24.2	24.2	24.2
Hungary	45.0	42.5	45.0	Mexico	39.6	39.6	41.7
Israel	45.8	45.8	45.8	Peru	23.3	23.3	25.0
Latvia	32.1	32.1	33.0	Uruguay	0.0	0.0	0.0
Poland	28.3	29.5	30.5	Venezuela	15.4	8.3	8.3
Russia	10.8	10.8	11.0				
Slovak Republic	15.0	17.5	25.0	**Middle East**			
Turkey	20.4	20.4	20.8	Egypt	22.9	22.9	22.9
Ukraine	8.3	8.3	8.3	Lebanon	33.3	33.3	33.3
				Morocco	35.8	35.8	35.8
Western Europe				Pakistan	5.0	9.6	9.6
Austria	61.7	61.7	62.9	Saudi Arabia	43.3	43.3	43.3
Belgium	75.0	75.0	75.0	Tunisia	16.7	16.7	16.7
Denmark	80.0	80.0	85.0				
Finland	73.3	73.3	73.3	**Africa**			
France	74.2	71.2	72.7	South Africa	49.0	50.0	50.0
Germany	54.2	46.7	47.2	**Other**			
Greece	40.0	44.8	45.8	Australia	72.5	72.5	72.5
Iceland	54.7	58.3	58.3	Canada	75.0	75.0	75.0
Ireland	70.0	71.7	72.5	Japan	12.9	12.0	20.6
Italy	63.3	63.3	63.3	United States	75.0	75.0	77.0

Source: Moody's.

[1]Constructed according to a numerical scale assigned to Moody's weighted average bank ratings by country. "0" indicates the lowest possible average rating and "100" indicates the highest possible average rating.

World Economic and Financial Surveys

This series (ISSN 0258-7440) contains biannual, annual, and periodic studies covering monetary and financial issues of importance to the global economy. The core elements of the series are the *World Economic Outlook* report, usually published in April and September, and the semiannual *Global Financial Stability Report*. Other studies assess international trade policy, private market and official financing for developing countries, exchange and payments systems, export credit policies, and issues discussed in the *World Economic Outlook*. Please consult the IMF *Publications Catalog* for a complete listing of currently available World Economic and Financial Surveys.

World Economic Outlook: A Survey by the Staff of the International Monetary Fund

The *World Economic Outlook*, published twice a year in English, French, Spanish, and Arabic, presents IMF staff economists' analyses of global economic developments during the near and medium term. Chapters give an overview of the world economy; consider issues affecting industrial countries, developing countries, and economies in transition to the market; and address topics of pressing current interest.

ISSN 0256-6877.

$49.00 (academic rate: $46.00); paper.

2004. (September). ISBN 1-58906-406-2. **Stock #WEOEA2004002.**
2004. (April). ISBN 1-58906-337-6. **Stock #WEOEA200401.**
2003. (April). ISBN 1-58906-212-4. **Stock #WEOEA0012003.**
2002. (Sep.). ISBN 1-58906-179-9. **Stock #WEOEA0022002.**

Global Financial Stability Report: Market Developments and Issues

The *Global Financial Stability Report*, published twice a year, examines trends and issues that influence world financial markets. It replaces two IMF publications—the annual *International Capital Markets* report and the electronic quarterly *Emerging Market Financing* report. The report is designed to deepen understanding of international capital flows and explores developments that could pose a risk to international financial market stability.

$49.00 (academic rate: $46.00); paper.

September 2004 ISBN 1-58906-378-3. **Stock #GFSREA2004002.**
April 2004 ISBN 1-58906-328-7. **Stock #GFSREA0012004.**
September 2003 ISBN 1-58906-236-1. **Stock #GFSREA0022003.**
March 2003 ISBN 1-58906-210-8. **Stock #GFSREA0012003.**
December 2002 ISBN-1-58906-192-6. **Stock #GFSREA0042002.**

Emerging Local Securities and Derivatives Markets

by Donald Mathieson, Jorge E. Roldos, Ramana Ramaswamy, and Anna Ilya

The volatility of capital flows since the mid-1990s has sparked an interest in the development of local securities and derivatives markets. This report examines the growth of these markets in emerging market countries and the key policy issues that have arisen as a result.

$42.00 (academic rate: $35.00); paper.

2004. ISBN 1-58906-291-4. **Stock #WEOEA0202004.**

Official Financing: Recent Developments and Selected Issues

by a staff team in the Policy Development and Review Department led by Martin G. Gilman and Jian-Ye Wang

This study provides information on official financing for developing countries, with the focus on low-income countries. It updates the 2001 edition and reviews developments in direct financing by official and multilateral sources.

$42.00 (academic rate: $35.00); paper.

2003. ISBN 1-58906-228-0. Stock #WEOEA0132003.
2001. ISBN 1-58906-038-5. **Stock #WEOEA0132001.**

Exchange Arrangements and Foreign Exchange Markets: Developments and Issues

by a staff team led by Shogo Ishii

This study updates developments in exchange arrangements during 1998–2001. It also discusses the evolution of exchange rate regimes based on de facto policies since 1990, reviews foreign exchange market organization and regulations in a number of countries, and examines factors affecting exchange rate volatility.

ISSN 0258-7440

$42.00 (academic rate $35.00)

2003 (March) ISBN 1-58906-177-2. **Stock #WEOEA0192003.**

World Economic Outlook Supporting Studies

by the IMF's Research Department

These studies, supporting analyses and scenarios of the *World Economic Outlook*, provide a detailed examination of theory and evidence on major issues currently affecting the global economy.

$25.00 (academic rate: $20.00); paper.

2000. ISBN 1-55775-893-X. **Stock #WEOEA0032000.**

Exchange Rate Arrangements and Currency Convertibility: Developments and Issues

by a staff team led by R. Barry Johnston

A principal force driving the growth in international trade and investment has been the liberalization of financial transactions, including the liberalization of trade and exchange controls. This study reviews the developments and issues in the exchange arrangements and currency convertibility of IMF members.

$20.00 (academic rate: $12.00); paper.

1999. ISBN 1-55775-795-X. **Stock #WEOEA0191999.**

Available by series subscription or single title (including back issues); academic rate available only to full-time university faculty and students. For earlier editions please inquire about prices.

The IMF *Catalog of Publications* is available on-line at the Internet address listed below.

Please send orders and inquiries to:
International Monetary Fund, Publication Services, 700 19th Street, N.W.
Washington, D.C. 20431, U.S.A.
Tel.: (202) 623-7430   Telefax: (202) 623-7201
E-mail: publications@imf.org
Internet: http://www.imf.org